CHILD SUPPORT –
THE NEW LAW

CHILD SUPPORT –
THE NEW LAW

Roger Bird LLB

District Judge, Bristol County Court and
District Registry

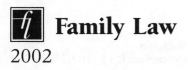 **Family Law**

2002

Published by
Family Law, a publishing
imprint of Jordan Publishing Limited
21 St Thomas Street
Bristol BS1 6JS

British Library Cataloguing-in-Publication Data

A catalogue record for this book is available
from the British Library.

ISBN 0 85308 761 X

Photoset by Mendip Communications Ltd, Frome, Somerset
Printed by Henry Ling Limited, The Dorset Press, Dorchester, DT1 1HD, UK

PREFACE

The fact that a fifth edition of this book is needed within eight years of publication of the first edition is, perhaps, indication enough of the struggles which successive governments have had in trying to implement the idea that there should be a State-administered system of calculating and enforcing the maintenance of children based on non-discretionary principles. Whether, as various commentators have suggested, the introduction and implementation of the Child Support Act 1991 was one of the greatest failures of public administration of the last century (and there was certainly plenty of competition for that melancholy distinction) or whether, as the present government appears to think, the Act was a good idea which needs amendment, remains to be seen. Be that as it may, practitioners now have to acquire the new knowledge and skills required by the new legislation. Hence the need for this book.

Readers should soon become familiar with the new terminology such as 'non-resident parent' in place of 'absent parent'; in this edition, unless otherwise indicated, a parent referred to in the male gender is the non-resident parent, and the female is the person with care. This is not intended to be a sexist assumption but is merely a convenient shorthand.

The law is correct as at the date given below.

ROGER BIRD
11 February 2002

CONTENTS

TABLE OF CASES

References are to paragraph numbers.

TABLE OF STATUTES

References are to paragraph and appendix numbers.

TABLE OF STATUTORY INSTRUMENTS

References are to paragraph and appendix numbers.

TABLE OF ABBREVIATIONS

BETEC	Business and Technology Education Council
CA 1989	Children Act 1989
CSA	Child Support Agency
CSA 1991	Child Support Act 1991
CS(CE)Regs 1992	Child Support (Collection and Enforcement) Regulations 1992
CS(CEMA)Regs 2000	Child Support (Collection and Enforcement and Miscellaneous Amendments) Regulations 2000
CSC(P)Regs 1992	Child Support Commissioners (Procedure) Regulations 1992
CS(IED)Regs 1992	Child Support (Information, Evidence and Disclosure) Regulations 1992
CS(MAJ)Regs 1992	Child Support (Maintenance Arrangements and Jurisdiction) Regulations 1992
CS(MASC)Regs 1992	Child Support (Maintenance Assessments and Special Cases) Regulations 1992
CS(MCP)Regs 2000	Child Support (Maintenance Calculation Procedure) Regulations 2000
CS(MCSC)Regs 2000	Child Support (Maintenance Calculations and Special Cases) Regulations 2000
CSO	child support officer
CSPSSA 2000	Child Support, Pensions and Social Security Act 2000
CS(V)Regs 2000	Child Support (Variations) Regulations 2000
DfES	Department for Education and Skills
DPMCA 1978	Domestic Proceedings and Magistrates' Courts Act 1978
DSS	Department of Social Security
FPR 1991	Family Proceedings Rules 1991
HFEA 1990	Human Fertilisation and Embryology Act 1990
LEA	Local Education Authority
MCA 1973	Matrimonial Causes Act 1973
MCA 1980	Magistrates' Courts Act 1980

MOD	Ministry of Defence
RSC 1965	Rules of the Supreme Court 1965
SQC	Scottish Qualifications Council
SSCS(DA)Regs 1999	Social Security and Child Support (Decisions and Appeals) Regulations 1999

CHAPTER ONE

The Background to and General Principles of the Act

Introduction

1.1 The Child Support, Pensions and Social Security Act 2000 (CSPSSA 2000) received Royal Assent on 28 July 2000. Part I of the Act represents the Government's attempt to reform the law relating to child support and came into force on 6 April 2002. The purpose of this book is to explain the law as it is now that the amendments made to the Child Support Act 1991 (CSA 1991) by the CSPSSA 2000 have come into force.

Although the CSPSSA 2000 makes extensive changes to the law of child support, the CSA 1991 remains the source of law, with many sections being amended and some entirely replaced. Accordingly, the CSA 1991 in its amended form is examined in detail and the implications of any changes are set out.

1.2 Before 1990, the idea that the courts were not the appropriate forum for decisions as to child maintenance when the parents could not agree would have seemed foreign to most lawyers and members of the public in this country. Maintenance of children was regarded as a branch of family law which fell naturally within the jurisdiction of the courts, and there were few who thought that it should be removed into some free-standing system. Nevertheless, this is what the CSA 1991 attempted to achieve. As will be seen, a complete assumption of the role of the court has not yet been accomplished, although the Act has been in force for eight years.

1.3 It is unnecessary in this book to set out a detailed account of the genesis and passage into law of this measure. Previous editions dealt in detail with the Antipodean origins of the concept, the White Paper 'Children Come First', the lively parliamentary debates, and the eventual enactment of the Bill; to dwell on these matters now might be of some academic interest, but would not help the reader who seeks a reliable guide to the workings of the Act and regulations. Accordingly, a more severely practical approach will be adopted here.

Having said that, it may be of interest briefly to bring up to date the historical section of the previous editions, before embarking on a more detailed analysis of the changes effected by the CSPSSA 2000.

1.4 In legal circles, the CSA 1991 was always a controversial measure. Nevertheless, at the outset, it enjoyed a generally favourable reception from the media and other opinion formers. Typical of such reactions was that of the then Bishop of Gloucester, speaking on behalf of the Church of England in one of the parliamentary debates. He said that he believed:

'that the creation of a single, powerful, and well-publicised Child Support Agency could be significant of the nation's will to grapple with the problem of the children who are at risk and suffering as a result of family breakdown.' (House of Lords, Official Report, 25 February 1991 col 808)

What was remarkable was the speed with which this goodwill evaporated. The press were not slow to publicise stories of men who had, allegedly, committed suicide because of what were regarded as extortionate assessments. More significantly, a series of both official and independent reports began to highlight serious deficiencies in the performance of the Child Support Agency (CSA), and hardships which resulted from the rigid application of the formula. A pattern emerged of critical Select Committee reports every autumn, followed by amended regulations the following spring. The CSA failed to meet its performance targets for 1993/94; the Select Committee report published in November 1994[1] was highly critical; the Ombudsman's Report[2] revealed serious maladministration.

The conclusions of one typical independent report[3] were similar. The authors' conclusions were that the Act had done nothing to improve the well-being of children in lone parent families on benefits; on the contrary, the emotional distress and material losses which had been experienced by a number of children were clearly damaging rather than beneficial to their welfare. As a consequence of the Act, some of the very poorest children in the UK had already experienced a net reduction in the material quality of their lives, and others were facing such reductions in the near future, as fathers became unable to pay for the treats, shoes, clothes and outings which afforded a temporary escape from the deprivations of life on the poverty line. Children witnessed renewed tension and arguments between parents; the Act threatened to undermine both the frequency and the quality of relationships between children and their fathers.

1.5　The government of the day attempted to improve the operation of the CSA 1991 and set out its proposals in a White Paper 'Improving Child Support' (Cm 2745, 1995). These proposals were translated into law by the Child Support Act 1995 and the various sets of regulations flowing therefrom. One of the features of these enactments seemed to be that it was recognised that the CSA 1991 had been unduly rigid and prescriptive and provision was made for the amelioration of the formula approach by means of, inter alia, Departure Directions. However, this did not stem the flow of criticism.

In 1998 in their book *Child Support in Action*,[4] three eminent academic authors succinctly recorded the drawbacks of the system.

'The media picture of the misery visited upon absent fathers is borne out in part, but even more striking is the evidence of a catastrophic administrative failure leading to the abandonment of many of the basic tenets of administrative justice. The reasons for this do not lie primarily in the perceived unfairness of the formula but rather in the failure of those drafting the Child Support Act 1991 to appreciate the impact of

---

1　The Operation of the Child Support Act; Proposals for Change (HC 470 1994–95, HMSO).
2　Investigation of Complaints against the Child Support Agency (HC 135 1994–95, HMSO).
3　Glendinning, Clarke and Craig 'The impact of the Child Support Act on lone mothers and their children' *Journal of Child Law* vol 7 no 1 p 18.
4　Gwynn Davis, Nick Whiteley and Richard Young (Hart Publishing, 1998).

such change upon the rest of our hugely complex benefit structure and their failure also to grasp that the problems of inadequate disclosure and ineffective enforcement – with which courts had grappled for decades – could not be tackled successfully by a distant bureaucracy.'[5]

The book concluded with some suggestions which seem to have been accepted, in principle at least, by those responsible for the recent legislative changes.

'One option worthy of serious consideration is a move closer to the Australian model. In the first place, this would involve simplifying the formula by abandoning the current shadowing of income support rates. Instead, the central principle would be the deduction of a specified percentage of income according to the number of children involved. The introduction of a disregard of maintenance payments when calculating Income Support entitlement would also provide a real incentive for mothers to co-operate and fathers to pay.'[6]

1.6 As will be seen, the recommendations of Davis et al have been incorporated in the new legislation (although it is only fair to them to point out that they also recommended[7] the abandonment of the element of discretion represented by departures, which has in fact been retained under the name of 'variation'). In the event, the Government's proposals were contained in a White Paper 'Children First' (Cm 3992, 1998). In the introduction the Prime Minister said 'the system of child support we inherited is a mess', and 'the system needs urgent reform'. He continued: 'we will replace the highly complicated formula for assessing maintenance by a radically simpler calculation. It will be transparent so that fathers [*sic*] will know in advance exactly how much they must pay.' The White Paper invited comments but, unsurprisingly perhaps, the draft legislation when published showed little sign of second thoughts.

The purpose of this book is to put the new provisions into context, that context being the CSA 1991. Part I of the CSPSSA 2000 does no more than amend the CSA 1991 by inserting large amounts of new material in substitution for the original material. Accordingly, this book will consist of an examination of the provisions of the CSA 1991 as amended and, where appropriate, to the all-important delegated legislation.

The General Principles and Characteristics of the Act

1.7 The long title of the CSA 1991 is 'An Act to make provision for the assessment, collection and enforcement of periodical maintenance payable by certain parents with respect to children of theirs who are not in their care; for the collection and enforcement of certain other kinds of maintenance; and for connected purposes'. The CSPSSA 2000 amends that Act.

In later chapters, the detail of the Act as amended and the way in which it is intended to work will be examined. Here, it is intended to set out in outline the general scheme of the Act, to consider its basic principles and to examine some of

---

5 Op cit, p v.
6 Ibid, p 232.
7 Ibid, p 223.

its key terms and concepts. It will be seen that some terms (eg 'parent') have a different meaning under this Act from that adopted in other legislation, even legislation as close in time and subject matter as the Children Act 1989 (CA 1989).

The Duty to Maintain

1.8   Section 1 of the CSA 1991 sets out the basic principle underlying the whole Act, namely that parents have an obligation to maintain their children, and then deals with how that obligation may be discharged. By s 1(1):

> '. . . each parent of a qualifying child is responsible for maintaining him.'

This defines the obligation in general terms. Section 1(2) then goes on to provide that for the purposes of the Act:

> '. . . a non-resident parent shall be taken to have met his responsibility to maintain any qualifying child of his by making periodical payments of maintenance with respect to the child of such amount, and at such intervals, as may be determined in accordance with the provisions of this Act.'

In other words, once the obligations imposed by the Act have been discharged, no further liability under the Act, or otherwise, exists.

Section 1(3) introduces the concept of the 'maintenance calculation'; and provides that:

> 'Where a maintenance calculation made under this Act requires the making of periodical payments, it shall be the duty of the non-resident parent with respect to whom the assessment was made to make those payments.'

In s 1, therefore, are found the statutory obligations to maintain (s 1(1)), and to pay the maintenance calculation (s 1(3)) and, in s 1(2), a statement of the sufficiency of making payments under the Act.

1.9   Section 1 introduces the terms 'qualifying child', 'non-resident parent' and 'maintenance calculation'. These are all terms new to English law, as are 'person with care', and 'child support maintenance', which appear in s 3. These terms are central to the philosophy of the Act and their meaning must be considered in detail.[8] This is dealt with in Chapter Two.

For the present purposes, however, the general principle of the CSA 1991 may be stated as follows: the Act imposes obligations upon the parents of children where:

(a)   the parents are or are presumed to be the natural or adoptive parents of the child;

(b)   one or both parents do not live in the same household as the child;

(c)   the child lives with a person with care who provides for the child.

---

8 It should be noted that the CSPSSA 2000 has changed some of the terminology, so that 'non-resident parent' replaces 'absent parent' and 'maintenance calculation' replaces 'maintenance assessment'.

Section 1(3) refers to a 'maintenance calculation', which, by s 54, is defined as 'a calculation of maintenance made under this Act'. There is no further definition in the Act but the meaning is clear in the context of the Act, since, as will be seen, a maintenance calculation can be made by only the Secretary of State or an officer under his authority. Section 3(6) provides that 'periodical payments which are required to be paid in accordance with a maintenance calculation are referred to in this Act as "child support maintenance"'.

The Welfare of the Children

1.10 The marginal note to s 2 of the CSA 1991 describes that section as 'welfare of the children: the general principle'. Section 2 itself provides that:

> 'Where, in any case which falls to be dealt with under this Act, the Secretary of State is considering the exercise of any discretionary power conferred by this Act, he shall have regard to the welfare of any child likely to be affected by his decision.'

Section 2 was not included in the original Bill and so represented the result of further thought on the part of the Government. In considering what this provision will mean it may be useful to begin with a comparison with two other statutory provisions in related fields.

Section 1(1) of the CA 1989 repeats a principle contained in earlier statutes, namely that in proceedings concerned with the upbringing of a child or the administration of a child's property or the application of any income arising from it:

> 'the child's welfare shall be the court's paramount consideration.'

Section 25(1) of the Matrimonial Causes Act 1973 (MCA 1973) was amended in 1984 to include the provision that, when considering any application for financial relief, whether for the parties to a marriage or their child, it is the duty of the court to have regard to all the circumstances of the case:

> 'first consideration being given to the welfare while a minor of any child of the family who has not attained the age of eighteen.'

Section 2 of the CSA 1991 differs from its predecessors in three important respects. First, it imposes obligations on the Secretary of State, reflecting the fact that it is officers acting under his authority rather than the courts who will be making decisions affecting children. This will be significant when the question of remedies for breach of the statutory obligations is considered.

Secondly, it does not make the welfare of children the first or paramount consideration; it merely says that regard is to be had to such welfare. It therefore carries less force than the other provisions.

Thirdly, s 2 has a wider ambit than the other provisions in that it directs attention to the welfare of any child likely to be affected by the decision. The other statutes require regard to be had to the welfare of a child who is directly involved in the litigation; the reference to 'any child' goes very much further than this.

1.11 There are many occasions on which the Secretary of State will have to have regard to the welfare of the children. A complete list is set out in para **8.20**. When making any of these decisions the Secretary of State (or officer under his authority) must 'have regard to' the welfare of any child. What does this mean? As has been seen, the welfare of children is not the first or paramount consideration. Would the production of a completed checklist showing that the officer concerned had gone through a prescribed procedure and applied his mind to the welfare of children be sufficient?

Only a tentative answer can be given to such questions. It is suggested that, where it could be shown that the consequences of any decision would be detrimental to the welfare of any child in question, it could then fairly be argued that the officer concerned had not had regard to the welfare of that child. It might be thought that the areas which are most likely to produce a challenge to the discretionary powers of the Secretary of State are reduced benefit directions, liability orders and distress.

The requirement to have regard to the welfare of any child likely to be affected by the decision is a wide one. It clearly includes not only the children in respect of whom maintenance calculations are being made or enforced but also the children in the home of the non-resident parent for whom that parent provides. The possibility might then arise of a conflict of interest between the child whose maintenance calculation was not being paid, and whose needs were therefore not being provided for, and the child of the non-resident parent who would suffer deprivation if the non-resident parent were forced to pay money which he could not afford or were committed to prison.

1.12 What is the remedy of a person who considers that the Secretary of State has failed to observe the statutory duty imposed by s 2? In principle, the answer is an application for judicial review. This is considered further in Chapter Eight and will not be discussed in detail here, save to say that judicial review is concerned with the propriety of the decision-making process rather than the merits of the decision itself, and that judicial review would not be appropriate where the structure of the Act itself contained a right of appeal.

The Child Support Agency

1.13 Moving the second reading of the Child Support Bill on 25 February 1991 the Lord Chancellor said:

> '. . . a Child Support Agency will be established as a next steps agency under the authority of . . . the Secretary of State for Social Security. The agency will trace absent parents, investigate the parents' means and assess, collect and enforce payments of child maintenance . . . [A]s a next steps agency, the agency will have no independent existence in statute. The powers that it will need to do its work are, therefore, expressed as powers of . . . the Secretary of State for Social Security.'

Although in reality the CSA looms large in any consideration of the new law and procedure it is nowhere mentioned in the Act, for the reason given above by the Lord Chancellor. Instead, the Act confers all the powers to be exercised by the Agency on the Secretary of State.

The CSA 1991 originally conferred certain authority on the child support officer. Since the Social Security Act 1998, all decisions, determinations and calculations previously falling to the child support officer are now to be made by the Secretary of State or an officer of the Secretary of State acting under his authority.

When procedure is considered in Chapter Two, it will be seen that, under s 4(1), applications for child support maintenance ('a maintenance calculation') must be made to the Secretary of State, on whom s 4 imposes certain obligations. It is the function of an officer under the authority of the Secretary of State to consider the application, to obtain such information as he requires, to make the calculation and, if necessary, to take steps to enforce it.

1.14   The other significant personnel to feature in the Agency's work will be the inspectors. By s 15(1), the Secretary of State may appoint 'on such terms as he thinks fit, persons to act as inspectors'. Section 15(2) provides that:

> 'The function of inspectors is to acquire information which the Secretary of State needs for any of the purposes of this Act.'

Their powers will be considered further in Chapter Two, but here it may be noted that they have wide powers of investigation and entry.

The Formula

1.15   We must now consider how maintenance calculations are to be made and what principles are to be employed.

Section 11(6) provides that:

> 'The amount of child support maintenance to be fixed by a maintenance calculation shall be determined in accordance with Part I of Schedule 1 unless an application for a variation has been made and agreed.'

Variation is then dealt with in s 11(7) which provides that:

> 'If the Secretary of State has agreed to a variation, the amount of child support maintenance to be fixed shall be determined on the basis he determines under section 28F(4).'

Section 11(8) provides that Part II of Sch 1 makes further provision with respect to maintenance calculations.

Schedule 1 will be considered in detail in Chapter Three. Here, it is only necessary to note the vital fact that it contains a formula for the determination of maintenance calculations. The formula which now exists as a result of the CSPSSA 2000 is a completely different formula from that which hitherto applied. The previous formula was based on a 'maintenance requirement' for the children of any family and the apportionment of that requirement between the parents on the basis of their respective incomes and allowable outgoings. The new formula is based entirely on a percentage of the non-resident parent's income, although, as will be seen, the calculation is not as simple as might have been hoped. However, provision is made for variation of the formula in certain cases, and this is at the discretion of the Secretary of State. Variation is considered in Chapter Five. Subject to variation, however, the intention of the CSA 1991 remains: by reference to the formula a 'correct' decision should be arrived at in every case.

1.16 The belief that the proper application of the formula would give an unchallengeable answer was given as the reason why the role of the courts had been rendered unnecessary and explains the thinking behind the system of revision and appeal. The formula was originally applied to the facts of a particular case in the same way as if calculating a benefit such as income support. This has now changed only in the sense that the formula is, ostensibly, easier to calculate since it requires only a pocket calculator. In the original 1991 formula, no element of discretion was possible. When the Act was amended in 1995 an element of discretion was introduced in the shape of departure directions. That element of discretion has been carried into the new law under the name of variation.

The purity of the original doctrine has therefore been sullied and made more unpredictable by the introduction of a discretionary element. However, in most cases the basic principle remains and the proponents of the amended Act envisage that the formula will reign undisturbed.

The Exclusion of the Court

1.17 One of the novel features of the new child support law introduced in 1991 was the virtual total exclusion of the jurisdiction of the courts.

Section 8 applies where the Secretary of State would have jurisdiction to make a maintenance calculation with respect to a qualifying child and a non-resident parent of his on an application duly made by a person entitled to apply (s 8(1)). The section applies, and the jurisdiction of the court is excluded, even where the circumstances of the case are such that the Secretary of State would not make a calculation if it were applied for (s 8(2)); this means that, for example, if the result of the formula is that no calculation should be made, there is no alternative remedy available to the person with care.

Therefore, where a person entitled to apply for a maintenance calculation in respect of a qualifying child and a non-resident parent wishes to apply for maintenance, it must be done by means of an application to the Secretary of State and not to the courts. The jurisdiction of the courts is completely excluded. Some of the possible reasons for this have already been discussed. Whatever the reason may be, the intention of the legislation is clear. Child maintenance is assessed by means of the formula which is certain and unchallengeable. To permit the courts to become involved, whether in making or reviewing calculations, would be to introduce an element of discretion which might result in departures from the formula. This could not be contemplated; hence the exclusion of the role of the courts. This is all discussed in more detail in Chapter Ten.

1.18 In the context of breakdown of marriage, there are certain implications. For example, a court dealing with an application for a property adjustment order pursuant to s 23 of the MCA 1973 cannot make an order in respect of the children of the marriage as part of its overall disposition except by consent and, even then, such an order may be set aside after one year; moreover, a parent with care who is, or will at any time in the future be, in receipt of benefit cannot contract out of the right to receive or the duty to pay child maintenance as part of a larger 'package deal'. Insofar as they can, the parties and the court have to predict what the liability of the non-resident parent is likely to be and bear that in mind when negotiating or ordering that part of the financial and other obligations and liabilities with which the court can deal.

The courts retain jurisdiction in respect of non-qualifying children such as stepchildren. In respect of qualifying children, the role of the court is limited. This is discussed in more detail in Chapter Ten.

The Link with State Benefits

1.19 The fact that the child support system introduced by the CSA 1991 is the creature of the Department of Social Security (DSS)[9] has never been concealed. The Secretary of State responsible is the Secretary of State for Social Security. The original system of child support officers, Chief Child Support Officer, inspectors, and tribunals was modelled on the social security system, and the amounts of maintenance calculations were originally based on social security rates of payment. However, there are further provisions in the Act which impose particular obligations on a person with care of a qualifying child who is in receipt of benefit.

Section 6 provides that where income support, an income-based jobseeker's allowance, or any other benefit of a prescribed kind, is claimed by or paid to the parent with care of a qualifying child, the Secretary of State may treat that parent as having applied for a maintenance calculation and take action to recover from the non-resident parent on the parent with care's behalf the child support maintenance so determined.

The remainder of the section will be considered in detail in Chapter Two but the basic principle is set out above.

1.20 The principle is therefore clear: a parent (normally a mother) who is in receipt of benefit must apply for a maintenance calculation. The specific benefits cited are of a non-contributory nature and so the DSS would gain from the making of a maintenance calculation by an appropriate reduction in the maintenance recovered. The other benefits which the Secretary of State has prescribed are of the same nature and do not include contributory benefits such as unemployment benefit or sickness benefit.

The duty to give information means that the mother has to name the father and give all necessary information to enable him to be traced.

The system is tailor-made for the parent on benefit; the whole organisation of calculation and enforcement makes it easier and more effective for such a parent (or, more accurately, the DSS, to which in fact the financial gain will accrue) to recoup money from a non-resident parent. However, a distinctive feature of the system is that the parent who is not in receipt of benefit has to go

---

9 The Department of Social Security's functions have since 2001 been taken over by the Department of Works and Pensions.

through exactly the same procedure, if maintenance is to be recovered other than by voluntary agreement.

The Role of Delegated Legislation

1.21 During the original parliamentary debates on the Bill, one criticism frequently made was that so much remained to be determined by statutory instrument. On dozens of occasions, power was conferred on the Secretary of State to make regulations to govern a particular implementation of the Act. The result was that it was sometimes difficult to predict exactly how the Act was going to work, although it must be said that some of the regulation-making powers are quite specific about what the regulations may provide (eg the regulations as to protected income provided for under Sch 1, para 6).

Whatever the reasons or justification for this state of affairs, it is a fact that the complete picture of how the Act works emerged only when all the regulations were made and published, and this is a process which continues from year to year.

General Summary

1.22 The CSA and the apparatus of law and regulations in which it operates have been a part of British law for approximately 10 years. In that time, the whole system of calculation and recovery of financial support for children has very radically changed. The Government admits that it has been a dismal failure and concedes that previous changes have not been for the better; however, it remains convinced that the amended version now enacted will solve the earlier problems. Only time will tell. However, the basic philosophy of the CSA 1991 remains.

The system of child maintenance under which parents pursue their remedies through the courts is, in principle, almost completely abolished. Subject to limited exceptions and transitional provisions, the only way to recover maintenance is to apply to an organ of the State which will calculate maintenance according to a predetermined formula with only limited scope for discretion. This State agency also has powers of investigation for the purposes of obtaining information for the calculation and is charged with the task of enforcing and recovering the money due under its calculation. Parents in receipt of State benefits are compelled to apply for calculations and, subject to statutory obligations, to provide information to the agency.

The CSA 1991 therefore clearly represented a major centralisation and extension of the role and powers of the State into what had hitherto been regarded as an area of private law.

CHAPTER TWO

Procedure for Obtaining Maintenance Calculations

Introduction

2.1 A person with care of a qualifying child who decides to apply for a calculation will probably do so for one of three reasons. First, she may have no choice; if she is in receipt of State benefits, the CSA 1991 imposes an obligation on her to do so (see para **2.11**). Secondly, the non-resident parent may be paying nothing, or not enough, for the support of the child. Thirdly, the parents may have agreed a figure but the person with care wishes to have the protection of a formal arrangement (although once a calculation is applied for the result will be determined by the formula rather than by any agreement which has been made; the relevance of agreements will be considered below at para **2.24** when those who may not apply are considered).

2.2 As was seen in Chapter One, the CSA 1991 establishes separate provisions for those persons with care who are in receipt of State benefits and those who are not; in effect, a two-tier system is established. This distinction will have to be borne in mind throughout this chapter.

As will be seen, the first two questions to be considered will be the jurisdiction of the Secretary of State, including whether the child is a qualifying child. Once those hurdles are crossed, the questions of who may, must, or may not apply will arise. The procedure, properly so called, is then introduced, with particulars of forms for application and reply, time-limits, the duty to co-operate, interim and default calculations, and so on. Then some of the other features in the system such as inspectors and, finally, termination of calculations, will be dealt with.

Jurisdiction

2.3 The first point to be established in any case is whether the Secretary of State has jurisdiction to make a calculation. Section 44(1) of the CSA 1991 provides that he has jurisdiction only with respect to a person who is:

(a) a person with care;
(b) a non-resident parent; or
(c) a qualifying child,

if that person is habitually resident in the UK, except in the case of a non-resident parent who falls within subsection (2A).

Section 44(2A) applies to a non-resident parent if he is not habitually resident within the UK but is:

(a) employed in the civil service of the Crown, including Her Majesty's Diplomatic Service and Her Majesty's Overseas Civil Service;
(b) a member of the naval, military or air forces of the Crown, including any person employed by an association established for the purposes of Part XI of the Reserve Forces Act 1996;
(c) employed by a company of a prescribed description registered under the Companies Act 1985 in England and Wales or in Scotland, or under the Companies (Northern Ireland) Order 1986, SI 1986/1032; or
(d) employed by a body of a prescribed description.

The detail as to the companies or bodies of a prescribed description referred to in (c) and (d) above is contained in reg 7A(1) and (2) of the Child Support (Maintenance Arrangements and Jurisdiction) Regulations 1992[1] (CS(MAJ) Regs 1992), SI 1992/2645. Companies covered by this regulation are those which employ employees to work outside the UK but make calculation and payment arrangements within the UK, so that a deduction from earnings order could be made. The prescribed bodies relate to various kinds of Health Service trust and local authorities.

Subject to the exception in subsection (2A), which is designed to 'catch' British public servants working overseas, therefore, it is necessary for all three persons (the essential players in the drama) to be habitually resident; if any of them is not habitually resident, the Secretary of State will not have jurisdiction. The term 'habitually resident' is not defined in the Act, probably because it appears in other legislation, for example the Domicile and Matrimonial Proceedings Act 1973, s 5(2)(b), and its meaning has been judicially considered and defined in many cases under that legislation. Habitual residence does not require continuous presence in a country but involves the establishment of a sufficient degree of settled residence in a country to justify the court, or, in this case, the Secretary of State, assuming jurisdiction. Each case has to be decided on its merits, and the overall picture will have to be considered.

The UK means Great Britain (England, Wales and Scotland) and Northern Ireland. It does not include, for example, the Channel Islands or the Isle of Man.

Where the person with care is not an individual, it is not necessary for that person to show habitual residence. Where both parents are absent, at least one of them must be habitually resident.

2.4 By s 44(3), the Secretary of State may make regulations to provide for the cancellation of any calculation where any of the three persons mentioned above ceases to be habitually resident. The regulations are contained in reg 7(1) and (2) of the CS(MAJ)Regs 1992.

Is the Child a Qualifying Child?

2.5 The question of whether the child is a qualifying child is, of course, part of the whole issue of the jurisdiction of the Secretary of State. If the child is not a

---

1 As amended by the Child Support (Information, Evidence and Disclosure and Maintenance Arrangements and Jurisdiction) (Amendment) Regulations 2000, SI 2001/161.

qualifying child, that is an end of the matter as far as the Secertary of State is concerned, and the person with care will have to apply to the courts.

By s 3(1), a child is a 'qualifying child' if:

'(a) one of his parents is, in relation to him, a non-resident parent; or
(b) both of his parents are, in relation to him, non-resident parents.'

Section 3(2) defines a 'non-resident parent' as follows:

'The parent of any child is a "non-resident parent", in relation to him, if –
(a) that parent is not living in the same household with the child; and
(b) the child has his home with a person who is, in relation to him, a person with care.'

This definition leads on to the definition of 'person with care'; by s 3(3), this is a person:

'(a) with whom the child has his home;
(b) who usually provides day to day care for the child (whether exclusively or in conjunction with any other person); and
(c) who does not fall within a prescribed category of person.'

Section 3(3)(c) requires clarification. By reg 21(1) of the Child Support (Maintenance Calculation Procedure) Regulations 2000 (CS(MCP)Regs 2000), SI 2001/157, the prescribed persons who may not be persons with care are:

'(a) a local authority;
(b) a person with whom a child who is looked after by a local authority is placed by that authority under the provisions of the CA 1989 except where that person is a parent of such child and the local authority allow the child to live with that parent under section 23(5) of that Act;
(c) [relates to Scotland only].'

'Child who is looked after by a local authority' has the same meaning as in s 22 of the CA 1989.

The Act also sets out a list of persons whom the Secretary of State may *not* prescribe as a category under s 3(4). They are:

'(a) parents;
(b) guardians;
(c) persons in whose favour residence orders under section 8 of the Children Act 1989 are in force;
(d) in Scotland, persons having the right to custody of a child.'

The result of this combination of double negatives is, therefore, that these persons are always capable of being persons with care.

2.6 This somewhat exhaustive examination has been necessary to establish what the CSA 1991 means by 'qualifying child'; at the same time, the meanings of 'non-resident parent' and 'person with care' have been established. However, two further terms remain to be defined, namely 'child' and 'parent'. Clearly, a person cannot be a qualifying child unless he is a child, or what the Act recognises as a child, and 'parent' needs some clarification.

Section 55(2) states clearly who is *not* a child for the purposes of the Act; this is a person who:

'(a) is or has been married;
 (b) has celebrated a marriage which is void; or
 (c) has celebrated a marriage in respect of which a decree of nullity has been granted.'

The essential excluding factor is, therefore, the participation in a ceremony of marriage whether or not this was a valid ceremony; a person under 16 who had taken part in a ceremony of marriage (which would be void *ab initio*) would be excluded from the provisions of the Act. 'Marriage' is not defined by the Act but, presumably, it means a ceremony which was intended to comply with the provisions of the Marriage Acts.

2.7 By s 55(1), a person *is* a child if he falls within any of the following:

'(a) he is under the age of 16;
 (b) he is under the age of 19 and receiving full-time education (which is not advanced education) –
     (i) by attendance at a recognised educational establishment; or
     (ii) elsewhere, if the education is recognised by the Secretary of State; or
 (c) he does not fall within paragraph (a) or (b) but –
     (i) he is under the age of 18, and
     (ii) prescribed conditions are satisfied with respect to him.'

Section 55(4) provides that the Secretary of State may recognise education provided otherwise than at a recognised educational establishment only if he is satisfied that education was being provided for the child immediately before the age of 16. Section 55(6) provides that, in determining whether a person falls within s 55(1)(b), no account shall be taken of such interruptions in his education as may be prescribed.

2.8 With the aid of the above, and of the regulations, the following framework emerges (it is assumed that the other requirements, eg as to non-resident parent etc, are satisfied).

(1) Person under 16

A person under 16 must be a qualifying child unless he has gone through a ceremony of marriage.

(2) Person over 16 but under 19

A person over 16 but under 19:

(a) is *not* a qualifying child if in advanced education (ie a course in preparation for a degree, a Diploma of Higher Education, HND or HNC of the Business and Technology Education Council (BETEC) or the Scottish Qualifications Council (SQC) or a teaching qualification, or any other course which is of a standard above that of an ordinary national diploma, a national diploma or a national certificate of BETEC or SQC, GCE 'A' level, or their Scottish equivalents). (See para 2 of Sch 1 to the CS(MCP)Regs 2000; as to the meaning of 'full-time education', see para 3);

(b) may not be a 'child' if he is engaged in training under work-based training for young people or if he is entitled to income support or an income-based jobseeker's allowance;

(c) *is* a qualifying child if in non-advanced education recognised by the Secretary of State;

(d) otherwise, *is not* a qualifying child *unless*:
    (i) he is under 18; and
    (ii) is registered for work or for training under work-based training for young people, (or, in Scotland, Skillseekers training) with the DfES (formerly the DEE), MOD, an LEA (in Scotland, an education authority), or any corresponding body in an EU Member State; and
    (iii) is not engaged in remunerative work other than work of a temporary nature that is due to cease before the end of the applicable extension period and the extension period has not expired; and immediately before the extension period he is a child for the purposes of the Act but for this regulation.

See generally CS(MCP)Regs 2000, Sch 1.

Interruptions in education of up to six months may be ignored, provided there is a reasonable excuse, for example sickness or holidays.

2.9 The other term to be defined is 'parent'. Section 54 defines parent, in relation to any child, as any person who is in law the mother or father of the child. To be a parent, therefore, it is necessary to be the biological mother or father of a child, or to have adopted the child (an adoption order in respect of a child of which a person is a parent will mean that that person ceases to be a parent).

However, because of advances in medical science, the matter does not end there. The position is governed both by common law and by ss 27 and 28 of the Human Fertilisation and Embryology Act 1990 (HFEA 1990), the combined effect of which is as follows:

(a) a woman who bears a child will, at the child's birth, always be regarded as the child's mother (HFEA 1990, s 27(1));

(b) in principle, the father of a child is the person who provides the sperm which leads to conception. However, this is subject to the following exceptions:
    (i) the husband of a woman who is artificially inseminated is treated as the father of the child unless it is proved that he did not consent to the treatment (HFEA 1990, s 28(2));
    (ii) where a woman has been artificially inseminated in the course of treatment provided for her and a man under the licensing procedure established by the HFEA 1990, then the man is treated as the father (HFEA 1990, s 28(3));

(c) a donor of sperm for the purposes of 'treatment services' provided under the HFEA 1990 is not to be treated as the child's father;

(d) at common law, a number of presumptions arise, all of which are capable of being rebutted, for example the husband of a married woman is the father of the child, and a man whose name is entered as father in the Register of Births is the father.

Who may Apply?

2.10 In order to reach this stage, it will have been established that there is:

- a qualifying child;
- a non-resident parent;
- a person with care.

The next question to be decided is whether a person intending to apply for a calculation is entitled to do so. Therefore, a distinction must be made between those who *may* apply and those who will be treated as having applied and, in effect therefore, *must* apply; this is the difference between applications under s 4 and s 6; or those where the applicant is not in receipt of State benefits and those where she is.

Section 4(1) of the CSA 1991 provides that either the person with care or the non-resident parent may apply to the Secretary of State for a calculation. However, s 4(9) provides that no application may be made under s 4 if there is in force a calculation made in response to an application made under s 6.

At this stage, therefore, matters relating to applications have to be subdivided as follows:

- Section 6 applications (see paras **2.11** to **2.21**).
- Section 4 applications (see paras **2.22** to **2.23**).

In addition, further subdivisions arise, as follows:

- The effect of court orders or agreements (see para **2.24**).
- Multiple applications (see para **2.25**).

Applications by Parents Receiving Benefit

2.11 The CSA 1991 distinguishes between those persons with care who are in receipt of benefit and those who are not; since, it may be argued, the Act is designed for the benefit of the former, it seems logical to deal with them first.

Section 6 applies where 'income support, an income-based jobseeker's allowance or any other benefit of a prescribed kind is claimed by or in respect of, or paid to or in respect of, the parent of a qualifying child who is also a person with care of the child.' In this section, that parent (ie the parent who is the person with care) is referred to as 'the parent'.

When the above conditions apply, s 6(3) applies. This provides that:

'The Secretary of State may –
(a) treat the parent as having applied for a maintenance calculation with respect to the qualifying child and all other children of the non-resident parent in relation to whom the parent is also a person with care; and
(b) take action under this Act to recover from the non-resident parent, on the parent's behalf, the child support maintenance so determined.'

The following initial points should be noted. First, s 6(6) provides that subsection (1) has effect regardless of whether any of the benefits mentioned are payable with respect to any qualifying child. Accordingly, the payment of benefit of a prescribed kind of any amount or nature empowers the Secretary of State to impose this requirement.

Secondly, although s 6(3) refers to the Secretary of State taking action, it is clear that when he does so he takes action on behalf of the parent with care; if the parent with care refuses to give him the necessary information or requests him not to proceed, there is nothing the Secretary of State can do except penalise the parent with care (see 'The requirement to co-operate', at para **2.13**). This is emphasised by s 6(4) which provides that, before taking action, the Secretary of State must notify the parent in writing of the effects of subsections (3) and (5) and of s 46. Subsection (5) provides that the Secretary of State may not act under subsection (3) if the parent asks him not to (a request which need not be in writing).

Section 6 refers to a 'parent' while s 4 refers to a 'person' with care. The distinction is important. Only a person with care who is a parent may be compelled to take action under s 6.

2.12   The procedure after an application is treated as having been made under s 6 is the same as when an application is made under s 4. This will be considered in more detail at para **2.26**. Here it is only necessary to note that, whereas in a s 4 application (which need not be in writing) the Secretary of State will first satisfy himself that he has all necessary information before proceeding, in a s 6 application he will make the decision to proceed and then give notice to the non-resident parent as he would in a s 4 application unless either he cannot do so because of lack of information or the parent with care has specifically requested him not to proceed.

The requirement to co-operate

2.13   By s 6(7), the parent with care must, unless she has made a request under subsection (5), comply with the regulations made by the Secretary of State 'so far as she reasonably can'. The regulations in question are those which are made with a view to the Secretary of State's being provided with the information which is required to enable:

'(a)   the non-resident parent to be identified or traced;
 (b)   the amount of child support maintenance payable by him to be calculated; and
 (c)   that amount to be recovered from him.'

The information to be supplied is prescribed by reg 3(2) of the Child Support (Information, Evidence and Disclosure) Regulations 1992 (CS(IED) Regs 1992), SI 1992/1812; it includes the following:

(a)   the habitual residence and name and address of the non-resident parent;
(b)   the name and address of any current or recent employer of a non-resident parent;
(c)   persons living in the same household as the non-resident parent.

It is also provided that the obligation to provide information which is required by subsection (7) does not apply in such circumstances as may be prescribed and may, in prescribed circumstances, be waived by the Secretary of State.

2.14 This raises few problems in the context of marriage breakdown where there is normally little doubt as to the identity of the non-resident parent. However, difficulties may arise in the case of a single mother, and the CSA 1991 contains sanctions to 'encourage' a parent with care to give the prescribed information. These provisions gave rise to controversy during the parliamentary passage of the Act, which was mentioned in previous editions of this book; this is now history and there seems little point in repeating it here.

The final sanction which the Secretary of State may apply is a reduced benefit direction. This is considered at para **2.19**, but there is a procedure which must be exhausted before that stage can be reached.

The procedure is contained in s 46. This comes into effect under s 46(1) where any person (referred to as 'the parent'):

'(a) has made a request under section 6(5);
 (b) fails to comply with any regulation made under section 6(7); or
 (c) having been treated as having applied for a maintenance calculation under section 6, refuses to take a scientific test (within the meaning of section 27A).'

It is made clear, therefore, that the section applies only to parents who come within s 6(1) and have either requested the Secretary of State to take no action, failed to supply the information required, or failed to co-operate when tests are required to ascertain paternity (as to which, see Chapter Six).

2.15 What follows is laid down in s 46(2). The Secretary of State may serve written notice on the parent requiring her, before the end of a specified period of four weeks thereafter (see CS(MCP)Regs 2000, reg 9):

(a) where she has made a request under s 6(5), 'to give him her reasons for making the request';
(b) where she has failed to comply with the regulations, 'to give him her reasons for failing to do so'; or
(c) where she refuses to take a scientific test, 'to give him her reasons for her refusal'.

2.16 When the period specified in the notice has expired, the Secretary of State must consider whether, if:

(a) he 'were to do what is mentioned in section 6(3)', ie to treat her as having applied for a maintenance calculation and take action to recover the sums so determined; or
(b) the parent 'were to be required to comply' with her obligations under s 6(7); or
(c) the parent took the scientific test,

'there would be a risk of her, or of any children living with her, suffering harm or undue distress as a result of his taking such action or her complying or taking the test'.

2.17 If the Secretary of State decides that there are no such reasonable grounds, he may, except in prescribed circumstances, make a reduced benefit decision with respect to the parent. Where the circumstances which have triggered this position are the parent's request to the Secretary of State not to take action on her behalf (under s 6(5)), the Secretary of State under s 46(6):

'may, from time to time, serve written notice on the parent requiring her, before the end of a specified period –
(a) to state whether her request under section 6(5) still stands; and
(b) if so, to give him her reasons for maintaining her request.'

This seems to be an effort by the Secretary of State to give the parent an opportunity to reflect on the error of her ways.

As to 'prescribed circumstances' mentioned in s 46(5), reg 10 of the CS(MCP)Regs 2000 provides that no reduced benefit direction may be given where income support is payable to, or in respect of, the parent in question, or where that parent is in receipt of an income-based jobseeker's allowance and the applicable amount of the claimant includes one or more of the amounts set out in para 20(4), (5) or (7) of Sch 1 to the Jobseeker's Allowance Regulations 1996, SI 1996/207.

2.18 Neither the CSA 1991 nor the present regulations give any guidance as to what may, or may not, constitute 'harm or undue distress'. It will be for the Secretary of State to make a value judgement, in the light of the ordinary meanings of those words.

The following cases would justify the Secretary of State in deciding not to proceed:

– the parent has been the victim of rape;
– the non-resident parent has sexually assaulted a child living in the household of the parent with care;
– the child was conceived as a result of incest;
– the non-resident parent is a 'celebrity' and unwelcome publicity might result which would be adverse to the welfare of parent and child.

In the following cases, the Secretary of State should proceed:

– the non-resident parent is seeking contact;
– the parent with care wants to sever all links with the non-resident parent;
– the non-resident parent is, or was at the time of conception of the child, under 16;
– the non-resident parent is married to someone else;
– a voluntary agreement exists.

2.19 If the Secretary of State is not satisfied that reasonable grounds are shown, a reduced benefit direction may be given. Section 46(10)(b) defines a reduced benefit direction as 'a decision that the amount payable by way of any relevant benefit to, or in respect of, the parent concerned be reduced by such amount, and for such period, as may be prescribed'. By s 46(10)(c) 'relevant benefit' means 'income support or an income-based jobseeker's allowance or any other benefit of a kind prescribed for the purposes of section 6'.

By s 46(7), the Secretary of State must send a copy of the reduced benefit direction to the parent concerned.

Revisions and appeals generally are dealt with in Chapter Seven.

2.20 The detail as to reduced benefit decisions is contained in regs 11 to 20 of the CS(MCP)Regs 2000, the important parts of which may be summarised as follows. The regulations provide for the benefit payable in respect of the parent herself to be reduced by 40%. This reduction may apply for a period of up to three years. Where there is already a reduced benefit decision in force, any further reduced benefit decision will take effect the day after the existing reduction expires. Only one reduced benefit decision in relation to a parent may be in force at any one time. No reduction may reduce the parent's benefit to less than the minimum benefit payable in respect of income support or income-based jobseekers' allowance; in such a case, the reduction will be adjusted accordingly.

2.21   When a parent subject to a reduced benefit decision ceases to receive benefit, the reduced benefit decision is suspended for 52 weeks and then ceases to have effect. However, if benefit again becomes payable within that 52-week period, the reduced benefit decision applies for its unexpired term.

A reduced benefit decision is suspended if there is in relation to that decision only one qualifying child and that child ceases to be a child within the meaning of the Act, or if the parent ceases to be a parent with care. The decision will terminate if the parent concerned either withdraws her request under s 6(5) (request not to proceed) or complies with her obligations.

Applications by Persons Not Receiving Benefits

2.22   A person with care who is not receiving benefits is in a different position from one who is receiving benefits, in that there is no compulsion on her to take or authorise action, nor is there any sanction, other than the abandoning of the claim, if she fails to supply the necessary information. Nevertheless, the procedure for applying for an assessment is broadly similar and the result will be calculated in the same way.

Either the person with care or the non-resident parent may apply to the Secretary of State for a maintenance calculation. There is a series of regional offices for the CSA, and application should be made to the office nearest to the applicant. Fees are payable (see para **2.44**).

2.23   The procedure for applying for a maintenance calculation under s 4 is governed by the CS(MCP)Regs 2000, Part II, which may be summarised as follows.

(a) Applications need not normally be in writing. However, if the Secretary of State directs that the application be made in writing, the application must be either on a form provided by the Secretary of State 'or in such other written form as the Secretary of State may accept as sufficient in the circumstances of any particular case' (reg 3(1)). It seems therefore that a telephone call to the CSA will normally be accepted as sufficient, but the Secretary of State retains a wide discretion over the form of the application.

(b) Provided that the application conforms to reg 3(1), it is deemed 'effective' (reg 3(2)). This seems to mean no more than that it is effective if the Secretary of State accepts it.

(c) Where an application is not effective (ie the Secretary of State does not accept it), the Secretary of State may request the applicant to provide such additional information or evidence as he may specify; where the application was made on a form, a fresh form may be required (reg 3(3)).

(d) In principle, an application is deemed to have been made on the day it is received (reg 3(2)). Where additional information has been requested and is received within 14 days of the request or on a later date where the Secretary of State is satisfied that the delay was unavoidable, the application will be treated as having been made on the day on which the application was received (reg 3(4)). Otherwise, it will be treated as having been made on the day the additional information or evidence was received (reg 3(5)).

(e) An effective application may be amended or withdrawn at any time before a maintenance calculation is made; such withdrawal or amendment need not be in writing unless the Secretary of State requires it to be (reg 3(6)). However, no amendment may relate to any change of circumstances arising after the effective date of a maintenance calculation (reg 3(7)).

The Effect of Court Orders or Agreements

2.24 The existence of a court order or agreement is relevant to be considered at this stage since it may have the effect of preventing a person from making an application for a calculation. The ability of the parties to make an agreement, and the jurisdiction of the courts, are considered in Chapter Ten.

The only purpose in mentioning the subject here, therefore, is to alert the reader to the fact that the existence of an order or agreement must be borne in mind when deciding whether or not an application may be made. The effect of the amendments to s 4 of the CSA 1991 made by the CSPSSA 2000 is that, if a court order is made after a prescribed date, it will not be possible to apply for a maintenance calculation under s 4 for 14 months. The prescribed date is 5 April 2002. Therefore, if a court order is in existence at that date, the pre-2002 position will apply and the CSA will have no jurisdiction under s 4. If there is no court order by that date, an application for an order (in the same circumstances as before that date) may be made, but it will only oust the jurisdiction of the CSA for 14 months, after which time the parent with care may make an application under s 4. This does not affect the rights of the Secretary of State under s 6.

Multiple Applications

2.25 More than one person may be a person with care in relation to a qualifying child (s 3(5)). The CSA 1991 provides that where more than one application for a calculation is made, regulations may provide for two or more applications to be treated as a single application, and for the replacement of a maintenance calculation made on the application of one person by a later calculation made on the application of that or any other person (Sch 1, Part II, para 14).

The existing regulations are contained in reg 4 of and Sch 2 to the CS(MCP)Regs 2000, and Sch 2 sets out the permutations which may apply. They appear complicated, but may be summarised as follows.

(a) The basic position is that only one application for a maintenance calculation should be proceeded with (s 5(2)).

(b) Where a person with care or a non-resident parent makes an effective application for a maintenance calculation (or in Scotland the child makes such an application) and, before the calculation is made, makes another application in respect of the same non-resident parent or person with care, as the case may be, the applications will be treated as a single application (Sch 2, paras 1 and 2).

(c) Applications by different persons are dealt with in Sch 2, para 3.

The table below shows how multiple applications are at present dealt with. It should be noted that in all these cases, where the applications are not in respect of identical qualifying children, the application with which the Secretary of State proceeds will be treated as a single application in respect of ALL the qualifying children with respect to whom applications have been made (para 3(13)). However, where the Secretary of State is satisfied that the same person with care does not provide the principal day to day care for all such qualifying children, he must make separate calculations in relation to each person with care providing such principal day to day care (para 3(14)).

Applications made by	*Applications to be proceeded with*
1. Person with care and non-resident parent	Person with care (para 3(2))
2. (In Scotland only)	
The child and either parent	The parent (para 3(31))
The child and both parents	The parent with care (para 3(4))
The child and the parents, and a person with parental responsibility	The parent with care (para 3(4))
More than one qualifying child	The eldest child (para 3(5))
3. Two non-resident parents	Both applications to be dealt with as one application (para 3(6))
4. Applications under s 6 by the person with care and under s 4 by another person with care who has parental responsibility	The parent with care (para 3(7))
5. More than one person with care, both having parental responsibility, one of whom falls to be treated as a non-resident parent	The one who is not to be treated as a non-resident parent (para 3(8))
6. As 5., but where there is more than one person who does not fall to be dealt with as a non-resident parent	As in 7. below
7. More than one person with care, neither having parental responsibility	The application of the principal provider of day to day care, as determined in accordance with para 3(11)

Note

Schedule 2, para 3(11) may be summarised as follows. Where the Secretary of State can establish with which person the child spends the greater part of its time (or, in the case of more than one child, the greatest proportion of their time, taking account of the time each child spends with each person with care), the application of that person will proceed. Where he cannot so determine, and child benefit is paid to one person with care but not both, the application of the person receiving child benefit will proceed. Where all else fails, the application of the applicant 'who in the opinion of the Secretary of State is the principal provider of day to day care . . .' will proceed.

Where there is more than one person with care of a qualifying child and one or more, but not all, of them have parental responsibility for (in Scotland, parental rights over) the child, only those persons with parental responsibility (rights) may apply (s 5(1)). 'Parental responsibility' is defined by s 3(1) of the CA 1989 as 'all the rights, duties, powers, responsibilities and authority which by law a parent has in relation to the child and his property'.

Notice of Application for Maintenance Calculation

2.26 When an effective application has been made under s 4, or is treated as having been made under s 6, the Secretary of State must, as soon as is reasonably practicable, notify the non-resident parent and any other relevant persons (not including the applicant or a person treated as the applicant) of the application and request such information as he may require. This notification may be oral or in writing (CS(MCP)Regs 2000, reg 5(1)). Once again, it seems that a telephone call will suffice. Such notice must specify the effective date of the maintenance calculation (as to which, see para **2.41**) and the ability to make a default maintenance decision (reg 5(2)).

The information to be supplied is dealt with in paras **2.27** to **2.35**.

Information Required from Non-Resident Parent

2.27 By s 11(1) of the CSA 1991, any application for a maintenance calculation (whether or not the person with care is receiving benefit) received by the Secretary of State shall be dealt with by him in accordance with the Act. In order to make a calculation, he needs information from the person with care and the non-resident parent. The obligation of the former to supply information has already been considered above.

Section 14(1) empowers the Secretary of State to make regulations requiring any information or evidence needed for the determination of any application under the Act, or any question arising in connection with such an application, to be furnished by such person as may be prescribed by regulations and in accordance with the regulations. A person who is required to comply with any regulations as to the supply of information who fails to comply with such a request is guilty of an offence. It is also an offence for such a person to make a statement or representation which he knows to be false, or to provide or knowingly cause or knowingly allow to be provided a document which he knows to be false in a material particular. It is a defence to prove that there was reasonable excuse for failure to comply with a request for information. The maximum penalty is a fine not exceeding level 3 on the standard scale.

2.28   The general duty to give information is set out in CS(IED)Regs 1992, reg 2(1). It covers many possibilities, and may be summarised as providing that where an application for a maintenance calculation has been received, a 'relevant person' (in this context, the non-resident parent or a person who is alleged to be the father of the qualifying child) shall furnish such information or evidence as is required by the Secretary of State, and which is needed to enable a determination to be made in relation to one or more of the matters listed in reg 3(1).

By reg 3(2), the information or evidence to be furnished may, in particular, include information as to (inter alia) the following:

(a)   the name and address of any current or recent employer of a non-resident parent;

(b)   the address from which a non-resident parent who is self-employed carries on his trade or business, the trading name, and the gross receipts and expenses and other outgoings of the trade or business;

(c)   any other income of a non-resident parent;

(d)   income of persons living in the same household as the non-resident parent;

(e)   housing costs;

(f)   the identifying details of any bank, building society or similar account held in the name of the non-resident parent and statements relating to any such account.

The maintenance enquiry form contains questions designed to elicit all this information.

2.29   In addition to the information which he obtains from the person with care and the non-resident parent, the Secretary of State may also obtain information from other persons. Not surprisingly, such other persons include government departments and other public bodies.

Section 14(2) provides that the Secretary of State may make use of any information in his possession which was acquired by him in connection with his functions under any of the benefit Acts. He may therefore inspect files relating to any other benefit application made by any person.

2.30   However, the clearest departure from what used to be regarded as the principle of confidentiality in government records occurs in Sch 2 to the Act. This provides for the provision of information to the Secretary of State from Inland Revenue records and local authority records.

Paragraph 1 of Sch 2 applies where the Secretary of State requires information for the purpose of tracing the current address of a non-resident parent or the current employer of a non-resident parent. Paragraph 1(2) states:

> 'In such a case, no obligation as to secrecy imposed by statute or otherwise on a person employed in relation to the Inland Revenue shall prevent any information obtained or held in connection with the assessment or collection of income tax from being disclosed to –
>
> (a)   the Secretary of State;
>
> (b)   the Department of Health and Social Services for Northern Ireland; or
>
> (c)   an officer of either of them authorised to receive such information in connection with the operation of this Act or of any corresponding Northern Ireland legislation.'

It will be seen that the obligation as to secrecy may be waived only if the current address or current employer of a non-resident parent is not known. Where such information is already known, no application to the Inland Revenue may be made. However, Sch 2 imposes no limit on the information which may be disclosed once it is established that information may be given; para 1(2) refers to 'any information obtained in connection with the assessment or collection of income tax'. This obviously includes details of the non-resident parent's earnings and entitlement to allowances, and it would seem that all this may be revealed once the obligation as to secrecy has been removed.

2.31 Paragraph 2 of Sch 2 deals with local authority records and applies, in effect, where the Secretary of State requires relevant information for the discharge of his functions under the Act; this is clearly a broad mandate, and means that the power can be invoked at will.

The Secretary of State may give a direction to the appropriate authority requiring it to give him such relevant information in connection with housing benefit or community charge benefit to which a non-resident parent or person with care is entitled as the Secretary of State considers necessary in connection with his determination of that person's income of any kind, housing costs or protected income. Under para 2(4), 'appropriate authority' means, in relation to housing benefit, the housing or local authority concerned, and, in relation to community charge benefit, the charging authority or, in Scotland, the levying authority. The community charge has been replaced by the council tax, to which similar principles apply.

As a kind of quid pro quo, reg 9 of the CS(IED)Regs 1992 permits the Secretary of State to disclose to the authorities mentioned above any information held for the purposes of the Act.

Finally, it should be noted that the parents or parties to the application do not have the right to obtain information from the Secretary of State. In *Re C (A Minor) (Child Support Agency: Disclosure)* [1995] 1 FLR 201, Ewbank J held that there was no power vested in the Secretary of State to disclose information about the address of a parent.

2.32 Given the very wide powers to collect information from a variety of sources, it is not surprising that the CSA 1991 contains sanctions against the unauthorised disclosure of information. Section 50 of the Act and reg 11 of the CS(IED)Regs 1992 contain a list of persons affected; this includes any child support officer (CSO) or any other civil servant involved in functions under the Act, Tribunal staff, and others ranging from the Comptroller and Auditor-General to anyone employed by the DSS.

Any such person is guilty of an offence if, without lawful authority, he discloses any information which was acquired by him in the course of his employment and relates to a particular person. A person guilty of an offence under s 50 is liable on conviction on indictment to imprisonment for up to two years or a fine or both, and on summary conviction to imprisonment for up to six months or a fine or both.

It is not an offence to disclose information in the form of a summary or collection of information in general terms (s 50(2)). Section 50(3) also provides a statutory defence to a prosecution under the section for an officer who believed that he was making the disclosure in question with lawful authority and had no reasonable cause to believe otherwise, or who believed that the information had been previously disclosed with lawful authority. Section 50(6) defines what is lawful authority, and should be referred to where the question arises.

2.33 Having dealt with the Secretary of State's powers to obtain information from other public authorities, his powers as to other persons, in particular members of the public, must now be considered. The Secretary of State has wide powers to require different classes of persons to furnish information or evidence. However, this can only be for a lawful purpose; reg 3(1) of the CS(IED)Regs 1992 provides that the information or evidence may only be required if needed to enable certain decisions to be made or purposes to be fulfilled. These purposes are set out in full in the regulation but may be summarised as decisions as to whether to proceed or whether there is jurisdiction on which application should proceed, identification and tracing of non-resident parents, calculating and enforcing child support maintenance, and identifying related proceedings.

2.34 The persons who may be required to furnish information are listed in reg 2(2). It will be noted that different classes of person may be required to give the information or evidence only if it is required for certain specific purposes; not all the matters listed in reg 3(1) apply to such persons.

The first class of person is 'the relevant person', defined as a person with care, a non-resident parent and a child who applies under s 7; such a person is liable in respect of all the purposes set out in reg 3(1).

A person who is alleged to be the parent of a child but who denies parentage is required to give information or evidence for the purpose of reg 3(1)(b), viz a decision to be made as to whether the Secretary of State has jurisdiction, and reg 3(1)(d), viz a non-resident parent to be identified.

A current or recent employer of a non-resident parent is so required for the purposes of identifying or tracing him, assessing and recovering child support maintenance, and enforcing court orders.

A local authority in whose area a non-resident parent lives is so required for the purpose of making a decision as to whether there exists a qualifying child or a non-resident parent.

Finally, in any case where, in relation to the qualifying child or children, or the non-resident parent, there is or has been a relevant court order, or there have been or are pending related proceedings before a court, certain information or evidence may be required. The persons liable to supply such information include the senior district judge, the district judge of a district registry, the proper officer of a county court, a clerk to the justices, and (in Scotland), the deputy principal clerk of session or the sheriff clerk, as the case may be. The requirement is limited to cases where the information or evidence is required for the purpose of ascertaining that the amount payable under a relevant court order, recovering the same from a non-resident parent, or identifying any related proceedings. By reg 1(2), 'related proceedings' are defined as proceedings in which a relevant court order was being sought, this in turn being defined as orders as to periodical or capital provision or variation of property rights made under one of the enactments set out in s 8(11) of the CSA 1991 (eg the MCA 1973, the Domestic Proceedings and Magistrates' Courts Act 1978 (DPMCA 1978), the CA 1989) in relation to a qualifying child or a relevant person. Similar provisions exist for Scotland.

2.35 As to the nature of the information or evidence to be supplied, reg 3(2) sets out a very detailed list of particular matters; when considering any particular case, it should be borne in mind that the information can be required only for the specified purposes contained in reg 3(1) and (2), as set out above.

The information or evidence listed in reg 3(2) includes such matters as the habitual residence of the parents or child, their marital status, where the child spends its time, matters relevant to disputes as to parentage, names and addresses of employers, gross and net earnings of parents, amounts payable under court orders, persons living in the same household as parents and details of their incomes, benefits payable, housing costs, details of bank or building society accounts.

Inspectors

2.36 The final weapon in the armoury of the Secretary of State is the use of inspectors; this is a familiar feature in the field of social security. The function of inspectors is stated to be 'to acquire information which the Secretary of State needs for any of the purposes of this Act'.

Under s 15(4):

'an inspector has power, at any reasonable time and either alone or accompanied by such other persons as he thinks fit, to enter any premises which –
(a) are liable to inspection under this section; and
(b) are premises to which it is reasonable for him to require entry in order that he may exercise his functions under this section,
and there may make such examination and enquiry as he considers appropriate.'

Under the previous law, the premises had to be specified in the certificate of appointment. This has now been changed, and s 15(4A) defines the premises which are liable to inspection under this section. They are:

'those which are not used wholly as a dwelling house and which the inspector has reasonable grounds for suspecting are –
(a) premises at which a non-resident parent is or has been employed;
(b) premises at which a non-resident parent carries out, or has carried out, a trade, profession, vocation or business;
(c) premises at which there is information held by a person ("A") whom the inspector has reasonable grounds for suspecting has information about a non-resident parent acquired in the course of A's own trade, profession, vocation or business.'

'Premises' includes moveable structures and vehicles, vessels, aircraft, offshore installations and 'places of all descriptions whether or not occupied as land or otherwise'. It is difficult to think of anywhere an inspector could not go. Subsection (4A)(a) and (b) are clear and need no elaboration. By (c), it seems that an inspector would be entitled to enter the offices of, say, a doctor or solicitor and require the production of files, records, etc which might contain details of the work record of a patient or client.

2.37 The inspector may, therefore, require entry to certain premises. Once there, he is empowered to question any person aged 18 or over whom he finds on the premises (s 15(5)).

Section 15(6) provides that, if required to do so by an inspector exercising his powers, any person who is within the definition above shall furnish to the inspector all such information and documents as the inspector may reasonably require:

> 'If required to do so by an inspector exercising his powers, any such person shall furnish to the inspector all such information and documents as the inspector may reasonably require.'

2.38 Anyone who fails to co-operate with the inspector is liable to a penalty. Section 15(7) provides that no person shall be required under s 15 to answer any question or give any evidence tending to incriminate himself, or, in the case of a person who is married, his or her spouse; however, 'incriminate' means render himself liable to criminal proceedings, and this would not normally apply.

Subject to this, under s 15(9):

> 'If any person –
> (a) intentionally delays or obstructs any inspector exercising his powers; or
> (b) without reasonable excuse, refuses or neglects to answer any question or furnish any information or to produce any document when required to do so under this section,
> he shall be guilty of an offence and liable on summary conviction to a fine not exceeding level 3 on the standard scale.'

The Calculation

2.39 Once the Secretary of State has sufficient information, he makes a calculation. This calculation must be made in accordance with Part I of Sch 1; the detail of how calculations are made is contained in Chapter Three.

Regulation 23(1) of the CS(MCP)Regs 2000 sets out what a notification of a maintenance calculation must contain. In addition to the maintenance calculation itself, it must set out:

(a) the effective date of the calculation (as to which, see para **2.41**);
(b) where relevant, the non-resident parent's weekly income;
(c) the number of qualifying children;
(d) the number of relevant other children;
(e) the weekly rate;
(f) the amounts calculated in accordance with Part 1 of Sch 1 to the Act and details of any variation;
(g) details of any adjustment or apportionment or shared care;
(h) any adjustments under regs 9 or 11 of the Child Support (Maintenance Calculations and Special Cases) Regulations 2000 (CS(MCSC)Regs 2000), SI 2001/155.

The effect of reg 23(3) is that no notice may contain the address of the person with care or any information which might lead to her being traced, except where her written consent has been given.

2.40 The notification of a default maintenance calculation (see para **2.42**) must set out the effective date, the default rate, the number of qualifying children, whether any apportionment has been applied, and the nature of the information required to enable a decision to be made under s 11 by way of s 16 (ie enabling the Secretary of State to make a decision in the usual way and not by default) (reg 23(2)).

2.41 The effective date of a calculation (ie the date on which the calculation takes effect for the purposes of the Act: reg 1(2)) is as follows.

(a) Where there is no maintenance calculation in force and application was made by the non-resident parent, the effective date of his application (reg 25(2)).

(b) Where there is no maintenance calculation in force, and the application is made under s 4 by a person with care or is treated as having been made by her under s 6, the date of notification of the calculation to the non-resident parent (reg 25(3)).

(c) Where the Secretary of State is satisfied that the non-resident parent has intentionally avoided receipt of a notice of maintenance calculation, he may determine the date of notification (reg 25(4)).

(d) Regulations 26 to 28 govern the position where there is or has been a court order. For the relationship between court orders and maintenance calculations generally, see Chapter Ten. The position as to effective dates may be summarised as follows:

   (i) where there is no maintenance calculation in force, a child maintenance order made on or after 5 April 2002 has been in force for at least one year, and an application for a maintenance calculation has been made under s 4 (or s 7 in Scotland), the effective date is two months and two days after the application is made (reg 26(2));

   (ii) where there is no maintenance calculation in force, an application for a maintenance calculation is treated as made under s 6, and there is a maintenance order in force, the effective date of the maintenance calculation is two days after the maintenance calculation is made, irrespective of the date of the maintenance order and whether or not it has been in force for a year (reg 27(2));

   (iii) where a maintenance calculation is made and there was a maintenance order in force which ceased to have effect after the date on which the application for the maintenance calculation was made but before the effective date provided for in (a) to (c) above, the effective date is the day following that in which the maintenance order ceased to have effect (reg 28).

Interim and Default Maintenance Decisions

2.42 Even with the wide powers available to him, the Secretary of State may find that he still has insufficient information to enable him to make an accurate calculation. Section 12 is designed to deal with this position. Under s 12, the Secretary of State has two distinct powers: the first is to make a default maintenance decision and the second is to make an interim decision. These must be considered separately.

The power to make a default maintenance decision arises where either the Secretary of State is required to make a maintenance calculation (ie where an application has been made under s 4 or is treated as having been made under s 6) or is proposing to make a decision under s 16 or s 17 (ie on a review) and 'it appears to him that he does not have sufficient information to enable him to do so'. In such circumstances, he may make a default decision and regulations will prescribe the procedure for doing so and the default rate.

The default rate replaces what used to be called an interim assessment under the old s 12. It was thought that the previous system of interim assessments was unduly harsh and resulted in very poor returns. The Government's intentions were explained in the following terms:

> 'we intend that default rates of maintenance will be put in place quickly and that they will be set according to whether there are one, two or three or more children to be maintained. We envisage rates of £30, £40 and £50 for those children, which reflects the average net income of the non-resident parent. In other words, they are not punitive. They are simply an averaging – a default payment which someone will pay until the final determination has been made. This will prevent large amounts of arrears building up and, because default rates will be put into place quickly, they will be easier to enforce.'[2]

The default rates are fixed by reg 7 of the CS(MCP)Regs 2000. As anticipated, these rates are £30 per week where there is one qualifying child of the non-resident parent, £40 per week for two children and £50 per week for three or more children. These sums may be apportioned where the non-resident parent has more than one qualifying child and there is, in relation to them, more than one person with care.

However, somewhat confusingly, interim assessments (now called interim decisions) have not been abolished altogether; they reappear in the context of applications for variation. Variations are dealt with in more detail in Chapter Five. Here, it is only necessary to note that s 12(2) provides that 'where an application for a variation has been made under section 28A(1) in connection with an application for a maintenance calculation (or in connection with such an application which is treated as having been made), the Secretary of State may make an interim maintenance decision'. Procedure will be prescribed by regulations but the amount of child support maintenance which may be fixed by an interim maintenance decision is determined by reference to Part I of Sch 1.

Part I of Sch 1 is the part of the Act which sets out the new formula; it is discussed in detail in Chapter Three. The provisions for variation are contained elsewhere in the Act. What this means, therefore, is that the interim decision would require payment of the 'standard rate', depending on the income of the non-resident parent but without regard to any of the matters which might permit a variation.

The significance of this is that the Secretary of State would be able to refuse to consider the application for a variation if the amount due under the interim decision were not paid. Since the application for variation would be based on the

---

2 Baroness Hollis, Official Report (HL) 8 May 2000, col 1327.

argument that the non-resident parent could not afford the 'going rate' this might seem harsh. However, this subject is examined in more detail in Chapter Five.

Termination of Calculations (Other than Interim Calculations)

2.43 The CSA 1991 and the regulations provide for circumstances in which a maintenance calculation may terminate or cease to have effect.

Paragraph 16(1) of Sch 1 to the Act provides that a calculation shall cease to have effect:

'(a) on the death of the non-resident parent, or of the person with care, with respect to whom it was made;

(b) on there no longer being a qualifying child with respect to whom it might have effect;

(c) on the non-resident parent with respect to whom it was made ceasing to be a parent of –

(i) the qualifying child with respect to whom it was made; or

(ii) where it was made with respect to more than one qualifying child, all of the qualifying children with respect to whom it was made.'

These provisions need little comment. A person would cease to be parent if an adoption order were made. A declaration of a court that an absent parent was not the father of the child would not, of itself, lead to termination, but would result in a review of the calculation.

Fees

2.44 By the Child Support Fees Regulations 1992, SI 1992/3094, the Secretary of State has power to charge fees for the use of the CSA. By reg 2, where a calculation is made following an application under ss 4, 6 or 7, fees shall be payable in accordance with regs 3 and 4.

Regulation 3 deals with the persons liable to pay the fees. These are the person with care and the non-resident parent with respect to whom the calculation was made. However, some people are exempt from paying fees. They are any person receiving income support, family credit or disability allowance, or who is under 16 or under 19 years of age and receiving full-time education which is not advanced education, or whose calculable income is nil, or is a non-resident parent whose protected income effects a reduction in any calculation.

The regulations do not specify which party is to pay the fee. However, the applicant must pay a fee to issue the application and the non-resident parent must pay a fee after a calculation is made, subject to exemption.

Regulation 1(2) defines 'collection fee' as a fee in respect of services provided by the Secretary of State for the collection of child support maintenance or for enforcing payment of such maintenance or for both collection and enforcement.

Repayment of Overpaid Maintenance

2.45 Section 41B(1) of the CSA 1991 makes provision for repayment of child support maintenance which has been overpaid by a non-resident parent. This applies where:

'(a) it would not be possible for the non-resident parent to recover the amount of the overpayment by way of an adjustment of the amount payable under a maintenance calculation; or

(b) it would be inappropriate to rely on an adjustment of the amount payable under a maintenance calculation as the means of enabling the non-resident parent to recover the amount of the overpayment.'

Section 41B(2) provides that, in such circumstances, the Secretary of State may make such payment to the non-resident parent by way of reimbursement or partial reimbursement as he considers appropriate. When he does so, he may require 'the relevant person' to pay to him the whole, or a specified proportion, of the amount of the payment (s 41B(3)).

'Relevant person' is defined by s 41B(8) as the person with care to whom the overpayment was made. It also applies under s 41B(1A):

'where the non-resident parent has made a voluntary payment and it appears to the Secretary of State –

(a) that he is not liable to pay child support maintenance; or

(b) that he is liable, but some or all of the payments amount to an overpayment.'

Where (b) applies, the Secretary of State must also be satisfied that subsection (1)(a) and (b) above apply.

CHAPTER THREE

How Child Support is Calculated

Introduction

3.1 The changes effected by the CSPSSA 2000 are brought about by amendments of the CSA 1991. In order to ascertain the 'formula' or process by which child maintenance is calculated, therefore, it is still necessary to look to Part I of Sch 1 to the CSA 1991, but in its amended form.

Certain new terms have been introduced by the Act. The absent parent is no more; he is now described as the 'non-resident parent'.[1] However, the person with care continues to be so called. A maintenance assessment is now a maintenance 'calculation'.[2]

The legislation also still refers to the children with respect to whom the maintenance calculation falls to be made as 'qualifying children'; this definition is explained at para **2.5**.

3.2 The basic principle of the current formula is that child maintenance is based entirely on a calculation of the income of the non-resident parent. No account is taken of the income or other means of the person with care. No attempt is made to determine a 'maintenance requirement' based on the needs of the child. The only material which may be used to determine the amount of child maintenance in any case is the income of the non-resident parent. Comment on this change will be found at para **3.22**.

The stages through which any calculation of child maintenance must go, and the questions which must be asked in each case, are as follows.

(1) Which rate applies (ie basic, reduced, flat or nil rates)?
(2) When basic or reduced rate applies, what sum is payable?
(3) Is any reduction to take account of any other dependent children of the non-resident parent appropriate?
(4) Should the result of (2) be apportioned?
(5) Is care shared? If so, how is the maintenance reduced?
(6) When the flat rate or nil rate applies, what sum is payable?

Each of these stages will be considered in this chapter. The chapter will conclude with a critical assessment of the current provisions and a model for assessing the maintenance liability in any case.

3.3 The usual rules for calculating child maintenance may be varied. Variation is a separate topic which will be considered in Chapter Five.

---

1 CSPSSA 2000, Sch 3, para 11(2).
2 Ibid, s 1(2).

Which Rate Applies?

3.4   The general rule is that the basic rate is applied,[3] and a fixed percentage of the non-resident parent's income is taken, as described in para **3.7**. However, this does not apply where that income falls below a certain level and in these cases a reduced rate, or even a flat or nil rate, may apply. The system is best described from the bottom upwards.

The nil rate

This applies (ie no child maintenance is payable) where the non-resident parent has a net income of below £5 or is of a prescribed description, namely:

(a)   a student;

(b)   a child;

(c)   a prisoner;

(d)   a person who is 16 or 17 years old and is either in receipt of income support or income-based job-seekers' allowance or is a member of a couple whose partner is in receipt of such benefit;

(e)   a person receiving an allowance in respect of work-based training for young people (or, in Scotland, skillseekers training);

(f)   certain persons in residential care homes or nursing homes or certain hospital patients in receipt of income support;

(g)   a person who would be liable to pay the flat rate were it not for the fact that his net weekly income (inclusive of any benefit received by his partner or himself) is less than £5 per week.[4]

The flat rate

This may be either a fixed amount of £5 or such sum as may be prescribed by regulations. The £5 fixed rate applies where the nil rate does not apply and either:

(a)   the non-resident parent's net weekly income is £100 or less; or

(b)   he receives any benefit, pension or allowance prescribed for this purpose; or

(c)   he or his partner (if any) receives any benefit prescribed for this purpose.

The list of benefits prescribed for this purpose is set out in reg 4 of the CS(MCSC)Regs 2000, which should be consulted for the full list. It includes category A retirement pension, category B retirement pension under s 48C of the Social Security Contributions and Benefits Act 1992, category C and D retirement pensions under s 78 of that Act, incapacity benefit, invalid care allowance, maternity allowance, contribution-based jobseeker's allowance, income support and income-based jobseeker's allowance.

The flat rate of a prescribed amount applies where the nil rate does not apply and:

(a)   the non-resident parent has a partner who is also a non-resident parent; and

(b)   the partner is a person with respect to whom a maintenance calculation is in force; and

---

3 CSA 1991, Sch 1, Part I, para 1(1).

4 CS(MCSC)Regs 2000, reg 5.

(c) the non-resident parent or his partner receives any benefit prescribed as above for this purpose.[5]

In these circumstances, the prescribed amount payable is one half of the flat rate (ie £2.50) where he has one partner and, where he has more than one partner, the sum of £5 divided by the number of partners.[6] (The latter position might apply where the non-resident parent had validly contracted a polygamous marriage, as to which see para **3.5** below.)

3.5 A person's partner is defined as 'if they are a couple, the other member of that couple'. Where a person is a husband or wife by virtue of a marriage entered into under a law which permits polygamy, his partner may be 'another party to the marriage who is of the opposite sex and is a member of the same household'.[7]

'Couple' means a man and a woman who are either married to each other and are members of the same household or are not married to each other but are living together as husband and wife.[8]

The Reduced Rate

3.6 The *reduced rate* is payable where:

(a) neither the nil rate nor a flat rate applies, and
(b) the non-resident parent's net weekly income is less than £200 but more than £100.[9]

The reduced rate is defined by the regulations[10] as $F + (A \times T)$, where:

F is the flat rate liability, ie £5;
A is the non-resident parent's net weekly income; and
T is a percentage determined in accordance with the following table.

	1 qualifying child				2 qualifying children				3 or more qualifying children			
Number of relevant other children	0	1	2	3 or more	0	1	2	3 or more	0	1	2	3 or more
T(%)	25	20.5	19	17.5	35	29	27	25	45	37.5	35	32.5

This is, in effect, a sliding scale which changes according to the number of qualifying children and the number of 'relevant other children' of the non-resident parent (as to which see paras **3.7** to **3.11**) of the non-resident parent. For

---

5 CSA 1991, Sch 1, Part I, para 4.
6 CS(MCSC)Regs 2000, reg 4(3).
7 CSA 1991, Sch 1, Part I, para 10C(4) and (5).
8 Ibid, para 10C(5).
9 Ibid, para 3.
10 CS(MCSC)Regs 2000, reg 3.

example, a non-resident parent earning a net income of £150 per week with two qualifying children would have to pay £22.50 (ie £5 plus 35% of £50) if he had no relevant other children, but this would be reduced to £19.50 (ie £5 plus 29% of £50) if he had one relevant other child and to £18.50 (£5 plus 27% of £50) if he had two relevant other children.

Calculation of the Basic Rate

3.7   The general rule is that the basic rate is a percentage of the weekly net income of the non-resident parent. This percentage is:

15% where he has one qualifying child;
20% where he has two qualifying children;
25% where he has three or more qualifying children.[11]

The method of calculating net income is discussed at para **3.11**.

This is, therefore, a simple calculation. A non-resident parent earning £300 per week net will pay £45 for one child and £75 for three children, irrespective of their ages. The calculation ignores the income of the resident parent. There is a 'cap' or limit on the maintenance, as a result of a last-minute change of heart by the Government. The effect of this cap is that net income of over £2000 per week is ignored.[12]

It was originally the Government's firm intention that there should be no cap or limit on the income a percentage of which would be taken in child maintenance. The official view was that '. . . having an upper limit to the amount of maintenance payable would result in an inconsistency of treatment between non-resident parents with relatively high levels of income and those on more modest sums'.[13] It was also said that 'maintenance for all children will be based on what a father can afford, not what he or anyone else believes the children need'.[14] 'Placing an upper limit on the amount paid in respect of any one child is inconsistent with the Government's plan for a simple and transparent system of rates that protects the rights of all children to support from non-resident parents in keeping with their ability to provide.'[15]

Had this proposal been enacted, surprising results might have followed. It would probably have seemed curious to most people that a non-resident parent earning £10,000 per week would be required to pay £1500 per week for a child, whether that child is 15 months old or 15 years old. Such a sum would greatly exceed any conceivable needs of the child (and, of course, no account would be taken of the income of the person with care).

Whatever the merits of the proposal, a different view eventually prevailed. When the Lords' amendments were finally considered (perhaps bearing in mind the extreme lack of parliamentary time), the Government decided not to try to undo the amendment which imposed the £2000 limit. The official view adopted latterly was that 'we have been persuaded, however, that in the case of very high

11 CSA 1991, Sch 1, Part I, para 2.
12 Ibid, para 10(3).
13 Baroness Hollis at Official Report (HL) 8 May 2000, col 1251.
14 Ibid.
15 Ibid, col 1252.

earners, the courts are better placed to unravel their financial affairs and to come to a sensible conclusion about the proper allocation of property, spousal maintenance, and child maintenance. Without a cap on child support liability, the courts might find it impossible to settle the family's financial affairs properly. With a cap, the courts will be able to work from a fixed maximum child support liability while settling other financial arrangements'.[16] The right to apply to the court for top-ups is maintained (see para **10.10**).

3.8 However, the calculation contains a further complication. It is provided that allowance may be made for any 'relevant other children' of the non-resident parent.[17] 'Relevant other children' are defined as children other than qualifying children in respect of whom the non-resident parent or his partner receives child benefit, and such other children as may be prescribed.[18] No other category of child has been so prescribed. These are therefore children living with the non-resident parent who are the children of either himself or his partner. No account is taken of any income of the partner nor of any income of the children.

The allowance which is made is by way of a percentage deduction from the net weekly income of the non-resident parent before the basic rate is calculated, and the percentages are:

15% where he has one relevant other child;
20% where he has two relevant other children;
25% where he has three or more relevant other children.[19]

3.9 If, therefore, the non-resident parent had a net weekly income of £300 and two relevant other children, 20% or £60 would first be notionally deducted from his net weekly income leaving £240. If there were two qualifying children he would have to pay 20% of the net figure of £240, namely £48 per week. Had he no relevant other children the sum payable would have been £60. The value which the scheme places on the support of the non-relevant children would therefore be £12 per week. It is important to remember that this reduction as to relevant other children applies only where the applicable rate is the basic rate. For the position when the reduced rate applies, see para **3.6** above.

3.10 The results of these rules could be curious and their inflexibility makes them somewhat arbitrary. A non-resident parent earning £300 per week would pay the sums set out above whether the person with care was earning nothing, £500 per week or £10,000 per week, or whether the natural (non-resident) parent of his partner's children was paying nothing or substantially more than the child support rate. Many will consider this bizarre.

3.11 Net weekly income is determined in such manner as prescribed by regulations.[20] These regulations may in particular provide for the Secretary of State to estimate any income or make an assumption as to any fact where, in his

16 Angela Eagle MP in Official Report (HC) 24 July 2000, cols 793 and 794.
17 CSA 1991, Sch 1, Part I, para 2(2).
18 Ibid, para 10C(2).
19 Ibid, para 2(2).
20 Ibid, para 10(1).

view, the information at his disposal is unreliable, insufficient, or relates to an untypical period in the life of the non-resident parent.[21]

It should be noted that the Secretary of State will have power to make his own judgement as to income if he does not accept the figures provided by the non-resident parent.

In addition, it is provided that the Secretary of State may by regulation provide that in such circumstances and to such extent as may be prescribed:

(a) where the Secretary of State is satisfied that a person has intentionally deprived himself of a source of income with a view to reducing the amount of his net weekly income, his net weekly income shall be taken to include income from that source of an amount estimated by the Secretary of State;
(b) a person is to be treated as possessing income which he does not possess;
(c) income which a person does possess is to be disregarded.[22]

These regulations are contained in detail in Parts II and III of the Schedule to the CS(MCSC)Regs 2000. They may be summarised as follows:

(a) *Employed earners (Part II)* Earnings comprise gross pay, including bonuses, overtime and pay in lieu of notice. They do not include benefits in kind, tips, expenses reimbursed, employer payments during a strike, or part-time earnings as a fireman, lifeboat operative, auxiliary coastguard, a member of the territorial army or income from childminding. To calculate net earnings, income tax, class 1 NIC contributions and pension contributions (save where there is a 'pension mortgage', when only 75% is allowed) are deducted.
(b) *Self-employed earners (Part III)* Earnings comprise taxable profits as returned to the Inland Revenue or, if the CSA chooses, as notified by the Revenue in the tax calculation notice, including childminding income where this is the only or main source of income. To calculate net earnings, income tax, class 2 and 4 NIC contributions, and contributions to a retirement annuity contract or personal pension (with the same restriction as above on 'pension mortgages') are deducted.
(c) *Investment income* This is ignored for the purposes of the formula. However, pension income is classed as 'other income' and is included.

Apportionment

3.12 Apportionment is applied where 'the non-resident parent has more than one qualifying child and in relation to them there is more than one person with care'.[23] In other words, the non-resident parent has two or more children who are living with different people. In such circumstances, the rate of maintenance liability is divided by the number of qualifying children and shared among the persons with care according to the number of qualifying children in relation to whom each is a person with care.[24]

---

21 CSA 1991, Sch 1, Part I, para 10(2).
22 Ibid, para 10B.
23 Ibid, para 6(1).
24 Ibid, para 6(2).

3.13 For example, if a non-resident parent had a net income of £400 per week and three qualifying children, one of whom lived with A and two of whom lived with B, the starting point would be that his maintenance liability would be £100 (25% of £400). A would receive one-third of this sum (£33.33) and B would receive two-thirds (£66.66). The ages of the children would be irrelevant.

Shared Care

3.14 Under the previous legislation, an attempt was made to give some relief to non-resident parents (then called absent parents) who had a qualifying child living with them for longer than a certain period in each year. The formula which was applied was to treat one person as a non-resident parent where there were two or more persons not living in the same household who each provided day to day care for a child. Day to day care meant 104 nights or more in any 12-month period. In these circumstances, an algebraic formula was applied to apportion the maintenance liability between the two persons.[25]

3.15 These provisions were sometimes criticised as providing a spurious encouragement to non-resident parents to apply to the court for overnight contact. However, they applied only when the non-resident parent had the child or children for more than every weekend in one year. The current law goes further and provides even more of an encouragement to such disruption; the exact effect depends on whether the maintenance liability is based on the basic or reduced rate on the one hand or the flat rate on the other hand. These must be considered separately.

Basic and reduced rate
3.16 These provisions apply when the rate of child maintenance payable is the basic rate or the reduced rate and '. . . the care of a qualifying child is shared between the non-resident parent and the person with care, so that the non-resident parent from time to time has care of the child overnight'. In these circumstances, 'the amount of child support maintenance which he would otherwise have been liable to pay the person with care . . . is to be decreased in accordance with this paragraph'.[26]

The first stage of the calculation is to calculate the decrease 'according to the number of such nights which the Secretary of State determines there to have been, or expects there to be, or both during a prescribed twelve-month period'.[27] The amount of decrease for one child is as follows.

---

25 See CS(MASC)Regs 1992, reg 20.
26 CSA 1991, Sch 1, Part I, para 7(1) and (2).
27 Ibid, para 7(3).

Number of nights	Fraction to subtract
52 to 103	One-seventh
104 to 155	Two-sevenths
156 to 174	Three-sevenths
175 or more	One-half[28]

3.17   It is then provided that, if the person with care is providing for more than one qualifying child of the non-resident parent, 'the applicable decrease is the sum of the appropriate fractions in the Table divided by the number of such qualifying children'.[29] There is then a further calculation to carry out in some cases. If the applicable fraction is one-half in relation to any qualifying child in the care of the person with care, the total amount payable to the person with care is then to be further decreased by £7 for each such child.[30]

Finally, if the application of these provisions would decrease the weekly amount of child support maintenance (or the aggregate of all such amounts) payable by the non-resident parent to the person with care (or all of them) to less than £5 per week, the non-resident parent is liable to pay only £5 per week.[31] In appropriate cases this would be apportioned as described in para **3.12**.

3.18   An example may assist. A and B have three children, C, D and E. The children live with A but have overnight contact with B in different proportions. C spends 70 nights per annum with B, D 140 nights and E 180.

The fractions to be aggregated are therefore one-seventh, two-sevenths and one-half. The result is thirteen-fourteenths. That fraction is then divided by three (the number of the children) so that the reduction is 4.33/14.

If the non-resident parent had a net income of £400 per week, the initial maintenance liability would have been £100. This would now be reduced by 4.33/14 resulting in a net figure of £69.08. Then that figure would be reduced by £7 because the fraction in respect of one of the children was one-half, so that the total sum payable would be £62.08.

Flat rate

3.19   Where the child maintenance payable is in accordance with the flat rate (except where this is so only because the non-resident parent's income is £100 or less), then if the care of a qualifying child is shared for at least 52 nights during a prescribed 12-month period, the amount of child support maintenance payable by the non-resident parent to the person with care of that child is nil.[32]

Miscellaneous matters

3.20   A few minor matters remain to be noted on the subject of shared care. First, the Secretary of State has to decide in any case what number of nights are to

---

28 CSA 1991, Sch 1, Part I, para 7(4).
29 Ibid, para 7(5).
30 Ibid, para 7(6).
31 Ibid, para 7(7).
32 Ibid, para 7(8).

be regarded as shared: this can be on the basis of the past record, a prediction of the future, or a combination of the two. It is not clear how a dispute between the parties would be resolved, except by the Secretary of State accepting the word of one of them and then leaving the matter to the Appeal Tribunal.

Secondly, regulations provide for which nights are to count for the purposes of shared care or for how it is to be determined whether a night counts, and for the calculation to be based on a period other than 12 months.[33] Under CS(MCSC) Regs 2000, reg 7, a night counts for the purpose of shared care where the non-resident parent has the care of a qualifying child overnight and the child stays at the same address as the non-resident parent. A non-resident parent 'has the care' of the child when he looking after the child.

In determining the number of nights for the purpose of shared care, the Secretary of State will consider the 12-month period ending with the relevant week. He may have regard to a shorter period where there has been no pattern for the frequency with which the non-resident parent looks after the child over the preceding 12 months, or he is aware that a change in that frequency is intended; in such circumstances the Secretary of State shall have regard to such lesser period as seems to him to be appropriate.

Where a child is a patient in hospital or is a boarder at a boarding school, the person who, but for those circumstances, would otherwise have care of the child overnight will be treated as providing that care during the periods in question.

The Flat Rate and the Nil Rate

3.21 When the flat rate applies (as to which see para **3.4**), the sum payable will depend on which of the circumstances described apply. When the nil rate applies, nothing is payable.

Some Comments on the Provisions Introduced in the CSPSSA 2000

3.22 When the Bill was going through Parliament it was subjected to a number of criticisms. Some of those criticisms related to enforcement provisions (as to which see Chapter Nine). As far as the formula itself was concerned, the principal original criticisms were, first, that there was no limit on the liability of the non-resident parent and, secondly, that no account was taken of the means of the parent with care. The Government purported to refute the first criticism by professing not to understand it; its view was that children were entitled as of right to share in the wealth of their parents, a view which most lawyers would think was unknown to English law and find somewhat alarming. In the event, disaster was avoided and a cap or limit was imposed, although as will be seen below, the Government's philosophy reappears in a different context.

As to the second criticism, it may seem to many that simple justice demands that some account be taken of the income of the person with care. The Government does not accept this view, and the proposal has been enacted. The

---

33 CSA 1991, Sch 1, Part I, para 9.

proposal was justified on three principal grounds. First, it was said that the cost of maintaining a child is on average 30% of family income, which ought to be divided equally between the parents. The person with care already provides her share by housing costs, food, heat, etc; that is her contribution. The non-resident parent's contribution, because he is not living there, is in cash.[34]

The second ground was, again, that the child was entitled to a share of its parent's income: 'the child has the right to maintenance from his or her father [*sic*] irrespective of the income of the mother, exactly as if they were part of an intact family'.[35] Finally, it was said that the numbers of people who might be adversely affected by these proposals were so few that it was not really worth making special arrangements to cater for them.[36] This argument had originally been applied also to the cap on the non-resident parent's liability.

3.23 Whatever the merits of the arguments, this principle is now part of child support law. It may well have an effect on ancillary relief settlements. However, another factor which seems even more likely to affect ancillary relief is the fact that, in average income cases, maintenance calculations under the new provisions will be lower than under the old system. A likely consequence of this is that, whereas there had been a growing trend to agree clean break orders with no spousal maintenance on the basis that the non-resident parent would in reality never be able to pay more than the child support demanded by the old formula, this will no longer be an attractive option. It may well be that at least nominal spousal orders will be required, which, whatever the merits of the arguments, will reverse one of the important social developments of recent years.

A Possible Model for Use

3.24 It has been seen in this chapter that the new provisions do not result in as simple a calculation as might have been expected. The following model may serve as an aid to calculation (NRP = non-resident parent and PWC = person with care).

Stage 1 Calculate NRP's net income (described as A).

Stage 2 Is A less than £5 per week or is NRP of a prescribed description, eg a prisoner? If YES, stop here; nil rate applies.

Stage 3 Does NRP have a partner who is also an NRP in respect of whom a maintenance calculation is in force and do either of them receive a prescribed benefit? If YES to all questions, flat rate of prescribed amount applies. If NO, proceed to Stage 4.

Stage 4 Is A less than £100 per week? If YES, flat rate of £5 per week applies.

---

34 See Baroness Hollis at Official Report (HL) 8 May 2000, col 1254. The Baroness expressed herself 'baffled' that this argument was not understood (see col 1255).

35 Ibid, col 1260.

36 Ibid, col 1262.

Stage 5 Do NRP or partner (if any) receive any benefit prescribed for this purpose? If YES, flat rate of £5 per week applies. If NO, proceed to Stage 6.

Stage 6 Is A more than £100 per week but less than £200 per week? If NO, proceed to Stage 7. If YES, reduced rate applies. Sum payable = B. See the detailed discussion at para **3.6** above.

Note: From this point, A is either the net income or £2000, whichever is the lower.

Stage 7 Does NRP have a 'relevant child' or children? If NO, A remains unchanged; proceed to Stage 8. If YES, deduct from A 15% for one such child, 20% for two and 25% for three or more such children. Now proceed to Stage 8 with the reduced A figure.

Stage 8 Multiply A by 15% for one child, 20% for two and 25% for three children. The result = C.

Stage 9 Is there more than one PWC in relation to the qualifying children? If NO, proceed to Stage 10. If YES, divide B or C by the number of children; result = D. How many children has each PWC? Multiply D by the number each PWC has.

Stage 10 Is the care of any qualifying child shared between PWC and NRP for more than 51 nights per year? If NO, B or C remains unchanged and is carried forward to Stage 11. If YES, in respect of EACH CHILD, reduce B or C as follows.

Number of nights	*Fraction to subtract*
52 to 103	One-seventh
104 to 155	Two-sevenths
156 to 174	Three-sevenths
175 or more	One-half

Now aggregate the total of the deductible fractions =
Divide this figure by the number of qualifying children of NRP with PWC =
Result = D
Now divide B or C (as the case may be) by D.
Carry forward result to Stage 11.

Stage 11 The figure brought forward from Stage 10 is the sum to be inserted in the maintenance calculation.

CHAPTER FOUR

Special Cases

Introduction

4.1   The rules for the making of maintenance calculations set out in Chapter Three were for the 'normal' case or set of circumstances in which liability for a calculation might arise. The CSA 1991 recognises that not all cases are normal, and accordingly provision is made for 'special cases' where the standard approach is modified.

Section 42(1) provides that the Secretary of State may by regulations provide that, in prescribed circumstances, a case is to be treated as a special case for the purposes of the Act. The Act itself sets out examples of circumstances which might be special cases, but this is not prescriptive and does not limit what may be prescribed by regulation. Indeed, the regulations as they now appear in Part III of the CS(MCSC)Regs 2000 depart quite extensively from what the Act gives as examples.

Accordingly, this chapter will concentrate on the regulations, since they contain the substantive law. The various kinds of special case will now be considered in turn.

Persons Treated as Non-Resident Parents (reg 8)

4.2   This special case relates to the position where two or more persons who do not live in the same household each provide day to day care for the same qualifying child, and at least one of them is a parent of the child. 'Day to day care' is defined by reg 1(2) as care of not less than 104 nights in total during the 12-month period ending with the relevant week (or such other period as the Secretary of State considers more representative of the current arrangements). In effect, therefore, this applies where a person has care of a child for more than an average of two nights each week. The purpose of this regulation is to enable the Secretary of State to decide who is the person with care and who is the non-resident parent. Regulation 8(2) provides, unsurprisingly, that the non-resident parent is the parent who provides care to a lesser extent than the other person who provides care. Where the persons concerned are both parents of the child, and each provides care to an equal extent but to a greater extent than or equal to any other person who provides care for the child, the non-resident parent will be the parent who does not receive child benefit for the child in question or, where neither of them receives child benefit, the person who, in the opinion of the Secretary of State, will not be the principal provider of day to day care for the child.

Where a child is a boarder at a boarding school or is a patient in hospital, the person who would, but for those circumstances, otherwise provide day to day care for the child will be treated as providing day to day care for the periods in question (reg 1(2)). One could foresee that, where the school holidays were equally shared, this could give rise to some debate.

Care Provided in Part by a Local Authority (reg 9)

4.3 This special case arises when the care of a qualifying child is shared between the person with care and a local authority and the child is in the care of the local authority for 52 nights or more during the 12-month period ending with the relevant week (or during such other period as the Secretary of State thinks is more representative on a pro rata basis), and it is intended that the child shall be in the care of the authority for a number of nights in a period from the effective date. It is limited to cases where the rate of child support maintenance payable is the basic rate or reduced rate (or has been calculated following agreement to a variation where the non-resident parent's liability would otherwise have been a flat rate or the nil rate).

In such cases, the amount of child support maintenance which the non-resident parent is liable to pay is adjusted. The first calculation is the number of nights spent or to be spent by the child in the care of the local authority (annualised where the period in question is less than 12 months). Then, the amount of child support maintenance is decreased in accordance with the following table:

Number of nights in care	Fraction to subtract
52–103	One-seventh
104–155	Two-sevenths
156–207	Three sevenths
209–259	Four-sevenths
260–262	Five-sevenths

If the non-resident parent and the person with care have more than one qualifying child, the applicable decrease is the sum of the appropriate fractions in the table divided by the number of such qualifying children.

4.4 Where the amount of child support maintenance which the non-resident parent is liable to pay in relation to the same person with care is to be decreased on account of shared care (as to which see para **3.16**), the applicable decrease is the sum of the appropriate fractions derived under those provisions.

Non-Resident Parent Liable to Pay Maintenance Under a Maintenance Order (reg 11)

4.5 This special case arises when an application for child support maintenance is made or treated as made with respect to a qualifying child and a non-resident parent and an application for a different child cannot be made (eg because he does not fall within the definition of qualifying child) but that non-resident parent is liable to pay maintenance under a maintenance order for that child. Pausing there, the most common example of this might be where the 'different child' was a stepchild or (in an application under s 4) where the court order itself prevented the making of a maintenance calculation (because it was made before April 2002 or had not been in force for a year).

The circumstances are limited to cases where the rate payable is the basic rate or the reduced rate or where it has been calculated following agreement to variation where the non-resident parent's liability would otherwise have been a flat rate or the nil rate.

In these circumstances, the amount of child support maintenance is calculated as follows.

(a) First, make the maintenance calculation as if the number of qualifying children included the different child (ie the child with respect to whom the non-resident parent is liable to make payments under the court order).
(b) Then, apportion the amount so calculated between the qualifying children and the different child (ie divide that maintenance calculation by the total number of children).
(c) The amount payable is the amount apportioned to the qualifying children.
(d) That amount is then payable to (each) parent with care subject to any apportionment required where there is more than one person with care in relation to one child or because of shared care.

Child who is a Boarder or an In-Patient in Hospital (reg 12)

4.6 This special case applies when a qualifying child is a boarder at a boarding school or is an in-patient in hospital. In such circumstances, since he is away from home, the person who would otherwise provide day to day care is not doing so. Regulation 12(2) provides that, in these circumstances, for the definition of 'person with care' contained in s 3(3)(b) of the CSA 1991 there is substituted a reference to the person who would usually be providing such care for that child but for the circumstances set out above.

Child who is Allowed to Live with his Parent under s 23(5) of the CA 1989 (reg 13)

4.7 This special case applies where a qualifying child who is in the care of a local authority is allowed by the local authority to live with a parent of his pursuant to s 23(5) of the CA 1989. In such circumstances, for the definition of 'person with care' in s 3(3)(b) of the CSA 1991 is substituted a reference to the parent of the child with whom the local authority allows the child to live.

Person with Part-Time Care who is not a Non-Resident Parent (reg 14)

4.8 A special case arises where two or more persons who do not live in the same household each provide day to day care for the same qualifying child but neither of them is a parent who is treated as a non-resident parent under reg 8(2). In such circumstances, the person whose application for a maintenance calculation is being proceeded with shall be entitled to receive all the child support maintenance in respect of the child in question. However, this is subject to the power of the Secretary of State, at the request of that person or any other person who is providing day to day care for the child, and after considering the interests of the child and the representations of all concerned, to divide the child support maintenance between such persons in the same ratio as it appears to him that each provides care.

CHAPTER FIVE

Variations

Introduction

5.1 The various attempts at establishing an administrative system for the calculation of child support maintenance since 1991 have all involved two elements. The first and principal element has been the creation of a rigid formula or system which will provide the answer to the amount of maintenance to be paid in any case and which can be operated and calculated by officials without any discretion. The second element recognises the fact that the application of a rigid formula may bring about injustice in some cases and seeks to provide a method of relief from such injustice. Accordingly, the original scheme had provision for 'special cases' to allow for unusual situations, although, even there, the amelioration was provided by means of another algebraic and equally unbending formula. In 1995 provision was made for 'departures', which allowed the CSO to depart from the formula in certain defined classes of case and introduced some element of discretion.

The CSPSSA 2000 further refines the position. It is intended that the new method of calculating child support will provide a fair answer in most cases but it is recognised that there may be cases where the rates do not properly reflect a non-resident parent's ability to support his children. In such cases, which it is intended should be exceptional, there is provision for the variation upwards and downwards of the standard rates. These exceptional cases are clearly defined and build on the provisions for departures introduced by the CSA 1995. Some of the cases in which variations may be allowed are remarkably similar to those in which a departure might previously have been permitted, but there are important differences.

5.2 The current rules as to variation will now be discussed. The procedures for applying for variations and dealing with the applications are discussed at paras **5.35** to **5.50**. It should also be noted that the consideration of an application for variation may be subject to a regular payments condition; this is discussed at para **5.43**.

Cases where Variation may be Allowed

The basic rule
5.3 It is provided that the Secretary of State may agree to a variation if:

(a) he is satisfied that the case is one which falls within one or more of the cases set out in Part I of Sch 4B to the CSA 1991 or in regulations made under that Part; and

(b) it is his opinion that, in all the circumstances of the case, it would be just and equitable to agree to a variation.[1]

This is, therefore, the basic statement of principle, and both parts of the principle must be satisfied. In deciding whether or not it would be just and equitable in any case to agree to a variation, the Secretary of State:

(a) must have regard, in particular, to the welfare of any child likely to be affected if he did agree to a variation; and
(b) must, or as the case may be, must not, take any prescribed factors into account, or must take them into account (or not) in prescribed circumstances.[2]

5.4 The factors which must, or must not, be taken into account in determining whether it would be just and equitable to agree to a variation in any case are prescribed by reg 21 of the Child Support (Variations) Regulations 2000 (CS(V)Regs 2000), SI 2001/156. The factors which must be taken into account are:

(a) where the application for a variation is made on any ground:
    (i) whether, in the opinion of the Secretary of State, agreeing to a variation would be likely to result in a relevant person ceasing paid employment;
    (ii) if the applicant is the non-resident parent, the extent, if any, of his liability to pay child maintenance under a court order or agreement in the period prior to the effective date of the maintenance calculation; and
(b) where the application is made on the ground of special expenses, whether, in the opinion of the Secretary of State:
    (i) the financial arrangements made by the non-resident parent could have been such as to enable the expenses to be paid without a variation being agreed; or
    (ii) the non-resident parent has at his disposal financial resources which are currently utilised for the payment of expenses other than those arising from essential everyday requirements and which could be used to pay the expenses.

5.5 The factors which may not be taken into account are:

(a) the fact that the conception of the child was not planned by one or both of the parents;
(b) whether the non-resident parent or the person with care was responsible for the breakdown of their relationship;
(c) the fact that the non-resident parent or person with care has formed a new relationship;
(d) the existence of any particular arrangements for contact, including whether any arrangements are being adhered to;
(e) the income or assets of any person other than the non-resident parent (other than any partner pursuant to reg 20(3), as to which see para **5.32** below);

---

1 CSA 1991, s 28F(1).
2 Ibid, s 28F(2).

(f) the failure by the non-resident parent to make payments of child support maintenance or payments under a court order; or

(g) representations made by persons other than the relevant persons (ie the non-resident parent and the person with care).

The cases contained in Sch 4B as amplified by the CS(V)Regs 2000 will now be considered.

Special expenses

5.6 A variation applied for by a non-resident parent may be agreed by reference to his special expenses.[3] Special expenses is not a term to be interpreted according to the general dictionary meaning of the words. Instead, the term is defined as:

> 'the whole, or any amount above a prescribed amount, or any prescribed part, of expenses which fall within a prescribed description of expenses.'[4]

The CS(V)Regs 2000 prescribe what expenses are and are not special. Schedule 4B itself[5] permits the Secretary of State to make particular provision for certain classes of expense. Experience of the earlier legislation shows that this is likely to be the complete list, namely:

(a) costs incurred by a non-resident parent in maintaining contact with the child, or with any of the children, with respect to whom the application for a maintenance calculation has been made (or treated as made);

(b) costs attributable to a long-term illness or disability of a relevant other child;

(c) debts of a prescribed nature incurred before the non-resident parent became a non-resident parent in relation to a child with respect to whom the maintenance calculation has been applied for (or treated as having been applied for):
  (i) for the joint benefit of both parents;
  (ii) for the benefit of any such child; or
  (iii) for the benefit of any other child falling within a prescribed category;

(d) boarding school fees for a child in relation to whom the application for a maintenance calculation has been made (or treated as made);

(e) the cost to the non-resident parent of making payments in relation to a mortgage on the home he and the parent with care shared, if he no longer has an interest in it, and she and a child in relation to whom the application for a maintenance calculation has been made (or treated as made) still live there.

Schedule 4B therefore sets out an exhaustive list of what may be classed as special expenses.

Thresholds

5.7 An important preliminary matter concerns the 'thresholds' for special expenses. Regulation 15(1) of the CS(V)Regs 2000 in effect imposes a financial 'bottom line' for expenses; if any expense is less than the threshold, no account will be taken of it. With the exception of reg 11 (special expenses due to illness or

---

3 CSA 1991, Sch 4B, para 2(1).
4 Ibid, para 2(2)
5 Ibid, para 2(3).

disability of a child) this limitation applies to all special expenses. It is provided that costs or repayments shall only be special expenses where they exceed the threshold amount, which is as follows:

(a) *where the relevant net weekly income of the non-resident parent is £200 or more:* £15 per week where the expenses fall within only one description of expenses or is the aggregate of those expenses; or

(b) *where the relevant net weekly income is below £200:* £10 per week where the description falls within only one description of expenses or in respect of the aggregate of those expenses.

Contact costs

5.8 Regulation 10 of the CS(V)Regs 2000 provides that certain costs 'incurred or reasonably expected to be incurred by the non-resident parent, whether in respect of himself or the qualifying child, or both, for the purpose of maintaining contact with that child shall constitute [special] expenses'. These costs are as follows:

(a) the cost of purchasing a ticket for travel;

(b) the cost of purchasing fuel where travel is by a vehicle which is not carrying fare-paying passengers;

(c) the taxi fare for a journey or part of a journey where the Secretary of State is satisfied that the disability or long-term illness of the non-resident parent or the qualifying child makes it impracticable for any other form of transport to be used for that journey or part of the journey;

(d) the cost of car hire where the cost of the journey would be less in total than it would be if public transport or taxis or a combination of both were used;

(e) where the Secretary of State considers a return journey on the same day is impracticable, or the established or intended pattern of contact with the child includes contact over two or more consecutive days, the cost of the non-resident parent's or, as the case may be, the child's, accommodation for the number of nights the Secretary of State considers appropriate in the circumstances of the case; and

(f) any minor incidental costs such as tolls or fees payable for the use of a particular road or bridge incurred in connection with such travel, including breakfast where it is included as part of the accommodation cost referred to at (e) above.

These costs may include the costs incurred by a person travelling with the non-resident parent or the qualifying child if the Secretary of State is satisfied that the presence of another person on the journey or part of the journey is necessary. The circumstances where this applies will include, but are not limited to, where it is necessary because of the young age of the qualifying child or the disability or long-term illness of the non-resident parent or the child.

5.9 These travel costs may only constitute special expenses to the extent that they are incurred in accordance with a set pattern of frequency of contact between the non-resident parent and the qualifying child which had been established at (or if it has ceased, which had been established before) the time that the variation application was made. Alternatively, they may be based on an intended set pattern of contact which the Secretary of State is satisfied has been agreed between the non-resident parent and the person with care (reg 10(3)(a)).

The costs must be calculated as a weekly average amount based on the expenses actually incurred over the previous 12 months (or such other period as the Secretary of State considers appropriate), or, where contact is anticipated, based on an average anticipated weekly cost over such period as the Secretary of State considers appropriate. Where contact has ceased, the costs are calculated as an average weekly amount based on the expenses actually incurred during the period from the first day of the maintenance period from which the variation would take effect to the last day of the maintenance period in relation to which the variation would take effect (reg 10(3)(b)).

5.10 By reg 10(4), costs of contact do not include costs which relate to periods when the non-resident parent has care of a qualifying child overnight as part of a shared care arrangement for which provision is made (as to which, see para **3.14**). In other words, once allowance has been made for shared care a further allowance under these provisions is not applicable. Any financial assistance (other than a loan) from any source which the non-resident parent receives to meet, wholly or in part, the costs of contact, will be deducted from the costs before they are taken into account (reg 10(5)). Presumably this means assistance from a charity or public body; a private gift would be difficult to monitor.

5.11 It is noticeable that no account may be taken of the cost of travel to work. This was one of the most glaring omissions from the original formula in 1991 and was one of the first parts of that scheme to be amended. Eventually, there were two complementary methods of making allowance for these costs. Under the new scheme, no account may be taken of such costs.

Illness or disability of relevant other child

5.12 Regulation 11 provides that expenses necessarily incurred by the non-resident parent in respect of certain items due to the long-term illness or disability of a relevant other child may be special expenses. A relevant other child is a child (other than a qualifying child) in respect of whom the non-resident parent or his partner receives child benefit (CSA 1991, Sch 1, para 10C).

The eligible expenses are set out in reg 11(1)(a)–(m) and need not be recited in full here.[6] They include the expenses of personal attendance, mobility, domestic help, medical aids and diet. To qualify the child, or someone on his behalf, must receive attendance allowance, disability living allowance or mobility allowance, be a patient, or be registered or treated as blind.

Where the non-resident parent receives financial assistance from any source in respect of the long-term illness or disability of the child, such assistance must be deducted from the special expenses (reg 11(3)).

Prior debts

5.13 Regulation 12(1) provides that the repayment of certain debts incurred before the non-resident parent became a non-resident parent in relation to the

---

6 See Appendix 2 where the CS(V) Regs 2000 are set out for the full list.

qualifying child and at the time when he and the person with care were a couple may constitute special expenses. In other words, the debts must have been incurred when both parents and the child were living together as a family; this could not therefore apply where eg a grandparent was the person with care.

The debts are limited to debts incurred:

(a) for the joint benefit of the non-resident parent and the person with care;
(b) for the benefit of the person with care where the non-resident parent remains legally liable to repay.the whole or part of the debt;
(c) for the benefit of any person who is not a child but who at the time the debt was incurred:
    (i) was a child;
    (ii) lived with the non-resident parent and the parent with care; and
    (iii) of whom the non-resident parent or the person with care is the parent, or both are the parents;
(d) for the benefit of the qualifying child; or
(e) for the benefit of any child, other than the qualifying child, who, at the time the debt was incurred, lived with the non-resident parent and the person with care and of whom the person with care is the parent.

5.14 This somewhat exhaustive definition is clear enough. The debt must have been incurred for the benefit of the family (which includes, for this purpose, non-qualifying children) when the family was living together. By reg 12(3) certain classes of debt are excluded and repayment of them cannot be special expenses. They include gambling debts, fines, credit card debts, unpaid legal costs in respect of separation or divorce (or debts incurred to repay any of the foregoing), or loans other than from a qualifying lender.[7] Also excluded are amounts payable under a mortgage or loan taken out on the security of any property except where that mortgage or loan was taken out to facilitate the purchase of, or pay for the repairs or improvements[8] to the home of the person with care and qualifying child.

5.15 Except where the repayment is of amounts due under a mortgage or loan or in respect of a policy of insurance taken out in connection with the purchase of, or repair or improvement to the home of the person with care and the qualifying child, repayment of a debt may not constitute special expenses where the non-resident parent has taken responsibility for the debt as part of a financial settlement with the person with care or by virtue of a court order (reg 12(4)). Care should therefore be exercised in the wording of undertakings given in ancillary relief orders.

Boarding school fees
5.16 By reg 13(1) 'the maintenance element of the costs incurred, or reasonably expected to be incurred, by the non-resident parent for the purpose of the attendance at a boarding school of the qualifying child' may constitute special expenses. Boarding school fees means 'the fees payable in respect of attendance

---

7 Within the meaning of s 376 of the Income and Corporation Taxes Act 1988.
8 As defined in CS(V)Regs 2000, reg 12(6)(b).

at a recognised educational establishment providing full-time education which is not advanced education for children under the age of 19 and where some or all of the pupils, including the qualifying child, are resident during the term time' (reg 13(5)).

At first sight, this is a surprising though (to many) welcome concession on the part of the authorities. The rationale is clearly that, where a child is at boarding school and the non-resident parent is paying the fees, the person with care is relieved of the cost of maintenance of that child while he is away. It is necessary to distinguish the maintenance costs from the educational costs. By reg 13(2), where the Secretary of State considers that the maintenance costs cannot be distinguished with reasonable certainty from the other costs, he may instead determine the amount of those costs which shall not exceed 35% of the total costs. It is also provided that no variation on these grounds shall reduce by more than 50% the income (of the non-resident parent) to which the Secretary of State would otherwise have regard in the calculation of the maintenance liability (reg 13(4)). Any financial assistance with the fees from any source, or any sharing of the fees, must be taken into account (reg 13(3)).

Payments in respect of certain mortgages, loans or insurance policies

5.17 Regulation 14 provides that certain payments made in respect of a mortgage, loan, or insurance policy may constitute special expenses. These are payments which are made to the mortgagee, lender or insurer or to the person with care. The significance of this is that this provision may be invoked when the person with care makes the payments and the non-resident parent reimburses her (under a settled arrangement).

In order to qualify as special expenses the payments must meet the following conditions.

(1) The mortgage or loan must have been taken out to facilitate the purchase of, or repairs or improvements to, a property by a person other than the non-resident parent; in most cases this means that the person with care will have taken out the loan.

(2) The payments may not apply to a debt incurred by the non-resident parent nor arise out of any other legal liability of the non-resident parent for the period in respect of which the variation is applied for.

(3) The property must have been the home of the applicant (non-resident parent) and the person with care when they were a couple and must remain the home of the person with care and the qualifying child.

(4) The non-resident parent must not have any legal or equitable interest in the property and no charge or right to have a charge over it.

Amounts payable under a policy of insurance taken out for the discharge of a mortgage or loan referred to above, including an endowment policy, may be allowable except where the non-resident parent is entitled to any part of the proceeds on the maturity of the policy.

Property or capital transfers

5.18 When what became the CSA 1991 was being debated, one of the pressing issues was the injustice that might be caused if a full maintenance calculation was levied on a person who, as part of a matrimonial settlement, had transferred his interest in a home or capital to his former spouse in return for some reduction in the periodical payments which he might have to pay for the person with care and any child. Such arrangements had been relatively common before that date. Various attempts were made to resolve this difficulty, culminating in a type of departure direction permissible after the 1995 changes. The present legislation is very similar to the previous position and, once again, restricts any relief to arrangements made before 5 April 1993.

5.19 It is provided that a variation may be agreed in certain circumstances if before 5 April 1993:

(a) a court order of a prescribed kind was in force with respect to the non-resident parent and either the person with care with respect to the application for the maintenance calculation or the child, or any of the children, with respect to whom that application was made; or

(b) an agreement of a prescribed kind between the non-resident parent and any of those persons was in force.[9]

The circumstances in which, given the above facts, a variation may be agreed (in other words, the essential conditions for their becoming relevant) are that in consequence of one or more transfers of property of a prescribed kind and exceeding (singly or in aggregate) a prescribed minimum value:

(a) the amount payable by the non-resident parent by way of maintenance was less than would have been the case had that transfer or those transfers not been made; or

(b) no amount was payable by the non-resident parent by way of maintenance.[10]

5.20 The detail is contained in Part IV of the CS(V)Regs 2000. The court orders prescribed for these purposes are the orders which are listed or prescribed as constituting a 'maintenance order' in s 8(11) of the 1991 Act, namely orders which require the making or securing of periodical payments to or for the benefit of the child made under the MCA 1973, the DPMCA 1978, Part III of the Matrimonial and Family Proceedings Act 1984 or Sch 1 to the CA 1989, or any order varying or reviving such orders. 'Transfer of property' means a transfer by the non-resident parent of his beneficial interest in any asset to the person with care, the qualifying child, or trustees where the purpose of the trust is the provision of maintenance (reg 16(2)).

An agreement for these purposes is a written agreement made in connection with the kind of transfer of property set out above (reg 16(1)(b)).

The minimum value of the asset transferred must be £5000 (reg 16(4)); anything less than that will not qualify.

5.21 Regulation 16(3) provides that, where a transfer of property would not have fallen within the definition above when made but the Secretary of State is satisfied that some or all of the amount of that property was subsequently

---

9 CSA 1991, Sch 4B, para 3.
10 Ibid, para 3(2).

transferred to the person currently with care of the qualifying child, the transfer to the person currently with care constitutes a transfer of property which qualifies under these provisions. Presumably, 'subsequently' means after the original transfer but before 5 April 1993.

5.22 Where the above conditions are satisfied, the value of the transfer of property will be taken as being that part of the transfer made by the non-resident parent (making allowances for any transfer by the person with care to the non-resident parent) which the Secretary of State is satisfied is in lieu of periodical payments of maintenance (reg 17(1)). In order to satisfy this requirement it will be necessary to produce the court order or agreement (which, ideally, should recite these facts) or the surrounding correspondence. In determining the value of a transfer of property, the Secretary of State must assume, unless evidence to the contrary is provided to him, that:

(a) the person with care and the non-resident parent had equal beneficial interests in the asset in relation to which the court order or agreement was made;

(b) where the person with care was married to the non-resident parent, one half of the value of the transfer was a transfer for the benefit of the person with care;

(c) where the person with care has never been married to the non-resident parent, none of the value of the transfer was for the benefit of the person with care (reg 17(2)).

5.23 The equivalent value of the transfer of property is then determined in accordance with the provisions of the Schedule to the CS(V)Regs 2000. The Schedule is set out in Appendix 2 and should be referred to there. It will be seen that the value of the transfer of property is multiplied by the 'relevant factor' set out in the Table. The relevant factor is the number in the Table at the intersection of the column for the statutory rate (in effect, the judgment rate of interest) and the number of years of liability beginning with the date of the order or agreement and ending with the date on which maintenance for the youngest child will cease or when that child reaches the age of 18.

Additional cases

5.24 It is contemplated that there may be cases other than those contained in the previous provisions set out above which could justify a variation. Accordingly, it is provided that 'the Secretary of State may by regulations prescribe other cases in which a variation may be agreed'.[11] However, it should not be thought that this confers carte blanche on the Secretary of State to do whatever is just; the provisions for departures in the earlier legislation contained a similar power and the regulations made followed precisely the examples given in the statute of cases which might be provided for. Accordingly, as before, the regulations deal with the following broad matters, the statute providing[12] that:

'regulations . . . may, for example, make provision with respect to cases where –

---

11 CSA 1991, Sch 4B, para 4(1).
12 Ibid, para 4(2).

   (a) the non-resident parent has assets which exceed a prescribed value;
   (b) a person's life-style is inconsistent with his income for the purposes of a calculation made under Part I of Schedule 1;
   (c) a person has income which is not taken into account in such a calculation;
   (d) a person has unreasonably reduced the income which is taken into account in such a calculation.'

It will be seen that, whereas the cases permitting variation under the previous headings are designed to assist a non-resident parent, these cases contemplate the opposite effect and are designed to prevent a non-resident parent from paying less than he should pay if his financial position is considered as a whole. The detailed regulations will now be considered.

Assets

5.25 Assets are defined by reg 18(2) of the CS(V)Regs 2000 as: money in cash or on deposit, or money due; interests in land; shares, stock, unit trusts and gilt-edged securities; choses in action; and any such asset outside Great Britain. Where any asset is held in the joint names of the non-resident parent and another person, the Secretary of State must assume, unless evidence to the contrary is provided to him, that the asset is held by them in equal shares (reg 18(4)).

    Where the assets have a total value of £65,000 or less (after deduction of amounts owing under any mortgage or charge) reg 18(2) does not apply. In other words, once the £65,000 threshold is crossed, all the assets are taken into account, but where they do not exceed that figure, no account is taken of them (reg 18(3)(a)).

    Certain other assets are also disregarded. These are:

(1) any asset which the Secretary of State is satisfied is being retained by the non-resident parent to be used for a purpose which the Secretary of State considers reasonable in all the circumstances of the case;
(2) any asset received by the non-resident parent as compensation for personal injuries;
(3) any asset used in the course of a trade or business; and
(4) property which is the home of the non-resident parent or any child of his (reg 18(3)(b) to (e)).

5.26 Regulation 18(1)(a) of the CS(V)Regs 2000 provides that the Secretary of State may agree (that is to say, impose) a variation where he is satisfied that there is an asset:

(a) in which the non-resident parent has the beneficial interest, or which the non-resident parent has the ability to control;
(b) which has been transferred by the non-resident parent to the trustees of a trust and which the non-resident parent is a beneficiary, in circumstances where the Secretary of State is satisfied that the transfer was made in order to reduce the amount of assets which would otherwise have been taken into account (this is to prevent the non-resident parent deliberately reducing his assets below the prescribed value);
(c) which has become subject to a trust created by legal implication of which the non-resident parent is a beneficiary (for similar reasons as given in (b) above).

5.27 Where a variation is agreed on the ground that the non-resident parent has relevant assets, reg 18(5) sets out the method of calculation which must be adopted. The statutory rate of interest (the judgment rate) is applied to the value of the assets and then divided by 52. The resulting figure is added to the non-resident parent's income for the purpose of the maintenance calculation. Thus, for example, if the assets were worth £80,000, the weekly amount to be added to the non-resident parent's income (calculated at a judgment rate of 7%) would be £107.69.

Income not taken into account and diversion of income

5.28 Regulation 19 in effect sets out two classes of case where the Secretary of State may agree a variation because the ostensible income of a non-resident parent does not produce the result the Secretary of State might want. The first relates to the relationship between the nil and flat rates and those on benefits or in a prescribed category.

Regulation 19(1) applies where the liability of the non-resident parent is, or would be, either the nil rate or a flat rate owing to the fact that he is in receipt of certain benefits or is of a prescribed category (for the types of benefits and prescribed categories, see para **3.4**), and the Secretary of State is satisfied that the non-resident parent is in receipt of income which would otherwise fall to be taken into account. This seems somewhat confusing, but the point is that if the non-resident parent is in receipt of benefit or, for example, is a student or prisoner, he automatically qualifies for the flat rate or a nil rate, as the case may be. The effect of this provision is that the Secretary of State may, when the actual net income exceeds £100 per week, take that as the income and not automatically apply the flat or nil rate (reg 19(2)).

When the non-resident parent is a student, his annual earned income is divided by 52 (or calculated over such other period as the Secretary of State considers representative).

5.29 The second category is contained in reg 19(4); the Secretary of State may agree a variation where he is satisfied that:

(a) the non-resident parent has the ability to control the amount of income he receives, including earnings from employment or self-employment, whether or not the whole of that income is derived from the company or business from which his earnings are derived, and

(b) the Secretary of State is satisfied that the non-resident parent has unreasonably reduced the amount of his income which would otherwise fall to be taken into account by diverting it to other persons or for purposes other than the provision of such income for himself in order to reduce his liability to pay child support maintenance.

5.30 In the first category, the additional income to be taken into account is the whole of the income referred to above, aggregated with any benefit, pension or allowance which the non-resident parent receives other than any benefits referred to in reg 26(3) (ie various constant attendance, exceptionally severe disablement or unemployability allowances). In the second category, the whole amount of any income by which the non-resident parent has reduced his income will be taken into account (reg 19(5)).

Lifestyle inconsistent with declared income

5.31   The regulations establish two categories of case where the Secretary of State may agree a variation under this head. First, reg 20(1)(b) provides that a variation may be agreed where the Secretary of State is satisfied that the income of the non-resident parent which has been, or would be, taken into account for the purposes of the maintenance calculation is substantially lower than the level of income required to support the overall lifestyle of the non-resident parent. By virtue of reg 20(1)(a) this seems to apply irrespective of the applicable rate, unless the second category applies.

The second category is where the Secretary of State is similarly satisfied but the liability of the non-resident parent is either a flat rate due to para 4(1)(b) of Sch 1 to the 1991 Act (because he receives a prescribed benefit or allowance) or is a flat rate or nil due to para 8 of Sch 1 (on flat rate reduced to nil because of shared care), or is at the nil rate because of para 5(a) of Sch 1 (non-resident parent is of a prescribed description, eg student or prisoner). The difference between the two categories lies in the exceptions to the general principle set out in reg 20(1)(b).

5.32   The first category does not apply where the Secretary of State is satisfied that the life-style of the non-resident parent is paid for from:

(a)   income which would be disregarded for the purpose of the maintenance calculation (as to which, see para **3.11**);
(b)   income which falls to be considered under reg 19(4) (diversion of income);
(c)   assets as defined for the purposes of reg 18, or income derived from those assets (ie no double jeopardy);
(d)   the income of any partner of the non-resident parent, except where the non-resident parent is able to influence or control the amount of income received by that partner; or
(e)   assets as defined by reg 18 of any partner of the non-resident parent, or any income derived from such assets, except where the non-resident parent is able to influence or control the assets, their use, or income derived from them (reg 20(3)).

5.33   The second category does not apply where the Secretary of State is satisfied that the life-style of the non-resident parent is paid for:

(a)   from any source referred to in para **5.32** above;
(b)   from net weekly income of £100 or less; or
(c)   from income which falls to be considered under reg 19(1) (ie diverted income; again, no double jeopardy) (reg 20(4)).

5.34   Where a variation is agreed under these provisions, the additional income to be taken into account is the difference between the income which the Secretary of State is satisfied the non-resident parent requires to support his overall life-style and the income which has been, or would be, taken into account for the purposes of the maintenance calculation, aggregated with any benefit, pension or allowance which the non-resident parent receives, other than any benefits referred to in reg 26(3).

Procedure for Applying for Variation

5.35 Having considered the circumstances in which a variation might be permitted, it is now necessary to consider how an application for a variation is made and how the Secretary of State will or may deal with it.

Who may apply?
5.36 Whether an application for a maintenance calculation is made under s 4 or is treated as having been made under s 6, 'the person with care or the non-resident parent . . . may apply to the Secretary of State for the rules by which the calculation is made to be varied in accordance with this Act'.[13]

When may application be made?
5.37 There are, in effect, two possibilities. First, it is provided[14] that an application for a variation may be made at any time before the Secretary of State has reached a decision under s 11 or s 12(2) on the application for a maintenance calculation (or the application having been treated as having been made under s 6). (Sections 11 and 12(2) are those which deal with the procedure for applying under s 4 of the CSA 1991.) In other words, if it is known that an application for a calculation has been made or is treated as having been made, either party may apply for a variation before the maintenance calculation is made. However, this need not be the end of the matter. It is also provided[15] that an application for a variation may be made when a maintenance calculation is in force, and when this happens the application will be treated as an application for a revision. The procedure for revision is considered in Chapter Four.

The principles which will be followed in either case are the same.

How is application made?
5.38 An application for a variation need not be in writing unless the Secretary of State directs that it must be.[16] In the first place, therefore, the application may be made orally (presumably, by telephone) and the Secretary of State will then decide whether or not written grounds are required. However, the application (whether oral or in writing) must say upon what grounds the application is made.[17] It is also provided that, in other respects, an application for a variation must be made in such manner as may be prescribed.[18] Regulation 4(1) of the CS(V)Regs 2000 provides that where the Secretary of State directs that the application must be in writing, the application may be either on an application form provided or in such other written form as he may accept. The application is

---

13 CSA 1991, s 28A(1).
14 By ibid, s 28A(3).
15 By ibid, s 28A(1).
16 Ibid, s 28A(4)(a).
17 Ibid, s 28A(4)(b).
18 Ibid, s 28A(5).

treated as having been made on the day of receipt of the written application or the date of notification otherwise.

Preliminary consideration

5.39   The first stage of any variation application is that the Secretary of State may give it a preliminary consideration.[19] This may lead to the rejection of the application *ad limine* with the Secretary of State proceeding to make his decision on the application for a maintenance calculation without any variation. The Secretary of State may do this only if it appears to him:

(a) that there are no grounds on which he could agree to a variation;
(b) that he has insufficient information to make a decision on the application for the maintenance calculation under s 11 (apart from any information needed in relation to the application for a variation) and therefore that his decision would be made under s 12(1); or
(c) that other prescribed circumstances apply.[20]

The first of these grounds is obvious enough and requires no comment. As to the second ground, what is meant is that there is insufficient information in any event so that even where there is no application for a variation the Secretary of State would make a default maintenance decision under s 12(1) (as to which see para **2.42**). This would, in effect, require the non-resident parent to pay £30 per week for one qualifying child, £40 for two children and £50 for three or more children.

5.40   Regulation 6(2) sets out further detail about the circumstances in which the Secretary of State may reject an application. These are:

(a) prescribed circumstances apply (see para **5.41** below);
(b) the application is made:
    (i) on the ground of special expenses and the amount or aggregate amount of the expenses does not exceed the relevant threshold (as to which see para **5.7**);
    (ii) on the ground of property or capital transfer and the value of the property does not exceed the minimum value (as to which see para **5.20**); or
    (iii) on the ground of assets under reg 18 or income under reg 19(1) and the respective thresholds are not exceeded;
(c) a request under reg 8 has not been complied with by the applicant and the Secretary of State is not able to determine the application without this information. Regulation 8 permits the Secretary of State to request further information.

None of these provisions requires any explanation.

5.41   The prescribed circumstances in which an application may be rejected on a preliminary consideration referred to in s 28B(2) of the CSA 1991 are

---

19 CSA 1991, s 28B(1).
20 Ibid, s 28B(2).

contained in reg 7. They apply where the application is made under s 28G of the 1991 Act, ie there is a maintenance calculation in force.

The regulation envisages four separate sets of circumstances which may be summarised as follows.

(1) The application is made by either the non-resident parent or the person with care and either:
   (a) a default maintenance decision is in force; or
   (b) the non-resident parent is liable to pay either the flat rate because he or his partner receives a prescribed benefit or less than the flat rate or nil because of shared care or the transitional regulations; or
   (c) the non-resident parent is liable to pay the flat rate of the prescribed amount because of having a partner who is also a non-resident parent and in respect of whom a maintenance calculation is in force and he or the partner receives a prescribed benefit, or would be so liable were it not for shared care.

(2) The non-resident parent applies and he is liable to pay either:
   (a) at the nil rate because he is of a prescribed description or his net weekly income is less than £5; or
   (b) at the flat rate because his net weekly income is less than £100 (including cases where it is less than £100 because of a variation); or
   (c) at the flat rate because he receives benefit or less because of shared care; or
   (d) £5 per week or some other prescribed rate due to shared care; or
   (e) equivalent to the flat rate because of the effect of a variation, or the transitional provisions.

(3) The application is made by the person with care, and either:
   (a) the weekly income taken into account was the capped amount (£2000); or
   (b) the non-resident parent or his partner is in receipt of working families' tax credit or disabled person's tax credit.

(4) The application is made by the non-resident parent on the ground of special expenses and (3)(a) above applies.

Interim maintenance decision

5.42 A default maintenance decision is not to be confused with an interim maintenance decision. This is in effect a maintenance calculation made in accordance with the normal rules in Part I of Sch 1 to the CSA 1991[21] but without regard to the application for a variation; presumably, this would be done where there was sufficient information on which to base a maintenance calculation but not for the variation application.

Regular payments condition

5.43 A regular payments condition may be imposed if two conditions are met. First, the non-resident parent must have applied for a variation. Secondly, the

---

21 CSA 1991, s 12(2) and (3).

Secretary of State must have made an interim maintenance decision.[22] The regular payments condition may take one of two forms, namely that either:

(a) the non-resident parent must make the payments of child support maintenance specified in the interim decision; or

(b) the non-resident parent must make such lesser payments of child support maintenance as may be determined in accordance with regulations made by the Secretary of State.[23]

Regulation 31(1) provides that the payments are those fixed in the interim maintenance decision or the maintenance calculation in force, as the case may be, adjusted to take account of the variation application as if that variation had been agreed. In other words, the non-resident parent must pay what he is, in effect, offering to pay, as a condition of the application for variation proceedings. If he fails to comply with the regular payments condition, and fails to make such payments which are due and unpaid within one month of being required to do so, the Secretary of State may refuse to consider the application (reg 31(2) and (3)).

The effect of non-compliance with the regular payments condition is that the Secretary of State may refuse to consider the application for a variation and instead reach his decision under s 11 (the application for a maintenance calculation) as if no application for a variation had been made.[24] This would, in effect, veto the variation application.

5.44 A regular payments condition will cease to have effect when the Secretary of State makes a decision on the application for a maintenance calculation, whether he agrees a variation or not, or when the application for a variation is withdrawn.[25] Provision is made for the written notification to all parties of any regular payments condition and of any determination of non-compliance with such a condition.

Determination of applications

5.45 If an application for a variation has not failed (in the sense of having been refused on preliminary consideration, or having lapsed or been withdrawn) the Secretary of State must determine it. He has three choices. He may agree the variation or not agree the variation. In either case, he will make a decision on the application for a maintenance calculation. Alternatively, he may refer the application to an appeal tribunal for the tribunal to determine what variation, if any, is to be made.[26] When the appeal tribunal deals with the application, it has the same powers as the Secretary of State would have had.

5.46 In determining any application for a variation, the Secretary of State must have regard to certain general principles. These are:

(a) that parents should be responsible for maintaining their children whenever they can afford to do so; and

22 CSA 1991, s 28C(1).
23 Ibid, s 28C(2).
24 Ibid, s 28C(5).
25 Ibid, s 28C(4).
26 Ibid, s 28D(1).

(b) where a parent has more than one child, his obligation to maintain any one of them should be no less of an obligation than his obligation to maintain any other of them.[27]

In addition, regard must be had to such other conditions as may be prescribed. No additional conditions have been prescribed.

5.47 The CSA 1991 contains provision for 'regulatory controls'. The basic principle is that 'no variations may be made other than those which are permitted under the regulations';[28] there is, therefore, no question of the Secretary of State enjoying a discretion such as might be exercised by a court. Instead, regulations will govern what he can do.

The regulations may in particular make provision for a variation to result in:

(a) a person's being treated as having more, or less, income than would be taken into account without the variation in a calculation under Part I of Sch 1;
(b) a person's being treated as liable to pay a higher, or a lower, amount of child support maintenance than would result without the variation from a calculation under that Part.[29]

These provisions require little comment. The 'normal' payment may be adjusted upwards or downwards. There is also provision for the regulations to specify, in effect, an upper limit on any special expenses which may be taken into account and for different provisions for different levels of income.[30] These have all been considered elsewhere.

5.48 The procedure where an application is not rejected is contained in reg 9, to which reference should be made. Its main effect may be summarised as follows:

(a) the Secretary of State must give notice to all parties of the application and invite representations;
(b) reg 9(2) prescribes information which need not be disclosed to all parties, eg medical evidence and information which might lead to a person or child being located;
(c) copies of any representations may be sent to the other parties;
(d) where no representations are received, the Secretary of State may proceed to determine the application.

5.49 The principles governing the Secretary of State's decision have already been summarised at para **5.4** above. It will be seen that, within the constraints of the regulations, the Secretary of State enjoys some discretion. In this respect, therefore, the system cannot be said to be certain.

5.50 The effect of a variation on the maintenance calculation and effective dates are contained in Part VII (regs 22 to 30) of the CS(V)Regs 2000. The detail is considerable and to repeat it all here would not add much to the reader's knowledge. The regulations are set out in Appendix 2.

---

27 CSA 1991, s 28F(1).
28 Ibid, Sch 4B, para 5(2).
29 Ibid, para 5(3).
30 Ibid, para 5(4).

CHAPTER SIX

Disputes as to Parentage

Introduction

6.1   This chapter is concerned with the manner in which a person alleged to be a non-resident parent may challenge the contention that he is a parent of the child concerned. Chapter Seven deals with the various other ways of challenging calculations etc; this chapter is limited to the issue of parentage.

Only a non-resident parent, or someone treated as such, can be required to pay a maintenance calculation under the provisions of the CSA 1991. 'Parent' is defined by s 54 as, in relation to any child, any person who is in law the mother or father of the child.

A person may become the mother or father of a child by virtue of an adoption order of the court. Apart from this, a woman is in law the mother of a child only if she has given birth to it, and a man is the father if he is the natural father in a biological sense; this statement may, to a limited extent, be qualified by the effect of the HFEA 1990, as to which see para **2.9**, but this will apply in only a very limited number of cases.

Accordingly, in the vast majority of cases, only a 'natural' father or mother will be liable under the CSA 1991. A dispute as to parentage is, therefore, of greater importance in this field than in any other area of family financial relief. In matrimonial proceedings before the courts, a person may be liable for child maintenance, even though that person is not a biological parent, if he or she has treated the child as a child of their family. This is not the case in relation to the Act, where the sole criterion is parentage.

6.2   In reality, this chapter is concerned almost entirely with the position of a man who denies that he is the father of a child. This is not because of any gender discrimination but because there is rarely any doubt as to whether a woman has given birth to a child. It is not impossible that a woman could deny being a non-resident parent, but that possibility will not be pursued further here.

The General Position

6.3   The general position is contained in s 26 of the CSA 1991. Section 26(1) provides that:

> 'Where a person who is alleged to be a parent of the child with respect to whom an application for a maintenance calculation has been made ("the alleged parent") denies that he is one of the child's parents, the Secretary of State shall not make a maintenance calculation on the assumption that the alleged parent is one of the child's parents unless the case falls within one of those set out in subsection (2).'

The effect of this is that where subsection (2) does not apply, the application for the calculation may not proceed until the issue of paternity has been determined. However, where subsection (2) does apply, the protests of the alleged parent will fall on deaf ears, and the calculation will be made.

In the event of a calculation being made, and the issue of parentage being raised thereafter for the first time, it would seem that the calculation would remain in force. However, this is dealt with at para **6.6**.

6.4 Section 26(2) sets out the cases in which a calculation may be made notwithstanding a denial of paternity. They are as follows.

'Case A1

Where –
(a) the child is habitually resident in England and Wales;
(b) the Secretary of State is satisfied that the alleged parent was married to the child's mother at some time in the period beginning with the conception and ending with the birth of the child; and
(c) the child has not been adopted.'

This is a new case added by the CSPSSA 2000. Here, it is sufficient for the alleged father to have been married to the mother at some time during the nine months ending with the birth; presumably, given the difficulty of establishing an exact date for conception, nine months before birth will be taken to be the date of conception.

'Case A2

Where –
(a) the child is habitually resident in England and Wales;
(b) the alleged parent has been registered as father of the child under section 10 or 10A of the Births and Deaths Registration Act 1953, or in any register kept under section 13 (register of births and still-births) or section 44 (Register of Corrections Etc) of the Registration of Births, Deaths and Marriages (Scotland) Act 1965, or under Article 14 or 18(1)(b)(ii) of the Births and Deaths Registration (Northern Ireland) Order 1976; and
(c) the child has not subsequently been adopted.'

Another addition in the CSPSSA 2000; little comment is needed here. Registration as father raises a presumption of paternity.

'Case A3

Where the result of a scientific test (within the meaning of section 27A) taken by the alleged parent would be relevant to determining the child's parent's parentage, and the alleged parent –
(a) refuses to take such a test; or
(b) has submitted to such a test, and it shows that there is no reasonable doubt that the alleged parent is a parent of the child.'

This too is a new case added by the CSPSSA 2000. The Secretary of State may, therefore, ask an alleged parent to take a test; presumably this could be based entirely on information received from the mother. If he refused to take the test, a maintenance calculation could be made. Paragraph (b) quite reasonably entitles the Secretary of State to follow the results of a test.

The procedure for testing, and the law thereon, is considered in more detail below.

'CASE A

Where the alleged parent is a parent of the child in question by virtue of having adopted him.'

This requires little comment. The production of the adoption order would be conclusive. By s 26(3), 'adopted' means adopted within the meaning of Part IV of the Adoption Act 1976, or, in relation to Scotland, Part IV of the Adoption (Scotland) Act 1978.

'CASE B

Where the alleged parent is a parent of the child in question by virtue of an order under section 30 of the Human Fertilisation and Embryology Act 1990 (parental orders in favour of gamete donors).'

For the general effect of the HFEA 1990, see para **2.9**. Section 30 enables a married couple who have provided the genetic material which has led to the conception of the child to apply to the court for a so-called 'parental order' which will provide for the child in question to be treated in law as their child. Production of the court's order would be a necessary prerequisite for this case to be applied.

'CASE B1

Where the Secretary of State is satisfied that the alleged parent is a parent of the child in question by virtue of section 27 or 28 of that Act (meaning of "mother" and of "father" respectively).'

This is another new case added by the CSPSSA 2000. Reference should be made to para **2.9** for further explanation of this point.

'CASE C

Where –
(a) either –
   (i) a declaration that the alleged parent is a parent of the child in question (or a declaration which has that effect) is in force under section 56 of the Family Law Act 1986 (declarations of parentage); or
   (ii) a declarator by a court in Scotland that the alleged parent is a parent of the child in question (or a declarator which has that effect) is in force; and
(b) the child has not subsequently been adopted.'

Section 56 of the Family Law Act 1986 (substituted by s 22 of the Family Law Reform Act 1987) deals with the right of an individual to apply to the court for a declaration that a named person is or was his parent or that he is the legitimate child of his parents. No one other than the 'child' can make the application; a parent cannot apply for a declaration in respect of his child.

'CASE D

Where –
(a) a declaration to the effect that the alleged parent is one of the parents of the child in question has been made under section 27; and
(b) the child has not subsequently been adopted.'

This prevents a non-resident parent from raising the issue of parentage more than once. Once the court has adjudicated as to paternity under s 27 (as to which see below) the issue cannot be raised again.

'CASE E

Where –
(a) the child is habitually resident in Scotland;
(b) the Secretary of State is satisfied that one or other of the presumptions set out in section 5(1) of the Law Reform (Parent and Child) (Scotland) Act 1986 applies; and
(c) the child has not subsequently been adopted.'

'CASE F

Where –
(a) the alleged parent has been found, or adjudged, to be the father of the child in question –
    (i) in proceedings before any court in England and Wales which are relevant proceedings for the purposes of section 12 of the Civil Evidence Act 1968 or in proceedings before any court in Northern Ireland which are relevant proceedings for the purposes of section 8 of the Civil Evidence Act (Northern Ireland) 1971; or
    (ii) in affiliation proceedings before any court in the United Kingdom,
(whether or not he offered any defence to the allegation of paternity) and that finding or adjudication still subsists; and
(b) the child has not subsequently been adopted.'

This requires little comment; the 1968 Act has been extended by the Courts and Legal Services Act 1990, Sch 16, para 2. The effect is, again, that once parentage has been determined by a competent court, the issue may not be re-opened.

6.5   It will be seen, therefore, that the class in s 26(2) are all cases where, in one way or another, a court order exists which governs the position as to parentage. The remedy of the non-resident parent in any of those cases who wished to continue to deny parentage could only be to appeal or to make some other application in the proceedings in which the order had been made.

Procedure

6.6   The procedure to be followed in the event of a dispute as to parentage which does not fall within s 26(2) is dictated by s 27. It provides that the Secretary of State or the person with care may apply to the court for a declaration as to whether an alleged parent is one of a child's parents in certain circumstances (s 27(1A)).

These circumstances are set out in s 27(1), which provides that s 27(1A) applies in any case where:

> '(a) an application for a maintenance calculation has been made, or a maintenance calculation is in force, with respect to a person ("the alleged parent") who denies that he is a parent of a child with respect to whom the application or calculation was made; and
>
> (b) the Secretary of State is not satisfied that the case falls within one of those set out in section 26(2).'

It will be seen that the Secretary of State may apply to the court even where a calculation has been made; the implication here is that the non-resident parent may not have denied parentage at the outset and only raised the issue at a subsequent time. On the other hand, this may be designed to cover the position where a calculation has been made with no co-operation from the non-resident parent.

The application to the court is not mandatory. The Secretary of State may apply, or leave it to the person with care to apply, or not apply at all. If the calculation had not yet been made, the Secretary of State could not proceed unless the application to the court were made (s 26(1)). However, if the calculation had been made, and the denial of parentage was made at a later stage, and the Secretary of State decided to do nothing, it would seem that the assessment would remain in force; there is no provision in the Act for a non-resident parent to apply to the court.

The only remedy of the non-resident parent would be to apply to the courts under other provisions, or to apply for judicial review.

6.7 Similar provisions to those set out above exist in relation to Scotland.

6.8 The effect of s 27(4) of the CSA 1991, Sch 11 to the CA 1989, and the Children (Allocation of Proceedings) (Amendment) Order 1993, SI 1993/624, is that the court to which the Secretary of State or person with care must apply is, in England and Wales, a magistrates' court. This follows the usual Children Act procedure; the magistrates' court may refer a case 'upwards' if appropriate.

The function of the court dealing with the matter is dealt with in s 27(2), which provides that:

> 'If, on hearing any application under subsection (1A), the court is satisfied that the alleged parent is, or is not, a parent of the child in question it shall make a declaration to that effect.'

By s 27(3), a declaration under this section shall have effect only for the purposes of the Act and proceedings in which a court is considering whether to make a maintenance order in the circumstances mentioned in s 8(6), (7) or (8). The s 8 cases are where the Act permits applications to the court of a 'top-up' or supplementary nature (see Chapter Ten).

6.9 Section 27A deals with the position as to fees for scientific tests. It applies in any case where:

> '(a) an application for a maintenance calculation has been made or treated as made or a maintenance calculation is in force;

(b) scientific tests have been carried out (otherwise than under a direction or in response to a request) in relation to bodily samples obtained from a person who is alleged to be a parent of a child with respect to whom the application or calculation is made or, as the case may be, treated as made;

(c) the results of the tests do not exclude the alleged parent from being one of the child's parents; and

(d) one of the conditions set out in subsection (2) is satisfied.'

The conditions in subsection (2) are as follows:

'(a) the alleged parent does not deny that he is one of the child's parents;

(b) in proceedings under section 27, a court has made a declaration that the alleged parent is a parent of the child in question; or

(c) *(applies to Scotland only).*'

When these conditions are met, s 27A(3) applies, the result of which is that the Secretary of State may recover any fees paid for the tests from the alleged parent as a debt due to the Crown.

Most of this is self-explanatory; s 27A(4) contains definitions of the various terms used in the section.

The broad thrust of the provision is that an alleged parent who is found to be, or admits to being, a parent of a child after tests have been carried out will be liable for the cost of the tests.

6.10   The question of blood tests was considered by the Court of Appeal in *Re A (A Minor) (Paternity: Refusal of Blood Test)* [1994] 2 FLR 463. Although this was not a case under the CSA 1991, it is worthy of consideration in this context since it deals with matters common to all cases of disputed paternity. The court has to consider the implications of a putative father's refusal to submit to blood tests which had been ordered by the court.

The court held that all issues of paternity now fell to be resolved within the framework of the CA 1989 by the courts, which have statutory freedom to deal with the evidence at large and to reach their own determination as to the significance to be attached to a person's refusal to consent to scientific tests directed by the court under the amended s 20 of the Family Law Reform Act 1990. A man who was unsure of his own paternity had it within his power to set all doubt at rest by submitting to a test. Against that background of law and scientific advance, it followed in justice and common sense that if someone chose to exercise his right not to be tested, the inference that he was the father should be virtually inescapable. He would have to advance very clear and cogent reasons for his refusal to be tested.

In *Re H (Paternity: Blood Test)* [1996] 2 FLR 65, CA, it was held that a mother's adamant refusal to undergo blood testing for herself and a child was not, of itself, determinative of the issue of paternity. Accordingly, the court made a direction for blood tests despite the mother's refusal; an inference adverse to the refusing party could be drawn irrespective of whether the refusal was before or after the court's direction. The welfare of the child was not the paramount consideration. Every child had a right to know the truth about its parentage, unless his welfare clearly justified a cover-up.

The law as to testing with a view to ascertaining parentage has now been changed by amendments made to the Family Law Reform Act 1969 by the

CSPSSA 2000. These came about largely as a result of the decision of Wall J in *Re O and J (Paternity: Blood Tests)* [2000] 1 FLR 418, where it was held that the person having care and control of a child has an absolute right to refuse to allow a sample of blood to be taken from the child for the purpose of determining paternity. Section 82(3) of the CSPSSA 2000 amends s 21 of the 1969 Act (which deals with consents required for the taking of blood samples) to add to the words 'if the person who has the care and control of him consents' the words 'or, (b) where that person does not consent, if the court considers that it would be in his best interests for the sample to be taken'.

The intentions of the legislature were explained by the Minister Mr Jeff Rooker as follows:

'A child will have a right to know who its parents are, and that is why taking a sample may be necessary. However, a court – and obviously not the child – will judge whether that is in the child's interests. . . . The amendment therefore focuses on the best interests of the child. In deciding whether to give a direction for tests to establish paternity the court will have the flexibility to distinguish between cases where establishing paternity is in the child's best interests and those where it might not be. It will be up to the court to make the decision.'[1]

---

1 Official Report (HC) 29 March 2000, cols 414 and 415.

CHAPTER SEVEN

Revisions

Introduction

7.1   The CSA 1991 contained quite complicated provisions for reviews (as they were then called). Reviews were always carried out by a child support officer and might result in an assessment (as it was then called) or refusal to make an assessment being altered. It might be a periodic review, or the means of the CSO correcting an error, or it might be the first stage of an attack on a decision of the CSO which could lead to an appeal.

These provisions were contained in ss 16–19 of the CSA 1991. These sections have now been changed in two ways. First, they were replaced by new ss 16 and 17 by virtue of the Social Security Act 1998, s 41. This introduced the term 'revision' in place of 'review' and created a simplified procedure in line with other aspects of social security. Secondly, ss 8 and 9 of the CSPSSA 2000 amend those provisions. The position is now, therefore, entirely different from the pre-1998 position.

Revision of Decisions

7.2   Section s 16(1A) sets out the decisions to which s 16 applies. They include:

'(a)   a decision of the Secretary of State under section 11, 12 or 17',

which are any decisions relating to maintenance calculations or default and interim calculations, or any decision made which supersedes an earlier decision (as to which, see para **7.7**). There is one specific provision relating to default maintenance decisions under s 12(1)(b). When the Secretary of State revises such a decision pursuant to s 16, he may (if appropriate) do so as if he were revising a decision under s 11 (a 'full' maintenance calculation); if he does so, his decision as revised is to be treated as one under s 11 rather than s 12 (in particular, for purposes of appeal).[1]

'(b)   a reduced benefit decision under section 46;'.

This is self-explanatory.

'(c)   a decision of an appeal tribunal on a referral under section 28D(1)(b).'

As will be seen when appeals are considered in Chapter Eight, s 28D(1)(b) applies where an application for what used to be called a departure direction and is now called a variation is referred by the Secretary of State rather than it being dealt with by him.

---

1   CSA 1991, s 16(1B).

7.3   In effect, s 16 enables the Secretary of State to revise, that is to say, change or modify, any of the decisions which fall within the section. He may do so either within a prescribed period or in prescribed cases or circumstances.[2] He may do so either on an application made by anyone entitled to apply or of his own initiative.[3]

7.4   The detail is contained in the Child Support (Decisions and Appeals) (Amendment) Regulations 2000, SI 2000/3185, which amend the Social Security and Child Support (Decisions and Appeals) Regulations 1999 (SSCS(DA)Regs 1999), SI 1999/991. Regulation 3A(1) of the SSCS(DA)Regs 1999 prescribes the circumstances in which the Secretary of State may revise any decision under s 16 of the CSA 1991. They may be summarised as follows:

(a) on receipt of an application for revision under s 16 or by way of an application under s 28G for a variation, provided such application is made within one month of notification of the decision (or such longer time as may be allowed; see para **7.5** below);

(b) where (a) applies, but the Secretary of State has notified the applicant that the application is unsuccessful because he is not in possession of all the information needed to make a decision, and the applicant reapplies within one month of such notification (or such longer period as the Secretary of State is satisfied is reasonable);

(c) where the Secretary of State is satisfied that the decision was erroneous due to a misrepresentation of, or failure to disclose, a material fact and that the decision was more advantageous to the person who misrepresented or failed to disclose that fact than it would have been but for that error;

(d) in any event, if the Secretary of State commences action leading to the revision of the decision within one month of the notification of the decision; or

(e) if the decision arose from an official error.

Items (a) to (d) above do not apply to changes of circumstances which have occurred since the date on which the decision had effect or which, according to information which the Secretary of State has, are expected to occur.[4]

7.5   Late applications are dealt with by reg 4 of the SSCS(DA)Regs 1999. The time-limit for applying for a revision may be extended where certain conditions are satisfied. The first conditions relate to the application itself and are as follows:

(a) an application for extension of time must be made;

(b) the application must contain particulars of the grounds on which the extension is sought and must identify the decision which is sought to be revised; and

(c) the application must be made within 13 months of the decision which it is sought to have revised.

---

2 CSA 1991, s 16(1)(a).
3 Ibid, s 16(1)(b).
4 SSCS(DA)Regs 1999, reg 3A(2).

Having cleared those formal hurdles, the application for extension will be considered. The Secretary of State must be satisfied that:

(a) it is reasonable to grant the application (for an extension of time);
(b) the application for revision has merit; and
(c) special circumstances are relevant to the application as a result of which it was not practicable for the application to be made within the normal time-limits.

7.6 In determining whether it is reasonable to grant an application for an extension, the Secretary of State must have regard to the principle that the greater the time that has elapsed since the expiry of the time prescribed for applying for the revision, the more compelling must be the special circumstances on which the application is based.[5] No account may be taken of the fact that the applicant or any person on his behalf was unaware of or misunderstood the law or the time-limits, nor that a Commissioner or a court has taken a different view of the law from that previously understood and applied.[6]

Decisions Superseding Earlier Decisions

7.7 Section 17 of the CSA 1991 makes provision for certain decisions to be superseded; the difference between revising and superseding would seem to be that the latter substitutes a completely new decision for the previous decision rather than merely changing it.

The decisions which may be superseded under s 17 are:

'(a) any decision of the Secretary of State under section 11 or 12 or [17], whether as originally made or as revised under section 16;'[7]

This covers any decision involving a maintenance calculation or interim or default calculation or any decision made under s 17 superseding such a decision.

'(b) any decision of an appeal tribunal under section 20;'[8]

The Secretary of State may, therefore, make a decision replacing the decision of an appeal tribunal.

'(c) any reduced benefit direction under section 46;
(d) any decision of an appeal tribunal on a referral under section 28D(1)(b);
(e) any decision of a Child Support Commissioner on an appeal from such a decision as is mentioned in paragraph (b) or (d).'[9]

This is self-explanatory.

7.8 The Secretary of State may make a decision under any of the above either on an application made by any person entitled to apply or on his own initiative.[10]

---

5 SSCS(DA) Regs 1999, reg 4(5).
6 Ibid, reg 4(6).
7 CSA 1991, s 17(1)(a).
8 Ibid, s 17(1)(b).
9 Ibid, s 17(1)(e).
10 Ibid, s 17(1).

He need not consider any issue that is not raised by the application or, as the case may be, did not cause him to act on his own initiative.[11]

The circumstances in which this jurisdiction may be exercised are set out in reg 6A of the SSCS(DA)Regs 1999. There are five sets of circumstances in which a decision may be superseded, as follows.

(1) A decision may be superseded by a decision made by the Secretary of State acting on his own initiative where:
  (a) there has been a relevant change of circumstances since the decision had effect; or
  (b) the decision was made in ignorance of, or was based on a mistake as to, some material fact.[12]
(2) A decision may be superseded by the Secretary of State where an application is made on the basis that:
  (a) there has been a change of circumstances since the date from which the decision had effect; or
  (b) it is expected that a change of circumstances will occur, and the Secretary of State is satisfied that the change of circumstances is or would be relevant.[13]
(3) A decision may be superseded by a decision made by the Secretary of State where an application is made on the basis that the decision was made in ignorance of or was based upon a mistake as to some fact, and the Secretary of State is satisfied that the fact is or would be material.[14]
(4) A decision, other than a decision made on appeal, may be superseded by a decision made by the Secretary of State acting on his own initiative or on application where he is satisfied that the decision was erroneous in point of law.[15]
(5) A decision may be superseded by a decision made by the Secretary of State where he receives an application for supersession by way of an application under s 28G (as to which, see Chapter Five).[16]

7.9 A decision may not be superseded where it might be revised.[17] The procedure for supersession does not apply to a decision to refuse an application for a maintenance calculation.[18] Regulation 6B prescribes circumstances in which a decision may not be superseded; these are too involved to be recited in full, but their broad thrust is to restrict supersessions to circumstances where a difference of more than 5% in the non-resident parent's income figure would be achieved. Where the Secretary of State proposes to supersede a decision under s 17 of his own initiative, he must notify the relevant persons who would be affected by his decision.[19]

---

11 CSA 1991, s 17(2).
12 SSCS(DA)Regs 1999, reg 6A(2).
13 Ibid, reg 6A(3).
14 Ibid, reg 6A(4).
15 Ibid, reg 6A(5).
16 Ibid, reg 6A(7).
17 Ibid, reg 6A(7).
18 Ibid, reg 6A(8).
19 Ibid, reg 7C.

7.10 For the detail of the dates on which a decision superseded under s 17 takes effect, see reg 7B. As to notification of decisions made under s 16 or s 17, see reg 15C.

Regulation 15B sets out the procedure to be adopted where an application is made under s 16 or s 17 in connection with a previously determined variation which has an effect on the maintenance calculation in force. Broadly, it requires the Secretary of State to give notice to all relevant persons and to invite representations, prescribes the information which must be given to the relevant persons, and prescribes the procedure which the Secretary of State must follow.

CHAPTER EIGHT

Appeals and Judicial Review

Introduction

8.1 As was seen in Chapter Seven, the normal first step for anyone aggrieved by a decision of the Secretary of State is an application for revision. Where the right to appeal exists, the first appellate tribunal is the appeal tribunal. From there, in certain cases, appeal lies to the Child Support Commissioner and thence, with permission, and on a point of law only, to the Court of Appeal.

Appeals as to disputed parentage are to the courts. Finally, although not an appeal as such, some decisions of the Secretary of State may be challenged by way of judicial review.

These possibilities will now be considered in turn. It should be noted that the system of appeals has changed quite radically since 1991, first as a result of changes in 1999 which affected all social security appeals, and now as a result of further changes effected by the CSPSSA 2000.

Appeal to an Appeal Tribunal

8.2 An appeal tribunal determining a misconceived appeal as a preliminary issue consists of one legally qualified panel member.[1] Otherwise, it must consist of one legally qualified member and one financially qualified member.[2] Each tribunal must have a clerk.

The right of appeal is restricted to 'a qualifying person',[3] defined[4] in different ways according to the type of appeal. The decisions in respect of which a right of appeal exists, and the persons who may appeal in each case, are as shown in the table below.

These provisions are clear enough. Sections 11 and 12 cover all maintenance calculations and this therefore provides a right of appeal against all such matters. Reduced benefit directions are dealt with in more detail in Chapter Two at para **2.19**. It should be noted, however, that no appeal will lie in respect of a reduced benefit direction unless the amount of the person's benefit is reduced in

---

1 SSCS(DA)Regs 1999, reg 36(1).
2 Ibid, reg 36(3).
3 CSA 1991, s 20(1).
4 By ibid, s 20(2).

Type of appeal[5]	Who may appeal[6]
Decision under ss 11, 12, or 17[5] (whether as originally made or as revised under s 16)	The person with care or non-resident parent[6] with respect to whom the decision was made
Decision not to make a maintenance calculation under s 11 or not to supersede a decision under s 17	Ditto
Reduced benefit decision	The person in respect of whom the benefits are payable
The imposition (under s 14A) of a requirement to make penalty payments, or their amount	The parent who has been required to make penalty payments
The imposition (under s 47) of a requirement to pay fees	The person required to pay fees

accordance with the reduced benefit direction.[7] This presumably covers the possibility that the Secretary of State might wish to make a reduced benefit direction but be prevented from doing so by one of the 'prescribed circumstances' under s 46(5). A person who was aggrieved by the principle, but who had suffered no loss, would not be able to appeal.

8.3 It is provided[8] that in deciding any appeal the tribunal need not consider any issue that is not raised by the appeal, and may not take into account any circumstances not obtaining at the time when the Secretary of State made the decision or imposed the requirement. The latter point means, clearly, that if the case is one where there might have been an application for revision, that is the remedy which should be sought rather than appeal.

If an appeal is allowed, the tribunal may either itself make such decision as it considers appropriate or remit the case to the Secretary of State with such directions (if any) as it considers appropriate.[9]

Procedural Matters

8.4 Procedure is governed by the SSCS(DA) Regs 1999 (as amended), and the parts of those regulations which apply to child support appeals are regs 30–58. The most important parts are as follows.

---

5 See CSA 1991, s 20(1).
6 See ibid, s 20(2).
7 Ibid, s 20(6).
8 By ibid, s 20(7).
9 Ibid, s 20(8).

(a) The notice

An appeal, or an application for an extension of time, must be in writing either on a form approved for the purpose by the Secretary of State or in such other form as may be accepted as sufficient for the purpose by him. It must be signed by either the person who has the right of appeal or a person who has written authority to act as their representative, contain particulars of the grounds on which it is made, and contain sufficient particulars of the decision appealed against to enable it to be identified (reg 33(1)).

(b) Service of the notice

The notice must be sent to 'an appropriate office' (reg 33(1)), defined as an office of the CSA (reg 33(2)(d)).

(c) Time-limits

The appeal must be brought within one month of the date of notification of the decision against which the appeal is brought, or, where a written statement of reasons for that decision is requested, within 14 days of the expiry of one month from notification of the decision (reg 31(1)). Disputes as to whether an appeal was brought within time must be referred to a legally qualified panel member (reg 31(4)).

(d) Late appeals

The time for appeal may be extended but no appeal may be brought more than one year after the time has expired (reg 32(1)). The procedure for giving notice is that set out under reg 33 (see *(a)* above). Any such application is determined by a legally qualified panel member. The panel member must be satisfied that if the application is granted there are reasonable prospects of success that the appeal will be successful and that it is in the interests of justice for the application to be granted (reg 32(4)). However, it cannot be found that it is in the interests of justice for the application to be granted unless either certain defined special circumstances exist or some other special circumstances exist which are wholly exceptional and relevant to the application, and as a result of those special circumstances it was not practicable for the application to be made within the time-limits (reg 32(5)).

The defined special circumstances are that the applicant or a spouse or dependant of the applicant has died or suffered serious illness, or that the applicant is not resident in the UK, or that normal postal services were disrupted (reg 32(6)). In determining whether it is in the interests of justice to grant the application, the principle to be observed is, in effect, that the greater the delay the more compelling must be the special circumstances (reg 32(7)). No account may be taken of ignorance or misunderstanding of the law nor of the fact that a Commissioner or a court has taken a different view of the law from that previously understood or applied (reg 32(8)).

(e) Further information

Where an application or appeal is made by letter and not on a prescribed form, and does not contain sufficient information, the Secretary of State may request further particulars (reg 33(6)).

(f) Directions

A legally qualified panel member may give directions at any stage, either of his own motion or at the request of one of the parties (reg 38(2)).

(g) Dispensing with hearings

The clerk to an appeal tribunal will direct the appellant and any other party to notify him in writing whether he wishes to have an oral hearing or whether he is content to proceed without an oral hearing (reg 39(1)). If the appellant does respond within 14 days the appeal may be struck out (reg 39(2)). Where a party requests an oral hearing there must be an oral hearing (reg 39(4)).

(h) Summoning of witnesses

A chairman of an appeal tribunal may by summons require any person in Great Britain to attend as a witness at a hearing to answer any questions or produce any documents in his custody or under his control. Fourteen days' notice is required (except where the witness agrees) and conduct money must be paid (reg 43(1)). No person may be compelled to give evidence or produce documents which he could not be compelled to give or produce in court proceedings (reg 43(2)). The chairman must take into account the need to protect matter relating to intimate personal or financial circumstances, which is commercially sensitive, or concerns national security (reg 43(3)).

(i) Oral hearings

Oral hearings must be in public unless the appellant requests a private hearing or the chairman is satisfied that intimate personal or financial circumstances may have to be disclosed or considerations of national security are involved (reg 49(5)). A chairman may require evidence to be given on oath (reg 43(5)). Any party to the proceedings is entitled to be present and to be heard (reg 49(7)). He may also call evidence, address the tribunal and put questions to any party (reg 49(11)).

(j) Misconceived appeals

A misconceived appeal may be struck out by a legally qualified member but not before the appellant has been given notice (reg 46(4)). An appellant to whom such notice is given may, within 14 days thereafter, request an oral hearing (reg 48(1)).

Appeal to Child Support Commissioners

8.5 Any person who is aggrieved by a decision of an appeal tribunal, and the Secretary of State (who, presumably, does not have to feel aggrieved), may appeal to a Child Support Commissioner on a question of law.[10] No such appeal may be brought without the leave of the person who was the chairman of, or constituted, the appeal tribunal (or such other person as may be determined by regulations) or a Child Support Commissioner.[11]

---

10 CSA 1991, s 24(1).
11 Ibid, s 24(6).

Before the question of leave is considered, s 23A should be mentioned. This applies where an application is made for leave and the person who constituted or was the chairman of the appeal tribunal considers that the decision was erroneous in law. In such circumstances, he may set aside the decision and refer the case either for redetermination by the tribunal or for determination by a differently constituted tribunal.[12] An unnecessary appeal to the Commissioner may, therefore, be avoided.

However, the section goes further. Where 'each of the principal parties to the case' (defined[13] as the Secretary of State and those who are qualifying persons under s 20(2) in relation to the decision) expresses the view that the decision was erroneous in point of law, the person to whom the application for leave is made must set aside the decision and refer the case for determination by a differently constituted tribunal.[14]

8.6 The Commissioner must set aside the decision in question if he holds that it was wrong in law.[15] He may then either give the decision which should have been given, make such findings and give such decision as he considers appropriate, (on an appeal by the Secretary of State) refer the case to an appeal tribunal with directions for its redetermination, or (in other cases) refer to the Secretary of State or an appeal tribunal with directions for redetermination.[16]

8.7 Sections 28ZA to 28ZB contain provisions concerning appeals which involve issues arising on other appeals. They are complicated and of marginal interest to most family lawyers, but their existence should be noted.

8.8 The relevant regulations are contained in the Child Support Commissioners (Procedure) Regulations 1992 (CSC(P)Regs 1992), SI 1992/2640, the most important of which are as follows.

(a) Time-limits for application for leave

An application for leave to appeal must be made:

(i) in the case of application to a tribunal chairman, within three months of the date on which notice of the decision was sent to the applicant; or

(ii) in the case of application to a Commissioner, within 42 days of the date of sending notice of the chairman's refusal of leave (reg 2(1)).

(b) To whom is application for leave made?

Application must be made to the chairman of the tribunal which made the decision under appeal (s 24(6)(a) and reg 2(1)). Where it would cause undue delay, or be impracticable for the application to be made to that chairman, the application may be determined by any other chairman (reg 2(2)).

An application for leave to appeal may be made to a Commissioner only where the applicant has been refused leave to appeal by a tribunal chairman

---

12 CSA 1991, s 23A(2).
13 By ibid, s 23A(4).
14 Ibid, s 23A(3).
15 Ibid, s 24(2).
16 Ibid, s 24(3).

(reg 2(3)); however, where there has been failure to apply to the chairman in time or at all, an application may be made to a Commissioner who may accept and deal with it 'for special reasons' if he thinks fit (reg 2(4)); such an application may be made outside the period of 42 days, for special reasons (reg 2(5)).

(c) The notice

Application for leave must be by notice in writing to the clerk to the tribunal at the Central Office. It must contain:

  (i) the name and address of the applicant;
 (ii) the ground on which the applicant intends to rely;
(iii) the applicant's address for service;
(iv) when the applicant is to be represented by someone who is not a barrister or solicitor, the written authority of that person to represent him;
 (v) the notice must have annexed to it a copy of the decision against which leave to appeal is sought. Where a chairman has refused leave, a copy of that decision must also be annexed, and the date on which notice of refusal was given must be stated. In the case of a late application, the reasons for delay must be stated (reg 3).

(d) Determination of application

A chairman will give a written determination which will be served on all parties (reg 4(1)). When a Commissioner grants leave, he may, with the consent of all parties, treat and determine any question arising as if it were a question arising on an appeal (reg 4(3)).

(e) Notice of appeal

Once leave to appeal has been granted, the appeal itself is by way of notice to a Commissioner, and the notice must contain:

  (i) the name and address of the appellant;
 (ii) the date on which leave to appeal was granted;
(iii) the ground on which the appellant intends to rely;
(iv) the appellant's address for service.

The notice must have annexed to it a copy of the determination granting leave to appeal and a copy of the decision appealed against (reg 5).

(f) Time-limit for appeal

The time-limit for appeal is 42 days from the date on which the applicant was given notice in writing that leave to appeal was granted (reg 6(2)). However, a Commissioner may accept a notice of appeal served after the expiry of 42 days if for special reasons he thinks fit (reg 6(2)).

(g) Directions

As soon as practicable after receipt of notice of appeal, a Commissioner must give such directions as appear necessary, specifying:

  (i) the parties who are to be respondents to the appeal; and
 (ii) the order in which and the time (not less than 30 days) within which any party is to be allowed to make written observations.

Where two or more parties appeal, the Commissioner will direct which of these is to be treated as appellant (reg 7). At any stage, a Commissioner of his own motion, or on application, may require any party to furnish such further particulars as may be reasonably required, or give such directions as may be necessary for the efficient and effective despatch of the proceedings. He may also direct any party to make such written representations as seem necessary. A party seeking a direction must do so in writing to the Commissioner (reg 10).

(h) Oral hearings

A Commissioner may determine any appeal, or application for leave to appeal, without an oral hearing (reg 11(1)). However, any party may request an oral hearing, and the Commissioner must grant such request unless he is satisfied that he can properly determine the appeal or application without a hearing. In that event, he must inform the party concerned, in writing, that the request for a hearing has been refused. He may then determine the matter. He may direct an oral hearing of his own motion (reg 11). Oral hearings are in public, unless otherwise directed, and all parties may attend and address the Commissioner. With the leave of the Commissioner, but not otherwise, they may give evidence, call witnesses, and question other witnesses (reg 13). A Commissioner may summon any person to attend or produce documents on not less than seven days' notice (reg 14).

(i) Decisions

Decisions of Commissioners are in writing. They may be set aside, under reg 20, on grounds similar to those in reg 15 of the Child Support Appeal Tribunals (Procedure) Regulations 1992, SI 1992/2641.

8.9 Paragraph 4A of Sch 4 to the CSA 1991 permits authorised officers, who are not Commissioners, to determine any questions which are determinable by a Commissioner and which do not include the determination of any appeal, application for leave to appeal, or reference. The detail is contained in reg 23A of the CSC(P)Regs 1992, which, in effect, delegates to 'nominated officers' (ie an officer authorised by the Lord Chancellor or, in Scotland, the Secretary of State) functions which may be summarised as follows:

– giving directions on notice of appeal, or any other directions;
– granting leave to Secretary of State to intervene;
– making orders for oral hearings;
– summoning witnesses;
– ordering the postponement of oral hearings;
– giving leave to withdraw;
– extending or abridging time.

Any party may, within 10 days of receiving notice of such a decision, request a Commissioner to consider and confirm or replace the decision.

8.10 Child support law is, essentially, social security law, and the structure of review, appeal to tribunal and thence to Commissioners is the same as in social security appeals; indeed, the individuals who sit as Child Support Commissioners are normally also Social Security Commissioners. It may, therefore, be helpful to consider two decisions of Commissioners in the field of social security law which indicate the approach of Commissioners to their task. In R(A)1/72 it was held that a decision was wrong in law if:

(a) it contained a false proposition of law on its face;
(b) it was supported by no evidence;
(c) the facts found were such that no person acting judicially and properly instructed as to the relevant law could have come to the determination in question.

Another decision, CSB29/81 cites R(I)14/75 as adding further grounds, namely breach of the requirements of natural justice and failure to state adequate reasons.

8.11 Section 24(2) provides that where, on an appeal under that section, a Child Support Commissioner holds that the decision appealed against was wrong in law he shall set it aside. If the decision is set aside, the Commissioner may adopt one of the four courses of action set out in s 24(3):

'(a) if he can do so without making fresh or further findings of fact, give the decision which he considers should have been given by the appeal tribunal;
(b) if he considers it expedient, make such findings and give such decision as he considers appropriate in the light of those findings; or
(c) on an appeal by the Secretary of State, refer the case to an appeal tribunal with directions for its determination; or
(d) on any other appeal, refer the case to the Secretary of State or, if he considers it appropriate, to an appeal tribunal with directions for its determination.'

When the Commissioner refers back to the Secretary of State, this must, subject to any direction of the Commissioner, be to one of his officers, or a person providing him with services, who has taken no part in the decision originally appealed against (s 24(4)), and when the matter is referred to an appeal tribunal, this must consist of persons who were not members of the tribunal which gave the decision which has been appealed against (s 24(5)).

Appeal from the Child Support Commissioner

8.12 The final stage of the appeal procedure provided by the CSA 1991 lies from the Child Support Commissioner, but only on a point of law.

Section 25(1) provides that an appeal on a question of law shall lie to the appropriate court from any decision of a Child Support Commissioner. 'Appropriate court' is defined by s 25(4) as either the Court of Appeal or the Court of Session depending on the circumstances of the case and, in particular, the convenience of the parties to the appeal.

8.13 By s 25(2), no appeal may be brought except:

'(a) with leave of the Child Support Commissioner who gave the decision or, where regulations made by the Lord Chancellor so provide, of a Child Support Commissioner selected in accordance with the regulations; or
(b) if the Child Support Commissioner refuses leave, with the leave of the appropriate court.'

The first application for leave must, therefore, always be to the Commissioner.

The parties who may apply for leave to appeal are specified in s 25(3); they are confined to:

'(a) a person who was a party to the proceedings in which the original decision, or appeal decision, was given;

(b) the Secretary of State; or

(c) any other person who is authorised to do so by regulations made by the Lord Chancellor.'

The reference to 'the original decision' means that a person cannot stand by and allow an appeal to reach this stage and then decide to join in. He must, at the very least, have been involved in the appeal procedure at the appeal tribunal stage.

8.14 The regulations governing these matters are contained in reg 25 of the CSC(P)Regs 1992. An application to a Commissioner under s 25 must be in writing and must be made within three months from the date on which the applicant was given notice of the decision. Where the Chief Child Support Commissioner decides that it is impracticable or would cause undue delay for the same Commissioner to determine the application for leave, a different Commissioner, or Tribunal of Commissioners, as the case may be, may determine the application.

8.15 The appeal to the Court of Appeal or Court of Session will follow the normal procedures for such appeals, which lie outside the scope of this book.

Appeals as to Parentage

8.16 As was seen in Chapter Seven, where a non-resident parent denies parentage at an early stage, the Secretary of State may not proceed to make an assessment except in certain specified cases; the issue of parentage has to be referred to a court for an adjudication.

It may be, however, that an assessment is made before the absent parent decides to raise the issue. In such a case, he would have to seek a revision under s 18. Normally, the next stage in the appeal process would be to the appeal tribunal, but there are special provisions for appeals as to parentage.

Section 45(1) of the CSA 1991 provides that the Lord Chancellor, or, in Scotland, the Lord Advocate, may by order make provision for certain appeals to be made to a court instead of an appeal tribunal. This provision is contained in the Child Support Appeals (Jurisdiction of Courts) Order 1993, SI 1993/961, which provides for appeals under s 20 to go to a court instead of an appeal tribunal, where the issue involved is whether a particular person is a parent of the child. No such order has been made, so that there is at present no right of appeal from such a decision.

'Court' means a magistrates' court; the Children Act system applies, so that there can be a transfer to a higher court, where appropriate.

Judicial Review

8.17   Although judicial review is not available as a routine method of challenging decisions of the Secretary of State or an appeal tribunal, it should be considered in certain cases. Before such cases are examined, the nature of judicial review must be briefly explained, with the warning that, as this is not a textbook on administrative law, the explanation is of the most basic nature.

Before 1977, a challenge to the actions of public authorities was made by one of the prerogative writs of certiorari, prohibition or mandamus. In 1977 this was changed by means of a radical revision of procedure and the substitution of a new Ord 53 of the RSC 1965, SI 1965/1776. This created a new procedure called an 'application for judicial review', under which it is unnecessary to select any one of the prerogative remedies. This procedure is designed to enable the High Court to exercise its powers to supervise the proceedings and decisions of, inter alia, public bodies and tribunals in a flexible and uniform manner. The procedure for judicial review is now governed by the Civil Procedure Rules 1998, Part 54 and the accompanying Practice Direction.

Applications for judicial review must be made promptly and, in any event, within three months of the act or omission complained of. Application for leave is made to a single judge, normally without a hearing. If the application is renewed, it may be made to a single judge in open court.

8.18   It is important to note that judicial review is concerned with the decision-making process, not the decision itself (*Chief Constable of North Wales Police v Evans* [1982] 1 WLR 1155, HL). Provided the procedures have been properly employed, judicial review cannot be employed as a method of appeal against the substantive decision. Judicial review is therefore limited to ensuring that the person or body in question has acted within its powers and that the rules of natural justice have not been breached.

Furthermore, judicial review will not normally be granted where there is another avenue of appeal. Save in the most exceptional cases, the jurisdiction to grant judicial review will not be exercised where other remedies are available (*R v Epping and Harlow General Commissioners, ex parte Goldstraw* [1983] 3 All ER 257).

Until 1980, the only way to challenge the decision of a Social Security Commissioner was by way of judicial review. In 1980 this was changed, and the right of appeal to the Court of Appeal, or, in Scotland, the Court of Session, was introduced. As has been seen, this right exists in CSA 1991 cases.

An allegation that the rules of natural justice had not been observed would be an allegation that a particular decision was 'wrong in law', and would, therefore, justify an application for review and thence to the appeal tribunal.

It might seem, therefore, that the occasions on which there could be an application for judicial review are limited.

8.19   However, this must be seen in the light of the 'welfare principle'. As was seen in Chapter One, s 2 of the CSA 1991 provides that:

> 'Where, in any case which falls to be dealt with under this Act, the Secretary of State is considering the exercise of any discretionary power conferred by this Act, he shall have regard to the welfare of any child likely to be affected by his decision.'

This section was considered by Thorpe J in *R v Secretary of State for Social Security, ex parte Biggin* [1995] 1 FLR 851. In this case, a father appealed to the Family Division against the dismissal by magistrates of his appeal against a deduction from earnings order made under the CSA 1991. His principal ground of complaint had been that the justices had failed to consider the welfare principle in dealing with the case. The Secretary of State contended that any assertion that a duty under s 2 had not been observed was a public law question open to judicial review and confined to the High Court. Thorpe J agreed; it was quite clear that the remedy for a breach of duty under s 2 was to apply to the Divisional Court, and not to the justices.

8.20 This decision makes clear the type of case which may form the basis of an application for judicial review. There are many occasions on which the Secretary of State has to exercise discretion. The most important may be summarised as decisions whether to:

(a) arrange for the collection and enforcement of maintenance (s 4(2) and (3));
(b) require a person with care to give the authorisation to apply for a maintenance calculation (s 6(2));
(c) make a default calculation (s 12(1));
(d) make a fresh calculation (s 19);
(e) arrange for the collection of child support maintenance (s 29(1));
(f) collect and enforce other forms of maintenance, and how sums should be allocated (s 30(1) and (3)(c));
(g) make a deduction from earnings order (s 31(2));
(h) apply to magistrates for a liability order (s 32(2));
(i) enforce a liability order by distress (s 35(1));
(j) apply to magistrates for commitment to prison (s 40);
(k) give a reduced benefit direction (s 46(5)).

Not all these decisions are automatically susceptible to judicial review. It is only where the person aggrieved alleges a failure to observe the welfare principle that this will be the case. It will be noted that the section refers to 'any child likely to be affected'; it is not limited to qualifying children. It could apply, for example, to the children of a non-resident parent's cohabitant.

CHAPTER NINE

Collection and Enforcement

The Role of the Agency

9.1   The function of the CSA is to 'bring together in one organisation all matters to do with the assessment, collection and enforcement of child maintenance in the great majority of cases' (Mr Tony Newton, then Secretary of State for Social Services, *Hansard* vol 192, para 179). Assessment (now calculation) has been considered in earlier chapters; the role of the Agency in collection and enforcement must now be considered.

As is often the case, the role of the CSA with respect to collection will depend on whether or not the person with care is in receipt of benefit. Under s 6(1) of the CSA 1991, a person receiving certain benefits must authorise the Secretary of State to recover child support maintenance from the non-resident parent; she has no choice. In the case of a non-benefit matter, under s 4(1), a person with care may apply to the Secretary of State for a maintenance calculation, and, by s 4(2), may request that the Secretary of State arrange for the collection of the child support maintenance in accordance with the calculation, and the enforcement of the obligation to pay. In the case of the person not receiving benefit, therefore, there is a choice as to whether the CSA deals with the collection, or whether a private arrangement is made. However, only the CSA may enforce a calculation.

Where a calculation has been made under s 4(1), the CSA will accept a request to collect in all cases.

9.2   The details as to collection are set out in paras **9.3** to **9.5**. Enforcement is dealt with in paras **9.6** et seq below, and it will be seen that the modes of enforcement available to the Secretary of State are as follows:

(a)   deduction from earnings order;
(b)   liability order;
(c)   distress;
(d)   county court enforcement;
(e)   imprisonment and disqualification from driving.

It must be emphasised that the Secretary of State is limited to the methods of enforcement authorised by the Act. In *Department of Social Security v Butler* [1996] 1 FLR 65, CA, the Secretary of State applied to the court for a *Mareva* injunction to restrain a non-resident parent, who owed large arrears of child support maintenance, from disposing of the proceeds of sale of a former matrimonial home which he had received from his solicitors. The judge refused this application, and the Court of Appeal upheld that decision. The CSA 1991 provided a detailed code for the collection of payments due under maintenance calculations. The duty under s 1(3) is not expressed as a civil debt, and may not be enforced by any means in a civil court, save as provided by the Act. Even if the court had jurisdiction, an injunction should not be ordered except in unusual and compelling cases; the DSS had ample powers to prevent arrears from accruing.

The remedies available to the Secretary of State will be considered in turn.

Collection

9.3 By s 29(2) of the CSA 1991, the Secretary of State may make regulations to govern how payments should be made. These regulations are contained in Part II of the Child Support (Collection and Enforcement) Regulations 1992[1] (CS(CE) Regs 1992), SI 1992/1889, the effect of which may be summarised as follows:

(a) the Secretary of State may specify to whom payments are to be made, for example to the person with care, to himself or to another person (reg 2(1));

(b) payment must be made by whatever method the Secretary of State specifies as appropriate, for example standing order, direct debit, cheque or postal order or cash. He may direct a liable person to take all reasonable steps to open an account from which payments can be made (reg 3);

(c) the Secretary of State shall specify the day and the interval (ie weekly, monthly etc) of payment, and may from time to time vary such interval. In so doing he must have regard to the needs of the person entitled to receive payment, when the liable person's income is normally received and any period necessary for the clearance of cheques (reg 4);

(d) the Secretary of State must, so far as is reasonably practicable, provide the liable person and the person entitled to receive payments with an opportunity to make representations about all the above matters, and must have regard to such representations when exercising his powers (reg 6);

(e) the Secretary of State must send the liable person a notice stating the amount of child support maintenance, to whom it must be paid, the method of payment and the day and interval of payment as soon as is reasonably practicable after the making of a maintenance calculation or any change in requirements (reg 7).

All this shows that the CSA enjoys very wide powers to control how payments are to be made.

9.4 The CSA also has the power to collect payments of maintenance other than child support maintenance in certain circumstances. The power derives from s 30(1) of the CSA 1991, which provides that when the Secretary of State is arranging for the collection of any payments under a maintenance calculation he may also arrange for the collection of periodical payments and secured periodical payments of a prescribed kind, and s 30(2), which makes similar provision for cases in which the Secretary of State is not collecting payments under a maintenance calculation.

The current regulations made under s 30 are the Child Support (Collection and Enforcement of other Forms of Maintenance) Regulations 1992,

---

1 As amended by the Child Support (Collection and Enforcement and Miscellaneous Amendments) Regulations 2000 (CS(CEMA)Regs 2000), SI 2001/162.

SI 1992/2643; by reg 2, the periodical payments and categories of person prescribed are as follows:

(a) payments under a maintenance order made in relation to a child in accordance with the provisions of:
   – s 8(6) (top-up orders);
   – s 8(7) (expenses for instruction or training);
   – s 8(8) (expenses due to disability);
(b) any periodical payments under a maintenance order which are payable to or for the benefit of a spouse or former spouse who is the person with care of a qualifying child in respect of whom a maintenance calculation is in force and the Secretary of State has arranged for its collection under s 29;
(c) any periodical payments under a maintenance order payable to, or for the benefit of a former child of the family of the person against whom the order is made, that child having his home with the person with care.

9.5 The classes of orders set out in (a) are clear enough; they are part of the structure of the Act. In theory, it would be possible in the other two cases for the Secretary of State to collect maintenance due under a court order when there was no maintenance calculation. However, the Secretary of State has a discretion as to whether or not to collect, and he might choose not to do so where there was no calculation. Paragraph (b) relates to the collection of spousal maintenance where there is also a calculation. Paragraph (c) extends this to collection of maintenance due in respect of non-qualifying children where there is a calculation.

Enforcement by Deduction from Earnings Order

9.6 Attachment of earnings is a well-known and much used process for enforcing payment of judgments and orders in England and Wales. Such orders are obtained in county courts under the provisions of the Attachment of Earnings Act 1971. The order stipulates a 'normal deduction rate', ie the weekly or monthly sum to be deducted by the employer from the debtor's earnings, and a 'protected earnings rate', ie the sum, calculated by reference to income support rates, below which the debtor's income must not be allowed to fall.

It is important to note that deduction from earnings orders under the CSA 1991 are not the same as attachment of earnings orders made by the court. They are a discrete form of enforcement arising only under this Act. Moreover, the order is made by an administrative agency (the Secretary of State) and not a court.

9.7 The statutory power to make a deduction from earnings order derives from s 31(2) of the CSA 1991, which provides that the Secretary of State may make a deduction from earnings order to secure the payment of any amount due under the maintenance calculation in question. Section 31(3) provides that such an order may be made to secure the payment of arrears of child support maintenance and amounts which will become due under the calculation.

It is not necessary to wait for arrears to accrue. The Secretary of State would be entitled to use deduction from earnings as a routine method of enforcement if he so chose. However, the general policy, as revealed in the DSS handbook *Notes to Advisers* is that this method of enforcement will be used only in limited circumstances where other forms of enforcement have failed.

9.8   The remainder of ss 31 and 32 deal with routine matters, the detail of which emerges in the regulations. These are currently contained in Part III of the CS(CE)Regs 1992, the most important parts of which are as follows.

(a)   'Earnings' are defined by reg 8(1), (3) and (4); the term includes wages, overtime and emoluments payable under a contract of service, private pensions, compensation for loss of office, and statutory sick pay. It does not include pay from HM Forces (although the Crown, generally, is not exempt), or pensions or benefits payable under any social security enactment.

(b)   By reg 9, an order must specify, inter alia, a protected earnings proportion and a normal deduction rate. The protected earnings proportion is 60% of the liable person's net earnings.

(c)   By reg 12(6), an employer may deduct a sum not exceeding £1 in respect of his administrative costs. However, this sum is to be collected from the liable person, and not as a deduction from the sum due under the order. Payments deducted under the order must be paid to the Secretary of State by the 19th day of the month following the month in which the deduction is made (reg 14(1)).

(d)   By reg 15(1), the Secretary of State may require a liable person to provide details of his employer, his current and anticipated earnings, and his place of work and pay number. Such details must be supplied within seven days of being given written notice to that effect. A liable person in respect of whom a deduction from earnings order is in effect must notify the Secretary of State in writing within seven days of every occasion on which he leaves employment or becomes employed or re-employed (reg 15(2)). Employers are under a similar duty (reg 16).

(e)   The regulations also include detailed provisions as to the power to review (reg 17), vary (reg 18), or discharge orders (reg 20) and lapse of orders (reg 21).

9.9   Since the Secretary of State is able to make a deduction from earnings order without warning to the liable person, there has to be a means of challenging such an order. This is provided by s 32(5), the effect of which is that a liable person may appeal to a magistrates' court (or, in Scotland, the sheriff) if he is aggrieved by a deduction from earnings order, or by the terms of any such order, or if there is a dispute as to whether payments constitute earnings or as to any other prescribed matter. By s 32(6), it is made clear that the court cannot question the assessment by reference to which the deduction from earnings order was made.

The regulations are contained in reg 22 of the CS(CE)Regs 1992. Appeal is by way of complaint, and must be made within 28 days of the date on which the matter appealed against arose.

Regulation 22(3) specifies the grounds on which an appeal may be made, namely:

'(a) that the deduction from earnings order is defective;
(b) that the payments in question do not constitute earnings.'

These are very limited grounds. 'Defective' must mean some technical defect; for example, it might be argued that the order specified an incorrect protected earnings rate (as not being the same as exempt income), or that the figures contained some arithmetical error.

Any dispute as to earnings would normally be concerned with whether a person was employed or self-employed. Here, the court would be guided by reg 8(2) which provides that:

'. . . the relationship of employer and employee shall be treated as subsisting between two persons if one of them, as a principal and not as a servant or agent, pays to the other any sum defined as earnings . . . [under these regulations].'

What the court may definitely not do is to consider the reasonableness or even the accuracy of the assessment nor the reasonableness of the Secretary of State's decision to make a deduction from earnings order. Where there might be room for such a challenge, it must be made by way of judicial review (see Chapter Eight).

By reg 22(4), where the court is satisfied that the appeal should be allowed, its powers are limited to either quashing the deduction from earnings order or specifying which, if any, of the payments in question do not constitute earnings. In *DSS v Taylor* [1996] 2 FLR 241, it was held that justices were not empowered to order repayment of sums wrongly recovered by the Secretary of State under a deduction from earnings order.

9.10 Regulation 24 contains provisions to govern priority as between different deduction from earnings orders or between deduction from earnings orders and attachment of earnings orders. Deduction from earnings orders are dealt with in date order, so that the net earnings are compared with the protected earnings rate on the later order or orders after deduction of the previous order or orders. Deduction from earnings orders have priority over attachment of earnings orders; in the case of an attachment of earnings order, the net earnings to be compared with the protected earnings are calculated after deduction of the sum due under a deduction from earnings order.

9.11 Persons who fail to comply with the requirements of a deduction from earnings order will, in the last resort, be liable to criminal sanctions. Section 32(8) of the CSA 1991, which applies to liable persons and their employers, provides that:

'If any person fails to comply with the requirements of a deduction from earnings order, or with any regulation under this section which is designated for the purposes of this subsection, he shall be guilty of an offence.'

Regulation 25 provides that the designated regulations are as follows:

– reg 14(1) (payment by employer to Secretary of State);
– reg 15(1) and (2) (failure to provide details of employer, place of work, or change of employment);
– reg 16(1), (2) and (3) (employer's duty to provide information); and
– reg 19(1) (employer's duty to comply with deduction from earnings order).

'Fails' imposes an absolute liability, but some relief is afforded by s 32(10) which provides that:

'It shall be a defence for a person charged with an offence under subsection (8) to prove that he took all reasonable steps to comply with the requirements in question.'

Once the failure has been established, therefore, the onus of proof is on the person charged. Under s 32(11), a person guilty of an offence under s 32(8) is liable on summary conviction to a fine not exceeding level 2 on the standard scale.

Liability Orders

9.12   It has been seen above that deduction from earnings orders are normally available as a useful means of securing payment of the sums due under a maintenance calculation. However, this can only be used where there are earnings from employment which may be attached. The CSA 1991, therefore, has to provide other means of enforcement, and the gateway to these is the liability order. A liability order is not a means of enforcement in itself, but is a prerequisite for other forms of enforcement. By s 33(5), a liability order is registered as a judgment for the purpose of s 73 of the County Courts Act 1984.

9.13   Unlike a deduction from earnings order, a liability order can be granted only when the liable person is in default. Section 33(1) of the CSA 1991 provides that s 33, which contains the relevant provisions as to liability orders, applies where:

'(a)   a person who is liable to make payments of child support maintenance ("the liable person") fails to make one or more of those payments; and
 (b)   it appears to the Secretary of State that –
        (i)   it is inappropriate to make a deduction from earnings order against him (because, for example, he is not employed); or
        (ii) although such an order has been made against him, it has proved ineffective as a means of securing that payments are made in accordance with the maintenance calculation in question.'

In order for the Secretary of State to make a valid decision to apply to the court for a liability order, therefore, two conditions have to be met. First, at least one payment of child support maintenance must be in arrear. Secondly, the Secretary of State must have addressed his mind to whether a deduction from earnings order could or should be made. Where the liable person is not employed, or where a deduction from earnings order has been made and proved unsuccessful, he will have no problem. However, he is not limited to these examples; he may decide that deduction from earnings would be inappropriate for other reasons. One such reason might be that the liable person had asked for there not to be a deduction from earnings order, because, for example, it might embarrass him with his employer.

9.14   By s 33(2), the Secretary of State may apply to a magistrates' court, or, in Scotland, the sheriff, for a liability order in respect of the liable person. Section 33(3) provides that the court, or sheriff:

' . . . shall make the order if satisfied that the payments in question have become payable by the liable person and have not been paid.'

The making of a liability order is therefore mandatory, provided the court is satisfied that the Secretary of State has proved the amount of the arrears. As in all such matters, the onus of proof is on the Secretary of State. Once the payments are in arrear, the court has to make a liability order if asked to do so. As was seen above, the Secretary of State has to go through a certain process before being able to make a valid decision as to whether to apply for a liability order; however, the magistrates, or sheriff, may not inquire into the validity of the order. Where grounds for challenge exist, they must be argued by way of an application for judicial review (see Chapter Eight).

9.15 Section 34 deals with the regulations about liability orders which the Secretary of State may make. These regulations are contained in Part IV of the CS(CE)Regs 1992. One of the most relevant here is reg 28(1), which provides that the Secretary of State must give the liable person at least seven days' notice of his intention to apply for a liability order. This notice must contain the amount of child support maintenance which it is alleged is unpaid.

Once a liability order specifying a sum of money which is unpaid has been made, it may be enforced in a variety of ways. These will now be considered.

Enforcement of Liability Orders by Distress

9.16 Distress means the seizure and sale of a person's goods to pay a debt. Section 35(1) provides that, where a liability order has been made against a liable person, the Secretary of State may:

' . . . levy the appropriate amount by distress and sale of the liable person's goods.'

By s 35(2), 'appropriate amount' is defined as the aggregate of the amount in respect of which the liability order was made, to the extent that it remains unpaid, and an amount for charges. The charges are prescribed by Sch 2 to the CS(CE)Regs 1992, and include, for example, a charge of £10 for writing a warning letter, and 10p per day for 'walking possession'.

The amount to be recovered, therefore, is the outstanding balance under the liability order, and the costs of the distress.

9.17 Section 35(3) sets out what the Secretary of State may seize when levying distress. This comprises:

'(a) any of the liable person's goods, except –
   (i) such tools, books, vehicles and other items of equipment as are necessary to him for use personally by him in his employment, business or vocation;
   (ii) such clothing, bedding, furniture, household equipment and provisions as are necessary for satisfying his basic domestic needs; and
(b) any money, banknotes, bills of exchange, promissory notes, bonds, specialties, or securities for money belonging to the liable person.'

By s 35(4), the liable person's domestic needs are to be taken to include those of any of his family with whom he resides.

9.18   Section 35(8)(c) provides for regulations to 'provide for an appeal to a magistrates' court by any person aggrieved by the levying of, or an attempt to levy, a distress under this section'. These regulations are contained in reg 31 of the CS(CE)Regs 1992.

Regulation 31(1) provides that:

> 'A person aggrieved by the levy of, or an attempt to levy, a distress may appeal to the magistrates' court having jurisdiction in the area in which he resides.'

Regulation 31(3) and (4) provides that, if the court is satisfied that the levy was irregular, it may order the goods to be discharged, award compensation equal to the value of the goods (if sold) or require the Secretary of State to desist from levy (in the case of attempted levy). The only ground on which appeal may be brought, therefore, is that the levy is 'irregular'. This can only apply to some procedural defect, and cannot go to the root of the decision to levy. The general merits of the matter cannot be addressed.

The right to appeal is conferred on 'any person aggrieved'. This could include, for example, the spouse, cohabitant or children of the liable person.

9.19   Section 37 contains provisions as to enforcement of liability orders in Scotland.

Enforcement of Liability Orders in County Courts

9.20   A liability order may be enforced through a county court, as if it were a judgment or order of that court. Section 36(1) provides that, where a liability order has been made against a person, the unpaid amount in respect of which the order was made shall, if a county court so orders, be recoverable by means of a third party debt order or a charging order as if it were payable under a county court order.

The powers of the county court are, therefore, limited to the two forms of enforcement stated above. There are no special regulations under the Act, so the procedure is determined by the County Court Rules 1981, SI 1981/1687. The Secretary of State initiates the proceedings by lodging at the court an affidavit by an authorised officer proving the liability order and the unpaid balance due. Provided all is in order, the district judge makes an order nisi, and this is the first warning the liable person receives. At the stage of order nisi, all the court has to be satisfied about is the existence of the liability and of the asset which it is sought to attach or charge.

The liable person may then 'shew cause' against the order, ie seek to convince the court that an order absolute should not be made. In the case of a garnishee order this might be done by showing that the money or fund attached was not, in fact, due to the liable person. In the case of a charging order, it is only possible to charge the liable person's interest in the property; it might, therefore, be argued that the interest of a joint owner was such as to render worthless the interest of the liable person, or that there was a negative equity in the property. In answer to this, it might be said that since the charging order was only over the liable person's interest, whatever that might be, it would be unnecessary to determine the extent of the interest at this stage.

In either case, the interests of other creditors must be considered. The decision as to whether to make an order absolute is a discretionary one, which rests with the district judge; such discretion must, of course, be exercised judicially, and it would seem that the merits of the original assessment or liability order should not be considered.

Finally, although the CSA 1991 does not say so, a charging order absolute may be enforced by an order for sale of the property charged; this is normally regarded as a last resort, to be ordered only where there is no other way of recovering the sum due.

Disqualification from Driving and/or Imprisonment

9.21   When all other means of enforcement have failed, the Secretary of State may adopt the final and drastic sanction of applying for the liable person to be committed to prison. This remedy has existed since 1991. However, one of the novelties introduced by the CSPSSA 2000 is the addition of disqualification from driving as one of the ultimate sanctions for non-payment of child support. The possibility of either of these sanctions being imposed may arise only where the Secretary of State has sought to levy an amount by distress or to recover an amount by virtue of s 36 of the CSA 1991 (ie third party debt proceedings or a charging order application in the county court) and that amount, or any portion of it, remains unpaid. In these circumstances, the Secretary of State may apply to a magistrates' court for an order under this section.[2]

9.22   An application under this section is for:

'. . . whichever the court considers most appropriate in all the circumstances of –

(a)   the issue of a warrant committing the liable person to prison; or

(b)   an order for him to be disqualified from holding or obtaining a driving licence.'[3]

The court will, therefore, be offered the choice of sanction. However, the Secretary of State may make representations to the court as to whether he thinks it more appropriate to commit to prison or to disqualify, and potentially liable persons will be pleased to learn that they 'may reply to those representations'.[4]

To arrive at this stage, therefore, the following conditions must have been fulfilled.

(1)   A liability order must have been made in a magistrates' court or by a sheriff. The following points may be noted:

(a)   the decision to apply for a liability order must have involved a determination by the Secretary of State that a deduction from earnings order was inappropriate, either because one had been made and proved ineffective, or for some other reason;

---

2   CSA 1991, s 39A(1).
3   Ibid, s 39A(2).
4   Ibid, s 39A(4).

(b) the magistrates' court may not look behind the liability order nor question its validity. Where there seems to be scope for challenge, this must be by way of judicial review.

(2) Either:

(a) distress must have been levied, and have failed to recover the whole sum due under the liability order; or

(b) there has been an unsuccessful application for a charging order or third party debt order in a county court; or

(c) a charging order or third party debt order has been made, but has failed to recover the whole sum due.

The only point to note here is that a charging order granted in a county court rarely results in immediate payment of the debt which it secured. As explained in para **9.20** above, orders for sale based on charging orders are quite rare; the point of a charging order is normally seen as giving a creditor some long-term or medium-term security.

(3) The amount of the sum due on the liability order, or some part of it, must still be outstanding. This will be for the Secretary of State to prove, and the magistrates are entitled to demand evidence.

Provisions applying to both remedies

9.23 Certain parts of these provisions apply both to imprisonment and to disqualification from driving. In both cases, the following must apply. The court must, in the presence of the liable person, inquire into:

(a) whether he needs a driving licence to earn his living;

(b) his means; and

(c) whether there has been wilful refusal or culpable neglect on his part.

9.24 The essential points appear to be as follows.

(1) The hearing must be in the presence of the liable person; if he is not there, it cannot proceed.

(2) The court must inquire into two matters. The first of these is the means of the liable person. It will therefore be necessary to take detailed evidence as to his income, outgoings, and liabilities. In *R v Liverpool City Justices, ex parte Lanckriet* [1977] RA 85, and *R v Richmond Justices, ex parte Atkins* [1983] RVR 148, which were cases concerned with enforcement of liability for rates and community charge, with provisions virtually identical to those in s 40, it was held that a committal is unlawful if a proper means inquiry is not carried out, or insufficient questions are put to the debtor to elicit his true financial position.

The second area of inquiry is as to whether the failure of the liable person to pay is due to his wilful refusal or culpable neglect. Here, the court must try to find out why the liable person has not paid, and make a judgment as to whether that amounts to wilful refusal or culpable neglect. Clearly, where the court is satisfied that the liable person has the funds to pay and has refused to do so, it will not be difficult to reach a decision. Similarly, where arrears have built up, but, at the date of the hearing, the liable person is without funds (eg unemployed) through no fault of his own, it would be difficult to find against him. In *R v Poole Magistrates, ex parte Benham* (1992) 156 JP 177, another community charge case, it was held that when considering whether there had been wilful refusal or culpable neglect, the court is confined to examining the conduct of the debtor between the bill and the liability order; as to means, the court may consider the debtor's means only on the day of the hearing.

As to proof of the liable person's income, CS(CE)Regs 1992, reg 33(2) (as amended) provides that a statement in writing as to the liable person's earnings, purporting to be signed by or on behalf of his employer, shall be evidence of the facts stated. This means that it is admissible in evidence, not that it is conclusive evidence; it would have to be weighed against anything said in evidence by the liable person.

9.25 If the magistrates decide that the failure to pay was not due to wilful refusal or culpable neglect, but was for some other reason which could not be brought into either of those categories, that would be an end of the matter, and the application would have to be dismissed. Where they find that the failure was for one of those reasons they then have to decide what to do.

Section 40(3) of the CSA 1991 provides that they 'may' issue a warrant of commitment; in other words, they have a discretion, which must be exercised judicially.

The proper approach of justices in very similar cases was considered in *R v Luton Magistrates' Court, ex parte Sullivan* [1992] 2 FLR 196, which was concerned with the power of justices to commit under s 76 of the Magistrates' Courts Act 1980 (MCA 1980) for arrears of maintenance.

Waite J observed that the power under s 76 to issue a writ committing a spouse to prison in such cases was 'a power of extreme severity'. He continued as follows:

'Indeed, it might be argued that the existence of such a power in a society which long ago closed the Marshalsea Prison and abandoned imprisonment as a remedy for enforcement of debts is anomalous. Certainly, Parliament has made it plain that the power is to be exercised sparingly and only as a last resort.'

Waite J emphasised that any order of commitment must be preceded by an inquiry, in the presence of the debtor, as to whether his default did indeed amount to wilful refusal or culpable neglect and that the court was expressly prohibited from exercising the power unless satisfied that all other methods of enforcing payment had been tried or considered and had proved unsuccessful or were likely to do so. He commented adversely on the fact that the justices had not allowed the debtor to obtain legal advice.

In *R v Birmingham Justices, ex parte Mansell* (1988) *The Independent*, April 21, another community charge case, it was held that justices had erred because they had failed to consider whether other enforcement proceedings could be used. In *R v Manchester City Magistrates' Court, ex parte Davis* [1988] 1 All ER 930, it was emphasised that no one, especially someone who had never been in prison, should ever be sent to prison lightly, and that where there were no means to pay the court should bear in mind that the application could always be renewed if the debtor's financial position improved.

9.26 When the court exercises its discretion in favour of issuing a warrant of commitment, it has the choice of making an outright order or a suspended order. In the light of the judicial dicta set out above, it might be argued that a suspended order would be the natural first choice for the court.

By s 40(4), the warrant must state the amount mentioned in s 35(1) (ie the amount to be levied on distress), or so much of it as remains outstanding, plus the prescribed amount in respect of the costs of commitment. By s 40(6), a warrant must order the liable person to be imprisoned for a specified period, but to be released on payment of the amount stated on the warrant (unless in custody for some other reason).

The maximum term of imprisonment which may be imposed is to be calculated in accordance with Sch 4 to the MCA 1980, but must not exceed six weeks (s 40(7)).

Regulation 34(5) of the CS(CE)Regs 1992 provides that where, after the issue of a warrant and part payment of the amount due in it is made, the period of imprisonment shall be reduced proportionately, so that for the period of imprisonment stated in the warrant there shall be substituted a period of such number of days as bears the same proportion to the number of days specified in the warrant as the amount remaining unpaid under the warrant bears to the amount specified in the warrant.

Provisions applying only to disqualification from driving

9.27 Section 40B provides further matters which deal only with disqualification from driving. However, before these are examined in detail, some consideration of why this penalty was introduced may be helpful. In the Second Reading debate in the House of Lords, Lord Stoddart of Swindon was clearly perplexed. He pointed out that 'the object of a driving licence is to ensure that people who drive have passed a relevant test. In my view – in many people's view, I should have thought – the withdrawal of a driving licence should not be used as a penalty for non-payment of this kind of maintenance or any other. Can the Minister explain?'[5]

The Minister was unabashed: 'We are seeking to introduce this provision at the moment because fathers who can and should pay maintenance are not doing so. For many of them, a gaol sentence is perhaps too heavy; and some of the other penalties – for example, restraint of goods (sic) or garnishee orders on their estates – take a very long time to kick in'.[6] Later, after referring to the experience of the State of Texas, the Minister said: '. . . it was not the taking away of licences that got the money flowing to children; it was the threat of taking away the driving licences that got the money flowing to children. That is what we want to ensure. If we have had real difficulty in some cases in getting a father who can pay to face up to his responsibilities, at the end of the day if the threat of removal of a driving licence ensures that he addresses his responsibilities for the first time, I am confident that I shall have the support of my noble friend.'[7]

---

5 Official Report (HL) 17 April 2000, col 464.
6 Ibid, per Baroness Hollis.
7 Ibid.

9.28   Regulation 35(1) of the CS(CE)Regs 1992, inserted by the CS(CEMA) Regs 2000, provides that, for the purpose of enabling an enquiry to be made under s 39A as to the liable person's livelihood, means and conduct, a Justice of the Peace may issue a summons to him to appear before a magistrates' court and to produce any driving licence held by him and, where applicable, its counterpart, and if he does not appear may issue a warrant for his arrest. In any such proceedings, a statement in writing to the effect that wages of any amount have been paid to the liable person during any period, purporting to be signed for or on behalf of his employer shall be evidence of the facts there stated (reg 35(2)). This cannot mean that such a statement is conclusive or irrefutable, but merely that it is admissible in evidence.

9.29   The court may, but only if it is of the opinion that there has been wilful refusal or culpable neglect on the part of the liable person:

(a)   order him to be disqualified for such period specified in the order but not exceeding two years from holding or obtaining a driving licence (a 'disqualification order');

(b)   make a disqualification order but suspend its operation until such time and on such conditions (if any) as it thinks just.[8] This disqualification order must be in the form prescribed by Sch 4 to the CS(CE)Regs 1992.

The court may not take action under both s 40 and s 40B; in other words, it may not both commit to prison and disqualify.

The disqualification order must state the amount in respect of which it is made, being, in effect, the sum stated in the liability order and costs.[9] The liable person must produce his driving licence to the court.[10]

9.30   If part of the amount due is paid, either the liable person or the Secretary of State may apply to the court for an order substituting a shorter period of disqualification or revoking the order.[11] If the amount due is paid in full, the court must make an order revoking the disqualification order.[12] The Secretary of State may make representations as to the amount which should be paid before an order is revoked.[13]

If the amount due has not been paid in full when the period of disqualification expires the Secretary of State may apply for a further disqualification order.[14]

9.31   Section 80 of the MCA 1980 applies in relation to a disqualification order.[15] The result of this is that a liable person against whom a disqualification order has been made may be searched and any money in his possession applied towards the amount due.

---

8 CSA 1991, s 40B(1).
9 Ibid, s 40B(3).
10 Ibid, s 40B(4).
11 Ibid, s 40B(5)(a).
12 Ibid, s 40B(5)(b).
13 Ibid, s 40B(6).
14 Ibid, s 40B(7).
15 Ibid, s 40B(10).

Arrears and Penalty Payments

9.32   Section 41 of the CSA 1991, which deals with arrears, has been amended by the CSPSSA 2000. The section applies where the Secretary of State is authorised to recover child support maintenance and the non-resident parent has failed to make one or more payments due. The new provisions relate to penalty payments, which replace the former provisions for interest on arrears.

The amount of a penalty payment may not exceed 25% of the amount of child support maintenance payable for that week, but otherwise is to be determined by regulations. [16] Payment of a penalty payment does not relieve the non-resident parent of the obligation to pay the child support maintenance.[17]

Any payments received are to be paid into the Consolidated Fund;[18] the parent with care will not benefit.

9.33   The regulations governing collection of penalty payments are contained in Part IIA of the CS(CE)Regs 1992 (reg 7A), inserted by the CS(CEMA)Regs 2000, and may be summarised as follows:

(a)   the regulation applies where the liable person is in arrears with payments of child support maintenance and the Secretary of State requires the liable person to pay penalty payments to him;

(b)   a payment of child support maintenance is overdue if not received by the time the next payment of child support maintenance is due;

(c)   the Secretary of State may require a penalty payment to be made if the outstanding amount of child support maintenance is not received within seven days of the notification or if the liable person fails to pay all outstanding amounts due on dates and of amounts as agreed between the liable person and the Secretary of State;

(d)   penalty payments must be paid within 14 days of notification.

---

16 CSA 1991, s 41A(2).
17 Ibid, s 41A(3).
18 Ibid, s 41A(6).

CHAPTER TEN

The Role of the Courts and Maintenance Agreements

Introduction

10.1   One of the fundamental objectives of the CSA 1991 was the removal from the courts of the task of assessing, collecting and enforcing child maintenance and the transfer of these matters to the CSA; the reasons for this were discussed in Chapter One and need not be examined here.

However, it would be wrong to assume that the courts are left with no functions in this field. Quite apart from those areas specifically delegated to the courts by the Act, there are certain residual areas of jurisdiction which may be exercised for the time being. These will be examined in this chapter, together with the ability of parents to enter into maintenance agreements in respect of their children.

The effect of the Act on other areas, such as spousal financial provision will also be considered.

The CSPSSA 2000 has made some important changes to the position relating to court orders. The first of these has already been discussed at para **2.24**. The fact that there is in force a court order made after a prescribed date no longer prevents the Secretary of State from making a maintenance calculation provided one year has elapsed from the date of the order. As has been seen, the CSPSSA 2000 amends s 4(10) of the CSA 1991.

The General Principle

10.2   The question which the practitioner will need to answer in any particular case is whether an application for a maintenance calculation may be made under s 4, or, alternatively, whether the parents may agree a figure or whether the court has any jurisdiction to make an order for a child. (There can never be any doubt about the right to apply under s 6; that overrides any agreement or order.)

The answer lies in the interlinked provisions of ss 4 and 8 of the CSA 1991. Section 4 deals with the right to apply for a calculation under s 4, and s 4(10) provides that:

'No application may be made at any time under this section [ie for a maintenance calculation under s 4] with respect to a qualifying child or any qualifying children if –

(a)   there is in force a written maintenance agreement made before 5th April 1993, or a maintenance order made before a prescribed date, in respect of that child or those children and the person who is, at that time, the non-resident parent; or

(aa) a maintenance order made on or after the date prescribed for the purposes of paragraph (a) is in force in respect of them, but has been so for less than the period of one year beginning with the date on which it was made; or

(b) benefit is being paid to, or in respect of, a parent with care of that child or those children.'

Paragraph (b) speaks for itself. Paragraph (a) is also self-explanatory as to maintenance agreements and this is likely to be of diminishing importance. The prescribed date has been fixed as 6 April 2002. The effect of that subsection is, therefore, that if an order is in existence on 5 April 2002 it will prevent any application under s 4.

If no order is in existence on 5 April 2002, subsection (aa) applies. This does not prevent the court from making an order (by consent) but the order will oust the jurisdiction of the CSA for one year only, after which either party may apply for a maintenance calculation.

10.3 Section 8 is designed to deal with the powers of the court. Section 8(3) of the CSA 1991 provides that:

'In any case where subsection (1) applies, no court shall exercise any power which it would otherwise have to make, vary or revive any maintenance order in relation to the child and absent parent concerned.'

Subsection (1) applies to any case where the Secretary of State would have jurisdiction to make an assessment (see Chapter Two). Accordingly, in cases where there is a qualifying child, a person with care and a non-resident parent, all within the United Kingdom, the Secretary of State has jurisdiction and the court may not exercise any jurisdiction which it would otherwise have.

Section 8(4) provides that these provisions do not prevent the court from revoking an order. By s 8(2), subs (1) (and, therefore, subs (3)) apply even though the circumstances of the case are such that the Secretary of State would not make a calculation if it were applied for; in other words, the courts may not be used as a fall-back position if the means of a non-resident parent are such that no calculation could be made.

10.4 The significant provision in relation to the interrelation of orders and maintenance calculations is s 8(3A) which provides that:

'Unless a maintenance calculation has been made with respect to the child concerned, subsection (3) does not prevent a court from varying a maintenance order in relation to that child and the non-resident parent concerned –

(a) if the maintenance order was made on or after the date prescribed for the purposes of section 4(1)(a) . . . ; or
(b) where the order was made before then, in any case in which s 4(10) . . . prevents the making of an application for a maintenance calculation with respect to . . . that child.'

In effect, therefore, an order, if validly made, may be varied. It must be emphasised that the court's power to make any order for a child is limited to orders in terms which the parties have agreed; if the parties do not agree, the court may not make the order (see para **10.28**). If an order made after 5 April 2002 is varied, the time-limit of one year during which the jurisdiction of the CSA is excluded does not start afresh, but expires one year after the date of the original order.

Differing views have been expressed as to whether a court, when varying an order (which must have been made by consent), is limited to making a variation by consent or whether it may deal with the case on a non-consensual basis. There is no binding authority on this.[1]

10.5　On the face of it, therefore, the position is simple; subject to what has been said above, the jurisdiction of the courts is excluded where the Secretary of State has jurisdiction. Unfortunately, the reality is a little more complicated. There are 11 instances where the courts may retain, or exercise, jurisdiction to make orders for child maintenance. Some of these instances are where the Secretary of State has no jurisdiction, which presents no problem, and some are where the CSA 1991 specifically confers jurisdiction on the court.

These exceptions to the rule may be summarised as follows:

(a)　the Secretary of State has no jurisdiction;
(b)　the child is not the adopted or 'natural' child of both parties;
(c)　the child is between 17 and 19 years old and not in full-time education;
(d)　the child is 19 years old or over;
(e)　topping-up orders under s 8(6);
(f)　orders for additional educational expenses under s 8(7);
(g)　orders for expenses of a disabled or blind child under s 8(8);
(h)　lump sum or property adjustment orders for child;
(i)　certain consent orders;
(j)　variation of existing orders;
(k)　orders against the person with care.

The various exceptions will now be considered in turn.

Exceptions to the General Rule

(a) Secretary of State has no jurisdiction because of residence

10.6　Jurisdiction is covered by s 44 of the CSA 1991 and is dealt with at para **2.3**. Briefly, the Secretary of State has jurisdiction where the qualifying child, the person with care and the non-resident parent are habitually resident within the UK. If any one of the three is not so resident, the Secretary of State lacks jurisdiction and any application will have to be brought in the courts.

(b) Stepchildren and 'children of the family'

10.7　In order to be a qualifying child, a child must be the adopted or 'natural' child of both parents. In cases to which the MCA 1973 applies, the position is different; a party to a marriage has obligations in respect of a child of whom he is not the father but has treated as a child of the family, as defined by s 52 of the MCA 1973. The most common example of a child of the family is a child of one party to a marriage who lives with her and her new husband after their marriage.

---

1 See Professor Gillian Douglas at [1998] Fam Law 394 and the ensuing correspondence with Nicholas Mostyn QC at [1998] Fam Law 510. The position is not free from doubt, but the present writer agrees with Mr Mostyn that the court is not so restricted.

Such a child is not a qualifying child and may not be the subject of a calculation. To obtain financial relief for such a child it is therefore necessary to apply to the court under the provisions of either the MCA 1973, the CA 1989, or the DPMCA 1978.

Where a calculation is made in respect of another child or children, the CSA may arrange for the collection of maintenance for a non-qualifying child (see para **9.4**).

(c) Child aged 17 or 18

10.8 'Child' is defined by s 55(1) of the CSA 1991, which is discussed at para **2.7**. A 17- or 18-year-old will be excluded from the ambit of the Act unless:

(i) he is in full-time education which is not advanced education; or
(ii) he is not in education at all.

(d) Child aged 19 or over

10.9 A person who is 19 years old or over cannot bring himself within any provision of the CSA 1991. However, it is not uncommon for such a person to be financially dependent on his parents, for example when pursuing full-time education. Local education authorities have regard to the means of parents when assessing eligibility for grants, assuming that grants are available, with the result that students have to look to their parents for support.

Any parent of a person of this age, or the person himself, who wishes to claim maintenance from a parent will, therefore, have to bring an application in the courts.

(e) Topping-up under s 8(6)

10.10 It was seen in Chapter Three that there is a 'cap' or limit on the amount of child support maintenance which can be required under a maintenance calculation. Net income of a non-resident parent exceeding £2000 per week must be disregarded, so that the maximum sum which could be required (for three or more children) would be £500. There may be circumstances where a greater figure would be reasonable, but the Government considers that the courts would be more appropriate vehicles for this kind of application.

Accordingly, the CSA 1991 permits applications to the court to 'top up'. This was permitted under the Act from the outset, but the changes to the formula made new provisions necessary.

Section 8(6), as amended, provides that s 8 shall not prevent a court from exercising any power which it has to make a maintenance order for a child if:

'(a) a maintenance calculation is in force with respect to the child;
(b) the non-resident parent's net weekly income exceeds the figure referred to in paragraph 10(3) of Schedule 1 (as it has effect from time to time pursuant to regulations made under paragraph 10A(1)(b)); and
(c) the court is satisfied that the circumstances of the case make it appropriate for the non-resident parent to make or secure the making of periodical payments under a maintenance order in addition to the child support maintenance payable by him in accordance with the maintenance calculation.'

10.11 In order to satisfy the court that it has jurisdiction to entertain an application, therefore, the applicant must prove that there has been a maintenance calculation based on a net income for the non-resident parent of £2000 per week and that his actual net income exceeds that figure. The court would then have to proceed to deal with the application according to the statute which gave it primary jurisdiction (viz MCA 1973, DPMCA 1978 or CA 1989). The primary factors would be the needs of the child and the ability of the parents to pay; unlike in the CSA calculations, the means of the person with care would be relevant.

(f) Additional educational expenses

10.12 Section 8(7) is what might be called the 'school fees exception', although, as will be seen, it is not limited to school fees. It provides that the court shall not be prevented from exercising any power which it has to make a maintenance order in relation to a child if:

'(a) the child is, will be or (if the order were to be made) would be receiving instruction at an educational establishment or undergoing training for a trade, profession or vocation (whether or not while in gainful employment); and

(b) the order is made solely for the purposes of requiring the person making or securing the making of periodical payments fixed by the order to meet some or all of the expenses incurred in connection with the provision of the instruction or training.'

The first point to be noted is that there is no question of additional maintenance or topping-up involved; this subsection does not contain the prerequisite that there be a maintenance calculation to provide for everyday needs, although it may be that there will be such a calculation. Secondly, 'educational establishment' is not defined by the Act (unlike 'recognised educational establishment', which is defined by s 55(3)). Accordingly, the normal plain meaning afforded by the English language applies, and the term must mean school, college or university.

Of course, the child must be 18 years old or under; if he is aged between 16 and 18, and not attending a 'recognised educational establishment', he will be outside the ambit of the CSA 1991 in any event, so that the court would have jurisdiction anyway.

10.13 Provided the child is a child within the meaning of s 55(1), various classes of expenses seem to be claimable under s 8(7). School fees and extra expenses incurred at school are obvious examples. The subsection could also include accommodation charges, travelling expenses, or the provision of special clothing, books or computer equipment. Whatever the nature of the expenses, it would be necessary to show that they were directly attributable to the provision of the education or training.

When the expenses arise out of training for a trade, profession or vocation, the fact that the child is in gainful employment is not a bar; whatever income the child derived from such gainful employment would be one of the factors to be taken into account in assessing the child's needs.

(g) Disabled or blind child

10.14 Disabled or blind children frequently have additional special needs and expenses which cannot be accommodated within the terms of a rigid formula. Accordingly, the CSA 1991 permits application to the courts.

Section 8(8) provides that a court shall not be prevented from exercising any power which it has to make a maintenance order in relation to a child if:

'(a) a disability living allowance is paid to or in respect of him; or
(b) no such allowance is paid but he is disabled,
and the order is made solely for the purpose of requiring the person making or securing the making of periodical payments fixed by the order to meet some or all of any expenses attributable to the child's disability.'

By s 8(9), a child is disabled if he is blind, deaf or dumb or is substantially and permanently handicapped by illness, injury, mental disorder or congenital deformity or such other disability as may be prescribed.

As with s 8(7), it is not a prerequisite of an application to the court that a maintenance calculation be in force. The purpose of the provision is limited to the recovery of expenses attributable to the child's disability.

(h) Lump sums or property adjustment orders

10.15 For the sake of completeness, it should be noted that s 8(1) and (3) exclude the jurisdiction of the courts in respect of 'a maintenance order in relation to a child'. The various other forms of financial relief for a child are not brought under the umbrella of the CSA 1991, and the powers of the courts in relation thereto are not affected.

The court is therefore entitled to make a lump sum order or a property adjustment order in favour of a child; such an order would be unusual (see, eg, *A v A (A Minor: Financial Provision)* [1994] 1 FLR 657).

(i) Certain consent orders

10.16 This topic is considered more fully at para **10.28**.

(j) Power to vary

10.17 The prohibition on the exercise of the court's powers contained in CSA 1991, s 8(3) extends to variation of an existing order; it might, therefore, be thought that the courts have no power to vary their orders. This is, in fact, not the case, as was seen in para **10.4** above.

(k) Orders against the person with care

10.18 Section 8(10) provides that the section does not prevent a court exercising its power to make a maintenance order in relation to a child if that order is made against a person with care of the child. Such cases will clearly be unusual; it is difficult to think of cases where an order for periodical payments for a child would be made against the person with whom the child lived. However, the power is there, to be exercised in suitable cases.

The Effect of the CSA 1991 on Related Court Proceedings

10.19 The related court proceedings with which this section deals are concerned entirely with the ancillary relief proceedings between spouses or former spouses brought under the MCA 1973. On or after the grant of a decree, the court has power to make orders for periodical payments or for capital provision, and these are intended to do justice as between the parties in the light of the factors set out in s 25 of the MCA 1973. The effect of the CSA 1991 is that one important aspect of the financial relations between spouses or former spouses, namely the maintenance of their children, has been removed from the jurisdiction of the court. Nevertheless, the court still has to proceed to deal with the remaining issues. The problem is, therefore, what influence the CSA 1991 should have on these remaining issues.

10.20 The first way in which the CSA 1991 impinges on the courts is the question of what relationship the calculation of orders for children in cases in which the court retains jurisdiction should have to the amounts which the formula calculation would produce. Should the courts have regard to the formula when assessing child maintenance?

In principle, the answer must be that the court cannot be guided by a statute other than that under which the application before it is brought. The various statutes under which an application for child maintenance may be made (MCA 1973, DPMCA 1978, CA 1989) all have provisions which direct the court to have regard to certain matters. It might be argued that it would not be proper for the court to look beyond for guidance.

However, the position is not entirely clear-cut. When deciding the amount of the needs of the child, the court has to use some 'raw material'; the court cannot exist in a vacuum and has to have some figures, such as income support or foster-care rates, to decide how much it costs to keep a child. It might be argued that the method of calculating the maintenance requirement prescribed by the CSA 1991 is as good a means as any of working out what the financial needs of the child are. However, this could only be a starting point.

10.21 Some guidance under the previous formula was provided by the decision of Douglas Brown J in *E v C (Child Maintenance)* [1996] 1 FLR 472. In this case, a family proceedings court made orders reducing a maintenance order against a father from £5 per week for each of two children to £1 per year each. He was unemployed and in receipt of benefit. On the appeal, the judge allowed the appeal. He said that the CSA would have produced a nil assessment in this case. While that assessment was not binding on the justices, it would have been strongly persuasive had they known about it. It was the practice of professional judges to ask about a CSA assessment, and it would be helpful to justices to do likewise.

From this case, one can draw high judicial approval for the proposition that a maintenance calculation which the CSA would make is a material factor in all cases involving maintenance of children, and should be produced in all such cases. It would, of course, then be open to the parties to argue that such calculation should be altered in the light of the facts of the case, and the statutory matters to which the court was directed to have regard.

10.22 One matter which caused concern when the CSA 1991 was in its infancy was the problem of the parent, normally a father, who had transferred his share of a matrimonial home to the other parent to secure a roof over the heads of the family, and whose liability for maintenance of the other parent had been dismissed, with a fairly nominal order for the children. The Act, as originally enacted, made little or no provision for such parents, and there is no doubt that injustice resulted; this is recognised by the fact that the Government has introduced the departure scheme (now 'variations') to take account of such cases.

Some of these arguments have come before the courts, and the more important decisions will now be set out.

In *Crozier v Crozier* [1994] 1 FLR 126, a consent order for ancillary relief was made in 1989; this provided for the transfer of the husband's interest in the former matrimonial home to the wife, in full and final settlement of all claims against him, save for child maintenance which was agreed in a nominal sum. The wife was in receipt of income support. In 1993, the Secretary of State applied to the magistrates for a contribution from the husband towards the child's maintenance; the husband was ordered to pay £4 per week; it was common ground that an application would be made to the CSA, and that the husband would then have to pay £29 per week. The husband applied to set aside or vary the consent order, to enable him to recoup his half-share in the house to meet his liabilities.

Booth J refused leave to appeal out of time. She said that the parties may never have reached the agreement they did had the husband known that he would have to pay for the child. However, although the clean break was available to spouses, different considerations applied to child maintenance. The ongoing responsibilities of parents remained a basic factor, and parents could not achieve a clean break in respect of their child. Furthermore, at the time of the consent order, the State was empowered to recover maintenance for the child under the Social Security Act 1986. The State was never bound by the parents' agreement. Accordingly, neither the existence of the order in 1993, nor the anticipated liability under the CSA 1991 constituted a new event in fact or law sufficient to invalidate the basis of the agreed order.

10.23 In *Mawson v Mawson* [1994] 2 FLR 985, the facts were that during an application for ancillary relief, the wife withdrew her claim for financial provision for the child pending an application to the CSA for an assessment. The assessment was for £596.70 per month, which was manifestly more than would have been ordered by the court. In the light of this, the district judge ordered the transfer to her of the matrimonial home and a lump sum of £2000, but only allowed a three-month term for periodical payments at the rate of £150 per month, with no right to make any further application. The wife appealed.

Thorpe J said that a s 28(1A) direction, prohibiting the wife from making any further application, was inappropriate where there was a young child, and that part of the order should be deleted. There should be a limited term order, which should be for nine months. Apart from that, the order of the district judge was unchanged.

10.24 Thorpe J was also the judge in *Smith v McInerney* [1994] 2 FLR 1077. Ostensibly, this case was concerned with the effects of a maintenance agreement on a subsequent application for ancillary relief. In 1990, the husband and wife made a separation agreement, pursuant to which the husband transferred his interest in the former matrimonial home to the wife; in return, he was released from any obligation to maintain the wife or the children, although, in fact, he continued to make payments for the children. He was subsequently made redundant, and, in 1993, applied for a property adjustment order. The district judge ordered that the property be charged with 35% of its net value in favour of the husband. The wife appealed.

Thorpe J asserted the general principle that what the parties had agreed at the time of separation should be upheld by the court; the circumstances of the present case fell far short of those which would justify the court in imposing terms other than those agreed. The appeal should therefore be allowed. However, that was not an end of the matter; since the wife asserted her rights under the agreement, the husband was also entitled to the benefits for which he had contracted. He was entitled to the money he had advanced prior to his redundancy. More significantly, from the point of view of this book, the judge accepted that, since the wife was now in receipt of State benefits, it was likely that the husband would be the subject of an assessment by the CSA. The judge said:

> 'It seems to me manifestly fair that if the husband parted with capital in February 1990, in part in commutation of his future obligations to maintain [the child], then he should have the right to look to the wife for indemnity in respect of any sums which are extracted from him in respect of [the child]'s maintenance. In reality, he would be paying twice to discharge the same obligation; once by capital, and secondly by periodical payments. While the wife would not herself have laid claim to that second payment, she would indirectly have triggered it by her application for income support for herself.'

The judge therefore adjourned the husband's application for a property adjustment order generally, for the single purpose of providing a means of pursuing a claim for indemnity if, and only if, the CSA extracted from him substantive periodical payments in respect of the child between the date of the order and the date of the child ceasing to be dependent. The quantification of the claim could not sensibly be attempted until the child was 'off cost'. At that stage, in the absence of agreement, the court could quantify the sums paid by the husband and do justice to him by fixing some percentage interest, or charge, in relation to the capital from which he parted in February 1990 to settle his obligations in respect of the child in part.

10.25 This case may seem, at first, to be contrary to the spirit of *Crozier*. However, the essential point seems to be that in *Crozier* there was an application to set aside a consent order of the court, which had to be considered in the light of the authorities on that subject, particularly *Barder v Caluori* [1988] AC 20; in *Smith v McInerney* (above), there was not yet a court order, and the issue before the court was the weight to be attached to an agreement, the relevant leading case being *Edgar v Edgar* (1981) FLR 19. The arguments which may be taken on behalf of parties in such cases may, therefore, depend on the substantive nature of the application under consideration.

10.26 The final case to be considered is a decision of a judge in a county court which, although not a binding authority, has some persuasive weight. In *B v M (Child Support: Revocation of Order)* [1994] 1 FLR 342, a father had been ordered in 1986 to pay maintenance for two children at the rate of £41 per month per child. In 1993, the mother sought the help of the CSA, and was told that she could apply for an assessment if the order were revoked. She applied for revocation, and the district judge revoked the order. The father appealed.

His Honour Judge Bryant said that an application to revoke an order was governed by s 31(7) of the MCA 1973, which set out a list of factors to be considered. He accepted that a CSA assessment would probably be higher than the court order. However, it did not follow that an assessment under the CSA 1991 was necessarily in the best interests of the child. It might be that other matters would outweigh the financial advantage. For example, a high maintenance figure might inhibit the father from exercising his right to contact. The result could only be reached by the court weighing up all relevant factors, bearing in mind the welfare of the children. It was not enough to come to the court and say 'I wish to go to the Child Support Agency. Please revoke the existing order'. In the present case, he had heard nothing to take it out of the ordinary run of cases for which the transitional provisions were designed.

10.27   It would be difficult to give a definitive summary of the way in which the CSA 1991 has impinged on the conduct of applications for ancillary relief. This may be partly because, despite the fears of many when the Act first came into force, the CSA has only impinged on the lives of a limited number of people, since its 'take-up' has not been as extensive as had been anticipated.[2]

However, the fact that orders made after the prescribed date, will last for only one year before they can be overtaken by a maintenance calculation, indicates that orders for children should, so far as possible, be based on the new formula contained in Sch 1.

Maintenance Agreements and Consent Orders

10.28   It has always been possible for parents to make agreements to regulate the maintenance payable in respect of their children. Such agreements could be incorporated into orders of the court but, if not, they established contractual obligations which could be sued upon like any other contract. The CSA 1991 does not affect the ability of parents to make maintenance agreements, but certain restrictions are placed on their enforceability.

10.29   Section 9(1) defines a maintenance agreement as:

' . . . any agreement for the making, or for securing the making, of periodical payments by way of maintenance, or in Scotland aliment, to or for the benefit of any child.'

Section 9(2) sets out the general principle:

---

2 It is also possible that, as a result of economic recession and decline in property prices, separating or divorcing couples have had less to argue about than in the mid-1980s. There has certainly been a decline in the numbers of applications for ancillary relief coming before the courts. Perhaps, like death, the CSA is something which most people know will come one day, but prefer not to think about now.

'Nothing in this Act shall be taken to prevent any person from entering into a maintenance agreement.'

Freedom of contract still exists. However, the CSA 1991 goes on to ensure that the jurisdiction of the CSA is not ousted, and that parents are unable to contract out of the Act.

Section 9(3) provides that:

'. . . the existence of a maintenance agreement shall not prevent any party to the agreement, or any other person, from applying for a maintenance calculation with respect to any child to or for whose benefit periodical payments are to be made or secured under the agreement.'

This is followed by s 9(4), which provides that any clause in an agreement purporting to restrict the right of any person to apply for a maintenance calculation shall be void. A person who makes a maintenance agreement may therefore resile from it at any time and apply to the CSA; where someone is in receipt of benefit she may be compelled to do so.

Finally, while parents are entitled to make agreements, they may not apply to the court to vary the agreement. Section 9(5)(b) prevents any such application where the Secretary of State has jurisdiction. Anyone dissatisfied with the amount payable under an agreement has no remedy except for an application for a calculation.

10.30 The CSA 1991 is also modified, again, ostensibly, on a temporary basis, by its provisions for consent order based on agreements. It will be remembered that s 8 purports to oust the jurisdiction of the court in all cases where the Secretary of State has jurisdiction. On the face of it, this prevents parties from applying to the court for a consent order for ancillary relief including an order for children. However, the rigour of this provision is modified by s 8(5) which empowers the Lord Chancellor (and, in Scotland, the Lord Advocate), to provide by order that the court shall not be prevented from exercising its powers if:

'(a) a written agreement (whether or not enforceable) provides for the making, or securing, by a non-resident parent of the child of periodical payments to or for the benefit of the child; and

(b) the maintenance order which the court makes is, in all material respects, in the same terms as that agreement.'

The order envisaged by the CSA 1991 is the Child Maintenance (Written Agreements) Order 1993, SI 1993/620.

The court may, therefore, make a maintenance order in respect of a child if there is before it an agreement in writing, and the order sought is in the same amounts as the amounts provided for in the agreement.[3] Most such applications will be by consent. However, notwithstanding the use of the word 'consent' in the title of the order, there seems to be no reason why one party could not seek an

---

3 Most courts require the agreement to be produced before making an order. Opinion is divided as to whether a separate agreement is necessary, or whether the agreement can be incorporated in the recitals in the consent application. The general practice (as adopted in the PRFD) is not to require such evidence of separate agreement.

order against the wishes of the other party, provided the order sought was in the same terms as those in the agreement.

It is to be noted that an order under s 8(5) does not require that the agreement was made before 5 April 1993; the agreement may be made at any time.

The Lord Chancellor's Department said originally that s 8(5) was intended to be a temporary provision, pending the assumption by the CSA of full jurisdiction in all cases. However, it remains intact after the changes effected by the CSPSSA 2000.

The Relationship Between Maintenance Calculations and Court Orders

10.31   Section 30 of the CSA 1991, and the regulations made thereunder, which deal with the power of the Secretary of State to collect some forms of child maintenance in addition to child support maintenance, have already been considered at para **9.4**. This section of this chapter is concerned with the way in which maintenance calculations and court orders impinge on each other, and the statutory provisions and regulations which govern this relationship.

The basic position under the existing regulations may be summarised as follows.

(1)   Certain types of court orders are prescribed by reg 3(1) of the CS(MAJ) Regs 1992 as coming within the regulations for the purpose of s 10(1). Twenty-six such types of order are prescribed; they are, in effect, any court order which might be made for, or in respect of, a child (a complete list of the statutes is set out in the regulation).

(2)   By reg 3(2), when a maintenance calculation is made in respect of all the children with respect to whom a prescribed order has been made, or in respect of one or more but not all such children and the amount payable under the order to or for the benefit of each child is separately stated, the order shall cease to have effect insofar as it relates to the child or children.

(3)   The exceptions to the rule set out in (2) above, are:
  (a)   where the order was made under s 8(7) or (8) (ie for educational expenses or where the child is disabled); and
  (b)   an exception relating to Scotland.

(4)   Where reg 3(1) and (2) apply, the maintenance calculation takes effect two days after it is made, and the order will cease to have effect on that day (reg 3(5) and (6)).

(5)   Similar provisions to those set out above exist in relation to maintenance agreements. By reg 4(2), where a maintenance calculation is made with respect to all the children with respect to whom an agreement is in force, or to one or more but not all such children but the amount payable to or for the benefit of each child is separately specified, the agreement shall become unenforceable insofar as it relates to the children who are the subject of the assessment from the effective date of the calculation. The agreement will remain unenforceable until such date as the Secretary of State no longer has jurisdiction to make a maintenance calculation with respect to that child (reg 4(3)).

10.32   Provision had to be made for the overlapping jurisdiction of the CSA and the courts. This is contained in the Maintenance Orders (Backdating) Order 1993, SI 1993/623. Its effect may be summarised as follows.

(1)   Amendments were made to s 29(5) of the MCA 1973, s 5(5) of the DPMCA 1978, and Sch 1, para 3(5) to the CA 1989, to enable a court to backdate any order made under s 8(6) (the top-up provisions) to the date of any maintenance calculation. However, as some protection for the non-resident parent, it was also provided that the backdating provision shall only apply where the application for the top-up order is made within six months of the assessment.

(2)   Amendments were made to s 31(2) of the MCA 1973, and s 20(9B) of the DPMCA 1978, to deal with the position where an order has been made for children and spouse, and a calculation supersedes the order insofar as it relates to the children. In such circumstances, one of the spouses might wish to apply to vary the spousal maintenance. It was provided that any variation may be backdated to the date of the calculation, with the same time-limit of six months.

(3)   Amendments were made to s 29(7) of the MCA 1973, s 5(7) of the DPMCA 1978, and Sch 1, para 3(7) to the CA 1989, to provide for the position where cases move out of the jurisdiction of the CSA and are either terminated automatically or cancelled by the Secretary of State. In such circumstances, any subsequent court order might be backdated to the date of cancellation or termination, with a time-limit of six months.

(4)   Amendments were made to s 31(11) of the MCA 1973, s 20(9A) of the DPMCA 1978, and Sch 1, para 6(9) to the CA 1989, to govern the position where a non-resident parent applies to vary an order covering more than one child following a calculation in respect of one or more but not all the children. The onus was on the non-resident parent to apply to vary, and, if a variation order is made, it may be backdated to the date when the calculation took effect.

10.33   Finally, procedures have been devised to deal with the position where there is a dispute as to whether the court or the Secretary of State has jurisdiction; these are contained in rr 10.24–10.26 of the Family Proceedings Rules 1991 (FPR 1991), SI 1991/1247. When a parent applies to a county court for a periodical payments order for a child, court staff sift and check the application. The form on which the application is made, normally Form A in App 1A of the FPR 1991, contains a 'tick box' checklist to identify which of the exceptions to the general rule in s 8 applies. Where either the proper officer or the district judge considers that the court does not have jurisdiction, the applicant is informed to that effect.

If the applicant persists with the application, the proper officer, if it was he who made the original decision, refers the matter to the district judge, who either informs the applicant that there appears to be no jurisdiction or gives directions for a hearing, which may be ex parte. At the hearing, if the district judge declines jurisdiction, the parties are given reasons in writing. That decision is subject to appeal to a circuit judge.

10.34 A practice has arisen of making orders for periodical payments in favour of a spouse, such sums to be reduced *pro tanto* by any sums payable under a CSA assessment or calculation. In *Dorney-Kingdom v Dorney-Kingdom* [2000] 2 FLR 855, CA, it was held that such a device was legitimate, since it did not seek to oust the CSA's jurisdiction, but it was crucial that there be a substantial element of spousal support in such an order.

CHAPTER ELEVEN

Transitional Provisions and Miscellaneous Matters

Transitional Provisions

11.1 The CSPSSA 2000 contains the usual provision that the Secretary of State may in regulations make such transitional and transitory provisions as he considers necessary or expedient in connection with the coming into force of Part I of the Act.[1] The matters for which these regulations may in particular provide are then set out.[2] They may be summarised as follows.

(a) There may be provision for the amount of child support maintenance payable by or to any person to be at a transitional rate.
(b) There may be more than one transitional rate, successively.
(c) There may be a phasing-in process by way of prescribed steps. This may result in an increase or a decrease in the amount payable.
(d) If a departure direction has been given under the previous arrangements, there may be regulations to ensure that this is taken into account under the new system.

The Government has stated that the new scheme will deal with new applications first. It is intended that existing cases will be transferred at a later date and the new rates will be phased in over a period of time.[3] It seems, therefore, that for some time the old system and the new system will run in tandem, after which there will be a period of phasing-in for old cases to be adapted to the new system.

11.2 The detailed regulations are contained in regs 11–28 of the Child Support (Transitional Provisions) Regulations 2000, SI 2000/3186, the effect of which may be summarised as follows. First, it must be said that existing or older cases may not be reviewed for some time, in view of the Government's intention to concentrate on new applications. However, once the Secretary of State is able to consider a particular case he may supersede any earlier decision pursuant to s 17 of the CSA 1991 and make a new maintenance calculation under the new formula. The conversion date relates back to 6 April 2002.

Once the new maintenance calculation has been fixed, the non-resident parent must pay at the new rate, unless he can take advantage of the phasing-in provisions.

Any increase or decrease is stepped over a maximum period of five years, at a rate depending on the non-resident parent's net income, as follows:

---

1 CSPSSA 2000, s 29(2).
2 In ibid, s 29(2)(a) and (b).
3 See *Notes for Guidance*, p 55.

Net income	Phasing amount
£100 or less per week	£2.50 per week
Over £100 but less than £400	£5 per week
£400 or more	£10 per week

These provisions are intended to ease the burden for both parties. It is likely that in many cases the result of the new formula will be less favourable to the person with care, and these provisions seek to soften the blow for her; whether it is logical that her payments should decrease faster when the non-resident parent is better off is debatable.

The Child Maintenance Bonus

11.3   The Child Support Act 1995 introduced a 'child maintenance bonus' to have effect as from April 1997. This was based on the 'back to work' bonus in the jobseeker's allowance and was intended to ensure that a person with care who was in receipt of income support would receive a credit for some of the child maintenance paid.

This has now been abolished and is replaced by a child maintenance premium which allows families in receipt of income support or jobseeker's allowance to keep up to £10 per week of the child maintenance paid.

An Overview of the New Child Support Regime

11.4   Some of the potentially controversial elements of the new regime, such as the disregard of the means of the person with care, have been discussed elsewhere in this book and need not be repeated here. However, it may be useful to consider how the child support system as it now exists will affect separated parents, particularly those who have been married and are divorced.

For the purposes of this discussion it is assumed that the net income of the non-resident parent does not exceed the cap of £104,000 per annum. Where the net income is that figure or a higher figure this would give rise, in principle, to a minimum liability of £15,600 per annum (where there is one child) and a maximum liability of £26,000 per annum (where there are three or more children), and the person with care would be able to apply to the court for a top-up. In addition, either party could apply to the court for a school fees order; this may be of assistance where a relatively high earner feels that an unreasonably large amount is being paid to the person with care, since the court would be able to take account of all factors and make such order in respect of school fees against either parent as it saw fit.

11.5   Such cases will not be the norm. However, in all cases, of whatever value, there will be ways in which the non-resident parent may legitimately reduce his net income for the purposes of the maintenance calculation. The most significant of these may be summarised as follows.

(1) If an employed person pays towards an occupational pension scheme or personal pension scheme, or a self-employed person pays towards a retirement annuity contract or personal pension scheme, 75% of the premiums are deducted before net income is calculated.

(2) If the non-resident parent is paying school fees, the maintenance element of the fees could constitute a special case and cause a reduction in net income.

(3) If the non-resident parent has a partner who has children living with her, the income of the non-resident parent is automatically adjusted to make allowance for those children. This is irrespective of any income of the partner or of any child maintenance which the natural father of the children is paying.

(4) A regrettable effect of the new rules as to shared care may be that non-resident parents will be encouraged to apply for shared care orders, or unrealistically generous amounts of staying contact so as to reduce their financial liability.

11.6   The effect on ancillary relief settlements may well be that orders will be agreed for children at the new rates, since there is little point after 6 April 2002 in attempting to fetter the jurisdiction of the CSA for longer than one year. In lower income cases, the effect of this might be that it is less easy to negotiate a clean break. The conventional wisdom in such cases has been that fathers will be unable to pay more than the child support figure demanded by the CSA. Now that, in lower income cases, the person with care may get less, this will not be a sustainable argument. Where the non-resident parent is a high earner it might affect the wife's settlement since there would be less left for her once the high child support figure had been deducted. In both sets of circumstances, the clean break may be more difficult to achieve.

APPENDIX 1

STATUTES

Child Support Act 1991, including prospective amendments by the Child Support, Pensions and Social Security Act 2000

ARRANGEMENT OF SECTIONS

The basic principles

The basic principles

1   The duty to maintain

(1) For the purposes of this Act, each parent of a qualifying child is responsible for maintaining him.

(2) For the purposes of this Act, a non-resident parent shall be taken to have met his responsibility to maintain any qualifying child of his by making periodical payments of maintenance with respect to the child of such amount, and at such intervals, as may be determined in accordance with the provisions of this Act.

(3) Where a maintenance calculation made under this Act requires the making of periodical payments, it shall be the duty of the non-resident parent with respect to whom the calculation was made to make those payments.

Amendments—Child Support, Pensions and Social Security Act 2000, s 1(2), Sch 3, para 11(2) – in force from a date to be appointed.

2   Welfare of children: the general principle

Where, in any case which falls to be dealt with under this Act, the Secretary of State is considering the exercise of any discretionary power conferred by this Act, he shall have regard to the welfare of any child likely to be affected by his decision.

Amendments—Social Security Act 1998, s 86(1), Sch 7, para 18.

3 Meaning of certain terms used in this Act

(1) A child is a 'qualifying child' if –

(a) one of his parents is, in relation to him, a non-resident parent; or
(b) both of his parents are, in relation to him, non-resident parents.

(2) The parent of any child is a 'non-resident parent', in relation to him, if –

(a) that parent is not living in the same household with the child; and
(b) the child has his home with a person who is, in relation to him, a person with care.

(3) A person is a 'person with care', in relation to any child, if he is a person –

(a) with whom the child has his home;
(b) who usually provides day to day care for the child (whether exclusively or in conjunction with any other person); and
(c) who does not fall within a prescribed category of person.

(4) The Secretary of State shall not, under subsection (3)(c), prescribe as a category –

(a) parents;
(b) guardians;
(c) persons in whose favour residence orders under section 8 of the Children Act 1989 are in force;
(d) (*applies to Scotland only*)

(5) For the purposes of this Act there may be more than one person with care in relation to the same qualifying child.

(6) Periodical payments which are required to be paid in accordance with a maintenance calculation are referred to in this Act as 'child support maintenance'.

(7) Expressions are defined in this section only for the purposes of this Act.

Amendments—Child Support, Pensions and Social Security Act 2000, s 1(2), Sch 3, para 11(2) – in force from a date to be appointed.

4 Child support maintenance

(1) A person who is, in relation to any qualifying child or any qualifying children, either the person with care or the non-resident parent may apply to the Secretary of State for a maintenance calculation to be made under this Act with respect to that child, or any of those children.

(2) Where a maintenance calculation has been made in response to an application under this section the Secretary of State may, if the person with care or non-resident parent with respect to whom the calculation was made applies to him under this subsection, arrange for –

(a) the collection of the child support maintenance payable in accordance with the calculation;
(b) the enforcement of the obligation to pay child support maintenance in accordance with the calculation.

(3) Where an application under subsection (2) for the enforcement of the obligation mentioned in subsection (2)(b) authorises the Secretary of State to take steps to enforce that obligation whenever he considers it necessary to do so, the Secretary of State may act accordingly.

(4) A person who applies to the Secretary of State under this section shall, so far as that person reasonably can, comply with such regulations as may be made by the Secretary of State with a view to the Secretary of State being provided with the information which is required to enable –

    (a) the non-resident parent to be identified or traced (where that is necessary);

    (b) the amount of child support maintenance payable by the non-resident parent to be calculated; and

    (c) that amount to be recovered from the non-resident parent.

(5) Any person who has applied to the Secretary of State under this section may at any time request him to cease acting under this section.

(6) It shall be the duty of the Secretary of State to comply with any request made under subsection (5) (but subject to any regulations made under subsection (8)).

(7) The obligation to provide information which is imposed by subsection (4) –

    (a) shall not apply in such circumstances as may be prescribed; and

    (b) may, in such circumstances as may be prescribed, be waived by the Secretary of State.

(8) The Secretary of State may by regulation make such incidental, supplemental or transitional provision as he thinks appropriate with respect to cases in which he is requested to cease to act under this section.

(9) No application may be made under this section if there is in force with respect to the person with care and non-resident parent in question a maintenance calculation made in response to an application treated as made under section 6.

(10) No application may be made at any time under this section with respect to a qualifying child or any qualifying children if –

    (a) there is in force a written maintenance agreement made before 5th April 1993, or a maintenance order made before a prescribed date, in respect of that child or those children and the person who is, at that time, the non-resident parent; or

    (aa) a maintenance order made on or after the date prescribed for the purposes of paragraph (a) is in force in respect of them, but has been so for less than the period of one year beginning with the date on which it was made; or

    (b) benefit is being paid to, or in respect of, a parent with care of that child or those children.

(11) In subsection (10) 'benefit' means any benefit which is mentioned in, or prescribed by regulations under, section 6(1).

Amendments—Child Support Act 1995, s 18(1); Social Security Act 1998, s 86(1), Sch 7, para 19; Child Support, Pensions and Social Security Act 2000, ss 1(2), 2, Sch 3, para 11(2), (3) – in force from a date to be appointed.

5 Child support maintenance: supplemental provisions

(1) Where –

    (a) there is more than one person with care of a qualifying child; and

    (b) one or more, but not all, of them have parental responsibility for the child;

no application may be made for a maintenance calculation with respect to the child by any of those persons who do not have parental responsibility for the child.

(2) Where more than one application for a maintenance calculation is made with respect to the child concerned, only one of them may be proceeded with.

(3) The Secretary of State may by regulation make provision as to which of two or more applications for a maintenance calculation with respect to the same child is to be proceeded with.

Amendments—Children (Scotland) Act 1995, s 105(4), Sch 4, para 52(1), (3); Child Support, Pensions and Social Security Act 2000, s 1(2) – in force from a date to be appointed.

6 Applications by those claiming or receiving benefit

(1) This section applies where income support, an income-based jobseeker's allowance or any other benefit of a prescribed kind is claimed by or in respect of, or paid to or in respect of, the parent of a qualifying child who is also a person with care of the child.

(2) In this section, that person is referred to as 'the parent'.

(3) The Secretary of State may –

    (a) treat the parent as having applied for a maintenance calculation with respect to the qualifying child and all other children of the non-resident parent in relation to whom the parent is also a person with care; and

    (b) take action under this Act to recover from the non-resident parent, on the parent's behalf, the child support maintenance so determined.

(4) Before doing what is mentioned in subsection (3), the Secretary of State must notify the parent in writing of the effect of subsections (3) and (5) and section 46.

(5) The Secretary of State may not act under subsection (3) if the parent asks him not to (a request which need not be in writing).

(6) Subsection (1) has effect regardless of whether any of the benefits mentioned there is payable with respect to any qualifying child.

(7) Unless she has made a request under subsection (5), the parent shall, so far as she reasonably can, comply with such regulations as may be made by the Secretary of State with a view to the Secretary of State's being provided with the information which is required to enable –

    (a) the non-resident parent to be identified or traced;

    (b) the amount of child support maintenance payable by him to be calculated; and

    (c) that amount to be recovered from him.

(8) The obligation to provide information which is imposed by subsection (7) –

    (a) does not apply in such circumstances as may be prescribed; and

    (b) may, in such circumstances as may be prescribed, be waived by the Secretary of State.

(9) If the parent ceases to fall within subsection (1), she may ask the Secretary of State to cease acting under this section, but until then he may continue to do so.

(10) The Secretary of State must comply with any request under subsection (9) (but subject to any regulations made under subsection (11)).

(11) The Secretary of State may by regulations make such incidental or transitional provisions as he thinks appropriate with respect to cases in which he is asked under subsection (9) to cease to act under this section.

(12) The fact that a maintenance calculation is in force with respect to a person with care does not prevent the making of a new maintenance calculation with respect to her as a result of the Secretary of State's acting under subsection (3).

Amendments—Child Support, Pensions and Social Security Act 2000, s 3 – in force from 10 November 2000 for the purpose only of making regulations.

7 *(applies to Scotland only)*

8 Role of the courts with respect to maintenance for children

(1) This subsection applies in any case where the Secretary of State would have jurisdiction to make a maintenance calculation with respect to a qualifying child and a non-resident parent of his on an application duly made (or treated as made) by a person entitled to apply for such a calculation with respect to that child.

(2) Subsection (1) applies even though the circumstances of the case are such that the Secretary of State would not make a calculation if it were applied for.

(3) Except as provided in subsection (3A), in any case where subsection (1) applies, no court shall exercise any power which it would otherwise have to make, vary or revive any maintenance order in relation to the child and non-resident parent concerned.

(3A) Unless a maintenance calculation has been made with respect to the child concerned, subsection (3) does not prevent a court from varying a maintenance order in relation to that child and the non-resident parent concerned –

    (a) if the maintenance order was made on or after the date prescribed for the purposes of section 4(1)(a) or 7(1)(a); or

    (b) where the order was made before then, in any case in which section 4(10) or 7(10) prevents the making of an application for a maintenance calculation with respect to or by that child.

(4) Subsection (3) does not prevent a court from revoking a maintenance order.

(5) The Lord Chancellor or in relation to Scotland the Lord Advocate may by order provide that, in such circumstances as may be specified by the order, this section shall not prevent a court from exercising any power which it has to make a maintenance order in relation to a child if –

    (a) a written agreement (whether or not enforceable) provides for the making, or securing, by a non-resident parent of the child of periodical payments to or for the benefit of the child; and

    (b) the maintenance order which the court makes is, in all material respects, in the same terms as that agreement.

(6) This section shall not prevent a court from exercising any power which it has to make a maintenance order in relation to a child if –

    (a) a maintenance calculation is in force with respect to the child;

    (b) the non-resident parent's net weekly income exceeds the figure referred to in paragraph 10(3) of Schedule 1 (as it has effect from time to time pursuant to regulations made under paragraph 10A(1)(b));

    (c) the court is satisfied that the circumstances of the case make it appropriate for the non-resident parent to make or secure the making of periodical payments under a maintenance order in addition to the child support maintenance payable by him in accordance with the maintenance calculation.

(7) This section shall not prevent a court from exercising any power which it has to make a maintenance order in relation to a child if –

(a) the child is, will be or (if the order were to be made) would be receiving instruction at an educational establishment or undergoing training for a trade, profession or vocation (whether or not while in gainful employment); and

(b) the order is made solely for the purposes of requiring the person making or securing the making of periodical payments fixed by the order to meet some or all of the expenses incurred in connection with the provision of the instruction or training.

(8) This section shall not prevent a court from exercising any power which it has to make a maintenance order in relation to a child if –

(a) a disability living allowance is paid to or in respect of him; or

(b) no such allowance is paid but he is disabled,

and the order is made solely for the purpose of requiring the person making or securing the making of periodical payments fixed by the order to meet some or all of any expenses attributable to the child's disability.

(9) For the purposes of subsection (8), a child is disabled if he is blind, deaf or dumb or is substantially and permanently handicapped by illness, injury, mental disorder or congenital deformity or such other disability as may be prescribed.

(10) This section shall not prevent a court from exercising any power which it has to make a maintenance order in relation to a child if the order is made against a person with care of the child.

(11) In this Act 'maintenance order', in relation to any child, means an order which requires the making or securing of periodical payments to or for the benefit of the child and which is made under –

(a) Part II of the Matrimonial Causes Act 1973;

(b) the Domestic Proceedings and Magistrates' Courts Act 1978;

(c) Part III of the Matrimonial and Family Proceedings Act 1984;

(d) the Family Law (Scotland) Act 1985;

(e) Schedule 1 to the Children Act 1989; or

(f) any other prescribed enactment,

and includes any order varying or reviving such an order.

Amendments—Child Support Act 1995, s 18(3); Social Security Act 1998, s 86(1), Sch 7, para 22; Child Support, Pensions and Social Security Act 2000, s 1(2), Sch 3, para 11(2), (5) – in force from a date to be appointed.

9 Agreements about maintenance

(1) In this section 'maintenance agreement' means any agreement for the making, or for securing the making, of periodical payments by way of maintenance, or in Scotland aliment, to or for the benefit of any child.

(2) Nothing in this Act shall be taken to prevent any person from entering into a maintenance agreement.

(3) Subject to section 4(10)(a) and section 7(10), the existence of a maintenance agreement shall not prevent any party to the agreement, or any other person, from

applying for a maintenance calculation with respect to any child to or for whose benefit periodical payments are to be made or secured under the agreement.

(4) Where any agreement contains a provision which purports to restrict the right of any person to apply for a maintenance calculation, that provision shall be void.

(5) Where section 8 would prevent any court from making a maintenance order in relation to a child and a non-resident parent of his, no court shall exercise any power that it has to vary any agreement so as –

(a) to insert a provision requiring that non-resident parent to make or secure the making of periodical payments by way of maintenance, or in Scotland aliment, to or for the benefit of that child; or
(b) to increase the amount payable under such a provision.

(6) In any case in which section 4(10) or 7(10) prevents the making of an application for a maintenance calculation, and –

(a) no parent has been treated under section 6(3) as having applied for a maintenance calculation with respect to the child; or
(b) a parent has been so treated but no maintenance calculation has been made,

subsection (5) shall have effect with the omission of paragraph (b).

Amendments—Child Support Act 1995, s 18(4); Child Support, Pensions and Social Security Act 2000, s 1(2), Sch 3, para 11(2), (6) – in force from a date to be appointed.

10 Relationship between maintenance calculations and certain court orders and related matters

(1) Where an order of a kind prescribed for the purposes of this subsection is in force with respect to any qualifying child with respect to whom a maintenance calculation is made, the order –

(a) shall, so far as it relates to the making or securing of periodical payments, cease to have effect to such extent as may be determined in accordance with regulations made by the Secretary of State; or
(b) where the regulations so provide, shall, so far as it so relates, have effect subject to such modifications as may be so determined.

(2) Where an agreement of a kind prescribed for the purposes of this subsection is in force with respect to any qualifying child with respect to whom a maintenance calculation is made, the agreement –

(a) shall, so far as it relates to the making or securing of periodical payments, be unenforceable to such extent as may be determined in accordance with regulations made by the Secretary of State; or
(b) where the regulations so provide, shall, so far as it so relates, have effect subject to such modifications as may be determined.

(3) Any regulations under this section may, in particular, make such provision with respect to –

(a) any case where any person with respect to whom an order or agreement of a kind prescribed for the purposes of subsection (1) or (2) has effect applies to the prescribed court, before the end of the prescribed period, for the order or agreement to be varied in the light of the maintenance calculation and of the provisions of this Act;

(b) the recovery of any arrears under the order or agreement which fell due before the coming into force of the maintenance calculation,

as the Secretary of State considers appropriate and may provide that, in prescribed circumstances, an application to any court which is made with respect to an order of a prescribed kind relating to the making or securing of periodical payments to or for the benefit of a child shall be treated by the court as an application for the order to be revoked.

(4) The Secretary of State may by regulation make provision for –

(a) notification to be given by the Secretary of State to the prescribed person in any case where he considers that the making of a maintenance calculation has affected, or is likely to affect, any order of a kind prescribed for the purposes of this subsection;

(b) notification to be given by the prescribed person to the Secretary of State in any case where a court makes an order which it considers has affected, or is likely to affect, a maintenance calculation.

(5) Rules may be made under section 144 of the Magistrates' Courts Act 1980 (rules of procedure) requiring any person who, in prescribed circumstances, makes an application to a magistrates' court for a maintenance order to furnish the court with a statement in a prescribed form, and signed by an officer of the Secretary of State, as to whether or not, at the time when the statement is made, there is a maintenance calculation in force with respect to that person or the child concerned.

In this subsection –

'maintenance order' means an order of a prescribed kind for the making or securing of periodical payments to or for the benefit of a child; and
'prescribed' means prescribed by the rules.

Amendments—Social Security Act 1998, s 86(1), Sch 7, para 23(1)(a), (b), (2); Child Support, Pensions and Social Security Act 2000, s 1(2) – in force from a date to be appointed.

Maintenance calculations

11   Maintenance calculations

(1) An application for a maintenance calculation made to the Secretary of State shall be dealt with by him in accordance with the provison made by or under this Act.

(2) The Secretary of State shall (unless he decides not to make a maintenance calculation in response to the application, or makes a decision under section 12) determine the application by making a decision under this section about whether any child support maintenance is payable and, if so, how much.

(3) Where –

(a) a parent is treated under section 6(3) as having applied for a maintenance calculation; but

(b) the Secretary of State becomes aware before determining the application that the parent has ceased to fall within section 6(1),

he shall, subject to subsection (4), cease to treat that parent as having applied for a maintenance calculation.

(4) If it appears to the Secretary of State that subsection (10) of section 4 would not have prevented the parent with care concerned from making an application for a maintenance calculation under that section he shall –

  (a) notify her of the effect of this subsection; and
  (b) if, before the end of the period of one month beginning with the day on which notice was sent to her, she asks him to do so, treat her as having applied not under section 6 but under section 4.

(5) Where subsection (3) applies but subsection (4) does not, the Secretary of State shall notify –

  (a) the parent with care concerned; and
  (b) the non-resident parent (or alleged non-resident parent), where it appears to him that that person is aware that the parent with care has been treated as having applied for a maintenance calculation.

(6) The amount of child support maintenance to be fixed by a maintenance calculation shall be determined in accordance with Part I of Schedule 1 unless an application for a variation has been made and agreed.

(7) If the Secretary of State has agreed to a variation, the amount of child support maintenance to be fixed shall be determined on the basis he determines under section 28F(4).

(8) Part II of Schedule 1 makes further provision with respect to maintenance calculations.

Amendments—Child Support, Pensions and Social Security Act 2000, s 1(1) – in force from a date to be appointed.

12 Default and interim maintenance decisions

(1) Where the Secretary of State –

  (a) is required to make a maintenance calculation; or
  (b) is proposing to make a decision under section 16 or 17,

and it appears to him that he does not have sufficient information to enable him to do so, he may make a default maintenance decision.

(2) Where an application for a variation has been made under section 28A(1) in connection with an application for a maintenance calculation (or in connection with such an application which is treated as having been made), the Secretary of State may make an interim maintenance decision.

(3) The amount of child support maintenance fixed by an interim maintenance decision shall be determined in accordance with Part I of Schedule 1.

(4) The Secretary of State may by regulations make provision as to default and interim maintenance decisions.

(5) The regulations may, in particular, make provision as to –

  (a) the procedure to be followed in making a default or an interim maintenance decision; and
  (b) a default rate of child support maintenance to apply where a default maintenance decision is made.

Amendments—Child Support, Pensions and Social Security Act 2000, s 4 – in force from 10 November 2000 for the purpose only of making regulations.

13 ...

Amendments—Social Security Act 1998, s 86(1), Sch 7, para 26.

Information

14 Information required by Secretary of State

(1) The Secretary of State may make regulations requiring any information or evidence needed for the determination of any application made or treated as made under this Act, or any question arising in connection with such an application (or application treated as made), or needed for the making of any decision or in connection with the imposition of any condition or requirement under this Act, or needed in connection with the collection or enforcement of child support or other maintenance under this Act, to be furnished –

    (a) by such persons as may be determined in accordance with regulations made by the Secretary of State; and

    (b) in accordance with the regulations.

(1A) Regulations under subsection (1) may make provision for notifying any person who is required to furnish any information or evidence under the regulations of the possible consequences of failing to do so.

(2)–(2A) ...

(3) The Secretary of State may by regulation make provision authorising the disclosure by him, in such circumstances as may be prescribed, of such information held by him for purposes of this Act as may be prescribed.

(4) The provisions of Schedule 2 (which relate to information which is held for purposes other than those of this Act but which is required by the Secretary of State) shall have effect.

Amendments—Child Support Act 1995, s 30(5), Sch 3, paras 2, 3(1), (2); Social Security Act 1998, s 86(1), Sch 7, para 27(a), (b); Child Support, Pensions and Social Security Act 2000, s 12, Sch 3, para 11(7) – in force from a date to be appointed.

14A Information – offences

(1) This section applies to –

    (a) persons who are required to comply with regulations under section 4(4) or 7(5); and

    (b) persons specified in regulations under section 14(1)(a).

(2) Such a person is guilty of an offence if, pursuant to a request for information under or by virtue of those regulations –

    (a) he makes a statement or representation which he knows to be false; or

    (b) he provides, or knowingly causes or knowingly allows to be provided, a document or other information which he knows to be false in a material particular.

(3) Such a person is guilty of an offence if, following such a request, he fails to comply with it.

(4) It is a defence for a person charged with an offence under subsection (3) to prove that he had a reasonable excuse for failing to comply.

(5) A person guilty of an offence under this section is liable on summary conviction to a fine not exceeding level 3 on the standard scale.

Amendments—Child Support, Pensions and Social Security Act 2000, s 13.

15 Powers of inspectors

(1) The Secretary of State may appoint, on such terms as he thinks fit, persons to act as inspectors under this section.

(2) The function of inspectors is to acquire information which the Secretary of State needs for any of the purposes of this Act.

(3) Every inspector is to be given a certificate of his appointment.

(4) An inspector has power, at any reasonable time and either alone or accompanied by such other persons as he thinks fit, to enter any premises which –

(a) are liable to inspection under this section; and
(b) are premises to which it is reasonable for him to require entry in order that he may exercise his functions under this section,

and may there make such examination and inquiry as he considers appropriate.

(4A) Premises liable to inspection under this section are those which are not used wholly as a dwelling house and which the inspector has reasonable grounds for suspecting are –

(a) premises at which a non-resident parent is or has been employed;
(b) premises at which a non-resident parent carries out, or has carried out, a trade, profession, vocation or business;
(c) premises at which there is information held by a person ('A') whom the inspector has reasonable grounds for suspecting has information about a non-resident parent acquired in the course of A's own trade, profession, vocation or business.

(5) An inspector exercising his powers may question any person aged 18 or over whom he finds on the premises.

(6) If required to do so by an inspector exercising his powers, any such person shall furnish to the inspector all such information and documents as the inspector may reasonably require.

(7) No person shall be required under this section to answer any question or to give any evidence tending to incriminate himself or, in the case of a person who is married, his or her spouse.

(8) On applying for admission to any premises in the exercise of his powers, an inspector shall, if so required, produce his certificate.

(9) If any person –

(a) intentionally delays or obstructs any inspector exercising his powers; or
(b) without reasonable excuse, refuses or neglects to answer any question or furnish any information or to produce any document when required to do so under this section,

he shall be guilty of an offence and liable on summary conviction to a fine not exceeding level 3 on the standard scale.

(10) In this section –

'certificate' means a certificate of appointment issued under this section;
'inspector' means an inspector appointed under this section;
'powers' means powers conferred by this section.

(11) In this section, 'premises' includes –

(a) moveable structures and vehicles, vessels, aircraft and hovercraft;

(b) installations that are offshore installations for the purposes of the Mineral Workings (Offshore Installations) Act 1971; and

(c) places of all other descriptions whether or not occupied as land or otherwise,

and references in this section to the occupier of premises are to be construed, in relation to premises that are not occupied as land, as references to any person for the time being present at the place in question.

Amendments—Social Security Act 1998, s 86(1), Sch 7, para 28; Child Support, Pensions and Social Security Act 2000, s 14(1)–(4).

Reviews and appeals

16   Revision of decisions

(1) Any decision to which subsection (1A) applies may be revised by the Secretary of State –

(a) either within the prescribed period or in prescribed cases or circumstances; and

(b) either on an application made for the purpose or on his own initiative;

and regulation may prescribe the procedure by which a decision of the Secretary of State may be so revised.

(1A) This subsection applies to –

(a) a decision of the Secretary of State under section 11, 12 or 17;

(b) a reduced benefit decision under section 46;

(c) a decision of an appeal tribunal on a referral under section 28D(1)(b).

(1B) Where the Secretary of State revises a decision under section 12(1) –

(a) he may (if appropriate) do so as if he were revising a decision under section 11; and

(b) if he does that, his decision as revised is to be treated as one under section 11 instead of section 12(1) (and, in particular, is to be so treated for the purposes of an appeal against it under section 20).

(2) In making a decision under subsection (1), the Secretary of State need not consider any issue that is not raised by the application or, as the case may be, did not cause him to act on his own initiative.

(3) Subject to subsections (4) and (5) and section 28ZC, a revision under this section shall take effect as from the date on which the original decision took (or was to take) effect.

(4) Regulations may provide that, in prescribed cases or circumstances, a revision under this section shall take effect as from such other date as may be prescribed.

(5) Where a decision is revised under this section, for the purpose of any rule as to the time allowed for bringing an appeal, the decision shall be regarded as made on the date on which it is so revised.

(6) Except in prescribed circumstances, an appeal against a decision of the Secretary of State shall lapse if the decision is revised under this section before the appeal is determined.

Amendments—Social Security Act 1998, s 40; Child Support, Pensions and Social Security Act 2000, s 8 – in force from a date to be appointed.

17 Decisions superseding earlier decisions

(1) Subject to subsection (2), the following, namely –

    (a) any decision of the Secretary of State under section 11 or 12 or this section, whether as originally made or as revised under section 16;

    (b) any decision of an appeal tribunal under section 20;

    (c) any reduced benefit decision under section 46;

    (d) any decision of an appeal tribunal on a referral under section 28D(1)(b);

    (e) any decision of a Child Support Commissioner on an appeal from such a decision as is mentioned in paragraph (b) or (d),

may be superseded by a decision made by the Secretary of State, either on an application made for the purpose or on his own initiative.

(2) In making a decision under subsection (1), the Secretary of State need not consider any issue that is not raised by the application or, as the case may be, did not cause him to act on his own initiative.

(3) Regulations may prescribe the cases and circumstances in which, and the procedure by which, a decision may be made under this section.

(4) Subject to subsection (5) and section 28ZC, a decision under this section shall take effect as from the beginning of the maintenance period in which it is made or, where applicable, the beginning of the maintenance period in which the application was made.

(4A) In subsection (4), a 'maintenance period' is (except where a different meaning is prescribed for prescribed cases) a period of seven days, the first one beginning on the effective date of the first decison made by the Secretary of State under section 11 or (if earlier) his first default or interim maintenance decision (under section 12) in relation to the non-resident parent in question, and each subsequent one beginning on the day after the last day of the previous one.

(5) Regulations may provide that, in prescribed cases or circumstances, a decision under this section shall take effect as from such other date as may be prescribed.

Amendments—Social Security Act 1998, s 41; Child Support, Pensions and Social Security Act 2000, s 9, Sch 9 – in force from 10 November 2000 for the purpose only of making regulations.

18–19 ...

Amendments—Social Security Act 1998, s 41.

20 Appeals to appeal tribunals

(1) A qualifying person has a right of appeal to an appeal tribunal against –

    (a) a decision of the Secretary of State under section 11, 12 or 17 (whether as originally made or as revised under section 16);

    (b) a decision of the Secretary of State not to make a maintenance calculation under section 11 or not to supersede a decision under section 17;

    (c) a reduced benefit decision under section 46;

    (d) the imposition (by virtue of section 41A) of a requirement to make penalty payments, or their amount;

    (e) the imposition (by virtue of section 47) of a requirement to pay fees.

(2) In subsection (1), 'qualifying person' means –

    (a) in relation to paragraphs (a) and (b) –

       (i)   the person with care, or non-resident parent, with respect to whom the Secretary of State made the decision, or

      (ii) in a case relating to a maintenance calculation which was applied for under section 7, either of those persons or the child concerned;

    (b) in relation to paragraph (c), the person in respect of whom the benefits are payable;

    (c) in relation to paragraph (d), the parent who has been required to make penalty payments; and

    (d) in relation to paragraph (e), the person required to pay fees.

(3) A person with a right of appeal under this section shall be given such notice as may be prescribed of –

    (a) that right; and

    (b) the relevant decision, or the imposition of the requirement.

(4) Regulations may make –

    (a) provision as to the manner in which, and the time within which, appeals are to be brought; and

    (b) such provision with respect to proceedings before appeal tribunals as the Secretary of State considers appropriate.

(5) The regulations may in particular make any provision of a kind mentioned in Schedule 5 to the Social Security Act 1998.

(6) No appeal lies by virtue of subsection (1)(c) unless the amount of the person's benefit is reduced in accordance with the reduced benefit decision; and the time within which such an appeal may be brought runs from the date of notification of the reduction.

(7) In deciding an appeal under this section, an appeal tribunal –

    (a) need not consider any issue that is not raised by the appeal; and

    (b) shall not take into account any circumstances not obtaining at the time when the Secretary of State made the decision or imposed the requirement.

(8) If an appeal under this section is allowed, the appeal tribunal may –

    (a) itself make such decision as it considers appropriate; or

    (b) remit the case to the Secretary of State, together with such directions (if any) as it considers appropriate.

Amendments—Child Support, Pensions and Social Security Act 2000, s 10 – in force from 10 November 2000 for the purpose only of making regulations.

20A, 21 ...

Amendments—Social Security Act 1998, s 42.

22 Child Support Commissioners

(1) Her Majesty may from time to time appoint a Chief Child Support Commissioner and such number of other Child Support Commissioners as she may think fit.

(2) The Chief Child Support Commissioner and the other Child Support Commissioners shall be appointed from among persons who –

    (a) have a 10 year general qualification; or

(b) *(applies to Scotland only)*

(3) The Lord Chancellor, after consulting the Lord Advocate, may make such regulation with respect to proceedings before Child Support Commissioners as he considers appropriate.

(4) The regulations –

  (a) may, in particular, make any provision of a kind mentioned in Schedule 5 to the Social Security Act 1998; and
  (b) shall provide that any hearing before a Child Support Commissioner shall be in public except in so far as the Commissioner for special reasons directs otherwise.

(5) Schedule 4 shall have effect with respect to Child Support Commissioners.

Amendments—Social Security Act 1998, s 86(1), Sch 7, para 29.

23 *(applies to Northern Ireland only)*

23A Redetermination of appeals

(1) This section applies where an application is made to a person under section 24(6)(a) for leave to appeal from a decision of an appeal tribunal.

(2) If the person who constituted, or was the chairman of, the appeal tribunal considers that the decision was erroneous in law, he may set aside the decision and refer the case either for redetermination by the tribunal or for determination by a differently constituted tribunal.

(3) If each of the principal parties to the case expresses the view that the decision was erroneous in point of law, the person shall set aside the decision and refer the case for determination by a differently constituted tribunal.

(4) The 'principal parties' are –

  (a) the Secretary of State; and
  (b) those who are qualifying persons for the purposes of section 20(2) in relation to the decision in question.

Amendments—Child Support, Pensions and Social Security Act 2000, s 11.

24 Appeal to Child Support Commissioner

(1) Any person who is aggrieved by a decision of an appeal tribunal, and the Secretary of State, may appeal to a Child Support Commissioner on a question of law.

(1A) ...

(2) Where, on an appeal under this section, a Child Support Commissioner holds that the decision appealed against was wrong in law he shall set it aside.

(3) Where a decision is set aside under subsection (2), the Child Support Commissioner may –

  (a) if he can do so without making fresh or further findings of fact, give the decision which he considers should have been given by the appeal tribunal;
  (b) if he considers it expedient, make such findings and give such decision as he considers appropriate in the light of those findings; or

    (c) on an appeal by the Secretary of State, refer the case to an appeal tribunal with directions for its determination; or

    (d) on any other appeal, refer the case to the Secretary of State or, if he considers it appropriate, to an appeal tribunal with directions for its determination.

(4) The reference under subsection (3) to the Secretary of State shall, subject to any direction of the Child Support Commissioner, be to an officer of his, or a person providing him with services, who has taken no part in the decision originally appealed against.

(5) On a reference under subsection (3) to an appeal tribunal, the tribunal shall, subject to any direction of the Child Support Commissioner, consist of persons who were not members of the tribunal which gave the decision which has been appealed against.

(6) No appeal lies under this section without the leave –

    (a) of the person who constituted, or was the chairman of, the appeal tribunal when the decision appealed against was given or of such other person as may be determined in accordance with regulations made by the Lord Chancellor; or

    (b) subject to and in accordance with regulations so made, of a Child Support Commissioner.

(7) The Lord Chancellor may by regulation make provision as to the manner in which, and the time within which, appeals under this section are to be brought and applications for leave under this section are to be made.

(8) Where a question which would otherwise fall to be determined by the Secretary of State first arises in the course of an appeal to a Child Support Commissioner, he may, if he thinks fit, determine it even though it has not been considered by the Secretary of State.

(9) Before making any regulations under subsection (6) or (7), the Lord Chancellor shall consult the Lord Advocate.

Amendments—Child Support Act 1995, s 30(5), Sch 3, paras 2, 7(2), (3); Social Security Act 1998, s 86(1), Sch 7, para 30(1), (2), (3)(a)–(c), (4)–(6)(a), (b), (7).

25   Appeal from Child Support Commissioner on question of law

(1) An appeal on a question of law shall lie to the appropriate court from any decision of a Child Support Commissioner.

(2) No such appeal may be brought except –

    (a) with leave of the Child Support Commissioner who gave the decision or, where regulations made by the Lord Chancellor so provide, of a Child Support Commissioner selected in accordance with the regulations; or

    (b) if the Child Support Commissioner refuses leave, with the leave of the appropriate court.

(3) An application for leave to appeal under this section against a decision of a Child Support Commissioner ('the appeal decision') may only be made by –

    (a) a person who was a party to the proceedings in which the original decision, or appeal decision, was given;

    (b) the Secretary of State; or

    (c) any other person who is authorised to do so by regulations made by the Lord Chancellor.

(3A) The Child Support Commissioner to whom an application for leave to appeal under this section is made shall specify as the appropriate court either the Court of Appeal or the Court of Session.

(3B) In determining the appropriate court, the Child Support Commissioner shall have regard to the circumstances of the case, and in particular the convenience of the persons who may be parties to the appeal.

(4) In this section –

'appropriate court', except in subsections (3A) and (3B), means the court specified in accordance with those subsections; and
'original decision' means the decision to which the appeal decision in question relates.

(5) The Lord Chancellor may by regulation make provision with respect to –

(a) the manner in which and the time within which applications must be made to a Child Support Commissioner for leave under this section; and
(b) the procedure for dealing with such applications.

(6) (*applies to Scotland only*)

Amendments—Child Support Act 1995, s 30(5), Sch 3, paras 2, 8(1), (2).

26 Disputes about parentage

(1) Where a person who is alleged to be a parent of the child with respect to whom an application for a maintenance calculation has been made or treated as made ('the alleged parent') denies that he is one of the child's parents, the Secretary of State shall not make a maintenance calculation on the assumption that the alleged parent is one of the child's parents unless the case falls within one of those set out in subsection (2).

(2) The Cases are –

CASE A1

Where –

(a) the child is habitually resident in England and Wales;
(b) the Secretary of State is satisfied that the alleged parent was married to the child's mother at some time in the period beginning with the conception and ending with the birth of the child; and
(c) the child has not been adopted.

CASE A2

Where –

(a) the child is habitually resident in England and Wales;
(b) the alleged parent has been registered as father of the child under section 10 or 10A of the Births and Deaths Registration Act 1953, or in any register kept under section 13 (register of births and still-births) or section 44 (Register of Corrections Etc) of the Registration of Births, Deaths and Marriages (Scotland) Act 1965, or under Article 14 or 18(1)(b)(ii) of the Births and Deaths Registration (Northern Ireland) Order 1976; and
(c) the child has not subsequently been adopted.

CASE A3

Where the result of a scientific test (within the meaning of section 27A) taken by the alleged parent would be relevant to determining the child's parentage, and the alleged parent –

(a) refuses to take such a test; or

(b) has submitted to such a test, and it shows that there is no reasonable doubt that the alleged parent is a parent of the child.

Case A

Where the alleged parent is a parent of the child in question by virtue of having adopted him.

Case B

Where the alleged parent is a parent of the child in question by virtue of an order under section 30 of the Human Fertilisation and Embryology Act 1990 (parental orders in favour of gamete donors).

Case B1

Where the Secretary of State is satisfied that the alleged parent is a parent of the child in question by virtue of section 27 or 28 of that Act (meaning of 'mother' and of 'father' respectively).

Case C

Where –

(a) either –

(i) a declaration that the alleged parent is a parent of the child in question (or a declaration which has that effect) is in force under section 55A or 56 of the Family Law Act 1986 or Article 32 of the Matrimonial and Family Proceedings (Northern Ireland) Order 1989 (declarations of parentage); or

(ii) *(applies to Scotland only)*; and

(b) the child has not subsequently been adopted.

...

Case E

Where –

(a) the child is habitually resident in Scotland;

(b) the Secretary of State is satisfied that one or other of the presumptions set out in section 5(1) of the Law Reform (Parent and Child) (Scotland) Act 1986 applies; and

(c) the child has not subsequently been adopted.

Case F

Where –

(a) the alleged parent has been found, or adjudged, to be the father of the child in question –

(i) in proceedings before any court in England and Wales which are relevant proceedings for the purposes of section 12 of the Civil Evidence Act 1968 or in proceedings before any court in Northern Ireland which are relevant proceedings for the purposes of section 8 of the Civil Evidence Act (Northern Ireland) 1971; or

(ii) in affiliation proceedings before any court in the United Kingdom, (whether or not he offered any defence to the allegation of paternity) and that finding or adjudication still subsists; and

(b) the child has not subsequently been adopted.

(3) In this section –

'adopted' means adopted within the meaning of Part IV of the Adoption Act 1976 or, in relation to Scotland, Part IV of the Adoption (Scotland) Act 1978; and 'affiliation proceedings', in relation to Scotland, means any action of affiliation and aliment.

Amendments—Children (Northern Ireland Consequential Amendments) Order 1995, SI 1995/756; Social Security Act 1998, s 86(1), Sch 7, para 31(1), (2); Child Support, Pensions and Social Security Act 2000, ss 1(2), 15, Sch 3, para 11(8), Sch 8, para 12.

27 Applications for declaration of parentage under Family Law Act 1986

(1) This section applies where –

(a) an application for a maintenance calculation has been made (or is treated as having been made), or a maintenance calculation is in force, with respect to a person ('the alleged parent') who denies that he is a parent of a child with respect to whom the application or calculation was made or treated as made;

(b) the Secretary of State is not satisfied that the case falls within one of those set out in section 26(2); and

(c) the Secretary of State or the person with care makes an application for a declaration under section 55A of the Family Law Act 1986 as to whether or not the alleged parent is one of the child's parents.

(2) Where this section applies –

(a) if it is the person with care who makes the application, she shall be treated as having a sufficient personal interest for the purposes of subsection (3) of that section; and

(b) if it is the Secretary of State who makes the application, that subsection shall not apply.

(3) This section does not apply to Scotland.

Amendments—Child Support, Pensions and Social Security Act 2000, Sch 8, para 13.

27A Recovery of fees for scientific tests

(1) This section applies in any case where –

(a) an application for a maintenance calculation has been made or treated as made or a maintenance calculation is in force;

(b) scientific tests have been carried out (otherwise than under a direction or in response to a request) in relation to bodily samples obtained from a person who is alleged to be a parent of a child with respect to whom the application or calculation is made or, as the case may be, treated as made;

(c) the results of the tests do not exclude the alleged parent from being one of the child's parents; and

(d) one of the conditions set out in subsection (2) is satisfied.

(2) The conditions are that –

(a) the alleged parent does not deny that he is one of the child's parents;

(b) in proceedings under section 55A of the Family Law Act 1986, a court has made a declaration that the alleged parent is a parent of the child in question; or

(c) *(applies to Scotland only)*.

(3) In any case to which this section applies, any fee paid by the Secretary of State in connection with scientific tests may be recovered by him from the alleged parent as a debt due to the Crown.

(4) In this section –

'bodily sample' means a sample of bodily fluid or bodily tissue taken for the purpose of scientific tests;

'direction' means a direction given by a court under section 20 of the Family Law Reform Act 1969 (tests to determine paternity);

'request' means a request made by a court under section 70 of the Law Reform (Miscellaneous Provisions) (Scotland) Act 1990 (blood and other samples in civil proceedings); and

'scientific tests' means scientific tests made with the object of ascertaining the inheritable characteristics of bodily fluids or bodily tissue.

(5) Any sum recovered by the Secretary of State under this section shall be paid by him into the Consolidated Fund.

Amendments—Child Support Act 1995, s 21; Child Support, Pensions and Social Security Act 2000, s 1(2), Sch 3, para 11(9).

28 *(applies to Scotland only)*

Decisions and appeals dependent on other cases

28ZA   Decisions involving issues that arise on appeal in other cases

(1) This section applies where –

(a) a decision by the Secretary of State falls to be made under section 11, 12, 16 or 17 or with respect to a reduced benefit decision under section 46; and

(b) an appeal is pending against a decision given in relation to a different matter by a Child Support Commissioner or a court.

(2) If the Secretary of State considers it possible that the result of the appeal will be such that, if it were already determined, it would affect the decision in some way –

(a) he need not, except in such cases or circumstances as may be prescribed, make the decision while the appeal is pending;

(b) he may, in such cases or circumstances as may be prescribed, make the decision on such basis as may be prescribed.

(3) Where the Secretary of State acts in accordance with subsection (2)(b), following the determination of the appeal he shall if appropriate revise his decision (under section 16) in accordance with that determination.

(4) For the purposes of this section, an appeal against a decision is pending if –

(a) an appeal against the decision has been brought but not determined;

(b) an application for leave to appeal against the decision has been made but not determined; or

(c) in such circumstances as may be prescribed, an appeal against the decision has not been brought (or, as the case may be, an application for leave to appeal against the decision has not been made) but the time for doing so has not yet expired.

(5) In paragraphs (a), (b) and (c) of subsection (4), any reference to an appeal, or an application for leave to appeal, against a decision includes a reference to –

(a) an application for, or for leave to apply for, judicial review of the decision under section 31 of the Supreme Court Act 1981; or

(b) an application to the supervisory jurisdiction of the Court of Session in respect of the decision.

Amendments—Social Security Act 1998, s 43; Child Support, Pensions and Social Security Act 2000, s 1(2), Sch 3, para 11(11) – in force from a date to be appointed.

28ZB   Appeals involving issues that arise on appeal in other cases

(1) This section applies where –

(a) an appeal ('appeal A') in relation to a decision or the imposition of a requirement falling within section 20(1), is made to an appeal tribunal, or from an appeal tribunal to a Child Support Commissioner; and

(b) an appeal ('appeal B') is pending against a decision given in a different case by a Child Support Commissioner or a court.

(2) If the Secretary of State considers it possible that the result of appeal B will be such that, if it were already determined, it would affect the determination of appeal A, he may serve notice requiring the tribunal or Child Support Commissioner –

(a) not to determine appeal A but to refer it to him; or

(b) to deal with the appeal in accordance with subsection (4).

(3) Where appeal A is referred to the Secretary of State under subsection (2)(a), following the determination of appeal B and in accordance with that determination, he shall if appropriate –

(a) in a case where appeal A has not been determined by the tribunal, revise (under section 16) his decision which gave rise to that appeal; or

(b) in a case where appeal A has been determined by the tribunal, make a decision (under section 17) superseding the tribunal's decision.

(4) Where appeal A is to be dealt with in accordance with this subsection, the appeal tribunal or Child Support Commissioner shall either –

(a) stay appeal A until appeal B is determined; or

(b) if the tribunal or Child Support Commissioner considers it to be in the interests of the appellant to do so, determine appeal A as if –

(i) appeal B had already been determined; and

(ii) the issues arising on appeal B had been decided in the way that was most unfavourable to the appellant.

In this subsection 'the appellant' means the person who appealed or, as the case may be, first appealed against the decision or the imposition of the requirement mentioned in subsection (1)(a).

(5) Where the appeal tribunal or Child Support Commissioner acts in accordance with subsection (4)(b), following the determination of appeal B the Secretary of State shall, if appropriate, make a decision (under section 17) superseding the decision of the tribunal or Child Support Commissioner in accordance with that determination.

(6) For the purposes of this section, an appeal against a decision is pending if –

(a) an appeal against the decision has been brought but not determined;

(b) an application for leave to appeal against the decision has been made but not determined; or

(c) in such circumstances as may be prescribed, an appeal against the decision has not been brought (or, as the case may be, an application for leave to appeal against the decision has not been made) but the time for doing so has not yet expired.

(7) In this section –

(a) the reference in subsection (1)(a) to an appeal to a Child Support Commissioner includes a reference to an application for leave to appeal to a Child Support Commissioner; and

(b) any reference in paragraph (a), (b) or (c) of subsection (6) to an appeal, or to an application for leave to appeal, against a decision includes a reference to –

(i) an application for, or for leave to apply for, judicial review of the decision under section 31 of the Supreme Court Act 1981; or

(ii) an application to the supervisory jurisdiction of the Court of Session in respect of the decision.

(8) Regulations may make provision supplementing that made by this section.

Amendments—Social Security Act 1998, s 43; Child Support, Pensions and Social Security Act 2000, Sch 3, para 11(12) – in force from a date to be appointed.

Cases of error

28ZC   Restrictions on liability in certain cases of error

(1) Subject to subsection (2), this section applies where –

(a) the effect of the determination, whenever made, of an appeal to a Child Support Commissioner or the court ('the relevant determination') is that the adjudicating authority's decision out of which the appeal arose was erroneous in point of law; and

(b) after the date of the relevant determination a decision falls to be made by the Secretary of State in accordance with that determination (or would, apart from this section, fall to be so made) –

(i) with respect to an application for a maintenance calculation (made after the commencement date) or one treated as having been so made, or under section 46 as to the reduction of benefit;

(ii) as to whether to revise, under section 16, any decision (made after the commencement date) referred to in section 16(1A); or

(iii) on an application under section 17 (made after the commencement date) for any decision (made after the commencement date) referred to in section 17(1).

(2) This section does not apply where the decision of the Secretary of State mentioned in subsection (1)(b) –

(a) is one which, but for section 28ZA(2)(a), would have been made before the date of the relevant determination; or

(b) is one made in pursuance of section 28ZB(3) or (5).

(3) In so far as the decision relates to a person's liability or the reduction of a person's benefit in respect of a period before the date of the relevant determination, it shall be made as if the adjudicating authority's decision had been found by the Commissioner or court not to have been erroneous in point of law.

(4) Subsection (1)(a) shall be read as including a case where –

    (a) the effect of the relevant determination is that part or all of a purported regulation or order is invalid; and

    (b) the error of law made by the adjudicating authority was to act on the basis that the purported regulation or order (or the part held to be invalid) was valid.

(5) It is immaterial for the purposes of subsection (1) –

    (a) where such a decision as is mentioned in paragraph (b)(i) falls to be made; or

    (b) where such a decision as is mentioned in paragraph (b)(ii) or (iii) falls to be made on an application under section 16 or (as the case may be) section 17,

whether the application was made before or after the date of the relevant determination.

(6) In this section –

'adjudicating authority' means the Secretary of State, or a child support officer or, in the case of a decision made on a referral under section 28D(1)(b), an appeal tribunal;

'the commencement date' means the date of the coming into force of section 44 of the Social Security Act 1998; and

'the court' means the High Court, the Court of Appeal, the Court of Session, the High Court or Court of Appeal in Northern Ireland, the House of Lords or the Court of Justice of the European Community.

(7) The date of the relevant determination shall, in prescribed cases, be determined for the purposes of this section in accordance with any regulation made for that purpose.

(8) Regulations made under subsection (7) may include provision –

    (a) for a determination of a higher court to be treated as if it had been made on the date of a determination of a lower court or a Child Support Commissioner; or

    (b) for a determination of a lower court or a Child Support Commissioner to be treated as if it had been made on the date of a determination of a higher court.

Amendments—Social Security Act 1998, s 44; Child Support, Pensions and Social Security Act 2000, Sch 3, para 11(13) – in force from a date to be appointed.

28ZD Correction of errors and setting aside of decisions

(1) Regulations may make provision with respect to –

    (a) the correction of accidental errors in any decision or record of a decision given under this Act; and

    (b) the setting aside of any such decision in a case where it appears just to set the decision aside on the ground that –

        (i) a document relating to the proceedings in which the decision was given was not sent to, or was not received at an appropriate time by, a party to the proceedings or a party's representative or was not received at an appropriate time by the body or person who gave the decision; or

        (ii) a party to the proceedings or a party's representative was not present at a hearing related to the proceedings.

(2) Nothing in subsection (1) shall be construed as derogating from any power to correct errors or set aside decisions which is exercisable apart from regulation made by virtue of that subsection.

Amendments—Social Security Act 1998, s 44.

Variations

28A Application for variation of usual rules for calculating maintenance

(1) Where an application for a maintenance calculation is made under section 4 or 7, or treated as made under section 6, the person with care or the non-resident parent or (in the case of an application under section 7) either of them or the child concerned may apply to the Secretary of State for the rules by which the calculation is made to be varied in accordance with this Act.

(2) Such an application is referred to in this Act as an 'application for a variation'.

(3) An application for a variation may be made at any time before the Secretary of State has reached a decision (under section 11 or 12(1)) on the application for a maintenance calculation (or the application treated as having been made under section 6).

(4) A person who applies for a variation –

(a) need not make the application in writing unless the Secretary of State directs in any case that he must; and
(b) must say upon what grounds the application is made.

(5) In other respects an application for a variation is to be made in such manner as may be prescribed.

(6) Schedule 4A has effect in relation to applications for a variation.

Amendments—Child Support, Pensions and Social Security Act 2000, s 5(2) – in force from 10 November 2000 for the purpose only of making regulations.

28B Preliminary consideration of applications

(1) Where an application for a variation has been duly made to the Secretary of State, he may give it a preliminary consideration.

(2) Where he does so he may, on completing the preliminary consideration, reject the application (and proceed to make his decision on the application for a maintenance calculation without any variation) if it appears to him –

(a) that there are no grounds on which he could agree to a variation;
(b) that he has insufficient information to make a decision on the application for the maintenance calculation under section 11 (apart from any information needed in relation to the application for a variation), and therefore that his decision would be made under section 12(1); or
(c) that other prescribed circumstances apply.

Amendments—Child Support, Pensions and Social Security Act 2000, s 5(2) – in force from 10 November 2000 for the purpose only of making regulations.

28C Imposition of a regular payments condition

(1) Where –

(a) an application for a variation is made by the non-resident parent; and
(b) the Secretary of State makes an interim maintenance decision,

the Secretary of State may also, if he has completed his preliminary consideration (under section 28B) of the application for a variation and has not rejected it under that section, impose on the non-resident parent one of the conditions mentioned in subsection (2) (a 'regular payments condition').

(2) The conditions are that –

    (a) the non-resident parent must make the payments of child support maintenance specified in the interim maintenance decision;

    (b) the non-resident parent must make such lesser payments of child support maintenance as may be determined in accordance with regulations made by the Secretary of State.

(3) Where the Secretary of State imposes a regular payments condition, he shall give written notice of the imposition of the condition and of the effect of failure to comply with it to –

    (a) the non-resident parent;

    (b) all the persons with care concerned; and

    (c) if the application for the maintenance calculation was made under section 7, the child who made the application.

(4) A regular payments condition shall cease to have effect –

    (a) when the Secretary of State has made a decision on the application for a maintenance calculation under section 11 (whether he agrees to a variation or not);

    (b) on the withdrawal of the application for a variation.

(5) Where a non-resident parent has failed to comply with a regular payments condition, the Secretary of State may in prescribed circumstances refuse to consider the application for a variation, and instead reach his decision under section 11 as if no such application had been made.

(6) The question whether a non-resident parent has failed to comply with a regular payments condition is to be determined by the Secretary of State.

(7) Where the Secretary of State determines that a non-resident parent has failed to comply with a regular payments condition he shall give written notice of his determination to –

    (a) that parent;

    (b) all the persons with care concerned; and

    (c) if the application for the maintenance calculation was made under section 7, the child who made the application.

Amendments—Child Support, Pensions and Social Security Act 2000, s 5(2) – in force from 10 November 2000 for the purpose only of making regulations.

28D Determination of applications

(1) Where an application for a variation has not failed, the Secretary of State shall, in accordance with the relevant provisions of, or made under, this Act –

    (a) either agree or not to a variation, and make a decision under section 11 or 12(1); or

    (b) refer the application to an appeal tribunal for the tribunal to determine what variation, if any, is to be made.

(2) For the purposes of subsection (1), an application for a variation has failed if –

    (a) it has been withdrawn; or

    (b) the Secretary of State has rejected it on completing a preliminary consideration under section 28B; or

(c) the Secretary of State has refused to consider it under section 28C(5).

(3) In dealing with an application for a variation which has been referred to it under subsection (1)(b), an appeal tribunal shall have the same powers, and be subject to the same duties, as would the Secretary of State if he were dealing with the application.

Amendments—Child Support Act 1995, s 4; Social Security Act 1998, s 86(1), Sch 7, para 36; Child Support, Pensions and Social Security Act 2000, s 5(3) – in force from 10 November 2000 for the purpose only of making regulations.

28E   Matters to be taken into account

(1) In determining whether to agree to a variation, the Secretary of State shall have regard both to the general principles set out in subsection (2) and to such other considerations as may be prescribed.

(2) The general principles are that –

> (a) parents should be responsible for maintaining their children whenever they can afford to do so;
> (b) where a parent has more than one child, his obligation to maintain any one of them should be no less of an obligation than his obligation to maintain any other of them.

(3) In determining whether to agree to a variation, the Secretary of State shall take into account any representations made to him –

> (a) by the person with care or non-resident parent concerned; or
> (b) *(applies to Scotland only)*

(4) In determining whether to agree to a variation, no account shall be taken of the fact that –

> (a) any part of the income of the person with care concerned is, or would be if the Secretary of State agreed to a variation, derived from any benefit; or
> (b) some or all of any child support maintenance might be taken into account in any manner in relation to any entitlement to benefit.

(5) In this section 'benefit' has such meaning as may be prescribed.

Amendments—Child Support Act 1995, s 5; Child Support, Pensions and Social Security Act 2000, s 5(4), Sch 3, para 11(2) – in force from 10 November 2000 for the purpose only of making regulations.

28F   Agreement to a variation

(1) The Secretary of State may agree to a variation if –

> (a) he is satisfied that the case is one which falls within one or more of the cases set out in Part I of Schedule 4B or in regulations made under that Part; and
> (b) it is his opinion that, in all the circumstances of the case, it would be just and equitable to agree to a variation.

(2) In considering whether it would be just and equitable in any case to agree to a variation, the Secretary of State –

> (a) must have regard, in particular, to the welfare of any child likely to be affected if he did agree to a variation; and
> (b) must, or as the case may be must not, take any prescribed factors into account, or must take them into account (or not) in prescribed circumstances.

(3) The Secretary of State shall not agree to a variation (and shall proceed to make his decision on the application for a maintenance calculation without any variation) if he is satisfied that –

    (a) he has insufficient information to make a decision on the application for the maintenance calculation under section 11, and therefore that his decision would be made under section 12(1); or

    (b) other prescribed circumstances apply.

(4) Where the Secretary of State agrees to a variation, he shall –

    (a) determine the basis on which the amount of child support maintenance is to be calculated in response to the application for a maintenance calculation (including an application treated as having been made); and

    (b) make a decision under section 11 on that basis.

(5) If the Secretary of State has made an interim maintenance decision, it is to be treated as having been replaced by his decision under section 11, and except in prescribed circumstances any appeal connected with it (under section 20) shall lapse.

(6) In determining whether or not to agree to a variation, the Secretary of State shall comply with regulations made under Part II of Schedule 4B.

Amendments—Child Support, Pensions and Social Security Act 2000, s 5(5) – in force from 10 November 2000 for the purpose only of making regulations.

28G Variations: revision and supersession

(1) An application for a variation may also be made when a maintenance calculation is in force.

(2) The Secretary of State may by regulations provide for –

    (a) sections 16, 17 and 20; and

    (b) sections 28A to 28F and Schedules 4A and 4B,

to apply with prescribed modifications in relation to such applications.

(3) The Secretary of State may by regulations provide that, in prescribed cases (or except in prescribed cases), a decision under section 17 made otherwise than pursuant to an application for a variation may be made on the basis of a variation agreed to for the purposes of an earlier decision without a new application for a variation having to be made.

Amendments—Child Support, Pensions and Social Security Act 2000, s 7.

28H, 28I   ...

Amendments—Child Support, Pensions and Social Security Act 2000, Sch 3, para 11(14) – in force from a date to be appointed.

Voluntary payments

28J Voluntary payments

(1) This section applies where –

    (a) a person has applied for a maintenance calculation under section 4(1) or 7(1), or is treated as having applied for one by virtue of section 6;

(b) the Secretary of State has neither made a decision under section 11 or 12 on the application, nor decided not to make a maintenance calculation; and

(c) the non-resident parent makes a voluntary payment.

(2) A 'voluntary payment' is a payment –

(a) on account of child support maintenance which the non-resident parent expects to become liable to pay following the determination of the application (whether or not the amount of the payment is based on any estimate of his potential liability which the Secretary of State has agreed to give); and

(b) made before the maintenance calculation has been notified to the non-resident parent or (as the case may be) before the Secretary of State has notified the non-resident parent that he has decided not to make a maintenance calculation.

(3) In such circumstances and to such extent as may be prescribed –

(a) the voluntary payment may be set off against arrears of child support maintenance which accrued by virtue of the maintenance calculation taking effect on a date earlier than that on which it was notified to the non-resident parent;

(b) the amount payable under a maintenance calculation may be adjusted to take account of the voluntary payment.

(4) A voluntary payment shall be made to the Secretary of State unless he agrees, on such conditions as he may specify, that it may be made to the person with care, or to or through another person.

(5) The Secretary of State may by regulations make provision as to voluntary payments, and the regulations may in particular –

(a) prescribe what payments or descriptions of payment are, or are not, to count as 'voluntary payments';

(b) prescribe the extent to which and circumstances in which a payment, or a payment of a prescribed description, counts.

Amendments—Child Support, Pensions and Social Security Act 2000, s 20 – in force from 10 November 2000 for the purpose only of making regulations.

Collection and enforcement

29 Collection of child support maintenance

(1) The Secretary of State may arrange for the collection of any child support maintenance payable in accordance with a maintenance calculation where –

(a) the calculation is made by virtue of section 6; or

(b) an application has been made to the Secretary of State under section 4(2) or 7(3) for him to arrange for its collection.

(2) Where a maintenance calculation is made under this Act, payments of child support maintenance under the calculation shall be made in accordance with regulations made by the Secretary of State.

(3) The regulation may, in particular, make provision –

(a) for payments of child support maintenance to be made –
   (i) to the person caring for the child or children in question;
   (ii) to, or through, the Secretary of State; or

    (iii) to, or through, such other person as the Secretary of State may, from time to time, specify;

  (b) as to the method by which payments of child support maintenance are to be made;

  (c) as to the intervals at which such payments are to be made;

  (d) as to the method and timing of the transmission of payments which are made, to or through the Secretary of State or any other person, in accordance with the regulations;

  (e) empowering the Secretary of State to direct any person liable to make payments in accordance with the calculation –

    (i) to make them by standing order or by any other method which requires one person to give his authority for payments to be made from an account of his to an account of another's on specific dates during the period for which the authority is in force and without the need for any further authority from him;

    (ii) to open an account from which payments under the calculation may be made in accordance with the method of payment which that person is obliged to adopt;

  (f) providing for the making of representations with respect to matters with which the regulations are concerned.

Amendments—Child Support, Pensions and Social Security Act 2000, s 1 (2) – in force from a date to be appointed.

30 Collection and enforcement of other forms of maintenance

(1) Where the Secretary of State is arranging for the collection of any payments under section 29 or subsection (2), he may also arrange for the collection of any periodical payments, or secured periodical payments, of a prescribed kind which are payable to or for the benefit of any person who falls within a prescribed category.

(2) The Secretary of State may, except in prescribed cases, arrange for the collection of any periodical payments, or secured periodical payments, of a prescribed kind which are payable for the benefit of a child even though he is not arranging for the collection of child support maintenance with respect to that child.

(3) Where –

  (a) the Secretary of State is arranging, under this Act, for the collection of different payments ('the payments') from the same non-resident parent;

  (b) an amount is collected by the Secretary of State from the non-resident parent which is less than the total amount due in respect of the payments; and

  (c) the non-resident parent has not stipulated how that amount is to be allocated by the Secretary of State as between the payments,

the Secretary of State may allocate that amount as he sees fit.

(4) In relation to England and Wales, the Secretary of State may by regulation make provision for sections 29 and 31 to 40 to apply, with such modifications (if any) as he considers necessary or expedient, for the purpose of enabling him to enforce any obligation to pay any amount which he is authorised to collect under this section.

(5) *(applies to Scotland only)*

(5A) Regulations made under subsection (1) or (2) prescribing payments which may be collected by the Secretary of State may make provision for the payment to him by such person or persons as may be prescribed of such fees as may be prescribed.

Amendments—Child Support, Pensions and Social Security Act 2000, Sch 3, para 11(2), (15) – in force from a date to be appointed.

31   Deduction from earnings orders

(1) This section applies where any person ('the liable person') is liable to make payments of child support maintenance.

(2) The Secretary of State may make an order ('a deduction from earnings order') against a liable person to secure the payment of any amount due under the maintenance calculation in question.

(3) A deduction from earnings order may be made so as to secure the payment of –

  (a) arrears of child support maintenance payable under the calculation;
  (b) amounts of child support maintenance which will become due under the calculation; or
  (c) both such arrears and such future amounts.

(4) A deduction from earnings order –

  (a) shall be expressed to be directed at a person ('the employer') who has the liable person in his employment; and
  (b) shall have effect from such date as may be specified in the order.

(5) A deduction from earnings order shall operate as an instruction to the employer to –

  (a) make deductions from the liable person's earnings; and
  (b) pay the amounts deducted to the Secretary of State.

(6) The Secretary of State shall serve a copy of any deduction from earnings order which he makes under this section on –

  (a) the person who appears to the Secretary of State to have the liable person in question in his employment; and
  (b) the liable person.

(7) Where –

  (a) a deduction from earnings order has been made; and
  (b) a copy of the order has been served on the liable person's employer,

it shall be the duty of that employer to comply with the order; but he shall not be under any liability for non-compliance before the end of the period of 7 days beginning with the date on which the copy was served on him.

(8) In this section and in section 32 'earnings' has such meaning as may be prescribed.

Amendments—Child Support, Pensions and Social Security Act 2000, s 1(2) – in force from a date to be appointed.

32   Regulations about deduction from earnings orders

(1) The Secretary of State may by regulation make provision with respect to deduction from earnings orders.

(2) The regulation may, in particular, make provision –

  (a) as to the circumstances in which one person is to be treated as employed by another;
  (b) requiring any deduction from earnings under an order to be made in the prescribed manner;

(bb) for the amount or amounts which are to be deducted from the liable person's earnings not to exceed a prescribed proportion of his earnings (as determined by the employer);

(c) requiring an order to specify the amount or amounts to which the order relates and the amount or amounts which are to be deducted from the liable person's earnings in order to meet his liabilities under the maintenance calculation in question;

(d) requiring the intervals between deductions to be made under an order to be specified in the order;

(e) as to the payment of sums deducted under an order to the Secretary of State;

(f) allowing the person who deducts and pays any amount under an order to deduct from the liable person's earnings a prescribed sum towards his administrative costs;

(g) with respect to the notification to be given to the liable person of amounts deducted, and amounts paid, under the order;

(h) requiring any person on whom a copy of an order is served to notify the Secretary of State in the prescribed manner and within a prescribed period if he does not have the liable person in his employment or if the liable person ceases to be in his employment;

(i) as to the operation of an order where the liable person is in the employment of the Crown;

(j) for the variation of orders;

(k) similar to that made by section 31(7), in relation to any variation of an order;

(l) for an order to lapse when the employer concerned ceases to have the liable person in his employment;

(m) as to the revival of an order in such circumstances as may be prescribed;

(n) allowing or requiring an order to be discharged;

(o) as to the giving of notice by the Secretary of State to the employer concerned that an order has lapsed or has ceased to have effect.

(3) The regulation may include provision that while a deduction from earnings order is in force –

(a) the liable person shall from time to time notify the Secretary of State, in the prescribed manner and within a prescribed period, of each occasion on which he leaves any employment or becomes employed, or re-employed, and shall include in such a notification a statement of his earnings and expected earnings from the employment concerned and of such other matters as may be prescribed;

(b) any person who becomes the liable person's employer and knows that the order is in force shall notify the Secretary of State, in the prescribed manner and within a prescribed period, that he is the liable person's employer, and shall include in such a notification a statement of the liable person's earnings and expected earnings from the employment concerned and of such other matters as may be prescribed.

(4) The regulation may include provision with respect to the priority as between a deduction from earnings order and –

(a) any other deduction from earnings order;

(b) any order under any other enactment relating to England and Wales which provides for deductions from the liable person's earnings;

(c) any diligence against earnings.

(5) The regulation may include a provision that a liable person may appeal to a magistrates' court (or in Scotland to the sheriff) if he is aggrieved by the making of a deduction from earnings order against him, or by the terms of any such order, or there is a

dispute as to whether payments constitute earnings or as to any other prescribed matter relating to the order.

(6) On an appeal under subsection (5) the court or (as the case may be) the sheriff shall not question the maintenance calculation by reference to which the deduction from earnings order was made.

(7) Regulations made by virtue of subsection (5) may include provision as to the powers of a magistrates' court, or in Scotland of the sheriff, in relation to an appeal (which may include provision as to the quashing of a deduction from earnings order or the variation of the terms of such an order).

(8) If any person fails to comply with the requirements of a deduction from earnings order, or with any regulation under this section which is designated for the purposes of this subsection, he shall be guilty of an offence.

(9) In subsection (8) 'designated' means designated by the regulation.

(10) It shall be a defence for a person charged with an offence under subsection (8) to prove that he took all reasonable steps to comply with the requirements in question.

(11) Any person guilty of an offence under subsection (8) shall be liable on summary conviction to a fine not exceeding level two on the standard scale.

Amendments—Child Support, Pensions and Social Security Act 2000, s 1(2), Sch 3, para 11(16) – in force from a date to be appointed.

33   Liability orders

(1) This section applies where –

    (a) a person who is liable to make payments of child support maintenance ('the liable person') fails to make one or more of those payments; and

    (b) it appears to the Secretary of State that –

        (i)   it is inappropriate to make a deduction from earnings order against him (because, for example, he is not employed); or

        (ii) although such an order has been made against him, it has proved ineffective as a means of securing that payments are made in accordance with the maintenance calculation in question.

(2) The Secretary of State may apply to a magistrates' court or, in Scotland, to the sheriff for an order ('a liability order') against the liable person.

(3) Where the Secretary of State applies for a liability order, the magistrates' court or (as the case may be) sheriff shall make the order if satisfied that the payments in question have become payable by the liable person and have not been paid.

(4) On an application under subsection (2), the court or (as the case may be) the sheriff shall not question the maintenance calculation under which the payments of child support maintenance fell to be made.

(5) If the Secretary of State designates a liability order for the purposes of this subsection it shall be treated as a judgment entered in a county court for the purposes of section 73 of the County Courts Act 1984 (register of judgments and orders).

(6) Where regulations have been made under section 29(3)(a) –

    (a) the liable person fails to make a payment (for the purposes of subsection (1)(a) of this section); and

    (b) a payment is not paid (for the purposes of subsection (3)), unless the payment is made to, or through, the person specified in or by virtue of those regulations for the case of the liable person in question.

Amendments—Child Support Act 1995, s 30(5), Sch 3, para 10; Child Support, Pensions and Social Security Act 2000, s 1(2), Sch 3, para 11(17).

34 Regulations about liability orders

(1) The Secretary of State may make regulation in relation to England and Wales –

(a) prescribing the procedure to be followed in dealing with an application by the Secretary of State for a liability order;

(b) prescribing the form and contents of a liability order; and

(c) providing that where a magistrates' court has made a liability order, the person against whom it is made shall, during such time as the amount in respect of which the order was made remains wholly or partly unpaid, be under a duty to supply relevant information to the Secretary of State.

(2) In subsection (1) 'relevant information' means any information of a prescribed description which is in the possession of the liable person and which the Secretary of State has asked him to supply.

35 Enforcement of liability orders by distress

(1) Where a liability order has been made against a person ('the liable person'), the Secretary of State may levy the appropriate amount by distress and sale of the liable person's goods.

(2) In subsection (1), 'the appropriate amount' means the aggregate of –

(a) the amount in respect of which the order was made, to the extent that it remains unpaid; and

(b) an amount, determined in such manner as may be prescribed, in respect of the charges connected with the distress.

(3) The Secretary of State may, in exercising his powers under subsection (1) against the liable person's goods, seize –

(a) any of the liable person's goods except –
  (i) such tools, books, vehicles and other items of equipment as are necessary to him for use personally by him in his employment, business or vocation;
  (ii) such clothing, bedding, furniture, household equipment and provisions as are necessary for satisfying his basic domestic needs; and

(b) any money, banknotes, bills of exchange, promissory notes, bonds, specialties or securities for money belonging to the liable person.

(4) For the purposes of subsection (3), the liable person's domestic needs shall be taken to include those of any member of his family with whom he resides.

(5) No person levying a distress under this section shall be taken to be a trespasser –

(a) on that account; or

(b) from the beginning, on account of any subsequent irregularity in levying the distress.

(6) A person sustaining special damage by reason of any irregularity in levying a distress under this section may recover full satisfaction for the damage (and no more) by proceedings in trespass or otherwise.

(7) The Secretary of State may make regulation supplementing the provisions of this section.

(8) The regulation may, in particular –

(a) provide that a distress under this section may be levied anywhere in England and Wales;

(b) provide that such a distress shall not be deemed unlawful on account of any defect or want of form in the liability order;

(c) provide for an appeal to a magistrates' court by any person aggrieved by the levying of, or an attempt to levy, a distress under this section;

(d) make provision as to the powers of the court on an appeal (which may include provision as to the discharge of goods distrained or the payment of compensation in respect of goods distrained and sold).

36 Enforcement in county courts

(1) Where a liability order has been made against a person, the amount in respect of which the order was made, to the extent that it remains unpaid, shall, if a county court so orders, be recoverable by means of garnishee proceedings or a charging order, as if it were payable under a county court order.

(2) In subsection (1) 'charging order' has the same meaning as in section 1 of the Charging Orders Act 1979.

37, 38 *(apply to Scotland only)*

39 Liability orders: enforcement throughout United Kingdom

(1) The Secretary of State may by regulation provide for –

(a) any liability order made by a court in England and Wales; or

(b) any corresponding order made by a court in Northern Ireland,

to be enforced in Scotland as if it had been made by the Sheriff.

(2) The power conferred on the Court of Session by section 32 of the Sheriff Courts (Scotland) Act 1971 (power of Court of Session to regulate civil procedure in the sheriff court) shall extend to making provision for the registration in the sheriff court for enforcement of any such order as is referred to in subsection (1).

(3) The Secretary of State may by regulation make provision for, or in connection with, the enforcement in England and Wales of –

(a) any liability order made by the sheriff in Scotland; or

(b) any corresponding order made by a court in Northern Ireland,

as if it had been made by a magistrates' court in England and Wales.

(4) Regulations under subsection (3) may, in particular, make provision for the registration of any such order as is referred to in that subsection in connection with its enforcement in England and Wales.

39A Commitment to prison and disqualification from driving

(1) Where the Secretary of State has sought –

(a) in England and Wales to levy an amount by distress under this Act; or

(b) to recover an amount by virtue of section 36 or 38,

and that amount, or any portion of it, remains unpaid he may apply to the court under this section.

(2) An application under this section is for whichever the court considers appropriate in all the circumstances of –

(a) the issue of a warrant committing the liable person to prison; or
(b) an order for him to be disqualified from holding or obtaining a driving licence.

(3) On any such application the court shall (in the presence of the liable person) inquire as to –

(a) whether he needs a driving licence to earn his living;
(b) his means; and
(c) whether there has been wilful refusal or culpable neglect on his part.

(4) The Secretary of State may make representations to the court as to whether he thinks it more appropriate to commit the liable person to prison or to disqualify him from holding or obtaining a driving licence; and the liable person may reply to those representations.

(5) In this section and section 40B, 'driving licence' means a licence to drive a motor vehicle granted under Part III of the Road Traffic Act 1988.

(6) In this section 'the court' means –

(a) in England and Wales, a magistrates' court;
(b) in Scotland, the sheriff.

Amendments—Child Support, Pensions and Social Security Act 2000, s 16(1).

40 Commitment to prison

(1), (2) ...

(3) If, but only if, the court is of the opinion that there has been wilful refusal or culpable neglect on the part of the liable person it may –

(a) issue a warrant of commitment against him; or
(b) fix a term of imprisonment and postpone the issue of the warrant until such time and on such conditions (if any) as it thinks just.

(4) Any such warrant –

(a) shall be made in respect of an amount equal to the aggregate of –
   (i) the amount mentioned in section 35(1) or so much of it as remains outstanding; and
   (ii) an amount (determined in accordance with regulations made by the Secretary of State) in respect of the costs of commitment; and
(b) shall state that amount.

(5) No warrant may be issued under this section against a person who is under the age of 18.

(6) A warrant issued under this section shall order the liable person –

(a) to be imprisoned for a specified period; but
(b) to be released (unless he is in custody for some other reason) on payment of the amount stated in the warrant.

(7) The maximum period of imprisonment which may be imposed by virtue of subsection (6) shall be calculated in accordance with Schedule 4 to the Magistrates' Courts Act 1980 (maximum periods of imprisonment in default of payment) but shall not exceed six weeks.

(8) The Secretary of State may by regulation make provision for the period of imprisonment specified in any warrant issued under this section to be reduced where there is part payment of the amount in respect of which the warrant was issued.

(9) A warrant issued under this section may be directed to such person or persons as the court issuing it thinks fit.

(10) Section 80 of the Magistrates' Courts Act 1980 (application of money found on defaulter) shall apply in relation to a warrant issued under this section against a liable person as it applies in relation to the enforcement of a sum mentioned in subsection (1) of that section.

(11) The Secretary of State may by regulation make provision –

- (a) as to the form of any warrant issued under this section;
- (b) allowing an application under this section to be renewed where no warrant is issued or term of imprisonment is fixed;
- (c) that a statement in writing to the effect that wages of any amount have been paid to the liable person during any period, purporting to be signed by or on behalf of his employer, shall be evidence of the facts stated;
- (d) that, for the purposes of enabling an inquiry to be made as to the liable person's conduct and means, a justice of the peace may issue a summons to him to appear before a magistrates' court and (if he does not obey) may issue a warrant for his arrest;
- (e) that for the purpose of enabling such an inquiry, a justice of the peace may issue a warrant for the liable person's arrest without issuing a summons;
- (f) as to the execution of a warrant for arrest.

(12) This section does not apply to Scotland.

Amendments—Child Support, Pensions and Social Security Act 2000, ss 16(2), 17(1), Sch 9, Pt I.

40A *(applies to Scotland only)*

40B Disqualification from driving: further provision

(1) If, but only if, the court is of the opinion that there has been wilful refusal or culpable neglect on the part of the liable person, it may –

- (a) order him to be disqualified, for such period specified in the order but not exceeding two years as it thinks fit, from holding or obtaining a driving licence (a 'disqualification order'); or
- (b) make a disqualification order but suspend its operation until such time and on such conditions (if any) as it thinks just.

(2) The court may not take action under both section 40 and this section.

(3) A disqualification order must state the amount in respect of which it is made, which is to be the aggregate of –

- (a) the amount mentioned in section 35(1), or so much of it as remains outstanding; and

(b) an amount (determined in accordance with regulations made by the Secretary of State) in respect of the costs of the application under section 39A.

(4) A court which makes a disqualification order shall require the person to whom it relates to produce any driving licence held by him, and its counterpart (within the meaning of section 108(1) of the Road Traffic Act 1988).

(5) On an application by the Secretary of State or the liable person, the court –

(a) may make an order substituting a shorter period of disqualification, or make an order revoking the disqualification order, if part of the amount referred to in subsection (3) (the 'amount due') is paid to any person authorised to receive it; and

(b) must make an order revoking the disqualification order if all of the amount due is so paid.

(6) The Secretary of State may make representations to the court as to the amount which should be paid before it would be appropriate to make an order revoking the disqualification order under subsection (5)(a), and the person liable may reply to those representations.

(7) The Secretary of State may make a further application under section 39A if the amount due has not been paid in full when the period of disqualification specified in the disqualification order expires.

(8) Where a court –

(a) makes a disqualification order;

(b) makes an order under subsection (5); or

(c) allows an appeal against a disqualification order,

it shall send notice of that fact to the Secretary of State; and the notice shall contain such particulars and be sent in such manner and to such address as the Secretary of State may determine.

(9) Where a court makes a disqualification order, it shall also send the driving licence and its counterpart, on their being produced to the court, to the Secretary of State at such address as he may determine.

(10) Section 80 of the Magistrates' Courts Act 1980 (application of money found on defaulter) shall apply in relation to a disqualification order under this section in relation to a liable person as it applies in relation to the enforcement of a sum mentioned in subsection (1) of that section.

(11) The Secretary of State may by regulations make provision in relation to disqualification orders corresponding to the provision he may make under section 40(11).

(12) *(applies to Scotland only)*

Amendments—Child Support, Pensions and Social Security Act 2000, s 16(3) – in force from a date to be appointed.

41 Arrears of child support maintenance

(1) This section applies where –

(a) the Secretary of State is authorised under section 4, 6 or 7 to recover child support maintenance payable by a non-resident parent in accordance with the maintenance calculation; and

(b) the non-resident parent has failed to make one or more payments of child support maintenance due from him in accordance with that calculation.

(2) Where the Secretary of State recovers any such arrears he may, in such circumstances as may be prescribed and to such extent as may be prescribed, retain them if he is satisfied that the amount of any benefit paid to or in respect of the person with care of the child or children in question would have been less had the non-resident parent made the payment or payments of child support maintenance in question.

(2A) In determining for the purposes of subsection (2) whether the amount of any benefit paid would have been less at any time than the amount which was paid at that time, in a case where the maintenance calculation had effect from a date earlier than that on which it was made, the calculation shall be taken to have been in force at that time.

(3)–(5) ...

(6) Any sums retained by the Secretary of State by virtue of this section shall be paid by him into the Consolidated Fund.

Amendments—Child Support Act 1995, s 30(3), Sch 3, para 11; Child Support, Pensions and Social Security Act 2000, ss 1(2), 18(1), Sch 3, para 11(2) – in force from 10 November 2000 for the purpose only of making regulations.

41A   Penalty payments

(1) The Secretary of State may by regulations make provision for the payment to him by non-resident parents who are in arrears with payments of child support maintenance of penalty payments determined in accordance with the regulations.

(2) The amount of a penalty payment in respect of any week may not exceed 25% of the amount of child support maintenance payable for that week, but otherwise is to be determined by the Secretary of State.

(3) The liability of a non-resident parent to make a penalty payment does not affect his liability to pay the arrears of child support maintenance concerned.

(4) Regulations under subsection (1) may, in particular, make provision –

(a) as to the time at which a penalty payment is to be payable;
(b) for the Secretary of State to waive a penalty payment, or part of it.

(5) The provisions of this Act with respect to –

(a) the collection of child support maintenance;
(b) the enforcement of an obligation to pay child support maintenance,

apply equally (with any necessary modifications) to penalty payments payable by virtue of regulations under this section.

(6) The Secretary of State shall pay penalty payments received by him into the Consolidated Fund.

Amendments—Child Support, Pensions and Social Security Act 2000, s 18(2) – in force from 10 November 2000 for the purpose only of making regulations.

41B   Repayment of overpaid child support maintenance

(1) This section applies where it appears to the Secretary of State that a non-resident parent has made a payment by way of child support maintenance which amounts to an overpayment by him of that maintenance and that –

(a) it would not be possible for the non-resident parent to recover the amount of the overpayment by way of an adjustment of the amount payable under a maintenance calculation; or

(b) it would be inappropriate to rely on an adjustment of the amount payable under a maintenance calculation as the means of enabling the non-resident parent to recover the amount of the overpayment.

(1A) This section also applies where the non-resident parent has made a voluntary payment and it appears to the Secretary of State –

(a) that he is not liable to pay child support maintenance; or

(b) that he is liable, but some or all of the payment amounts to an overpayment,

and, in a case falling within paragraph (b), it also appears to him that subsection (1)(a) or (b) applies.

(2) The Secretary of State may make such payment to the non-resident parent by way of reimbursement, or partial reimbursement, of the overpayment as the Secretary of State considers appropriate.

(3) Where the Secretary of State has made a payment under this section he may, in such circumstances as may be prescribed, require the relevant person to pay him the whole, or a specified proportion, of the amount of that payment.

(4) Any such requirement shall be imposed by giving the relevant person a written demand for the amount which the Secretary of State wishes to recover from him.

(5) Any sum which a person is required to pay to the Secretary of State under this section shall be recoverable from him by the Secretary of State as a debt due to the Crown.

(6) The Secretary of State may by regulation make provision in relation to any case in which –

(a) one or more overpayments of child support maintenance are being reimbursed to the Secretary of State by the relevant person; and

(b) child support maintenance has continued to be payable by the non-resident parent concerned to the person with care concerned, or again becomes so payable.

(7) For the purposes of this section –

(a) a payment made by a person under a maintenance calculation which was not validly made; and

(b) a voluntary payment made in the circumstances set out in subsection (1A)(a),

shall be treated as an overpayment of child support maintenance made by a non-resident parent.

(8) In this section 'relevant person', in relation to an overpayment, means the person with care to whom the overpayment was made.

(9) Any sum recovered by the Secretary of State under this section shall be paid by him into the Consolidated Fund.

Amendments—Child Support Act 1995, s 23; Child Support, Pensions and Social Security Act 2000, ss 1(2), 20(3), (4) – in force from 20 November 2000 for the purpose only of making regulations.

Special cases

42   Special cases

(1) The Secretary of State may by regulation provide that in prescribed circumstances a case is to be treated as a special case for the purposes of this Act.

(2) Those regulations may, for example, provide for the following to be special cases –

(a) each parent of a child is a non-resident parent in relation to the child;

(b) there is more than one person who is a person with care in relation to the same child;

(c) there is more than one qualifying child in relation to the same non-resident parent but the person who is the person with care in relation to one of those children is not the person who is the person with care in relation to all of them;

(d) a person is a non-resident parent in relation to more than one child and the other parent of each of those children is not the same person;

(e) the person with care has care of more than one qualifying child and there is more than one non-resident parent in relation to those children;

(f) a qualifying child has his home in two or more separate households.

(3) The Secretary of State may by regulation make provision with respect to special cases.

(4) Regulations made under subsection (3) may, in particular –

(a) modify any provision made by or under this Act, in its application to any special case or any special case falling within a prescribed category;

(b) make new provision for any such case; or

(c) provide for any prescribed provision made by or under this Act not to apply to any such case.

Amendments—Child Support, Pensions and Social Security Act 2000, Sch 3, para 11(2) – in force from a date to be appointed.

43   Recovery of child support maintenance by deduction from benefit

(1) This section applies where –

(a) a non-resident parent is liable to pay a flat rate of child support maintenance (or would be so liable but for a variation having been agreed to), and that rate applies (or would have applied) because he falls within paragraph 4(1)(b) or (c) or 4(2) of Schedule 1; and

(b) such conditions as may be prescribed for the purposes of this section are satisfied.

(2) The power of the Secretary of State to make regulations under section 5 of the Social Security Administration Act 1992 by virtue of subsection (1)(p) (deductions from benefits) may be exercised in relation to cases to which this section applies with a view to securing that payments in respect of child support maintenance are made or that arrears of child support maintenance are recovered.

(3) For the purposes of this section, the benefits to which section 5 of the 1992 Act applies are to be taken as including war disablement pensions and war widows' pensions (within the meaning of section 150 of the Social Security Contributions and Benefits Act 1992 (interpretation)).

Amendments—Child Support, Pensions and Social Security Act 2000, s 21 – in force from 10 November 2000 for the purpose only of making regulations.

Jurisdiction

44 Jurisdiction

(1) The Secretary of State shall have jurisdiction to make a maintenance calculation with respect to a person who is –

    (a) a person with care;
    (b) a non-resident parent; or
    (c) a qualifying child,

only if that person is habitually resident in the United Kingdom, except in the case of a non-resident parent who falls within subsection (2A).

(2) Where the person with care is not an individual, subsection (1) shall have effect as if paragraph (a) were omitted.

(2A) A non-resident parent falls within this subsection if he is not habitually resident in the United Kingdom, but is –

    (a) employed in the civil service of the Crown, including Her Majesty's Diplomatic Service and Her Majesty's Overseas Civil Service;
    (b) a member of the naval, military or air forces of the Crown, including any person employed by an association established for the purposes of Part XI of the Reserve Forces Act 1996;
    (c) employed by a company of a prescribed description registered under the Companies Act 1985 in England and Wales or in Scotland, or under the Companies (Northern Ireland) Order 1986; or
    (d) employed by a body of a prescribed description.

(3) ...

Amendments—Social Security Act 1998, s 86(1), Sch 7, para 41; Child Support, Pensions and Social Security Act 2000, ss 1(2), 22, Sch 3, para 11(2).

45 Jurisdiction of courts in certain proceedings under this Act

(1) The Lord Chancellor or, in relation to Scotland, the Lord Advocate may by order make such provision as he considers necessary to secure that appeals, or such class of appeals as may be specified in the order –

    (a) shall be made to a court instead of being made to an appeal tribunal; or
    (b) shall be so made in such circumstances as may be so specified.

(2) In subsection (1), 'court' means –

    (a) in relation to England and Wales and subject to any provision made under Schedule 11 to the Children Act 1989 (jurisdiction of courts with respect to certain proceedings relating to children) the High Court, a county court or a magistrates' court; and
    (b) in relation to Scotland, the Court of Session or the sheriff.

(3) Schedule 11 to the Act of 1989 shall be amended in accordance with subsections (4) and (5).

(4) The following sub-paragraph shall be inserted in paragraph 1, after sub-paragraph (2) –

    '(2A) Sub-paragraph (1) and (2) shall also apply in relation to proceedings –

(a) under section 27 of the Child Support Act 1991 (reference to court for declaration of parentage); or

(b) which are to be dealt with in accordance with an order made under section 45 of that Act (jurisdiction of courts in certain proceedings under that Act)'.

(5) In paragraphs 1(3) and 2(3), the following shall be inserted after 'Act 1976' –

'(bb) section 20 (appeals) or 27 (reference to court for declaration of parentage) of the Child Support Act 1991;'

(6) Where the effect of any order under subsection (1) is that there are no longer any appeals which fall to be dealt with by appeal tribunals, the Lord Chancellor after consultation with the Lord Advocate may by order provide for the abolition of those tribunals.

(7) Any order under subsection (1) or (6) may make –

(a) such modifications of any provision of this Act or of any other enactment; and

(b) such transitional provision,

as the Minister making the order considers appropriate in consequence of any provision made by the order.

Amendments—Social Security Act 1998, s 86(1), Sch 7, para 42(1).

Miscellaneous and supplemental

46 Reduced benefit decisions

(1) This section applies where any person ('the parent') –

(a) has made a request under section 6(5);

(b) fails to comply with any regulation made under section 6(7); or

(c) having been treated as having applied for a maintenance calculation under section 6, refuses to take a scientific test (within the meaning of section 27A).

(2) The Secretary of State may serve written notice on the parent requiring her, before the end of a specified period –

(a) in a subsection (1)(a) case, to give him her reasons for making the request;

(b) in a subsection (1)(b) case, to give him her reasons for failing to do so; or

(c) in a subsection (1)(c) case, to give him her reasons for her refusal.

(3) When the specified period has expired, the Secretary of State shall consider whether, having regard to any reasons given by the parent, there are reasonable grounds for believing that –

(a) in a subsection (1)(a) case, if the Secretary of State were to do what is mentioned in section 6(3);

(b) in a subsection (1)(b) case, if she were to be required to comply; or

(c) in a subsection (1)(c) case, if she took the scientific test,

there would be a risk of her, or of any children living with her, suffering harm or undue distress as a result of his taking such action, or her complying or taking the test.

(4) If the Secretary of State considers that there are such reasonable grounds, he shall –

(a) take no further action under this section in relation to the request, the failure or the refusal in question; and

(b) notify the parent, in writing, accordingly.

(5) If the Secretary of State considers that there are no such reasonable grounds, he may, except in prescribed circumstances, make a reduced benefit decision with respect to the parent.

(6) In a subsection (1)(a) case, the Secretary of State may from time to time serve written notice on the parent requiring her, before the end of a specified period –

(a) to state whether her request under section 6(5) still stands; and
(b) if so, to give him her reasons for maintaining her request,

and subsections (3) to (5) have effect in relation to such a notice and any response to it as they have effect in relation to a notice under subsection (2)(a) and any response to it.

(7) Where the Secretary of State makes a reduced benefit decision he must send a copy of it to the parent.

(8) A reduced benefit decision is to take effect on such date as may be specified in the decision.

(9) Reasons given in response to a notice under subsection (2) or (6) need not be given in writing unless the Secretary of State directs in any case that they must.

(10) In this section –

(a) 'comply' means to comply with the requirement or with the regulation in question; and 'complied' and 'complying' are to be construed accordingly;
(b) 'reduced benefit decision' means a decision that the amount payable by way of any relevant benefit to, or in respect of, the parent concerned be reduced by such amount, and for such period, as may be prescribed;
(c) 'relevant benefit' means income support or an income-based jobseeker's allowance or any other benefit of a kind prescribed for the purposes of section 6; and
(d) 'specified', in relation to a notice served under this section, means specified in the notice; and the period to be specified is to be determined in accordance with regulations made by the Secretary of State.

Amendments—Child Support, Pensions and Social Security Act 2000, s 19 – in force from 10 November 2000 for the purpose only of making regulations.

46A   Finality of decisions

(1) Subject to the provisions of this Act, any decision of the Secretary of State or an appeal tribunal made in accordance with the foregoing provisions of this Act shall be final.

(2) If and to the extent that regulations so provide, any finding of fact or other determination embodied in or necessary to such a decision, or on which such a decision is based, shall be conclusive for the purposes of –

(a) further such decisions;
(b) decisions made in accordance with sections 8 to 16 of the Social Security Act 1998, or with regulations under section 11 of that Act; and
(c) decisions made under the Vaccine Damage Payments Act 1979.

Amendments—Social Security Act 1998, s 86(1), Sch 7, para 44.

46B   Matters arising as respects decisions

(1) Regulations may make provision as respects matters arising pending –

(a) any decision of the Secretary of State under section 11, 12 or 17;

(b) any decision of an appeal tribunal under section 20; or

(c) any decision of a Child Support Commissioner under section 24.

(2) Regulations may also make provision as respects matters arising out of the revision under section 16, or on appeal, of any such decision as is mentioned in subsection (1).

(3) ...

Amendments—Social Security Act 1998, s 86(1), Sch 7, para 44; Child Support, Pensions and Social Security Act 2000, Sch 9, Part I.

47 Fees

(1) The Secretary of State may by regulation provide for the payment, by the non-resident parent or the person with care (or by both), such fees as may be prescribed in cases where the Secretary of State takes any action under section 4 or 6.

(2) The Secretary of State may by regulation provide for the payment, by the non-resident parent, the person with care or the child concerned (or by any or all of them), of such fees as may be prescribed in cases where the Secretary of State takes action under section 7.

(3) Regulations made under this section –

(a) may require any information which is needed for the purpose of determining the amount of any such fee to be furnished, in accordance with the regulations, by such person as may be prescribed;

(b) shall provide that no such fees shall be payable by any person to or in respect of whom income support, an income-based jobseeker's allowance, working families' tax credit or any other benefit of a prescribed kind is paid; and

(c) may, in particular, make provision with respect to the recovery by the Secretary of State of any fees payable under the regulations.

(4) The provisions of this Act with respect to –

(a) the collection of child support maintenance;

(b) the enforcement of any obligation to pay child support maintenance,

shall apply equally (with any necessary modifications) to fees payable by virtue of regulations made under this section.

Amendments—Jobseekers Act 1995, s 41(4), Sch 2, para 20; Tax Credits Act 1999, s 1(2), Sch 1, para 6(f)(i); Child Support, Pensions and Social Security Act 2000, Sch 3, para 11(2), (18) – in force from 10 November 2000 for the purpose only of making regulations.

48 Right of audience

(1) Any officer of the Secretary of State who is authorised by the Secretary of State for the purposes of this section shall have, in relation to any proceedings under this Act before a magistrates' court, a right of audience and the right to conduct litigation.

(2) In this section 'right of audience' and 'right to conduct litigation' have the same meaning as in section 119 of the Courts and Legal Services Act 1990.

Amendments—Child Support Act 1995, s 30(5), Sch 3, para 14.

49 (*applies to Scotland only*)

50 Unauthorised disclosure of information

(1) Any person who is, or has been, employed in employment to which this section applies is guilty of an offence if, without lawful authority, he discloses any information which –

    (a) was acquired by him in the course of that employment; and

    (b) relates to a particular person.

(2) It is not an offence under this section –

    (a) to disclose information in the form of a summary or collection of information so framed as not to enable information relating to any particular person to be ascertained from it; or

    (b) to disclose information which has previously been disclosed to the public with lawful authority.

(3) It is a defence for a person charged with an offence under this section to prove that at the time of the alleged offence –

    (a) he believed that he was making the disclosure in question with lawful authority and had no reasonable cause to believe otherwise; or

    (b) he believed that the information in question had previously been disclosed to the public with lawful authority and had no reasonable cause to believe otherwise.

(4) A person guilty of an offence under this section shall be liable –

    (a) on conviction on indictment, to imprisonment for a term not exceeding two years or a fine or both; or

    (b) on summary conviction, to imprisonment for a term not exceeding six months or a fine not exceeding the statutory maximum or both.

(5) This section applies to employment as –

    (a) the Chief Child Support Officer;

    (b) any other child support officer;

    (c) any clerk to, or other officer of, an appeal tribunal or a child support appeal tribunal;

    (d) any member of the staff of such a tribunal;

    (e) a civil servant in connection with the carrying out of any functions under this Act,

and to employment of any other kind which is prescribed for the purposes of this section.

(6) For the purposes of this section a disclosure is to be regarded as made with lawful authority if, and only if, it is made –

    (a) by a civil servant in accordance with his official duty; or

    (b) by any other person either –

        (i) for the purposes of the function in the exercise of which he holds the information and without contravening any restriction duly imposed by the responsible person; or

        (ii) to, or in accordance with an authorisation duly given by, the responsible person;

    (c) in accordance with any enactment or order of a court;

(d) for the purpose of instituting, or otherwise for the purposes of, any proceedings before a court or before any tribunal or other body or person mentioned in this Act; or

(e) with the consent of the appropriate person.

(7) 'The responsible person' means –

(a) the Lord Chancellor;

(b) the Secretary of State;

(c) any person authorised by the Lord Chancellor, or Secretary of State, for the purposes of this subsection; or

(d) any other prescribed person, or person falling within a prescribed category.

(8) 'The appropriate person' means the person to whom the information in question relates, except that if the affairs of that person are being dealt with –

(a) under a power of attorney;

(b) by a receiver appointed under section 99 of the Mental Health Act 1983;

(c) *(applies to Scotland only)*; or

(d) by a mental health appointee, that is to say –

    (i) a person directed or authorised as mentioned in sub-paragraph (a) of rule 41(1) of the Court of Protection Rules 1984; or

    (ii) a receiver ad interim appointed under sub-paragraph (b) of that rule;

the appropriate person is the attorney, receiver, custodian or appointee (as the case may be) or, in a case falling within paragraph (a), the person to whom the information relates.

Amendments—Social Security Act 1998, s 86(1), Sch 7, para 45.

51   Supplementary powers to make regulations

(1) The Secretary of State may by regulation make such incidental, supplemental and transitional provision as he considers appropriate in connection with any provision made by or under this Act.

(2) The regulation may, in particular, make provision –

(a) as to the procedure to be followed with respect to –

    (i) the making of applications for maintenance calculations;

    (ii) the making of decisions under section 11;

    (iii) the making of decisions under section 16 or 17;

(b) extending the categories of case to which section 16, 17 or 20 applies;

(c) as to the date on which an application for a maintenance calculation is to be treated as having been made;

(d) for attributing payments made under maintenance calculations to the payment of arrears;

(e) for the adjustment, for the purpose of taking account of the retrospective effect of a maintenance calculation, of amounts payable under the calculation;

(f) for the adjustment, for the purpose of taking account of over-payments or under-payments of child support maintenance, of amounts payable under a maintenance calculation;

(g) as to the evidence which is to be required in connection with such matters as may be prescribed;

(h) as to the circumstances in which any official record or certificate is to be conclusive (or in Scotland, sufficient) evidence;

(i) with respect to the giving of notices or other documents;

(j) for the rounding up or down of any amounts calculated, estimated or otherwise arrived at in applying any provision made by or under this Act.

(3) No power to make regulations conferred by any other provision of this Act shall be taken to limit the powers given to the Secretary of State by this section.

Amendments—Social Security Act 1998, s 86(1), Sch 7, para 46(a), (b); Child Support, Pensions and Social Security Act 2000, s 1(2), Sch 3, para 11(19) – in force from a date to be appointed.

52 Regulations and orders

(1) Any power conferred on the Lord Chancellor, or Lord Advocate or the Secretary of State by this Act to make regulations or orders (other than a deduction from earnings order) shall be exercisable by statutory instrument.

(2) No statutory instrument containing (whether alone or with other provisions) regulations made under –

(a) section 6(1), 12(4) (so far as the regulations make provision for the default rate of child support maintenance mentioned in section 12(5)(b)), 28C(2)(b), 28F(2)(b), 30(5A), 41(2), 41A, 41B(6), 43(1), 44(2A)(d), 46 or 47;

(b) paragraph 3(2) or 10A(1) of Part I of Schedule 1; or

(c) Schedule 4B,

or an order made under section 45(1) or (6), shall be made unless a draft of the instrument has been laid before Parliament and approved by a resolution of each House of Parliament.

(2A) No statutory instrument containing (whether alone or with other provisions) the first set of regulations made under paragraph 10(1) of Part I of Schedule 1 as substituted by section 1(3) of the Child Support, Pensions and Social Security Act 2000 shall be made unless a draft of the instrument has been laid before Parliament and approved by a resolution of each House of Parliament.

(3) Any other statutory instrument made under this Act (except an order made under section 58(2)) shall be subject to annulment in pursuance of a resolution of either House of Parliament.

(4) Any power of a kind mentioned in subsection (1) may be exercised –

(a) in relation to all cases to which it extends, in relation to those cases but subject to specified exceptions or in relation to any specified cases or classes of case;

(b) so as to make, as respects the cases in relation to which it is exercised –

(i) the full provision to which it extends or any lesser provision (whether by way of exception or otherwise);

(ii) the same provision for all cases, different provision for different cases or classes of case or different provision as respects the same case or class of case but for different purposes of this Act;

(iii) provision which is either unconditional or is subject to any specified condition;

(c) so to provide for a person to exercise a discretion in dealing with any matter.

Amendments—Child Support, Pensions and Social Security Act 2000, s 25 – in force from 10 November 2000 for the purpose only of making regulations.

53 Financial provisions

Any expenses of the Lord Chancellor or the Secretary of State under this Act shall be payable out of money provided by Parliament.

54 Interpretation

In this Act –

'non-resident parent', has the meaning given in section 3(2);

'appeal tribunal' means an appeal tribunal constituted under Chapter I of Part I of the Social Security Act 1998;

'application for a variation' means an application under section 28A or 28G;

'benefit Acts' means the Social Security Contributions and Benefits Act 1992 and the Social Security Administration Act 1992;

'child benefit' has the same meaning as in the Child Benefit Act 1975;

'child support maintenance' has the meaning given in section 3(6);

'deduction from earnings order' has the meaning given in section 31(2);

'default maintenance decision' has the meaning given in section 12;

'disabled person's tax credit' has the same meaning as in the benefit Acts;

'working families' tax credit' has the same meaning as in the benefit Acts;

'general qualification' shall be construed in accordance with section 71 of the Courts and Legal Services Act 1990 (qualification for judicial appointments);

'income support' has the same meaning as in the benefit Acts;

'income-based jobseeker's allowance' has the same meaning as in the Jobseekers Act 1995;

'interim maintenance decision' has the meaning given in section 12;

'liability order' has the meaning given in section 33(2);

'maintenance agreement' has the meaning given in section 9(1);

'maintenance calculation' means a calculation of maintenance made under this Act and, except in prescribed circumstances, includes a default maintenance decision and an interim maintenance decision;

'maintenance order' has the meaning given in section 8(11);

'parent', in relation to any child, means any person who is in law the mother or father of the child;

'parent with care' means a person who is, in relation to a child, both a parent and a person with care;

'parental responsibility', in the application of this Act –

> (a) to England and Wales, has the same meaning as in the Children Act 1989; and
>
> (b) *(applies to Scotland only)*;

'person with care' has the meaning given in section 3(3);

'prescribed' means prescribed by regulations made by the Secretary of State;

'qualifying child' has the meaning given in section 3(1);

'voluntary payment' has the meaning given in section 28J.

Amendments—Social Security (Consequential Provisions) Act 1992, s 4, Sch 2, para 114; Child (Scotland) Act 1995, s 105(4), Sch 4, para 52(1), (4); Jobseekers Act 1995, s 41(4), Sch 2, para 20; Child Support Act 1995, s 30(5), Sch 3, para 16; Social Security Act 1998, s 86(1), Sch 7, para 47(a), (b); Tax Credits Act 1999, s 1(2), Sch 1, paras 1, 6(i); Child Support, Pensions and Social Security Act 2000, Sch 3, para 11(2), (20) – in force from a date to be appointed.

55 Meaning of 'child'

(1) For the purposes of this Act a person is a child if –

> (a) he is under the age of 16;
> (b) he is under the age of 19 and receiving full-time education (which is not advanced education) –

(i) by attendance at a recognised educational establishment; or

(ii) elsewhere, if the education is recognised by the Secretary of State; or

(c) he does not fall within paragraph (a) or (b) but –

(i) he is under the age of 18, and

(ii) prescribed conditions are satisfied with respect to him.

(2) A person is not a child for the purposes of this Act if he –

(a) is or has been married;

(b) has celebrated a marriage which is void; or

(c) has celebrated a marriage in respect of which a decree of nullity has been granted.

(3) In this section –

'advanced education' means education of a prescribed description; and

'recognised educational establishment' means an establishment recognised by the Secretary of State for the purposes of this section as being, or as comparable to, a university, college or school.

(4) Where a person has reached the age of 16, the Secretary of State may recognise education provided for him otherwise than at a recognised educational establishment only if the Secretary of State is satisfied that education was being so provided for him immediately before he reached the age of 16.

(5) The Secretary of State may provide that in prescribed circumstances education is or is not to be treated for the purposes of this section as being full-time.

(6) In determining whether a person falls within subsection (1)(b), no account shall be taken of such interruptions in his education as may be prescribed.

(7) The Secretary of State may by regulation provide that a person who ceases to fall within subsection (1) shall be treated as continuing to fall within that subsection for a prescribed period.

(8) No person shall be treated as continuing to fall within subsection (1) by virtue of regulations made under subsection (7) after the end of the week in which he reaches the age of 19.

56 *(applies to Northern Ireland only)*

57 Application to Crown

(1) The power of the Secretary of State to make regulations under section 14 requiring prescribed persons to furnish information may be exercised so as to require information to be furnished by persons employed in the service of the Crown or otherwise in the discharge of Crown functions.

(2) In such circumstances, and subject to such conditions, as may be prescribed, an inspector appointed under section 15 may enter any Crown premises for the purpose of exercising any powers conferred on him by that section.

(3) Where such an inspector duly enters any Crown premises for those purposes, section 15 shall apply in relation to persons employed in the service of the Crown or otherwise in the discharge of Crown functions as it applies in relation to other persons.

(4) Where a liable person is in the employment of the Crown, a deduction from earnings order may be made under section 31 in relation to that person; but in such a case

subsection (8) of section 32 shall apply only in relation to the failure of that person to comply with any requirement imposed on him by regulations made under section 32.

58   Short title, commencement and extent, etc

(1) This Act may be cited as the Child Support Act 1991.

(2) Section 56(1) and subsections (1) to (11) and (14) of this section shall come into force on the passing of this Act but otherwise this Act shall come into force on such date as may be appointed by order made by the Lord Chancellor, the Secretary of State or Lord Advocate, or by any of them acting jointly.

(3) Different dates may be appointed for different provisions of this Act and for different purposes (including, in particular, for different cases or categories of case).

(4) An order under subsection (2) may make such supplemental, incidental or transitional provision as appears to the person making the order to be necessary or expedient in connection with the provisions brought into force by the order, including such adaptations or modifications of –

    (a) the provisions so brought into force;
    (b) any provisions of this Act then in force; or
    (c) any provision of any other enactment,

as appear to him to be necessary or expedient.

(5) Different provision may be made by virtue of subsection (4) with respect to different periods.

(6) Any provision made by virtue of subsection (4) may, in particular, include provision for –

    (a) the enforcement of a maintenance calculation (including the collection of sums payable under the calculation) as if the calculation were a court order of a prescribed kind;
    (b) the registration of maintenance calculations with the appropriate court in connection with any provision of a kind mentioned in paragraph (a);
    (c) the variation, on application made to a court, of the provisions of a maintenance calculation relating to the method of making payments fixed by the calculation or the intervals at which such payments are to be made;
    (d) a maintenance calculation, or an order of a prescribed kind relating to one or more children, to be deemed, in prescribed circumstances, to have been validly made for all purposes or for such purposes as may be prescribed.

In paragraph (c) 'court' includes a single justice.

(7) The Lord Chancellor, the Secretary of State or the Lord Advocate may by order make such amendments or repeals in, or such modifications of, such enactments as may be specified in the order, as appear to him to be necessary or expedient in consequence of any provision made by or under this Act (including any provision made by virtue of subsection (4)).

(8) This Act shall, in its application to the Isles of Scilly, have effect subject to such exceptions, adaptations and modifications as the Secretary of State may by order prescribe.

(9) Sections 27, 35, 40 and 48 and paragraph 7 of Schedule 5 do not extend to Scotland.

(10) Sections 7, 28, 40A and 49 extend only to Scotland.

(11) With the exception of sections 23 and 56(1), subsections (1) to (3) of this section and Schedules 2 and 4, and (in so far as it amends any enactment extending to Northern Ireland) Schedule 5, this Act does not extend to Northern Ireland.

(12) Until Schedule 1 to the Disability Living Allowance and Disability Working Allowance Act 1991 comes into force, paragraph 1(1) of Schedule 3 shall have effect with the omission of the words 'and disability appeal tribunals' and the insertion, after 'social security appeal tribunals', of the word 'and'.

(13) The consequential amendments set out in Schedule 5 shall have effect.

(14) In Schedule 1 to the Children Act 1989 (financial provision for children), paragraph 2(6)(b) (which is spent) is hereby repealed.

Amendments—Child Support, Pensions and Social Security Act 2000, s 1(2), Sch 3, para 11(21) – in force from a date to be appointed.

SCHEDULE 1

MAINTENANCE CALCULATIONS

PART I

CALCULATION OF WEEKLY AMOUNT OF CHILD SUPPORT MAINTENANCE

1 General rule

(1) The weekly rate of child support maintenance is the basic rate unless a reduced rate, a flat rate or the nil rate applies.

(2) Unless the nil rate applies, the amount payable weekly to a person with care is –

  (a) the applicable rate, if paragraph 6 does not apply; or
  (b) if paragraph 6 does apply, that rate as apportioned between the persons with care in accordance with paragraph 6,

as adjusted, in either case, by applying the rules about shared care in paragraph 7 or 8.

2 Basic rate

(1) The basic rate is the following percentage of the non-resident parent's net weekly income –

  15% where he has one qualifying child;
  20% where he has two qualifying children;
  25% where he has three or more qualifying children.

(2) If the non-resident parent also has one or more relevant other children, the appropriate percentage referred to in sub-paragraph (1) is to be applied instead to his net weekly income less –

  15% where he has one relevant other child;
  20% where he has two relevant other children;
  25% where he has three or more relevant other children.

3 Reduced rate

(1) A reduced rate is payable if –

  (a) neither a flat rate nor the nil rate applies; and

(b) the non-resident parent's net weekly income is less than £200 but more than £100.

(2) The reduced rate payable shall be prescribed in, or determined in accordance with, regulations.

(3) The regulations may not prescribe, or result in, a rate of less than £5.

4 Flat rate

(1) Except in a case falling within sub-paragraph (2), a flat rate of £5 is payable if the nil rate does not apply and –

(a) the non-resident parent's net weekly income is £100 or less; or
(b) he receives any benefit, pension or allowance prescribed for the purposes of this paragraph of this sub-paragraph; or
(c) he or his partner (if any) receives any benefit prescribed for the purposes of this paragraph of this sub-paragraph.

(2) A flat rate of a prescribed amount is payable if the nil rate does not apply and –

(a) the non-resident parent has a partner who is also a non-resident parent;
(b) the partner is a person with respect to whom a maintenance calculation is in force; and
(c) the non-resident parent or his partner receives any benefit prescribed under sub-paragraph (1)(c).

(3) The benefits, pensions and allowances which may be prescribed for the purposes of sub-paragraph (1)(b) include ones paid to the non-resident parent under the law of a place outside the United Kingdom.

5 Nil rate

The rate payable is nil if the non-resident parent –

(a) is of a prescribed description; or
(b) has a net weekly income of below £5.

6 Apportionment

(1) If the non-resident parent has more than one qualifying child and in relation to them there is more than one person with care, the amount of child support maintenance payable is (subject to paragraph 7 or 8) to be determined by apportioning the rate between the persons with care.

(2) The rate of maintenance liability is to be divided by the number of qualifying children, and shared among the persons with care according to the number of qualifying children in relation to whom each is a person with care.

7 Shared care – basic and reduced rate

(1) This paragraph applies only if the rate of child support maintenance payable is the basic rate or a reduced rate.

(2) If the care of a qualifying child is shared between the non-resident parent and the person with care, so that the non-resident parent from time to time has care of the child

overnight, the amount of child support maintenance which he would otherwise have been liable to pay the person with care, as calculated in accordance with the preceding paragraphs of this Part of this Schedule, is to be decreased in accordance with this paragraph.

(3) First, there is to be a decrease according to the number of such nights which the Secretary of State determines there to have been, or expects there to be, or both during a prescribed twelve-month period.

(4) The amount of that decrease for one child is set out in the following Table –

Number of nights	Fraction to subtract
52 to 103	One-seventh
104 to 155	Two-sevenths
156 to 174	Three-sevenths
175 or more	One-half

(5) If the person with care is caring for more than one qualifying child of the non-resident parent, the applicable decrease is the sum of the appropriate fractions in the Table divided by the number of such qualifying children.

(6) If the applicable fraction is one-half in relation to any qualifying child in the care of the person with care, the total amount payable to the person with care is then to be further decreased by £7 for each such child.

(7) If the application of the preceding provisons of this paragraph would decrease the weekly amount of child support maintenance (or the aggregate of all such amounts) payable by the non-resident parent to the person with care (or all of them) to less than £5, he is instead liable to pay child support maintenance at the rate of £5 a week, apportioned (if appropriate) in accordance with paragraph 6.

8 Shared care – flat rate

(1) This paragraph applies only if –

    (a) the rate of child support maintenance payable is a flat rate; and

    (b) that rate applies because the non-resident parent falls within paragraph 4(1)(b) or (c) or 4(2).

(2) If the care of a qualifying child is shared as mentioned in paragraph 7(2) for at least 52 nights during a prescribed 12-month period, the amount of child support maintenance payable by the non-resident parent to the person with care of that child is nil.

9 Regulations about shared care

The Secretary of State may by regulations provide –

    (a) for which nights are to count for the purposes of shared care under paragraphs 7 and 8, or for how it is to be determined whether a night counts;

    (b) for what counts, or does not count, as 'care' for those purposes; and

    (c) for paragraph 7(3) or 8(2) to have effect, in prescribed circumstances, as if the period mentioned there were other than 12 months, and in such circumstances for the Table in paragraph 7(4) (or that Table as modified pursuant to regulations made under paragraph 10A(2)(a)), or the period mentioned in paragraph 8(2), to have effect with prescribed adjustments.

10   Net weekly income

(1) For the purposes of this Schedule, net weekly income is to be determined in such manner as is provided for in regulations.

(2) The regulations may, in particular, provide for the Secretary of State to estimate any income or make an assumption as to any fact where, in his view, the information at his disposal is unreliable, insufficient, or relates to an atypical period in the life of the non-resident parent.

(3) Any amount of net weekly income (calculated as above) over £2,000 is to be ignored for the purposes of this Schedule.

10A   Regulations about rates, figures, etc.

(1) The Secretary of State may by regulations provide that –

   (a) paragraph 2 is to have effect as if different percentages were substituted for those set out there;
   (b) paragraph 3(1) or (3), 4(1), 5, 7(7) or 10(3) is to have effect as if different amounts were substituted for those set out there.

(2) The Secretary of State may by regulations provide that –

   (a) the Table in paragraph 7(4) is to have effect as if different numbers of nights were set out in the first column and different fractions were substituted for those set out in the second column;
   (b) paragraph 7(6) is to have effect as if a different amount were substituted for that mentioned there, or as if the amount were an aggregate amount and not an amount for each qualifying child, or both.

10B   Regulations about income

The Secretary of State may by regulations provide that, in such circumstances and to such extent as may be prescribed –

   (a) where the Secretary of State is satisfied that a person has intentionally deprived himself of a source of income with a view to reducing the amount of his net weekly income, his net weekly income shall be taken to include income from that source of an amount estimated by the Secretary of State;
   (b) a person is to be treated as possessing income which he does not possess;
   (c) income which a person does possess is to be disregarded.

10C   References to various terms

(1) References in this Part of this Schedule to 'qualifying children' are to those qualifying children with respect to whom the maintenance calculation falls to be made.

(2) References in this Part of this Schedule to 'relevant other children' are to –

   (a) children other than qualifying children in respect of whom the non-resident parent or his partner receives child benefit under Part IX of the Social Security Contributions and Benefits Act 1992; and
   (b) such other description of children as may be prescribed.

(3) In this Part of this Schedule, a person 'receives' a benefit, pension, or allowance for any week if it is paid or due to be paid to him in respect of that week.

(4) In this Part of this Schedule, a person's 'partner' is –

    (a) if they are a couple, the other member of that couple;

    (b) if the person is a husband or wife by virtue of a marriage entered into under a law which permits polygamy, another party to the marriage who is of the opposite sex and is a member of the same household.

(5) In sub-paragraph (4)(a), 'couple' means a man and a woman who are –

    (a) married to each other and are members of the same household; or

    (b) not married to each other but are living together as husband and wife.

PART II

GENERAL PROVISIONS ABOUT MAINTENANCE CALCULATIONS

11 Effective date of calculation

(1) A maintenance calculation shall take effect on such date as may be determined in accordance with regulations made by the Secretary of State.

(2) That date may be earlier than the date on which the calculation is made.

12 Form of calculation

Every maintenance calculation shall be made in such form and contain such information as the Secretary of State may direct.

13 ...

14 Consolidated applications and calculations

(1) The Secretary of State may by regulation provide –

    (a) for two or more applications for maintenance calculations to be treated, in prescribed circumstances, as a single application; and

    (b) for the replacement, in prescribed circumstances, of a maintenance calculation made on the application of one person by a later maintenance calculation made on the application of that or any other person.

(2) In sub-paragraph (1), the references (however expressed) to applications for maintenance calculations include references to applications treated as made.

15 Separate calculation for different periods

Where the Secretary of State is satisfied that the circumstances of a case require different amounts of child support maintenance to be calculated in respect of different periods, he may make separate maintenance calculations each expressed to have effect in relation to a different specified period.

16 Termination of calculations

(1) A maintenance calculation shall cease to have effect –

    (a) on the death of the non-resident parent, or of the person with care, with respect to whom it was made;

  (b) on there no longer being any qualifying child with respect to whom it would have effect;

  (c) on the non-resident parent with respect to whom it was made ceasing to be a parent of –

    (i) the qualifying child with respect to whom it was made; or

    (ii) where it was made with respect to more than one qualifying child, all of the qualifying children with respect to whom it was made.

  (d) ...

  (e) ...

(2)–(9) ...

(10) A person with care with respect to whom a maintenance calculation is in force shall provide the Secretary of State with such information, in such circumstances, as may be prescribed, with a view to assisting the Secretary of State in determining whether the calculation has ceased to have effect.

(11) The Secretary of State may by regulation make such supplemental, incidental or transitional provision as he thinks necessary or expedient in consequence of the provisions of this paragraph.

Amendments—Child Support Act 1995, s 14; Social Security Act 1998, s 86(1), Sch 7, para 48(3), (4), (5)(a)(c); Child Support, Pensions and Social Security Act 2000, s 1(3), Sch 1, Sch 3, para 11(2), (22) – in force from 10 November 2000 for the purpose only of making regulations.

SCHEDULE 2

PROVISION OF INFORMATION TO SECRETARY OF STATE

1 Inland Revenue records

(1) This paragraph applies where the Secretary of State or the Department of Health and Social Services for Northern Ireland requires information for the purpose of tracing –

  (a) the current address of a non-resident parent; or

  (b) the current employer of a non-resident parent.

(2) In such a case, no obligation as to secrecy imposed by statute or otherwise on a person employed in relation to the Inland Revenue shall prevent any information obtained or held in connection with the calculation or collection of income tax from being disclosed to –

  (a) the Secretary of State;

  (b) the Department of Health and Social Services for Northern Ireland; or

  (c) an officer of either of them authorised to receive such information in connection with the operation of this Act or of any corresponding Northern Ireland legislation.

(3) This paragraph extends only to disclosure by or under the authority of the Commissioners of Inland Revenue.

(4) Information which is the subject of disclosure to any person by virtue of this paragraph shall not be further disclosed to any person except where the further disclosure is made –

  (a) to a person to whom disclosure could be made by virtue of sub-paragraph (2); or

  (b) for the purposes of any proceedings (civil or criminal) in connection with the operation of this Act or of any corresponding Northern Ireland legislation.

1A Supply of information for child support purposes

(1) This paragraph applies to any information which –

    (a) relates to any earnings or other income of a non-resident parent in respect of a tax year in which he is or was a self-employed earner, and

    (b) is required by the Secretary of State or the Department of Health and Social Services for Northern Ireland for any purposes of this Act.

(2) No obligation as to secrecy imposed by statute or otherwise on a person employed in relation to the Inland Revenue shall prevent any such information obtained or held in connection with the calculation or collection of income tax from being disclosed to –

    (a) the Secretary of State;

    (b) the Department of Health and Social Services for Northern Ireland; or

    (c) an officer of either of them authorised to receive such information in connection with the operation of this Act.

(3) This paragraph extends only to disclosure by or under the authority of the Commissioners of Inland Revenue.

(4) Information which is the subject of disclosure to any person by virtue of this paragraph shall not be further disclosed to any person except where the further disclosure is made –

    (a) to a person to whom disclosure could be made by virtue of sub-paragraph (2); or

    (b) for the purposes of any proceedings (civil or criminal) in connection with the operation of this Act.

(5) For the purposes of this paragraph 'self-employed earner' and 'tax year' have the same meaning as in Parts I to VI of the Social Security Contributions and Benefits Act 1992.

2 ...

Amendments—Social Security Act 1998, s 86(1), Sch 7, para 49; Welfare Reform and Pensions Act 1999, s 80; Child Support, Pensions and Social Security Act 2000, s 1(2), Sch 3, para 11(2) – in force from a date to be appointed.

SCHEDULE 3

...

Amendments—Social Security Act 1998, s 86, Sch 7, para 50.

SCHEDULE 4

CHILD SUPPORT COMMISSIONERS

1 Tenure of office

(1) Every Child Support Commissioner shall vacate his office on the date on which he reaches the age of 70; but this sub-paragraph is subject to section 26(4) to (6) of the Judicial Pensions and Retirement Act 1993 (power to authorise continuance in office up to the age of 75).

(2) ...

(3) A Child Support Commissioner may be removed from office by the Lord Chancellor on the ground of misbehaviour or incapacity.

2   Commissioners' remuneration and their pensions

(1) The Lord Chancellor may pay, or make such payments towards the provision of such remuneration, pension, allowances or gratuities to or in respect of persons appointed as Child Support Commissioners as, with the consent of the Treasury, he may determine.

(2) The Lord Chancellor shall pay to a Child Support Commissioner such expenses incurred in connection with his work as such a Commissioner as may be determined by the Treasury.

(3) Sub-paragraph (1), so far as relating to pensions, allowances or gratuities, shall not have effect in relation to any person to whom Part I of the Judicial Pensions and Retirement Act 1993 applies, except to the extent provided by or under that Act.

2A   Expenses of other persons

(1) The Lord Chancellor or, in Scotland, the Secretary of State may pay to any person who attends any proceedings before a Child Support Commissioner such travelling and other allowances as he may determine.

(2) In sub-paragraph (1), references to travelling and other allowances include references to compensation for loss of remunerative time.

(3) No compensation for loss of remunerative time shall be paid to any person under this paragraph in respect of any time during which he is in receipt of other remuneration so paid.

3   Commissioners barred from legal practice

Section 75 of the Courts and Legal Services Act 1990 (judges etc barred from legal practice) shall apply to any person appointed as a Child Support Commissioner as it applies to any person holding as a full-time appointment any of the offices listed in Schedule 11 to that Act.

4   Deputy Child Support Commissioners

(1) The Lord Chancellor may appoint persons to act as Child Support Commissioners (but to be known as deputy Child Support Commissioners) in order to facilitate the disposal of the business of Child Support Commissioners.

(2) A deputy Child Support Commissioner shall be appointed –

   (a)   from among persons who have a 10 year general qualification or are advocates or solicitors in Scotland of 10 years' standing; and
   (b)   for such period or on such occasions as the Lord Chancellor thinks fit.

(3) Paragraph 2 applies to deputy Child Support Commissioners as if the reference to pensions were omitted and paragraph 3 does not apply to them.

4A   Determination of questions by other officers

(1) The Lord Chancellor may by regulation provide –

   (a)   for officers authorised –
       (i)   by the Lord Chancellor; or
       (ii)   (*applies to Scotland only*),
       to determine any question which is determinable by a Child Support Commissioner and which does not involve the determination of any appeal, application for leave to appeal or reference;

(b) for the procedure to be followed by any such officer in determining any such question;

(c) for the manner in which determinations of such questions by such officers may be called in question.

(2) A determination which would have the effect of preventing an appeal, application for leave to appeal or reference being determined by a Child Support Commissioner is not a determination of the appeal, application or reference for the purposes of sub-paragraph (1).

5 Tribunals of Commissioners

(1) If it appears to the Chief Child Support Commissioner (or, in the case of his inability to act, to such other of the Child Support Commissioners as he may have nominated to act for the purpose) that –

(a) an application for leave under section 24(6)(b); or

(b) an appeal,

falling to be heard by one of the Child Support Commissioners involves a question of law of special difficulty, he may direct that the application or appeal be dealt with by a tribunal consisting of any three or more of the Child Support Commissioners.

(2) If the decision of such a tribunal is not unanimous, the decision of the majority shall be the decision of the tribunal; and the presiding Child Support Commissioner shall have a casting vote if the votes are equally divided.

(3) Where a direction is given under sub-paragraph (1)(a), section 24(6)(b) shall have effect as if the reference to a Child Support Commissioner were a reference to such a tribunal as is mentioned in sub-paragraph (1).

6 Finality of decisions

(1) Subject to section 25, the decision of any Child Support Commissioner shall be final.

(2) If and to the extent that regulations so provide, any finding of fact or other determination which is embodied in or necessary to a decision, or on which a decision is based, shall be conclusive for the purposes of any further decision.

7 Consultation with Lord Advocate

(1) Before exercising any of his powers under paragraph 1(2) or (3), 4(1) or (2)(b) or 4A(1), the Lord Chancellor shall consult the Lord Advocate.

8 (*applies to Northern Ireland only*)

Amendments—Judicial Pensions and Retirement Act 1993, s 3, Sch 8, para 21; Child Support Act 1995, ss 17–18, 30(5), Sch 3, para 18; Social Security Act 1998, s 86(1), Sch 7, paras 51, 52.

SCHEDULE 4A

APPLICATIONS FOR A VARIATION

1 Interpretation

In this Schedule, 'regulations' means regulations made by the Secretary of State.

2 Applications for a variation

Regulations may make provision –

(a) as to the procedure to be followed in considering an application for a variation;

(b) as to the procedure to be followed when an application for a variation is referred to an appeal tribunal under section 28D(1)(b).

3 Completion of preliminary consideration

Regulations may provide for determining when the preliminary consideration of an application for a variation is to be taken to have been completed.

4 Information

If any information which is required (by regulations under this Act) to be furnished to the Secretary of State in connection with an application for a variation has not been furnished within such period as may be prescribed, the Secretary of State may nevertheless proceed to consider the application.

5 Joint consideration of applications for a variation and appeals

(1) Regulations may provide for two or more applications for a variation with respect to the same application for a maintenance calculation to be considered together.

(2) In sub-paragraph (1), the reference to an application for a maintenance calculation includes an application treated as having been made under section 6.

(3) An appeal tribunal considering an application for a variation under section 28D(1)(b) may consider it at the same time as an appeal under section 20 in connection with an interim maintenance decision, if it considers that to be appropriate.

Amendments—Child Support, Pensions and Social Security Act 2000, s 6(1) – in force from 10 November 2000 for the purpose only of making regulations.

SCHEDULE 4B

APPLICATIONS FOR A VARIATION: THE CASES AND CONTROLS

PART I

THE CASES

1 General

(1) The cases in which a variation may be agreed are those set out in this Part of this Schedule or in regulations made under this Part.

(2) In this Schedule 'applicant' means the person whose application for a variation is being considered.

2 Special expenses

(1) A variation applied for by a non-resident parent may be agreed with respect to his special expenses.

(2) In this paragraph 'special expenses' means the whole, or any amount above a prescribed amount, or any prescribed part, of expenses which fall within a prescribed description of expenses.

(3) In prescribing descriptions of expenses for the purposes of this paragraph, the Secretary of State may, in particular, make provision with respect to –

- (a) costs incurred by a non-resident parent in maintaining contact with the child, or with any of the children, with respect to whom the application for a maintenance calculation has been made (or treated as made);
- (b) costs attributable to a long-term illness or disability of a relevant other child (within the meaning of paragraph 10C(2) of Schedule 1);
- (c) debts of a prescribed description incurred, before the non-resident parent became a non-resident parent in relation to a child with respect to whom the maintenance calculation has been applied for (or treated as having been applied for) –

  - (i) for the joint benefit of both parents;
  - (ii) for the benefit of any such child; or
  - (iii) for the benefit of any other child falling within a prescribed category;

- (d) boarding school fees for a child in relation to whom the application for a maintenance calculation has been made (or treated as made);
- (e) the cost to the non-resident parent of making payments in relation to a mortgage on the home he and the person with care shared, if he no longer has an interest in it, and she and a child in relation to whom the application for a maintenance calculation has been made (or treated as made) still live there.

(4) For the purposes of sub-paragraph (3)(b) –

- (a) 'disability' and 'illness' have such meaning as may be prescribed; and
- (b) the question whether an illness or disability is long-term shall be determined in accordance with regulations made by the Secretary of State.

(5) For the purposes of sub-paragraph (3)(d), the Secretary of State may prescribe –

- (a) the meaning of 'boarding school fees'; and
- (b) components of such fees (whether or not itemised as such) which are, or are not, to be taken into account,

and may provide for estimating any such component.

3 Property or capital transfers

(1) A variation may be agreed in the circumstances set out in sub-paragraph (2) if before 5th April 1993 –

- (a) a court order of a prescribed kind was in force with respect to the non-resident parent and either the person with care with respect to the application for the maintenance calculation or the child, or any of the children, with respect to whom that application was made; or
- (b) an agreement of a prescribed kind between the non-resident parent and any of those persons was in force.

(2) The circumstances are that in consequence of one or more transfers of property of a prescribed kind and exceeding (singly or in aggregate) a prescribed minimum value –

- (a) the amount payable by the non-resident parent by way of maintenance was less than would have been the case had that transfer or those transfers not been made; or
- (b) no amount was payable by the non-resident parent by way of maintenance.

(3) For the purposes of sub-paragraph (2), 'maintenance' means periodical payments of maintenance made (otherwise than under this Act) with respect to the child, or any of the children, with respect to whom the application for a maintenance calculation has been made.

4 Additional cases

(1) The Secretary of State may by regulations prescribe other cases in which a variation may be agreed.

(2) Regulations under this paragraph may, for example, make provision with respect to cases where –

(a) the non-resident parent has assets which exceed a prescribed value;
(b) a person's lifestyle is inconsistent with his income for the purposes of a calculation made under Part I of Schedule 1;
(c) a person has income which is not taken into account in such a calculation;
(d) a person has unreasonably reduced the income which is taken into account in such a calculation.

PART II

REGULATORY CONTROLS

5—(1) The Secretary of State may by regulations make provision with respect to the variations from the usual rules for calculating maintenance which may be allowed when a variation is agreed.

(2) No variations may be made other than those which are permitted by the regulations.

(3) Regulations under this paragraph may, in particular, make provision for a variation to result in –

(a) a person's being treated as having more, or less, income than would be taken into account without the variation in a calculation under Part I of Schedule 1;
(b) a person's being treated as liable to pay a higher, or a lower, amount of child support maintenance than would result without the variation from a calculation under that Part.

(4) Regulations may provide for the amount of any special expenses to be taken into account in a case falling within paragraph 2, for the purposes of a variation, not to exceed such amounts as may be prescribed or as may be determined in accordance with the regulations.

(5) Any regulations under this paragraph may in particular make different provision with respect to different levels of income.

6 The Secretary of State may by regulations provide for the application, in connection with child support maintenance payable following a variation, of paragraph 7(2) to (7) of Schedule 1 (subject to any prescribed modifications).

Amendments—Child Support, Pensions and Social Security Act 2000, s 6(2) – in force from 10 November 2000 for the purpose only of making regulations.

SCHEDULE 4C

. . .

Amendments—Child Support, Pensions and Social Security Act 2000, Sch 9, Part I – in force from 10 November 2000 for the purpose only of making regulations.

SCHEDULE 5

CONSEQUENTIAL AMENDMENTS

1 The Tribunals and Inquiries Act 1971 (c 62)

(1) In section 7(3) of the Tribunals and Inquiries Act 1971 (chairman of certain tribunals to be drawn from panels) after 'paragraph' there shall be inserted '4A'.

(2) In Schedule 1 to that Act (tribunals under the general supervision of the Council on Tribunals) the following entry shall be inserted at the appropriate place –

'Child support maintenance	4A (a) The child support appeal tribunals established under section 21 of the Child Support Act 1991. (b) A Child Support Commissioner appointed under section 22 of the Child Support Act 1991 and any tribunal presided over by such a Commissioner.'

2 (*applies to Northern Ireland only*)

3 The House of Commons Disqualification Act 1975 (c 24)

(1) The House of Commons Disqualification Act 1975 shall be amended as follows.

(2) In Part I (disqualifying judicial offices), the following entries shall be inserted at the appropriate places –

'Chief or other Child Support Commissioner (excluding a person appointed under paragraph 4 of Schedule 4 to the Child Support Act 1991).'
'Chief or other Child Support Commissioner for Northern Ireland (excluding a person appointed under paragraph 4 of Schedule 4 to the Child Support Act 1991).'

(3) In Part III (other disqualifying offices), the following entry shall be inserted at the appropriate place –

'Regional or other full-time chairman of a child support appeal tribunal established under section 21 of the Child Support Act 1991'.

4 (*applies to Northern Ireland only*)

5 (*applies to Scotland only*)

6 (*applies to Scotland only*)

7 The Insolvency Act 1986 (c 45)

In section 281(5)(b) of the Insolvency Act 1986 (effect of discharge of bankrupt), after 'family proceedings' there shall be inserted 'or under a maintenance calculation made under the Child Support Act 1991'.

8 (*applies to Scotland only*)

Amendments—Child Support, Pensions and Social Security Act 2000, s 1(2) – in force from a date to be appointed.

Child Support Act 1995, including prospective amendments by the Child Support, Pensions and Social Security Act 2000

1–9 (*amend Child Support Act 1991*)

10 ...

Amendments—Child Support, Pensions and Social Security Act 2000, s 23 – in force from a date to be appointed.

11–17 (*amend Child Support Act 1991*)

Miscellaneous

18 Deferral of right to apply for maintenance assessment

(1)–(4) (*amend Child Support Act 1991*)

(5) ...

(6) Neither section 4(10) nor section 7(10) of the 1991 Act shall apply in relation to a maintenance order made in the circumstances mentioned in subsection (7) or (8) of section 8 of the 1991 Act.

(7) The Secretary of State may by regulations make provision for subsection 4(10), or section 7(10), of the 1991 Act not to apply in relation to such other cases as may be prescribed.

(8) Part I of the Schedule to the Child Support Act 1991 (Commencement No 3 and Transitional Provisions) Order 1992 (phased take-on of certain cases) is hereby revoked.

(9) At any time before 7th April 1997, neither section 8(3), nor section 9(5)(b), of the 1991 Act shall apply in relation to any case which fell within paragraph 5(2) of the Schedule to the 1992 Order (pending cases during the transitional period set by that Order).

Amendments—Child Support, Pensions and Social Security Act 2000, Sch 3, para 13(2).

19–23 (*amend Child Support Act 1991*)

24 ...

Amendments—Child Support, Pensions and Social Security Act 2000, Sch 3, para 13(3).

25 (*amends Social Security Administration Act 1992*)

Supplemental

26 Regulations and orders

(1) Any power under this Act to make regulations or orders shall be exercisable by statutory instrument.

(2) Any such power may be exercised to make different provision for different cases, including different provision for different areas.

(3) Any such power includes power –

(a) to make such incidental, supplemental, consequential or transitional provision as appears to the Secretary of State to be expedient; and
(b) to provide for a person to exercise a discretion in dealing with any matter.

(4) Subsection (5) applies to –

(a) the first regulations made under section 10;
(b) any order made under section 18(5).

(5) No regulations or order to which this subsection applies shall be made unless a draft of the statutory instrument containing the regulations or order has been laid before Parliament and approved by a resolution of each House.

(6) Any other statutory instrument made under this Act, other than one made under section 30(4), shall be subject to annulment in pursuance of a resolution of either House of Parliament.

27   Interpretation

(1) In this Act 'the 1991 Act' means the Child Support Act 1991.

(2) Expressions in this Act which are used in the 1991 Act have the same meaning in this Act as they have in that Act.

28   Financial provisions

There shall be paid out of money provided by Parliament –

(a) any expenditure incurred by the Secretary of State under or by virtue of this Act;
(b) any increase attributable to this Act in the sums payable out of money so provided under or by virtue of any other enactment.

29   *(applies to Northern Ireland only)*

30   Short title, commencement, extent etc

(1) This Act may be cited as the Child Support Act 1995.

(2) This Act and the 1991 Act may be cited together as the Child Support Acts 1991 and 1995.

(3) Section 29 and this section (apart from subsection (5)) come into force on the passing of this Act.

(4) The other provisions of this Act come into force on such day as the Secretary of State may by order appoint and different days may be appointed for different purposes.

(5) Schedule 3 makes minor and consequential amendments.

(6) This Act, except for –

(a) sections 17, 27 and 29,
(b) this section, and
(c) paragraphs 1, 18, 19 and 20 of Schedule 3,

does not extend to Northern Ireland.

[Schedules 1 and 2 amend Child Support Act 1991; Schedule 3 makes minor and consequential amendments.]

APPENDIX 2

STATUTORY INSTRUMENTS

Child Support (Maintenance Arrangements and Jurisdiction) Regulations 1992

SI 1992/2645

1 Citation, commencement and interpretation

(1) These Regulations may be cited as the Child Support (Maintenance Arrangements and Jurisdiction) Regulations 1992 and shall come into force on 5 April 1993.

(2) In these Regulations –

'the Act' means the Child Support Act 1991;
'Maintenance Calculation Procedure Regulations' means the Child Support (Maintenance Calculation Procedure) Regulations 2000;
'Maintenance Calculations and Special Cases Regulations' means the Child Support (Maintenance Calculations and Special Cases) Regulations 2000;
'effective date' means the date on which a maintenance calculation takes effect for the purposes of the Act;
'maintenance order' has the meaning given in section 8(11) of the Act.

(3) In these Regulations, unless the context otherwise requires, a reference –

(a) to a numbered regulation is to the regulation in these Regulations bearing that number;
(b) in a regulation to a numbered paragraph is to the paragraph in that regulation bearing that number;
(c) in a paragraph to a lettered or numbered sub-paragraph is to the sub-paragraph in that paragraph bearing that letter or number.

2 Prescription of enactments for the purposes of section 8(11) of the Act

The following enactments are prescribed for the purposes of section 8(11)(f) of the Act –

(a) the Conjugal Rights (Scotland) Amendment Act 1861;
(b) the Court of Session Act 1868;
(c) the Sheriff Courts (Scotland) Act 1907;
(d) the Guardianship of Infants Act 1925;
(e) the Illegitimate Children (Scotland) Act 1930;
(f) the Children and Young Persons (Scotland) Act 1932;
(g) the Children and Young Persons (Scotland) Act 1937;
(h) the Custody of Children (Scotland) Act 1939;
(i) the National Assistance Act 1948;
(j) the Affiliation Orders Act 1952;
(k) the Affiliation Proceedings Act 1957;
(l) the Matrimonial Proceedings (Children) Act 1958;
(m) the Guardianship of Minors Act 1971;
(n) the Guardianship Act 1973;
(o) the Children Act 1975;
(p) the Supplementary Benefits Act 1976;
(q) the Social Security Act 1986;
(r) the Social Security Administration Act 1992.

3 Relationship between maintenance calculations and certain court orders

(1) Orders made under the following enactments are of a kind prescribed for the purposes of section 10(1) of the Act –

    (a)   the Conjugal Rights (Scotland) Amendment Act 1861;
    (b)   the Court of Session Act 1868;
    (c)   the Sheriff Courts (Scotland) Act 1907;
    (d)   the Guardianship of Infants Act 1925;
    (e)   the Illegitimate Children (Scotland) Act 1930;
    (f)   the Children and Young Persons (Scotland) Act 1932;
    (g)   the Children and Young Persons (Scotland) Act 1937;
    (h)   the Custody of Children (Scotland) Act 1939;
    (i)   the National Assistance Act 1948;
    (j)   the Affiliation Orders Act 1952;
    (k)   the Affiliation Proceedings Act 1957;
    (l)   the Matrimonial Proceedings (Children) Act 1958;
    (m) the Guardianship of Minors Act 1971;
    (n)   the Guardianship Act 1973;
    (o)   Part II of the Matrimonial Causes Act 1973;
    (p)   the Children Act 1975;
    (q)   the Supplementary Benefits Act 1976;
    (r)   the Domestic Proceedings and Magistrates' Courts Act 1978;
    (s)   Part III of the Matrimonial and Family Proceedings Act 1984;
    (t)   the Family Law (Scotland) Act 1985;
    (u)   the Social Security Act 1986;
    (v)   Schedule 1 to the Children Act 1989;
    (w) the Social Security Administration Act 1992.

(2) Subject to paragraphs (3) and (4), where a maintenance calculation is made with respect to –

    (a) all of the children with respect to whom an order falling within paragraph (1) is in force; or
    (b) one or more but not all of the children with respect to whom an order falling within paragraph (1) is in force and where the amount payable under the order to or for the benefit of each child is separately specified,

that order shall, so far as it relates to the making or securing of periodical payments to or for the benefit of the children with respect to whom the maintenance calculation has been made, cease to have effect on the effective date of the maintenance calculation.

(3) The provisions of paragraph (2) shall not apply where a maintenance order has been made in accordance with section 8(7) or (8) of the Act.

(4) In Scotland, where –

    (a) an order has ceased to have effect by virtue of the provisions of paragraph (2) to the extent specified in that paragraph; and
    (b) the Secretary of State no longer has jurisdiction to make a maintenance calculation with respect to a child with respect to whom the order ceased to have effect,

that order shall, so far as it relates to that child, again have effect from the date the Secretary of State no longer has jurisdiction to make a maintenance calculation with respect to that child.

4 Relationship between maintenance calculations and certain agreements

(1) Maintenance agreements within the meaning of section 9(1) of the Act are agreements of a kind prescribed for the purposes of section 10(2) of the Act.

(2) Where a maintenance calculation is made with respect to –

    (a) all of the children with respect to whom an agreement falling within paragraph (1) is in force; or

    (b) one or more but not all of the children with respect to whom an agreement falling within paragraph (1) is in force and where the amount payable under the agreement to or for the benefit of each child is separately specified,

that agreement shall, so far as it relates to the making or securing of periodical payments to or for the benefit of the children with respect to whom the maintenance calculation has been made, become unenforceable from the effective date of the calculation.

(3) Where an agreement becomes unenforceable under the provisions of paragraph (2) to the extent specified in that paragraph, it shall remain unenforceable in relation to a particular child until such date as the Secretary of State no longer has jurisdiction to make a maintenance calculation with respect to that child.

5 Notifications by the Secretary of State

(1) Where the Secretary of State is aware that an order of a kind prescribed in paragraph (2) is in force and considers that the making of a maintenance calculation has affected, or is likely to affect, that order, he shall notify the persons prescribed in paragraph (3) in respect of whom that maintenance calculation is in force, and the persons prescribed in paragraph (4) holding office in the court where the order in question was made or subsequently registered, of the calculation and its effective date.

(2) The prescribed orders are those made under an enactment mentioned in regulation 3(1).

(3) The prescribed persons in respect of whom the maintenance calculation is in force are –

    (a) a person with care;

    (b) a non-resident parent;

    (c) a person who is treated as a non-resident parent under regulation 8 of the Maintenance Calculations and Special Cases Regulations;

    (d) a child who has made an application for a maintenance calculation under section 7 of the Act.

(4) The prescribed person holding office in the court where the order in question was made or subsequently registered is –

    (a) in England and Wales –

        (i) in relation to the High Court, the senior district judge of the principal registry of the Family Division or, where proceedings were instituted in a district registry, the district judge;

        (ii) in relation to a county court, the proper officer of that court within the meaning of Order 1, Rule 3 of the County Court Rules 1981;

        (iii) in relation to a magistrates' court, the justices' chief executive for that court;

    (b) in Scotland –

        (i) in relation to the Court of Session, the Deputy Principal Clerk of Session;

        (ii) in relation to a sheriff court, the sheriff clerk.

6   Notification by the court

(1) Where a court is aware that a maintenance calculation is in force and makes an order mentioned in regulation 3(1) which it considers has affected, or is likely to affect, that calculation, the person prescribed in paragraph (2) shall notify the Secretary of State to that effect.

(2) The prescribed person is the person holding the office specified below in the court where the order in question was made or subsequently registered –

   (a) in England and Wales –
     (i)   in relation to the High Court, the senior district judge of the principal registry of the Family Division or, where proceedings were instituted in a district registry, the district judge;
     (ii) in relation to a county court, the proper officer of that court within the meaning of Order 1, Rule 3 of the County Court Rules 1981;
     (iii) in relation to a magistrates' court, the justices' chief executive for that court;
   (b) in Scotland –
     (i)   in relation to the Court of Session, the Deputy Principal Clerk of Session;
     (ii) in relation to a sheriff court, the sheriff clerk.

7A   Prescription for the purposes of jurisdiction

(1) The companies prescribed for the purposes of section 44(2A)(c) of the Act (non-resident parents not habitually resident in the United Kingdom but employed by prescribed companies) are companies which employ employees to work outside the United Kingdom but make calculations and payment arrangements in relation to the earnings of those employees in the United Kingdom so that a deduction from earnings order may be made under section 31 of the Act in respect of the earnings of any such employee who is a liable person for the purposes of that section.

(2) The following bodies are prescribed for the purposes of section 44(2A)(d) of the Act (non-resident parents not habitually resident in the United Kingdom but employed by a prescribed body) –

   (a) a National Health Service Trust established by order made under section 5 of the National Health Service and Community Care Act 1990 ('the 1990 Act') or under section 12A of the National Health Service (Scotland) Act 1978 ('the 1978 Act');
   (b) a Primary Care Trust established by order made under section 16A of the National Health Service Act 1977;
   (c) a Health Authority established under section 8 of the National Health Service Act 1977 ('the 1977 Act');
   (d) a Special Health Authority established under section 11 of the 1977 Act;
   (e) a local authority, and for this purpose 'local authority' means, in relation to England, a county council, a district council, a London borough council, the Common Council of the City of London or the Council of the Isles of Scilly and, in relation to Wales, a county council or a county borough council and, in relation to Scotland, a council constituted under section 2 of the Local Government etc (Scotland) Act 1994;
   (f) a Health and Social Service Trust established by order made under Article 10 of the Health and Personal Social Services (Northern Ireland) Order 1991;
   (g) a Health and Social Services Board established by order made under Article 16 of the Health and Personal Social Services (Northern Ireland) Order 1972 ('the 1972 Order');
   (h) the Central Services Agency established by order made under Article 26 of the 1972 Order;

(i) a Special Agency established by order made under Article 3 of the Health and Personal Social Services (Special Agencies) (Northern Ireland) Order 1990;

(j) a Health Board constituted under section 2 of the 1978 Act; and

(k) a Special Health Board constituted under section 2 of the 1978 Act.

8 Maintenance calculations and maintenance orders made in error

(1) Where –

(a) at the time that a maintenance calculation with respect to a qualifying child was made a maintenance order was in force with respect to that child;

(aa) the maintenance order has ceased to have effect by virtue of the provisions of regulation 3;

(b) the non-resident parent has made payments of child support maintenance due under that calculation; and

(c) the Secretary of State revises the decision as to the maintenance calculation under section 16 of the Act and decides that no child support maintenance was payable on the ground that the previous decision was made in error,

the payments of child support maintenance shall be treated as payments under the maintenance order and that order shall be treated as having continued in force.

(2) Where –

(a) at the time that a maintenance order with respect to a qualifying child was made a maintenance calculation was in force with respect to that child;

(aa) the maintenance calculation ceases to have effect;

(b) the non-resident parent has made payments of maintenance due under that order; and

(c) the maintenance order is revoked by the court on the grounds that it was made in error,

the payments under the maintenance order shall be treated as payments of child support maintenance and the maintenance calculation shall be treated as not having ceased to have effect.

9 Cases in which application may be made under section 4 or 7 of the Act

The provisions of section 4(10) or 7(10) of the Act shall not apply to prevent an application being made under those sections after 22 January 1996 where a decision has been made by the relevant court either that it has no power to vary or that it has no power to enforce a maintenance order in a particular case.

Child Support (Maintenance Calculation Procedure) Regulations 2000

SI 2001/157

PART I

GENERAL

1 Citation, commencement and interpretation

(1) These Regulations may be cited as the Child Support (Maintenance Calculation Procedure) Regulations 2000.

(2) In these Regulations, unless the context otherwise requires –

'the Act' means the Child Support Act 1991;
'date of notification to the non-resident parent' means the date on which the non-resident parent is first given notice of a maintenance application;
'effective application' means as provided for in regulation 3;
'date of receipt' means the date on which the information or document is actually received;
'effective date' means the date on which a maintenance calculation takes effect for the purposes of the Act;
'notice of a maintenance application' means notice by the Secretary of State under regulation 5(1) that an application for a maintenance calculation has been made, or treated as made, in relation to which the non-resident parent is named as a parent of the child to whom the application relates;
'Maintenance Calculations and Special Cases Regulations' means the Child Support (Maintenance Calculations and Special Cases) Regulations 2000;
'maintenance period' has the same meaning as in section 17(4A) of the Act;
'relevant person' means –
- (a) a person with care;
- (b) a non-resident parent;
- (c) a parent who is treated as a non-resident parent under regulation 8 of the Maintenance Calculations and Special Cases Regulations;
- (d) where the application for a maintenance calculation is made by a child under section 7 of the Act, that child, in respect of whom a maintenance calculation has been applied for, or has been treated as applied for under section 6(3) of the Act, or is or has been in force.

(3) The provisions in Schedule 1 shall have effect to supplement the meaning of 'child' in section 55 of the Act.

(4) In these Regulations, unless the context otherwise requires, a reference –

- (a) to a numbered Part is to the Part of these Regulations bearing that number;
- (b) to a numbered Schedule is to the Schedule to these Regulations bearing that number;
- (c) to a numbered regulation is to the regulation in these Regulations bearing that number;
- (d) in a regulation or Schedule to a numbered paragraph is to the paragraph in that regulation or Schedule bearing that number; and

(e) in a paragraph to a lettered or numbered sub-paragraph is to the sub-paragraph in that paragraph bearing that letter or number.

(5) These Regulations shall come into force in relation to a particular case on the day on which the amendments to sections 5, 6, 12, 46, 51, 54 and 55 of the Act made by the Child Support, Pensions and Social Security Act 2000 come into force in relation to that type of case.

2 Documents

Except where otherwise stated, where –

(a) any document is given or sent to the Secretary of State, that document shall be treated as having been so given or sent on the day that it is received by the Secretary of State; and

(b) any document is given or sent to any other person, that document shall, if sent by post to that person's last known or notified address, be treated as having been given or sent on the day that it is posted.

PART II

APPLICATIONS FOR A MAINTENANCE CALCULATION

3 Applications under section 4 or 7 of the Act

(1) A person who applies for a maintenance calculation under section 4 or 7 of the Act need not normally do so in writing, but if the Secretary of State directs that the application be made in writing, the application shall be made either by completing and returning, in accordance with the Secretary of State's instructions, a form provided for that purpose, or in such other written form as the Secretary of State may accept as sufficient in the circumstances of any particular case.

(2) An application for a maintenance calculation is effective if it complies with paragraph (1) and, subject to paragraph (4), is made on the date it is received.

(3) Where an application for a maintenance calculation is not effective the Secretary of State may request the person making the application to provide such additional information or evidence as the Secretary of State may specify and, where the application was made on a form, the Secretary of State may request that the information or evidence be provided on a fresh form.

(4) Where the additional information or evidence requested is received by the Secretary of State within 14 days of the date of his request, or at a later date in circumstances where the Secretary of State is satisfied that the delay was unavoidable, he shall treat the application as made on the date on which the earlier or earliest application would have been treated as made had it been effective.

(5) Where the Secretary of State receives the additional information or evidence requested by him more than 14 days from the date of the request and in circumstances where he is not satisfied that the delay was unavoidable, the Secretary of State shall treat the application as made on the date of receipt of the information or evidence.

(6) Subject to paragraph (7), a person who has made an effective application may amend or withdraw the application at any time before a maintenance calculation is made and such amendment or withdrawal need not be in writing unless, in any particular case, the Secretary of State requires it to be.

(7) No amendment made under paragraph (6) shall relate to any change of circumstances arising after the effective date of a maintenance calculation resulting from an effective application.

4   Multiple applications

(1) The provisions of Schedule 2 shall apply in cases where there is more than one application for a maintenance calculation.

(2) The provisions of paragraphs 1, 2 and 3 of Schedule 2 relating to the treatment of two or more applications as a single application shall apply where no request is received for the Secretary of State to cease acting in relation to all but one of the applications.

(3) Where, under the provisions of paragraph 1, 2 or 3 of Schedule 2, two or more applications are to be treated as a single application, that application shall be treated as an application for a maintenance calculation to be made with respect to all of the qualifying children mentioned in the applications, and the effective date of that maintenance calculation shall be determined by reference to the earlier or earliest application.

5   Notice of an application for a maintenance calculation

(1) Where an effective application has been made under section 4 or 7 of the Act, or is treated as made under section 6(3) of the Act, as the case may be, the Secretary of State shall as soon as is reasonably practicable notify, orally or in writing, the non-resident parent and any other relevant persons (other than the person who has made, or is treated as having made, the application) of that application and request such information as he may require to make the maintenance calculation in such form and manner as he may specify in the particular case.

(2) Where the person to whom notice is being given under paragraph (1) is a non-resident parent, that notice shall specify the effective date of the maintenance calculation if one is to be made, and the ability to make a default maintenance decision.

(3) Subject to paragraph (4), a person who has provided information under paragraph (1) may amend the information he has provided at any time before a maintenance calculation is made and such information need not be in writing unless, in any particular case, the Secretary of State requires it to be.

(4) No amendment under paragraph (3) shall relate to any change of circumstances arising after the effective date of any maintenance calculation made in response to the application in relation to which the information was requested.

6   Death of a qualifying child

(1) Where the Secretary of State is informed of the death of a qualifying child with respect to whom an application for a maintenance calculation has been made or has been treated as made, he shall –

   (a) proceed with the application as if it had not been made with respect to that child if he has not yet made a maintenance calculation;
   (b) treat any maintenance calculation already made by him as not having been made if the relevant persons have not been notified of it and proceed with the application as if it had not been made with respect to that child.

(2) Where all of the qualifying children with respect to whom an application for a maintenance calculation has been made have died, and either the calculation has not been

made or the relevant persons have not been notified of it, the Secretary of State shall treat the application as not having been made.

PART III

DEFAULT MAINTENANCE DECISIONS

7 Default rate

(1) Where the Secretary of State makes a default maintenance decision under section 12(1) of the Act (insufficient information to make a maintenance calculation or to make a decision under section 16 or 17 of the Act) the default rate is as set out in paragraph (2).

(2) The default rate for the purposes of section 12(5)(b) of the Act shall be –

£30 where there is one qualifying child of the non-resident parent;
£40 where there are two qualifying children of the non-resident parent;
£50 where there are three or more qualifying children of the non-resident parent,

apportioned, where the non-resident parent has more than one qualifying child and in relation to them there is more than one person with care, as provided in paragraph 6(2) of Part I of Schedule 1 to the Act.

(3) Subject to paragraph (4), where any apportionment made under this regulation results in a fraction of a penny that fraction shall be treated as a penny if it is either one half or exceeds one half, otherwise it shall be disregarded.

(4) If, in making the apportionment required by this regulation, the effect of the application of paragraph (3) would be such that the aggregate amount of child support maintenance payable by a non-resident parent would be different from the aggregate amount payable before any apportionment, the Secretary of State shall adjust that apportionment so as to eliminate that difference; and that adjustment shall be varied from time to time so as to secure that, taking one week with another and so far as is practicable, each person with care receives the amount which she would have received if no adjustment had been made under this paragraph.

PART IV

REDUCED BENEFIT DECISIONS

8 Interpretation of Part IV

(1) For the purposes of this Part –

'applicable amount' is to be construed in accordance with Part IV of the Income Support Regulations and regulations 83 to 86 of the Jobseeker's Allowance Regulations;
'benefit week', in relation to income support has the same meaning as in the Income Support Regulations, and in relation to jobseeker's allowance has the same meaning as in the Jobseeker's Allowance Regulations;
'Income Support Regulations' means the Income Support (General) Regulations 1987;
'Jobseeker's Allowance Regulations' means the Jobseeker's Allowance Regulations 1996;
'parent concerned' means the parent with respect to whom a reduced benefit decision is given;
'reduced benefit decision ' has the same meaning as in section 46(10)(b) of the Act; and
'relevant benefit' has the same meaning as in section 46(10)(c) of the Act.

(2) In this Part references to a reduced benefit decision as being 'in operation', 'suspended' or 'in force' shall be construed as follows –

    (a) a reduced benefit decision is 'in operation' if, by virtue of that decision, relevant benefit is currently being reduced;

    (b) a reduced benefit decision is 'suspended' if –

        (i) after that decision has been given, relevant benefit ceases to be payable, or becomes payable at one of the rates indicated in regulation 14(4) or, as the case may be, regulation 15(4);

        (ii) at the time the reduced benefit decision is given, relevant benefit is payable at one of the rates indicated in regulation 15(4) or, as the case may be, regulation 16(4),

    and these Regulations provide for relevant benefit payable from a later date to be reduced by virtue of the same reduced benefit decision; and

    (c) a reduced benefit decision is 'in force' if it is either in operation or suspended and cognate terms shall be construed accordingly.

9 Period within which reasons are to be given

The period specified for the purposes of section 46(2) of the Act (for the parent to supply her reasons) is 4 weeks from the date on which the Secretary of State serves notice under that subsection.

10 Circumstances in which a reduced benefit decision shall not be given

The Secretary of State shall not give a reduced benefit decision where –

    (a) income support is paid to, or in respect of, the parent in question and the applicable amount of the claimant for income support includes one or more of the amounts set out in paragraph 15(3), (4) or (6) of Part IV of Schedule 2 to the Income Support Regulations; or

    (b) an income-based jobseeker's allowance is paid to, or in respect of, the parent in question and the applicable amount of the claimant for an income-based jobseeker's allowance includes one or more of the amounts set out in paragraph 20(4), (5) or (7) of Schedule 1 to the Jobseeker's Allowance Regulations.

11 Amount of and period of reduction of relevant benefit under a reduced benefit decision

(1) The reduction in the amount payable by way of a relevant benefit to, or in respect of, the parent concerned and the period of such reduction by virtue of a reduced benefit decision shall be determined in accordance with paragraphs (2) to (8) below.

(2) Subject to paragraph (6) and regulations 12, 13, 14, and 15, there shall be a reduction for a period of 156 weeks from the day specified in the reduced benefit decision under the provisions of section 46(8) of the Act in respect of each such week equal to –

$$0.4 \times B$$

where

B is an amount equal to the weekly amount in relation to the week in question, specified in column (2) of paragraph 1(1) (e) of Schedule 2 to the Income Support Regulations.

(3) Subject to paragraph (4), a reduced benefit decision shall come into operation on the first day of the second benefit week following the date of the reduced benefit decision.

(4) Subject to paragraph (5), where a reduced benefit decision ('the subsequent decision') is made on a day when a reduced benefit decision ('the earlier decision') is in

force in respect of the same parent, the subsequent decision shall come into operation on the day immediately following the day on which the earlier decision ceased to be in force.

(5) Where the relevant benefit is income support and the provisions of regulation 26(2) of the Social Security (Claims and Payments) Regulations 1987 (deferment of payment of different amount of income support) apply, a reduced benefit decision shall come into operation on such later date as may be determined by the Secretary of State in accordance with those provisions.

(6) Where the benefit payable is income support or an income-based jobseeker's allowance and there is a change in the benefit week whilst a reduced benefit decision is in operation, the period of the reduction specified in paragraph (2) shall be a period greater than 155 weeks but less than 156 weeks and ending on the last day of the last benefit week falling entirely within the period of 156 weeks specified in that paragraph.

(7) Where the weekly amount specified in column (2) of paragraph 1(1)(e) of Schedule 2 to the Income Support Regulations changes on a day when a reduced benefit decision is in operation, the amount of the reduction of income support or income-based jobseeker's allowance shall be changed from the first day of the first benefit week to commence for the parent concerned on or after the day that weekly amount changes.

(8) Only one reduced benefit decision in relation to a parent concerned shall be in force at any one time.

12 Modification of reduction under a reduced benefit decision to preserve minimum entitlement to relevant benefit

Where in respect of any benefit week the amount of the relevant benefit that would be payable after it has been reduced following a reduced benefit decision would, but for this regulation, be nil or less than the minimum amount of that benefit that is payable as determined –

(a) in the case of income support, by regulation 26(4) of the Social Security (Claims and Payments) Regulations 1987;
(b) in the case of an income-based jobseeker's allowance, by regulation 87A of the Jobseeker's Allowance Regulations,

the amount of that reduction shall be decreased to such extent as to raise the amount of that benefit to the minimum amount that is payable.

13 Suspension of a reduced benefit decision when relevant benefit ceases to be payable

(1) Where relevant benefit ceases to be payable to, or in respect of, the parent concerned at a time when a reduced benefit decision is in operation, that reduced benefit decision shall, subject to paragraph (2), be suspended for a period of 52 weeks from the date the relevant benefit ceases to be payable.

(2) Where a reduced benefit decision has been suspended for a period of 52 weeks and no relevant benefit is payable at the end of that period, it shall cease to be in force.

(3) Where a reduced benefit decision is suspended and relevant benefit again becomes payable to, or in respect of, the parent concerned, the amount payable by way of that benefit shall, subject to regulations 14 and 15, be reduced in accordance with that reduced benefit decision for the balance of the reduction period.

(4) The amount or, as the case may be, the amounts of that reduction to be made during the balance of the reduction period shall be determined in accordance with regulation 11(2).

(5) No reduction in the amount of benefit under paragraph (3) shall be made before the expiry of a period of 14 days from service of the notice specified in paragraph (6), and the provisions of regulation 11(3) shall apply as to the date the reduced benefit decision again comes into operation.

(6) Where relevant benefit again becomes payable to, or in respect of, a parent with respect to whom a reduced benefit decision is suspended, she shall be notified in writing by the Secretary of State that the amount of relevant benefit paid to, or in respect of, her will again be reduced, in accordance with the provisions of paragraph (3), if she falls within section 46(1) of the Act.

14 Suspension of a reduced benefit decision when a modified applicable amount is payable (income support)

(1) Where a reduced benefit decision is given or is in operation at a time when income support is payable to, or in respect of, the parent concerned but her applicable amount falls to be calculated under the provisions mentioned in paragraph (4), that decision shall be suspended for so long as her applicable amount falls to be calculated under the provisions mentioned in that paragraph, or 52 weeks, whichever period is the shorter.

(2) Where a reduced benefit decision is given or is in operation at a time when income support is payable to, or in respect of, the parent concerned, but her applicable amount includes a residential allowance under regulation 17 of, and paragraph 2A of Schedule 2 to, the Income Support Regulations (applicable amounts for persons in residential care and nursing homes), that decision shall be suspended for as long as her applicable amount includes a residential allowance under that regulation and Schedule 2, or 52 weeks, whichever period is the shorter.

(3) Where a case falls within paragraph (1) or (2) and a reduced benefit decision has been suspended for 52 weeks, it shall cease to be in force.

(4) The provisions of paragraph (1) shall apply where the applicable amount in relation to the parent concerned falls to be calculated under –

- (a) regulation 19 of, and Schedule 4 to, the Income Support Regulations (applicable amounts for persons in residential care and nursing homes);
- (b) regulation 21 of, and paragraphs 1 to 3 of Schedule 7 to, the Income Support Regulations (patients);
- (c) regulation 21 of, and paragraphs 10B, 10C and 13 of Schedule 7 to, the Income Support Regulations (persons in local authority or residential accommodation).

15 Suspension of a reduced benefit decision when a modified applicable amount is payable (income-based jobseeker's allowance)

(1) Where a reduced benefit decision is given or is in operation at a time when an income-based jobseeker's allowance is payable to, or in respect of, the parent concerned but her applicable amount falls to be calculated under the provisions mentioned in paragraph (4), that reduced benefit decision shall be suspended for so long as the applicable amount falls to be calculated under those provisions, or 52 weeks, whichever is the shorter.

(2) Where a reduced benefit decision is given or is in operation at a time when an income-based jobseeker's allowance is payable to, or in respect of, the parent concerned but her applicable amount includes a residential allowance under regulation 83(c) of, and paragraph 3 of Schedule 1 to, the Jobseeker's Allowance Regulations (persons in residential care or nursing homes), that reduced benefit decision shall be suspended for so long as the applicable amount includes such a residential allowance, or 52 weeks, whichever is the shorter.

(3) Where a case falls within paragraph (1) or (2) and a reduced benefit decision has been suspended for 52 weeks, it shall cease to be in force.

(4) The provisions of paragraph (1) shall apply where the applicable amount in relation to the parent concerned falls to be calculated under –

(a) regulation 85 of, and paragraph 1 or 2 of Schedule 5 to, the Jobseeker's Allowance Regulations (patients);

(b) regulation 85 of, and paragraphs 8, 9 or 15 of Schedule 5 to, the Jobseeker's Allowance Regulations (persons in local authority or residential accommodation); or

(c) regulation 86 of, and Schedule 4 to, the Jobseeker's Allowance Regulations (applicable amounts for persons in residential care and nursing homes).

16　Termination of a reduced benefit decision

A reduced benefit decision shall cease to be in force –

(a) where the parent concerned –
   (i)　withdraws her request under section 6(5) of the Act;
   (ii)　complies with her obligation under section 6(7) of the Act; or
   (iii)　consents to take a scientific test (within the meaning of section 27A of the Act);

(b) where following written notice under section 46(6)(b) of the Act, the parent concerned responds to such notice and the Secretary of State considers there are reasonable grounds;

(c) subject to regulation 13, where relevant benefit ceases to be payable to, or in respect of, the parent concerned; or

(d) where a qualifying child with respect to whom a reduced benefit decision is in force applies for a maintenance calculation to be made with respect to him under section 7 of the Act and a calculation is made in response to that application in respect of all the qualifying children in relation to whom the parent concerned falls within section 46(1) of the Act.

17　Reduced benefit decisions where there is an additional qualifying child

(1) Where a reduced benefit decision is in operation, or would be in operation but for the provisions of regulations 14 and 15, and the Secretary of State gives a further reduced benefit decision with respect to the same parent concerned in relation to an additional qualifying child of whom she is a parent with care, the earlier reduced benefit decision shall cease to be in force.

(2) Where a further reduced benefit decision comes into operation in a case falling within paragraph (1), the provisions of regulation 11 shall apply to it.

(3) Where –

(a) a reduced benefit decision ('the earlier decision') has ceased to be in force by virtue of regulation 13(2); and

(b) the Secretary of State gives a further reduced benefit decision ('the further decision') with respect to the same parent concerned where that parent falls within section 46(1) of the Act,

as long as the further decision remains in force, no additional reduced benefit decision shall be brought into force with respect to that parent in relation to one or more children to whom the earlier decision was given.

(4) Where a case falls within paragraph (1) or (3) and the further decision, but for the provisions of this paragraph, would cease to be in force by virtue of the provisions of

regulation 16, but the earlier decision would not have ceased to be in force by virtue of the provisions of regulation 16, the further reduced benefit decision shall remain in force for a period calculated in accordance with regulation 11.

(5) In this regulation 'additional qualifying child' means a qualifying child of whom the parent concerned is a parent with care and who was either not such a qualifying child at the time the earlier decision was given or had not been born at the time the earlier decision was given.

18 Suspension and termination of a reduced benefit decision where the sole qualifying child ceases to be a child or where the parent concerned ceases to be a person with care

(1) Where a reduced benefit decision is in operation and –

    (a) there is, in relation to that decision, only one qualifying child, and that child ceases to be a child within the meaning of the Act; or

    (b) the parent concerned ceases to be a person with care,

the decision shall be suspended from the last day of the benefit week during the course of which the child ceases to be a child within the meaning of the Act, or the parent concerned ceases to be a person with care, as the case may be.

(2) Where, under the provisions of paragraph (1), a decision has been suspended for a period of 52 weeks and no relevant benefit is payable at that time, it shall cease to be in force.

(3) If during the period specified in paragraph (2) the former child again becomes a child within the meaning of the Act or the parent concerned again becomes a person with care and relevant benefit is payable to, or in respect of, that parent, a reduction in the amount of that benefit shall be made in accordance with the provisions of paragraphs (3) to (6) of regulation 13.

19 Notice of termination of a reduced benefit decision

Where a reduced benefit decision ceases to be in force under the provisions of regulation 16, 17 or 18 the Secretary of State shall serve notice of this on the parent concerned and shall specify the date on which the reduced benefit decision ceases to be in force.

20 Rounding provisions

Where any calculation made under this Part results in a fraction of a penny, that fraction shall be treated as a penny if it exceeds one half and shall otherwise be disregarded.

PART V

MISCELLANEOUS PROVISIONS

21 Persons who are not persons with care

(1) For the purposes of the Act the following categories of person shall not be persons with care –

    (a) a local authority;

    (b) a person with whom a child who is looked after by a local authority is placed by that authority under the provisions of the Children Act 1989, except where that person is a parent of such a child and the local authority allow the child to live with that parent under section 23(5) of that Act;

    (c) in Scotland, a family or relative with whom a child is placed by a local authority under the provisions of section 26 of the Children (Scotland) Act 1995.

(2) In paragraph (1) above –

'family' means family other than such family defined in section 93(1) of the Children (Scotland) Act 1995;

'local authority' means, in relation to England, a county council, a district council, a London borough council, the Common Council of the City of London or the Council of the Isles of Scilly and, in relation to Wales, a county council or a county borough council, and, in relation to Scotland, a council constituted under section 2 of the Local Government etc (Scotland) Act 1994; and

'a child who is looked after by a local authority' has the same meaning as in section 22 of the Children Act 1989 or section 17(6) of the Children (Scotland) Act 1995 as the case may be.

22   Authorisation of representative

(1) A person may authorise a representative, whether or not legally qualified, to receive notices and other documents on his behalf and to act on his behalf in relation to the making of applications and the supply of information under any provisions of the Act or these Regulations.

(2) Where a person has authorised a representative for the purposes of paragraph (1) who is not legally qualified, he shall confirm that authorisation in writing to the Secretary of State.

PART VI

NOTIFICATIONS FOLLOWING CERTAIN DECISIONS

23   Notification of a maintenance calculation

(1) A notification of a maintenance calculation made under section 11 or 12(2) of the Act (interim maintenance decision) shall set out, in relation to the maintenance calculation in question –

    (a)   the effective date of the maintenance calculation;

    (b)   where relevant, the non-resident parent's net weekly income;

    (c)   the number of qualifying children;

    (d)   the number of relevant other children;

    (e)   the weekly rate;

    (f)   the amounts calculated in accordance with Part I of Schedule 1 to the Act and, where there has been agreement to a variation or a variation has otherwise been taken into account, the Child Support (Variations) Regulations 2000;

    (g)   where the weekly rate is adjusted by apportionment or shared care, or both, the amount calculated in accordance with paragraph 6, 7 or 8, as the case may be, of Part I of Schedule 1 to the Act; and

    (h)   where the amount of child support maintenance which the non-resident parent is liable to pay is decreased in accordance with regulation 9 or 11 of the Maintenance Calculations and Special Cases Regulations (care provided in part by local authority and non-resident parent liable to pay maintenance under a maintenance order), the adjustment calculated in accordance with that regulation.

(2) A notification of a maintenance calculation made under section 12(1) of the Act (default maintenance decision) shall set out the effective date of the maintenance calculation, the default rate, the number of qualifying children on which the rate is based,

whether any apportionment has been applied under regulation 7 and shall state the nature of the information required to enable a decision under section 11 of the Act to be made by way of section 16 of the Act.

(3) Except where a person gives written permission to the Secretary of State that the information in relation to him, mentioned in sub-paragraphs (a) and (b) below, may be conveyed to other persons, any document given or sent under the provisions of paragraph (1) or (2) shall not contain –

(a) the address of any person other than the recipient of the document in question (other than the address of the office of the officer concerned who is exercising functions of the Secretary of State under the Act) or any other information the use of which could reasonably be expected to lead to any such person being located;

(b) any other information the use of which could reasonably be expected to lead to any person, other than a qualifying child or a relevant person, being identified.

(4) Where a decision as to a maintenance calculation is made under section 11 or 12 of the Act, a notification under paragraph (1) or (2) shall include information as to the provisions of sections 16, 17 and 20 of the Act.

24 Notification when an applicant under section 7 of the Act ceases to be a child

Where a maintenance calculation has been made in response to an application by a child under section 7 of the Act and that child ceases to be a child for the purposes of the Act, the Secretary of State shall immediately notify, so far as that is reasonably practicable –

(a) the other qualifying children who have attained the age of 12 years and the non-resident parent with respect to whom that maintenance calculation was made; and

(b) the person with care.

PART VII

EFFECTIVE DATES OF MAINTENANCE CALCULATIONS

25 Effective dates of maintenance calculations

(1) Subject to regulations 26 to 29, where no maintenance calculation is in force with respect to the person with care or the non-resident parent, the effective date of a maintenance calculation following an application made under section 4 or 7 of the Act, or treated as made under section 6(3) of the Act, as the case may be, shall be the date determined in accordance with paragraphs (2) to (4) below.

(2) Where the application for a maintenance calculation is made under section 4 of the Act by a non-resident parent, the effective date of the maintenance calculation shall be the date that an effective application is made or treated as made under regulation 3.

(3) Where the application for a maintenance calculation is –

(a) made under section 4 of the Act by a person with care;
(b) treated as made under section 6(3) of the Act; or
(c) made by a child under section 7 of the Act,

the effective date of the maintenance calculation shall be the date of notification to the non-resident parent.

(4) For the purposes of this regulation, where the Secretary of State is satisfied that a non-resident parent has intentionally avoided receipt of a notice of a maintenance

application he may determine the date of notification to the non-resident parent as the date on which the notification would have been given to him but for such avoidance.

(5) Where in relation to a decision made under section 11 of the Act a maintenance calculation is made to which paragraph 15 of Schedule 1 to the Act applies, the effective date of the calculation shall be the beginning of the maintenance period in which the change of circumstance to which the calculation relates occurred or is expected to occur.

26   Effective dates of maintenance calculations – maintenance order and application under section 4 or 7

(1) This regulation applies, subject to regulation 28, where –

  (a) no maintenance calculation is in force with respect to the person with care or the non-resident parent;
  (b) an application for a maintenance calculation is made under section 4 or 7 of the Act; and
  (c) there is a maintenance order in force, made on or after the date prescribed for the purposes of section 4(10)(a) of the Act, in relation to the person with care and the non-resident parent and that order has been in force for at least one year prior to the date the application for a maintenance calculation is made.

(2) The effective date of the maintenance calculation shall be two months and two days after the application is made.

27   Effective dates of maintenance calculations – maintenance order and application under section 6

(1) This regulation applies, subject to regulation 28, where –

  (a) the circumstances set out in regulation 26(1)(a) apply;
  (b) an application for a maintenance calculation is treated as made under section 6(3) of the Act; and
  (c) there is a maintenance order in force in relation to the person with care and the non-resident parent.

(2) The effective date of the maintenance calculation shall be 2 days after the maintenance calculation is made.

28   Effective dates of maintenance calculations – maintenance order ceases

Where –

  (a) a maintenance calculation is made; and
  (b) there was a maintenance order in force in relation to the person with care and the non-resident parent which ceased to have effect after the date on which the application for the maintenance calculation was made but before the effective date provided for in regulation 25 or 26 as the case may be,

the effective date of the maintenance calculation shall be the day following that on which the maintenance order ceased to have effect.

29   Effective dates of maintenance calculations in specified cases

Where an application for a maintenance calculation is made under section 4 or 7 of the Act, or treated as made under section 6(3) of the Act –

  (a) except where the parent with care has made a request under section 6(5) of the Act, where in the period of 8 weeks immediately preceding the date the application is made, or treated as made under regulation 3, there has been in force a maintenance calculation in respect of the same non-resident parent and child but a different person with care, the effective date of the maintenance calculation made in respect of the application shall be the day following the day on which the previous maintenance calculation ceased to have effect;

(b) where a maintenance calculation ('the existing calculation') is in force with respect to the person who is the person with care in relation to the application but who is the non-resident parent in relation to the existing calculation, the effective date of the calculation shall be a date not later than 7 days after the date of notification to the non-resident parent which is the day on which a maintenance period in respect of the existing calculation begins.

PART VIII

REVOCATION, SAVINGS AND TRANSITIONAL PROVISIONS

30   Revocation and savings

(1) Subject to paragraph (2), the Child Support (Maintenance Assessment Procedure) Regulations 1992 shall be revoked with respect to a particular case with effect from the date that these Regulations come into force with respect to that type of case ('the commencement date').

(2) Subject to regulation 31(2), where before the commencement date in respect of a particular case –

(a) an application was made and not determined for –
    (i)   a maintenance assessment;
    (ii) a departure direction; or
    (iii) a revision or supersession of a decision;
(b) the Secretary of State had begun but not completed a revision or supersession of a decision on his own initiative;
(c) any time limit provided for in Regulations for making an application for a revision or a departure direction had not expired; or
(d) any appeal was made but not decided or any time limit for making an appeal had not expired,

the provisions of the Child Support (Maintenance Assessment Procedure) Regulations 1992 shall continue to apply for the purposes of –

(aa)   the decision on the application referred to in sub-paragraph (a);
(bb)   the revision or supersession referred to in sub-paragraph (b);
(cc)   the ability to apply for the revision or the departure direction referred to in sub-paragraph (c) and the decision whether to revise or to give a departure direction following any such application;
(dd)   any appeal outstanding or made during the time limit referred to in sub-paragraph (d); or
(ee)   any revision, supersession, appeal or application for a departure direction in relation to a decision, ability to apply or appeal referred to in sub-paragraphs (aa) to (dd) above.

(3) Where immediately before the commencement date in respect of a particular case an interim maintenance assessment was in force, the provisions of the Child Support (Maintenance Assessment Procedure) Regulations 1992 shall continue to apply for the purposes of the decision under section 17 of the Act to make a maintenance assessment calculated in accordance with Part I of Schedule 1 to the 1991 Act before its amendment by the 2000 Act and any revision, supersession or appeal in relation to that decision.

(4) Where after the commencement date a maintenance assessment is revised, cancelled or ceases to have effect from a date which is prior to the commencement date, the Child Support (Maintenance Assessment Procedure) Regulations 1992 shall apply for the purposes of that cancellation or cessation.

(5) Where under regulation 28(1) of the Child Support (Transitional Provisions) Regulations 2000 an application for a maintenance calculation is treated as an application for a maintenance assessment, the provisions of the Child Support (Maintenance Assessment Procedure) Regulations 1992 shall continue to apply for the purposes of the determination of the application and any revision, supersession or appeal in relation to any such assessment made.

(6) For the purposes of this regulation –

    (a) 'departure direction', 'maintenance assessment' and 'interim maintenance assessment' have the same meaning as in section 54 of the Act before its amendment by the 2000 Act;

    (b) 'revision or supersession' means a revision or supersession of a decision under section 16 or 17 of the Act before their amendment by the 2000 Act;

    (c) '2000 Act' means the Child Support, Pensions and Social Security Act 2000.

31 Transitional provision – effective dates and reduced benefit decisions

(1) Where a maintenance assessment is in force with respect to a non-resident parent or a parent with care and an application for a maintenance calculation is made to which regulation 29 applies, that regulation shall apply as if references to a maintenance calculation in force were to a maintenance assessment in force.

(2) Where –

    (a) the application for a maintenance assessment was made before the date prescribed for the purposes of section 4(10)(a) of the Act; and

    (b) the effective date of the maintenance assessment, if it were a maintenance assessment to which the Assessment Procedure Regulations applied ('the assessment effective date') would be later than the effective date provided for in these Regulations,

the application shall be treated as an application for a maintenance calculation and the effective date of that maintenance calculation shall be the assessment effective date.

(3) Paragraphs (4) to (7) shall apply where, on or before the commencement date, section 6 of the former Act applied to the parent with care.

(4) Where a maintenance assessment was made with an effective date, applying the Assessment Procedure Regulations, or the Maintenance Arrangements and Jurisdiction Regulations, which is before the prescribed date and on or after the commencement date the parent with care notifies the Secretary of State that she is withdrawing her authorisation under subsection (1) of that section, these Regulations shall apply as if the notification were a request not to act under section 6(5) of the Act.

(5) Where a maintenance assessment was not made because section 6(2) of the former Act applied, these Regulations shall apply as if section 6(5) of the Act applied.

(6) Where a maintenance assessment was not made, section 6(2) of the former Act did not apply and a reduced benefit direction was given under section 46(5) of the former Act, these Regulations shall apply as if the reduced benefit direction were a reduced benefit

decision made under section 46(5) of the Act, from the same date and with the same effect as the reduced benefit direction.

(7) Where a maintenance assessment was not made, the parent with care failed to comply with a requirement imposed on her under section 6(1) of the former Act and the Secretary of State was in the process of serving a notice or considering reasons given by the parent with care under section 46(2) or (3) of the former Act, these Regulations shall apply as if the Secretary of State was in the process of serving a notice or considering reasons under section 46(2) or (3) of the Act.

(8) For the purposes of this regulation –

    (a) '2000 Act' means the Child Support, Pensions and Social Security Act 2000;
       'Assessment Procedure Regulations' means the Child Support (Maintenance Assessment Procedure) Regulations 1992;
       'commencement date' means with respect to a particular case the date these Regulations come into force with respect to that type of case;
       'former Act' means the Act before its amendment by the 2000 Act;
       'Maintenance Arrangements and Jurisdiction Regulations' means the Child Support (Maintenance Arrangements and Jurisdiction) Regulations 1992;
       'maintenance assessment' has the meaning given in the former Act; and
       'prescribed date' means the date prescribed for the purposes of section 4(10)(a) of the Act;
    (b) references in paragraphs (4) to (7) to sections 6(5), 46(5) and 46(2) and (3) of the Act mean those provisions as substituted by the 2000 Act; and
    (c) in the application of the Assessment Procedure Regulations for the purposes of paragraph (4) where, on or after the prescribed date, no maintenance enquiry form, as defined in those Regulations, is given or sent to the absent parent, the Regulations shall be applied as if references in regulation 30 –
       (i) to the date when the maintenance enquiry form was given or sent to the absent parent were to the date of notification to the non-resident parent;
       (ii) to the return by the absent parent of the maintenance enquiry form containing his name, address and written confirmation that he is the parent of the child or children in respect of whom the application was made were to the provision of this information by the non-resident parent; and
    (d) in the application of the Maintenance Arrangements and Jurisdiction Regulations for the purposes of paragraph (4), where, on or after the prescribed date no maintenance enquiry form, as defined in the Assessment Procedure Regulations, is given or sent to the absent parent, regulation 3(8) shall be applied as if the reference to the date when the maintenance enquiry form was given or sent were a reference to the date of notification to the non-resident parent.

SCHEDULE 1

Regulation 1(3)

MEANING OF 'CHILD' FOR THE PURPOSES OF THE ACT

1 Persons of 16 or 17 years of age who are not in full-time non-advanced education

(1) Subject to sub-paragraph (3), the conditions which must be satisfied for a person to be a child within section 55(1)(c) of the Act are –

    (a) the person is registered for work or for training under work-based training for young people or, in Scotland, Skillseekers training with –
       (i) the Department for Education and Employment;

   (ii)   the Ministry of Defence;
   (iii) in England and Wales, a local education authority within the meaning of the
          Education Acts 1944 to 1992;
   (iv)   in Scotland, an education authority within the meaning of section 135(1) of
          the Education (Scotland) Act 1980 (interpretation); or
   (v)   for the purposes of applying Council Regulation (EEC) No. 1408/71, any
          corresponding body in another member State;
   (b) the person is not engaged in remunerative work, other than work of a temporary
        nature that is due to cease before the end of the extension period which applies in
        the case of that person;
   (c) the extension period which applies in the case of that person has not expired; and
   (d) immediately before the extension period begins, the person is a child for the
        purposes of the Act without regard to this paragraph.

(2) For the purposes of heads (b), (c) and (d) of sub-paragraph (1), the extension
period –

   (a) begins on the first day of the week in which the person would no longer be a child
        for the purposes of the Act but for this paragraph; and
   (b) where a person ceases to fall within section 55(1)(a) of the Act or within
        paragraph 5 –
        (i)   on or after the first Monday in September, but before the first Monday in
               January of the following year, ends on the last day of the week which falls
               immediately before the week which includes the first Monday in January in
               that year;
        (ii)   on or after the first Monday in January but before the Monday following
               Easter Monday in that year, ends on the last day of the week which falls 12
               weeks after the week which includes the first Monday in January in that
               year;
        (iii) at any other time of the year, ends on the last day of the week which falls 12
               weeks after the week which includes the Monday following Easter Monday
               in that year.

(3) A person shall not be a child for the purposes of the Act under this paragraph if –

   (a) he is engaged in training under work-based training for young people or, in
        Scotland, Skillseekers training; or
   (b) he is entitled to income support or an income-based jobseeker's allowance.

2   Meaning of 'advanced education' for the purposes of section 55 of the Act

For the purposes of section 55 of the Act 'advanced education' means education of the
following description –

   (a) a course in preparation for a degree, a Diploma of Higher Education, a higher
        national diploma, a higher national diploma or higher national certificate of the
        Business and Technology Education Council or the Scottish Qualifications
        Council or a teaching qualification; or
   (b) any other course which is of a standard above that of an ordinary national
        diploma, a national diploma or a national certificate of the Business and
        Technology Education Council or the Scottish Qualifications Authority, the
        advanced level of the General Certificate of Education, a Scottish certificate of
        education (higher level), a Scottish certificate of sixth year studies, or a Scottish
        National Qualification at Higher Level.

3   Circumstances in which education is to be treated as full-time education

For the purposes of section 55 of the Act education shall be treated as being full-time if it is received by a person attending a course of education at a recognised educational establishment and the time spent receiving instruction or tuition, undertaking supervised study, examination of practical work or taking part in any exercise, experiment or project for which provision is made in the curriculum of the course, exceeds 12 hours per week, so however that in calculating the time spent in pursuit of the course, no account shall be taken of time occupied by meal breaks or spent on unsupervised study, whether undertaken on or off the premises of the educational establishment.

4   Interruption of full-time education

(1) Subject to sub-paragraph (2), in determining whether a person falls within section 55(1)(b) of the Act no account shall be taken of a period (whether beginning before or after the person concerned attains age 16) of up to 6 months of any interruption to the extent to which it is accepted that the interruption is attributable to a cause which is reasonable in the particular circumstances of the case; and where the interruption or its continuance is attributable to the illness or disability of mind or body of the person concerned, the period of 6 months may be extended for such further period as the Secretary of State considers reasonable in the particular circumstances of the case.

(2) The provisions of sub-paragraph (1) shall not apply to any period of interruption of a person's full-time education which is likely to be followed immediately or which is followed immediately by a period during which –

(a) provision is made for the training of that person, and for an allowance to be payable to that person, under work-based training for young people or, in Scotland, Skillseekers training; or

(b) he is receiving education by virtue of his employment or of any office held by him.

5   Circumstances in which a person who has ceased to receive full-time education is to be treated as continuing to fall within section 55(1) of the Act

(1) Subject to sub-paragraphs (2) and (5), a person who has ceased to receive full-time education (which is not advanced education) shall, if –

(a) he is under the age of 16 when he so ceases, from the date on which he attains that age; or

(b) he is 16 or over when he so ceases, from the date on which he so ceases,

be treated as continuing to fall within section 55(1) of the Act up to and including the week including the terminal date, or if he attains the age of 19 on or before that date, up to and including the week including the last Monday before he attains that age.

(2) In the case of a person specified in sub-paragraph (1)(a) or (b) who had not attained the upper limit of compulsory school age when he ceased to receive full-time education, the terminal date shall be that specified in head (a), (b) or (c) of sub-paragraph (3), whichever next follows the date on which he would have attained that age.

(3) In this paragraph the 'terminal date' means –

(a) the first Monday in January; or

(b) the Monday following Easter Monday; or

(c) the first Monday in September,

whichever first occurs after the date on which the person's said education ceased.

(4) In this paragraph 'compulsory school age' means –

(a) in England and Wales, compulsory school age as determined in accordance with section 9 of the Education Act 1962;

(b) in Scotland, school age as determined in accordance with sections 31 and 33 of the Education (Scotland) Act 1980.

(5) A person shall not be treated as continuing to fall within section 55(1) of the Act under this paragraph if he is engaged in remunerative work, other than work of a temporary nature that is due to cease before the terminal date.

(6) Subject to sub-paragraphs (5) and (8), a person whose name was entered as a candidate for any external examination in connection with full-time education (which is not advanced education), which he was receiving at the time, shall so long as his name continued to be so entered before ceasing to receive such education be treated as continuing to fall within section 55(1) of the Act for any week in the period specified in sub-paragraph (7).

(7) Subject to sub-paragraph (8), the period specified for the purposes of sub-paragraph (6) is the period beginning with the date when that person ceased to receive such education ending with –

(a) whichever of the dates in sub-paragraph (3) first occurs after the conclusion of the examination (or the last of them, if there is more than one); or

(b) the expiry of the week which includes the last Monday before his 19th birthday,

whichever is the earlier.

(8) The period specified in sub-paragraph (7) shall, in the case of a person who had not attained the age of 16 when he so ceased, begin with the date on which he did attain that age.

6 Interpretation

In this Schedule –

'Education Acts 1944 to 1992' has the meaning prescribed in section 94(2) of the Further and Higher Education Act 1992;

'remunerative work' means work of not less than 24 hours a week –

(a) in respect of which payment is made; or

(b) which is done in expectation of payment;

'week' means a period of 7 days beginning with a Monday;

'work-based training for young people or, in Scotland, Skillseekers training' means –

(a) arrangements made under section 2 of the Employment and Training Act 1973 (functions of the Secretary of State) or section 2 of the Enterprise and New Towns (Scotland) Act 1990;

(b) arrangements made by the Secretary of State for the persons enlisted in Her Majesty's forces for any special term of service specified in regulations made under section 2 of the Armed Forces Act 1966(power of Defence Council to make regulations as to engagement of persons in regular forces); or

(c) for the purposes of the application of Council Regulation (EEC) No. 1408/71, any corresponding provisions operated in another member State, for purposes which include the training of persons who, at the beginning of their training, are under the age of 18.

SCHEDULE 2

Regulation 4(1)

MULTIPLE APPLICATIONS

1   No maintenance calculation in force: more than one application for a maintenance calculation by the same person under section 4 or 6 or under sections 4 and 6 of the Act

(1) Where an effective application is made or treated as made, as the case may be, for a maintenance calculation under section 4 or 6 of the Act and, before that calculation is made, the applicant makes a subsequent effective application under that section with respect to the same non-resident parent or person with care, as the case may be, those applications shall be treated as a single application.

(2) Where an effective application for a maintenance calculation is made, or treated as made, as the case may be, by a person with care –

    (a) under section 4 of the Act; or
    (b) under section 6 of the Act,

and, before that maintenance calculation is made, the person with care –

    (i) in a case falling within head (a), is treated as making an application under section 6 of the Act; or
    (ii) in a case falling within head (b), makes a subsequent effective application under section 4 of the Act,

with respect to the same non-resident parent, those applications shall, if the person with care does not cease to fall within section 6(1) of the Act, be treated as a single application under section 6 of the Act, and shall otherwise be treated as a single application under section 4 of the Act.

2   No maintenance calculation in force: more than one application by a child under section 7 of the Act

Where a child makes an effective application for a maintenance calculation under section 7 of the Act and, before that calculation is made, makes a subsequent effective application under that section with respect to the same person with care and non-resident parent, both applications shall be treated as a single application for a maintenance calculation.

3   No maintenance calculation in force: applications by different persons for a maintenance calculation

(1) Where the Secretary of State receives more than one effective application for a maintenance calculation with respect to the same person with care and non-resident parent, he shall, if no maintenance calculation has been made in relation to any of the applications, determine which application he shall proceed with in accordance with sub-paragraphs (2) to (11).

(2) Where an application by a person with care is made under section 4 of the Act or is treated as made under section 6 of the Act, and an application is made by a non-resident parent under section 4 of the Act, the Secretary of State shall proceed with the application of the person with care.

(3) Where there is an application for a maintenance calculation by a qualifying child under section 7 of the Act and a subsequent application is made with respect to that child by a person who is, with respect to that child, a person with care or a non-resident parent,

the Secretary of State shall proceed with the application of that person with care or non-resident parent, as the case may be.

(4) Where, in a case falling within sub-paragraph (3), there is made more than one subsequent application, the Secretary of State shall apply the provisions of sub-paragraphs (2), (7), (8), or (10), as is appropriate in the circumstances of the case, to determine which application he shall proceed with.

(5) Where there is an application for a maintenance calculation by more than one qualifying child under section 7 of the Act in relation to the same person with care and non-resident parent, the Secretary of State shall proceed with the application of the elder or, as the case may be, eldest of the qualifying children.

(6) Where there are two non-resident parents in respect of the same qualifying child and an effective application is received from each such person, the Secretary of State shall proceed with both applications, treating them as a single application for a maintenance calculation.

(7) Where an application is treated as having been made by a parent with care under section 6 of the Act and there is an application under section 4 of the Act by another person with care who has parental responsibility for (or, in Scotland, parental rights over) the qualifying child or qualifying children with respect to whom the application under section 6 of the Act was treated as made, the Secretary of State shall proceed with the application under section 6 of the Act by the parent with care.

(8) Where –

    (a) more than one person with care makes an application for a maintenance calculation under section 4 of the Act in respect of the same qualifying child or qualifying children (whether or not any of those applications is also in respect of other qualifying children);

    (b) each such person has parental responsibility for (or, in Scotland, parental rights over) that child or children; and

    (c) under the provisions of regulation 8 of the Maintenance Calculations and Special Cases Regulations one of those persons is to be treated as a non-resident parent,

the Secretary of State shall proceed with the application of the person who does not fall to be treated as a non-resident parent under the provisions of regulation 8 of those Regulations.

(9) Where, in a case falling within sub-paragraph (8), there is more than one person who does not fall to be treated as a non-resident parent under the provisions of regulation 8 of those Regulations, the Secretary of State shall apply the provisions of paragraph (10) to determine which application he shall proceed with.

(10) Where –

    (a) more than one person with care makes an application for a maintenance calculation under section 4 of the Act in respect of the same qualifying child or qualifying children (whether or not any of those applications is also in respect of other qualifying children); and

    (b) either –

        (i) none of those persons has parental responsibility for (or, in Scotland, parental rights over) that child or children; or

        (ii) the case falls within sub-paragraph (8)(b) but the Secretary of State has not been able to determine which application he is to proceed with under the provisions of sub-paragraph (8), the Secretary of State shall proceed with the application of the principal provider of day to day care, as determined in accordance with sub-paragraph (11).

(11) Where –

    (a) the applications are in respect of one qualifying child, the application of that person with care to whom child benefit is paid in respect of that child;

    (b) the applications are in respect of more than one qualifying child, the application of that person with care to whom child benefit is paid in respect of those children;

    (c) the Secretary of State cannot determine which application he is to proceed with under head (a) or (b) the application of that applicant who in the opinion of the Secretary of State is the principal provider of day to day care for the child or children in question.

(12) Subject to sub-paragraph (13), where, in any case falling within sub-paragraphs (2) to (10), the applications are not in respect of identical qualifying children, the application that the Secretary of State is to proceed with as determined by those sub-paragraphs shall be treated as an application with respect to all of the qualifying children with respect to whom the applications were made.

(13) Where the Secretary of State is satisfied that the same person with care does not provide the principal day to day care for all of the qualifying children with respect to whom an application would but for the provisions of this paragraph be made under sub-paragraph (12), he shall make separate maintenance calculations in relation to each person with care providing such principal day to day care.

(14) For the purposes of this paragraph 'day to day care' has the same meaning as in the Maintenance Calculations and Special Cases Regulations.

4   Maintenance calculation in force: subsequent application with respect to the same persons

Where a maintenance calculation is in force and a subsequent application is made or treated as made, as the case may be, under the same section of the Act for a maintenance calculation with respect to the same person with care, non-resident parent, and qualifying child or qualifying children as those with respect to whom the maintenance calculation in force has been made, that application shall not be proceeded with.

Child Support (Maintenance Calculations and Special Cases) Regulations 2000

SI 2001/155

PART I

GENERAL

1 Citation, commencement and interpretation

(1) These Regulations may be cited as the Child Support (Maintenance Calculations and Special Cases) Regulations 2000.

(2) In these Regulations, unless the context otherwise requires –

'the Act' means the Child Support Act 1991;

'Contributions and Benefits Act' means the Social Security Contributions and Benefits Act 1992;

'Contributions and Benefits (Northern Ireland) Act' means the Social Security Contributions and Benefits (Northern Ireland) Act 1992;

'couple' means a man and a woman who are –

(a) married to each other and are members of the same household; or

(b) not married to each other but are living together as husband and wife;

'course of advanced education' means –

(a) a full-time course leading to a postgraduate degree or comparable qualification, a first degree or comparable qualification, a Diploma of Higher Education, a higher national diploma, a higher national diploma or higher national certificate of the Business and Technology Education Council or the Scottish Qualifications Authority or a teaching qualification; or

(b) any other full-time course which is a course of a standard above that of an ordinary national diploma, a national diploma or national certificate of the Business and Technology Education Council or the Scottish Qualifications Authority, the advanced level of the General Certificate of Education, a Scottish certificate of education (higher level), a Scottish certificate of sixth year studies or a Scottish National Qualification at Higher Level;

'day' includes any part of a day;

'day to day care' means –

(a) care of not less than 104 nights in total during the 12 month period ending with the relevant week; or

(b) where, in the opinion of the Secretary of State, a period other than 12 months is more representative of the current arrangements for the care of the child in question, care during that period of not less in total than the number of nights which bears the same ratio to 104 nights as that period bears to 12 months, and for the purpose of this definition –

(i) where a child is a boarder at a boarding school or is a patient in a hospital or other circumstances apply, such as where the child stays with a person who is not a parent of the child, and which the Secretary of State regards as temporary, the person who, but for those circumstances, would otherwise provide day to day care of the child shall be treated as providing day to day care during the periods in question; and

(ii) 'relevant week' shall have the meaning ascribed to it in the definition in this paragraph, except that in a case where notification is given under regulation 7C of the Decisions and Appeals Regulations to the relevant persons on different dates, 'relevant week' means the period of 7 days immediately preceding the date of the latest notification;

'Decisions and Appeals Regulations' means the Social Security and Child Support (Decisions and Appeals) Regulations 1999;

'disabled person's tax credit' means a disabled person's tax credit under section 129 of the Contributions and Benefits Act;

'effective date' means the date on which a maintenance calculation takes effect for the purposes of the Act;

'employed earner' has the same meaning as in section 2(1)(a) of the Contributions and Benefits Act except that it shall include –

(a) a person gainfully employed in Northern Ireland; and

(b) a person to whom section 44(2A) of the Act applies;

'family' means –

(a) a couple (including the members of a polygamous marriage) and any member of the same household for whom one or more of them is responsible and who is a child; or

(b) a person who is not a member of a couple and a member of the same household for whom that person is responsible and who is a child;

'home' means –

(a) the dwelling in which a person and any family of his normally live; or

(b) if he or they normally live in more than one home, the principal home of that person and any family of his, and for the purpose of determining the principal home in which a person normally lives no regard shall be had to residence in a residential care home or a nursing home during a period which does not exceed 52 weeks or, where it appears to the Secretary of State that the person will return to his principal home after that period has expired, such longer period as the Secretary of State considers reasonable to allow for the return of that person to that home;

'Income Support Regulations' means the Income Support (General) Regulations 1987;

'the Jobseekers Act' means the Jobseekers Act 1995;

'Maintenance Calculation Procedure Regulations' means the Child Support (Maintenance Calculation Procedure) Regulations 2000;

'net weekly income' has the meaning given in the Schedule to these Regulations;

'nursing home' has the same meaning as in regulation 19(3) of the Income Support Regulations;

'occupational pension scheme' means such a scheme within the meaning in section 1 of the Pension Schemes Act 1993 and which is approved for the purposes of Part XIV of the Income and Corporation Taxes Act 1988;

'partner' means –

(a) in relation to a member of a couple, the other member of that couple;

(b) in relation to a member of a polygamous marriage, any other member of that marriage with whom he lives;

'patient' means a person (other than a person who is serving a sentence of imprisonment or detention in a young offender institution within the meaning of the Criminal Justice Act 1982 or the Prisons (Scotland) Act 1989 who is regarded as receiving free in-patient treatment within the meaning of the Social Security (Hospital In-Patients) Regulations 1975;

'person' does not include a local authority;

'personal pension scheme' means such a scheme within the meaning in section 1 of the Pension Schemes Act 1993 and which is approved for the purposes of Part XIV of the Income and Corporation Taxes Act 1988;

'polygamous marriage' means any marriage during the subsistence of which a party to it is married to more than one person and in respect of which any ceremony of marriage took place under the law of a country which at the time of that ceremony permitted polygamy;

'prisoner' means a person who is detained in custody pending trial or sentence upon conviction or under a sentence imposed by a court other than a person whose detention is under the Mental Health Act 1983 or the Mental Health (Scotland) Act 1984;

'relevant week' means –

   (a) in relation to an application for child support maintenance –

       (i)   where the application is made by a non-resident parent, the period of 7 days immediately before the application is made; and

      (ii) in any other case, the period of 7 days immediately before the date of notification to the non-resident parent and for this purpose 'the date of notification to the non-resident parent' means the date on which the non-resident parent is first given notice by the Secretary of State under the Maintenance Calculation Procedure Regulations that an application for a maintenance calculation has been made, or treated as made, as the case may be, in relation to which the non-resident parent is named as the parent of the child to whom the application relates;

   (b) where a decision ('the original decision') is to be –

       (i)   revised under section 16 of the Act; or

      (ii) superseded by a decision under section 17 of the Act on the grounds that the original decision was made in ignorance of, or was based upon a mistake as to, some material fact or was erroneous in point of law, the period of 7 days which was the relevant week for the purposes of the original decision;

   (c) where a decision ('the original decision') is to be superseded under section 17 of the Act –

       (i)   on an application made for the purpose on the basis that a material change of circumstances has occurred since the original decision was made, the period of 7 days immediately preceding the date on which that application was made;

      (ii) subject to sub-paragraph (b), in a case where a relevant person is given notice under regulation 7C of the Decisions and Appeals Regulations, the period of 7 days immediately preceding the date of that notification,

except that where, under paragraph 15 of Schedule 1 to the Act, the Secretary of State makes separate maintenance calculations in respect of different periods in a particular case, because he is aware of one or more changes of circumstances which occurred after the date which is applicable to that case, the relevant week for the purposes of each separate maintenance calculation made to take account of each such change of circumstances shall be the period of 7 days immediately before the date on which notification was given to the Secretary of State of the change of circumstances relevant to that separate maintenance calculation;

'residential care home' has the same meaning as in regulation 19(3) of the Income Support Regulations;

'retirement annuity contract' means an annuity contract for the time being approved by the Board of Inland Revenue as having for its main object the provision of a life annuity in old age or the provision of an annuity for a partner or dependant and in respect of which relief from income tax may be given on any premium;

'self-employed earner' has the same meaning as in section 2(1)(b) of the Contributions and Benefits Act except that it shall include a person gainfully employed in Northern Ireland otherwise than in employed earner's employment (whether or not he is also employed in such employment);

'student' means a person, other than a person in receipt of a training allowance, who is aged less than 19 and attending a full-time course of advanced education or who is aged 19 or over and attending a full-time course of study at an educational establishment; and for the purposes of this definition –

    (a) a person who has started on such a course shall be treated as attending it throughout any period of term or vacation within it, until the last day of the course or such earlier date as he abandons it or is dismissed from it;

    (b) a person on a sandwich course (within the meaning of paragraph 1(1) of Schedule 5 to the Education (Mandatory Awards) (No 2) Regulations 1993) shall be treated as attending a full-time course of advanced education or, as the case may be, of study;

'training allowance' means an allowance payable under section 2 of the Employment and Training Act 1973, or section 2 of the Enterprise and New Towns (Scotland) Act 1990;

'work-based training for young people or, in Scotland, Skillseekers training' means –

    (a) arrangements made under section 2 of the Employment and Training Act 1973 or section 2 of the Enterprise and New Towns (Scotland) Act 1990; or

    (b) arrangements made by the Secretary of State for persons enlisted in Her Majesty's forces for any special term of service specified in regulations made under section 2 of the Armed Forces Act 1966 (power of Defence Council to make regulations as to engagement of persons in regular forces),

for purposes which include the training of persons who, at the beginning of their training, are under the age of 18;

'working families' tax credit' means a working families' tax credit under section 128 of the Contributions and Benefits Act; and

'year' means a period of 52 weeks.

(3) The following other description of children is prescribed for the purposes of paragraph 10C(2)(b) of Schedule 1 to the Act (relevant other children) –

children other than qualifying children in respect of whom the non-resident parent or his partner would receive child benefit under Part IX of the Contributions and Benefits Act but who do not solely because the conditions set out in section 146 of that Act (persons outside Great Britain) are not met.

(4) Subject to paragraph (5), these Regulations shall come into force in relation to a particular case on the day on which Part I of Schedule 1 to the 1991 Act as amended by the Child Support, Pensions and Social Security Act 2000 comes into force in relation to that type of case.

(5) Paragraphs (1) and (2) of regulation 4 and, for the purposes of those provisions, this regulation shall come into force on 31st January 2001.

PART II

CALCULATION OF CHILD SUPPORT MAINTENANCE

2 Calculation of amounts

(1) Where any amount is to be considered in connection with any calculation made under these Regulations or under Schedule 1 to the Act, it shall be calculated as a weekly amount and, except where the context otherwise requires, any reference to such an amount shall be construed accordingly.

(2) Subject to paragraph (3), where any calculation made under these Regulations or under Schedule 1 to the Act results in a fraction of a penny that fraction shall be treated as a penny if it is either one half or exceeds one half, otherwise it shall be disregarded.

(3) Where the calculation of the basic rate of child support maintenance or the reduced rate of child support maintenance results in a fraction of a pound that fraction shall be treated as a pound if it is either one half or exceeds one half, otherwise it shall be disregarded.

(4) In taking account of any amounts or information required for the purposes of making a maintenance calculation, the Secretary of State shall apply the dates or periods specified in these Regulations as applicable to those amounts or information, provided that if he becomes aware of a material change of circumstances occurring after such date or period, but before the effective date, he shall take that change of circumstances into account.

(5) Information required for the purposes of making a maintenance calculation in relation to the following shall be the information applicable at the effective date –

- (a) the number of qualifying children;
- (b) the number of relevant other children;
- (c) whether the non-resident parent receives a benefit, pension or allowance prescribed for the purposes of paragraph 4(1)(b) of Schedule 1 to the Act;
- (d) whether the non-resident parent or his partner receives a benefit prescribed for the purposes of paragraph 4(1)(c) of Schedule 1 to the Act; and
- (e) whether paragraph 5(a) of Schedule 1 to the Act applies to the non-resident parent.

3 Reduced rate

The reduced rate is an amount calculated as follows –

$$F + (A \times T)$$

where –
F is the flat rate liability applicable to the non-resident parent under paragraph 4 of Schedule 1 to the Act;
A is the amount of the non-resident parent's net weekly income between £100 and £200; and
T is the percentage determined in accordance with the following Table –

	1 qualifying child of the non-resident parent				2 qualifying children of the non-resident parent				3 or more qualifying children on the non-resident parent			
Number of relevant other children of the non-resident parent	0	1	2	3 or more	0	1	2	3 or more	0	1	2	3 or more
T (%)	25	20.5	19	17.5	35	29	27	25	45	37.5	35	32.5

4 Flat rate

(1) The following benefits, pensions and allowances are prescribed for the purposes of paragraph 4(1)(b) of Schedule 1 to the Act –

    (a) under the Contributions and Benefits Act –
        (i)   bereavement allowance under section 39B;
        (ii)   category A retirement pension under section 44;
        (iii)   category B retirement pension under section 48C;
        (iv)   category C and category D retirement pensions under section 78;
        (v)   incapacity benefit under section 30A;
        (vi)   invalid care allowance under section 70;
        (vii)   maternity allowance under section 35;
        (viii) severe disablement allowance under section 68;
        (ix)   industrial injuries benefit under section 94;
        (x)   widowed mother's allowance under section 37;
        (xi)   widowed parent's allowance under section 39A; and
        (xii)   widow's pension under section 38;
    (b) contribution-based jobseeker's allowance under section 1 of the Jobseekers Act;
    (c) a social security benefit paid by a country other than the United Kingdom;
    (d) a training allowance (other than work-based training for young people or, in Scotland, Skillseekers training); and
    (e) a war disablement pension or war widow's pension within the meaning of section 150(2) of the Contributions and Benefits Act or a pension which is analogous to such a pension paid by the government of a country outside Great Britain.

(2) The benefits prescribed for the purposes of paragraph 4(1)(c) of Schedule 1 to the Act are –

    (a) income support under section 124 of the Contributions and Benefits Act; and
    (b) income-based jobseeker's allowance under section 1 of the Jobseekers Act.

(3) Where the non-resident parent is liable to a pay a flat rate by virtue of paragraph 4(2) of Schedule 1 to the Act –

    (a) if he has one partner, then the amount payable by the non-resident parent shall be half the flat rate; and
    (b) if he has more than one partner, then the amount payable by the non-resident parent shall be the result of apportioning the flat rate equally among him and his partners.

5   Nil rate

The rate payable is nil where the non-resident parent is –

(a) a student;

(b) a child within the meaning given in section 55(1) of the Act;

(c) a prisoner;

(d) a person who is 16 or 17 years old and –

    (i)   in receipt of income support or income-based jobseeker's allowance; or

    (ii) a member of a couple whose partner is in receipt of income support or income-based jobseeker's allowance;

(e) a person receiving an allowance in respect of work-based training for young people or, in Scotland, Skillseekers training;

(f) a person in a residential care home or nursing home who –

    (i)   is in receipt of a pension, benefit or allowance specified in regulation 4(1) or (2); or

    (ii) has the whole or part of the cost of his accommodation met by a local authority;

(g) a patient in hospital who is in receipt of income support whose applicable amount includes an amount under paragraph 1(a) or (b) of Schedule 7 to the Income Support Regulations (patient for more than 6 weeks);

(h) a person in receipt of a benefit specified in regulation 4(1) the amount of which has been reduced in accordance with the provisions of regulations 4(d) and 6 of the Social Security Hospital In-Patients Regulations 1975 (circumstances in which personal benefit is to be adjusted and adjustment of personal benefit after 52 weeks in hospital); or

(i) a person who would be liable to pay the flat rate because he satisfies the description in paragraph 4(1)(c) of Schedule 1 to the Act but his net weekly income, inclusive of –

    (aa) any benefit, pension or allowance that he receives which is prescribed for the purposes of paragraph 4(1)(b) of Schedule 1 to the Act; and

    (bb) any benefit that he or his partner receives which is prescribed for the purposes of paragraph 4(1)(c) of Schedule 1 to the Act,

    is less than £5 a week.

6   Apportionment

If, in making the apportionment required by regulation 4(3) or paragraph 6 of Part I of Schedule 1 to the Act, the effect of the application of regulation 2(2) (rounding) would be such that the aggregate amount of child support maintenance payable by a non-resident parent would be different from the aggregate amount payable before any apportionment, the Secretary of State shall adjust that apportionment so as to eliminate that difference; and that adjustment shall be varied from time to time so as to secure that, taking one week with another and so far as is practicable, each person with care receives the amount which she would have received if no adjustment had been made under this paragraph.

7   Shared care

(1) For the purposes of paragraphs 7 and 8 of Part I of Schedule 1 to the Act a night will count for the purposes of shared care where the non-resident parent –

(a) has the care of a qualifying child overnight; and

(b) the qualifying child stays at the same address as the non-resident parent.

(2) For the purposes of paragraphs 7 and 8 of Part I of Schedule 1 to the Act, a non-resident parent has the care of a qualifying child when he is looking after the child.

(3) Subject to paragraph (4), in determining the number of nights for the purposes of shared care, the Secretary of State shall consider the 12 month period ending with the relevant week and for this purpose 'relevant week' has the same meaning as in the definition of day to day care in regulation 1 of these Regulations.

(4) The circumstances in which the Secretary of State may have regard to a number of nights over less than a 12 month period are where there has been no pattern for the frequency with which the non-resident parent looks after the qualifying child for the 12 months preceding the relevant week, or the Secretary of State is aware that a change in that frequency is intended, and in that case he shall have regard to such lesser period as may seem to him to be appropriate, and the Table in paragraph 7(4) and the period in paragraph 8(2) of Schedule 1 to the Act shall have effect subject to the adjustment described in paragraph (5).

(5) Where paragraph (4) applies, the Secretary of State shall adjust the number of nights in that lesser period by applying to that number the ratio which the period of 12 months bears to that lesser period.

(6) Where a child is a boarder at a boarding school, or is a patient in a hospital, the person who, but for those circumstances, would otherwise have care of the child overnight shall be treated as providing that care during the periods in question.

PART III

SPECIAL CASES

8   Persons treated as non-resident parents

(1) Where the circumstances of a case are that –

    (a) two or more persons who do not live in the same household each provide day to day care for the same qualifying child; and

    (b) at least one of those persons is a parent of the child,

that case shall be treated as a special case for the purposes of the Act.

(2) For the purposes of this special case a parent who provides day to day care for a child of his is to be treated as a non-resident parent for the purposes of the Act in the following circumstances –

    (a) a parent who provides such care to a lesser extent than the other parent, person or persons who provide such care for the child in question; or

    (b) where the persons mentioned in paragraph (1)(a) include both parents and the circumstances are such that care is provided to the same extent by both but each provides care to an extent greater than or equal to any other person who provides such care for that child –

        (i) the parent who is not in receipt of child benefit for the child in question; or

        (ii) if neither parent is in receipt of child benefit for that child, the parent who, in the opinion of the Secretary of State, will not be the principal provider of day to day care for that child.

(3) For the purposes of this regulation and regulation 10 'child benefit' means child benefit payable under Part IX of the Contributions and Benefits Act.

9   Care provided in part by a local authority

(1) This regulation applies where paragraph (2) applies and the rate of child support maintenance payable is the basic rate, or the reduced rate, or has been calculated following agreement to a variation where the non-resident parent's liability would otherwise have been a flat rate or the nil rate.

(2) Where the circumstances of a case are that the care of the qualifying child is shared between the person with care and a local authority and –

- (a) the qualifying child is in the care of the local authority for 52 nights or more in the 12 month period ending with the relevant week; or
- (b) where, in the opinion of the Secretary of State, a period other than the 12 month period mentioned in sub-paragraph (a) is more representative of the current arrangements for the care of the qualifying child, the qualifying child is in the care of the local authority during that period for no fewer than the number of nights which bears the same ratio to 52 nights as that period bears to 12 months; or
- (c) it is intended that the qualifying child shall be in the care of the local authority for a number of nights in a period from the effective date,

that case shall be treated as a special case for the purposes of the Act.

(3) In a case where this regulation applies, the amount of child support maintenance which the non-resident parent is liable to pay the person with care of that qualifying child is the amount calculated in accordance with the provisions of Part I of Schedule 1 to the Act and decreased in accordance with this regulation.

(4) First, there is to be a decrease according to the number of nights spent or to be spent by the qualifying child in the care of the local authority during the period under consideration.

(5) Where paragraph (2)(b) or (c) applies, the number of nights in the period under consideration shall be adjusted by the ratio which the period of 12 months bears to the period under consideration.

(6) After any adjustment under paragraph (5), the amount of the decrease for one child is set out in the following Table –

Number of nights in care of local authority	*Fraction to subtract*
52–103	One-seventh
104–155	Two-sevenths
156–207	Three-sevenths
208–259	Four-sevenths
260–262	Five-sevenths

(7) If the non-resident parent and the person with care have more than one qualifying child, the applicable decrease is the sum of the appropriate fractions in the Table divided by the number of such qualifying children.

(8) In a case where the amount of child support maintenance which the non-resident parent is liable to pay in relation to the same person with care is to be decreased in accordance with the provisions of both this regulation and of paragraph 7 of Part I of Schedule 1 to the Act, read with regulation 7 of these Regulations, the applicable decrease is the sum of the appropriate fractions derived under those provisions.

(9) If the application of this regulation would decrease the weekly amount of child support maintenance (or the aggregate of all such amounts) payable by the non-resident parent to less than the rate stated in or prescribed for the purposes of paragraph 4(1) of Part I of Schedule 1 to the Act, he is instead liable to pay child support maintenance at a rate equivalent to that rate, apportioned (if appropriate) in accordance with paragraph 6 of Part I of Schedule 1 to the Act and regulation 6.

(10) Where a qualifying child is a boarder at a boarding school or is an in-patient at a hospital, the qualifying child shall be treated as being in the care of the local authority for any night that the local authority would otherwise have been providing such care.

(11) A child is in the care of a local authority for any night in which he is being looked after by the local authority within the meaning of section 22 of the Children Act 1989 or section 17(6) of the Children (Scotland) Act 1995.

10   Care provided for relevant other child by a local authority

Where a child other than a qualifying child is cared for in part or in full by a local authority and the non-resident parent or his partner receives child benefit for that child, the child is a relevant other child for the purposes of Schedule 1 to the Act.

11   Non-resident parent liable to pay maintenance under a maintenance order

(1) Subject to paragraph (2), where the circumstances of a case are that –

(a) an application for child support maintenance is made or treated as made, as the case may be, with respect to a qualifying child and a non-resident parent; and

(b) an application for child support maintenance for a different child cannot be made under the Act but that non-resident parent is liable to pay maintenance under a maintenance order for that child,

that case shall be treated as a special case for the purposes of the Act.

(2) This regulation applies where the rate of child support maintenance payable is the basic rate, or the reduced rate, or has been calculated following agreement to a variation where the non-resident parent's liability would otherwise have been a flat rate or the nil rate.

(3) Where this regulation applies, the amount of child support maintenance payable by the non-resident parent shall be ascertained by –

(a) calculating the amount of maintenance payable as if the number of qualifying children of that parent included any children with respect to whom he is liable to make payments under the order referred to in paragraph (1)(b); and

(b) apportioning the amount so calculated between the qualifying children and the children with respect to whom he is liable to make payments under the order referred to in paragraph (1)(b),

and the amount payable shall be the amount apportioned to the qualifying children, and the amount payable to each person with care shall be that amount subject to the application of apportionment under paragraph 6 of Schedule 1 to the Act and the shared care provisions in paragraph 7 of Part I of that Schedule.

(4) In a case where this regulation applies paragraph 7 of Part I of Schedule 1 to the Act (shared care) and regulation 10 (care provided in part by local authority) shall not apply in relation to a child in respect of whom the non-resident parent is liable to make payments under a maintenance order as provided in paragraph (1)(b).

12   Child who is a boarder or an in-patient in hospital

(1) Where the circumstances of the case are that –

(a) a qualifying child is a boarder at a boarding school or is an in-patient in a hospital; and

(b) by reason of those circumstances, the person who would otherwise provide day to day care is not doing so, that case shall be treated as a special case for the purposes of the Act.

(2) For the purposes of this case, section 3(3)(b) of the Act shall be modified so that for the reference to the person who usually provides day to day care for the child there shall be substituted a reference to the person who would usually be providing such care for that child but for the circumstances specified in paragraph (1).

13 Child who is allowed to live with his parent under section 23(5) of the Children Act 1989

(1) Where the circumstances of a case are that a qualifying child who is in the care of a local authority in England and Wales is allowed by the authority to live with a parent of his under section 23(5) of the Children Act 1989, that case shall be treated as a special case for the purposes of the Act.

(2) For the purposes of this case, section 3(3)(b) of the Act shall be modified so that for the reference to the person who usually provides day to day care for the child there shall be substituted a reference to the parent of the child with whom the local authority allow the child to live with under section 23(5) of the Children Act 1989.

14 Person with part-time care who is not a non-resident parent

(1) Where the circumstances of a case are that –

   (a) two or more persons who do not live in the same household each provide day to day care for the same qualifying child; and
   (b) those persons do not include any parent who is treated as a non-resident parent of that child by regulation 8(2),

that case shall be treated as a special case for the purposes of the Act.

(2) For the purposes of this case –

   (a) the person whose application for a maintenance calculation is being proceeded with shall, subject to sub-paragraph (b), be entitled to receive all of the child support maintenance payable under the Act in respect of the child in question;
   (b) on request being made to the Secretary of State by –
      (i) that person; or
      (ii) any other person who is providing day to day care for that child and who intends to continue to provide that care,
   the Secretary of State may make arrangements for the payment of any child support maintenance payable under the Act to the persons who provide such care in the same ratio as that in which it appears to the Secretary of State that each is to provide such care for the child in question;
   (c) before making an arrangement under sub-paragraph (b), the Secretary of State shall consider all of the circumstances of the case and in particular the interests of the child, the present arrangements for the day to day care of the child in question and any representations or proposals made by the persons who provide such care for that child.

PART IV

REVOCATION AND SAVINGS

15 Revocation and savings

(1) Subject to paragraphs (2), (3) and (4), the Child Support (Maintenance Assessments and Special Cases) Regulations 1992 ('the 1992 Regulations') shall be revoked with

respect to a particular case with effect from the date that these Regulations come into force with respect to that type of case ('the commencement date').

(2) Where before the commencement date in respect of a particular case –

    (a) an application was made and not determined for –
        (i) a maintenance assessment;
        (ii) a departure direction; or
        (iii) a revision or supersession of a decision;
    (b) the Secretary of State had begun but not completed a revision or supersession of a decision on his own initiative;
    (c) any time limit provided for in Regulations for making an application for a revision or a departure direction had not expired; or
    (d) any appeal was made but not decided or any time limit for making an appeal had not expired,

the provisions of the 1992 Regulations shall continue to apply for the purposes of –

    (aa) the decision on the application referred to in sub-paragraph (a);
    (bb) the revision or supersession referred to in sub-paragraph (b);
    (cc) the ability to apply for the revision or the departure direction referred to in sub-paragraph (c) and the decision whether to revise or to give a departure direction following any such application;
    (dd) any appeal outstanding or made during the time limit referred to in sub-paragraph (d); or
    (ee) any revision, supersession, appeal or application for a departure direction in relation to a decision, ability to apply or appeal referred to in sub-paragraphs (aa) to (dd) above.

(3) Where immediately before the commencement date in respect of a particular case an interim maintenance assessment was in force, the provisions of the 1992 Regulations shall continue to apply for the purposes of the decision under section 17 of the Act to make a maintenance assessment calculated in accordance with Part I of Schedule 1 to the Act before its amendment by the 2000 Act and any revision, supersession or appeal in relation to that decision.

(4) Where under regulation 28(1) of the Child Support (Transitional Provisions) Regulations 2000 an application for a maintenance calculation is treated as an application for a maintenance assessment, the provisions of the 1992 Regulations shall continue to apply for the purposes of the determination of the application and any revision, supersession or appeal in relation to any such assessment made.

(5) Where after the commencement date a maintenance assessment is revised from a date which is prior to the commencement date the 1992 Regulations shall apply for the purposes of that revision.

(6) For the purposes of this regulation –

    (a) 'departure direction', 'maintenance assessment' and 'interim maintenance assessment' have the same meaning as in section 54 of the Act before its amendment by the 2000 Act;
    (b) 'revision or supersession' means a revision or supersession of a decision under section 16 or 17 of the Act before their amendment by the 2000 Act; and
    (c) '2000 Act' means the Child Support, Pensions and Social Security Act 2000.

SCHEDULE

Regulation 1(2)

NET WEEKLY INCOME

PART I

GENERAL

1 Net weekly income

Net weekly income means the aggregate of the net weekly income of the non-resident parent provided for in this Schedule.

2 Amounts to be disregarded when calculating income

The following amounts shall be disregarded when calculating the net weekly income of the non-resident parent –

(a) where a payment is made in a currency other than sterling, an amount equal to any banking charge or commission payable in converting that payment to sterling;

(b) any amount payable in a country outside the United Kingdom where there is a prohibition against the transfer to the United Kingdom of that amount.

PART II

EMPLOYED EARNER

3 Net weekly income of employed earner

(1) The net weekly income of the non-resident parent as an employed earner shall be –

(a) his earnings provided for in paragraph 4 less the deductions provided for in paragraph 5 and calculated or estimated by reference to the relevant week as provided for in paragraph 6; or

(b) where the Secretary of State is satisfied that the person is unable to provide evidence or information relating to the deductions provided for in paragraph 5, the non-resident parent's net earnings estimated by the Secretary of State on the basis of information available to him as to the non-resident parent's net income.

(2) Where any provision of these Regulations requires the income of a person to be estimated, and that or any other provision of these Regulations requires that the amount of such estimated income is to be taken into account for any purpose, after deducting from it a sum in respect of income tax, or of primary Class 1 contributions under the Contributions and Benefits Act or, as the case may be, the Contributions and Benefits (Northern Ireland) Act, or contributions paid by that person towards an occupational pension scheme or personal pension scheme, then,

(a) subject to sub-paragraph (c), the amount to be deducted in respect of income tax shall be calculated by applying to that income the rates of income tax applicable at the effective date less only the personal relief to which that person is entitled under Chapter I of Part VII of the Income and Corporation Taxes Act 1988 (personal relief); but if the period in respect of which that income is to be estimated is less than a year, the amount of the personal relief deductible under this paragraph shall be calculated on a pro-rata basis and the amount of income to which each tax rate applies shall be determined on the basis that the ratio of that amount to the full amount of the income to which each tax rate applies is the same as the ratio of the proportionate part of that personal relief to the full personal relief;

(b) subject to sub-paragraph (c), the amount to be deducted in respect of Class 1 contributions under the Contributions and Benefits Act or, as the case may be, the Contributions and Benefits (Northern Ireland) Act, shall be calculated by applying to that income the appropriate primary percentage applicable on the effective date;

(c) in relation to any bonus or commission which may be included in that person's income –

   (i) the amount to be deducted in respect of income tax shall be calculated by applying to the gross amount of that bonus or commission the rate or rates of income tax applicable at the effective date;

   (ii) the amount to be deducted in respect of primary Class 1 contributions under the Contributions and Benefits Act or, as the case may be, the Contributions and Benefits (Northern Ireland) Act, shall be calculated by applying to the gross amount of that bonus or commission the appropriate main primary percentage applicable on the effective date but no deduction shall be made in respect of the portion (if any) of the bonus or commission which, if added to the estimated income, would cause such income to exceed the upper earnings limit for Class 1 contributions as provided for in section 5(1)(b) of the Contributions and Benefits Act or, as the case may be, the Contributions and Benefits (Northern Ireland) Act;

(d) the amount to be deducted in respect of any sums or contributions towards an occupational pension scheme or personal pension scheme shall be the full amount of any such payments made or, where that scheme is intended partly to provide a capital sum to discharge a mortgage secured upon that parent's home, 75 per centum of any such payments made.

4 Earnings

(1) Subject to sub-paragraph (2), 'earnings' means, in the case of employment as an employed earner, any remuneration or profit derived from that employment and includes –

   (a) any bonus, commission, payment in respect of overtime, royalty or fees;
   (b) any holiday pay except any payable more than 4 weeks after termination of the employment;
   (c) any payment by way of a retainer;
   (d) any statutory sick pay under Part XI of the Contributions and Benefits Act or statutory maternity pay under Part XII of the Contributions and Benefits Act; and
   (e) any payment in lieu of notice, and any compensation in respect of the absence or inadequacy of any such notice, but only in so far as such payment or compensation represents loss of income.

(2) Earnings for the purposes of this Part of Schedule 1 do not include –

   (a) any payment in respect of expenses wholly, exclusively and necessarily incurred in the performance of the duties of the employment;
   (b) any tax-exempt allowance made by an employer to an employee;
   (c) any gratuities paid by customers of the employer;
   (d) any payment in kind;
   (e) any advance of earnings or any loan made by an employer to an employee;

    (f) any amount received from an employer during a period when the employee has withdrawn his services by reason of a trade dispute;

    (g) any payment made in respect of the performance of duties as –

        (i)   an auxiliary coastguard in respect of coast rescue activities;

        (ii) a part-time fireman in a fire brigade maintained in pursuance of the Fire Services Acts 1947 to 1959;

        (iii) a person engaged part-time in the manning or launching of a lifeboat;

        (iv) a member of any territorial or reserve force prescribed in Part I of Schedule 3 to the Social Security (Contributions) Regulations 1979;

    (h) any payment made by a local authority to a member of that authority in respect of the performance of his duties as a member;

    (i) any payment where –

        (i)   the employment in respect of which it was made has ceased; and

        (ii) a period of the same length as the period by reference to which it was calculated has expired since that cessation but prior to the effective date; or

    (j) where, in any week or other period which falls within the period by reference to which earnings are calculated, earnings are received both in respect of a previous employment and in respect of a subsequent employment, the earnings in respect of the previous employment.

5 Deductions

(1) The deductions to be taken from gross earnings to calculate net income for the purposes of this Part of the Schedule are any amount deducted from those earnings by way of –

    (a) income tax;

    (b) primary Class 1 contributions under the Contributions and Benefits Act or under the Contributions and Benefits (Northern Ireland) Act; or

    (c) any sums paid by the non-resident parent towards an occupational pension scheme or personal pension scheme or, where that scheme is intended partly to provide a capital sum to discharge a mortgage secured upon that parent's home, 75 per centum of any such sums.

(2) For the purposes of sub-paragraph (1)(a), amounts deducted by way of income tax shall be the amounts actually deducted, including in respect of payments which are not included as earnings in paragraph 4.

6 Calculation or estimate

(1) Subject to sub-paragraphs (2) to (4), the amount of earnings to be taken into account for the purpose of calculating net income shall be calculated or estimated by reference to the average earnings at the relevant week having regard to such evidence as is available in relation to that person's earnings during such period as appears appropriate to the Secretary of State, beginning not earlier than 8 weeks before the relevant week and ending not later than the date of the calculation, and for the purposes of the calculation or estimate he may consider evidence of that person's cumulative earnings during the period beginning with the start of the year of assessment (within the meaning of section 832 of the Income and Corporation Taxes Act 1988) in which the relevant week falls and ending with a date no later than the date when the calculation is made.

(2) Subject to sub-paragraph (4), where a person has claimed, or has been paid, working families' tax credit or disabled person's tax credit on any day during the period beginning not earlier than 8 weeks before the relevant week and ending not later than the date on which the calculation is made, the Secretary of State may have regard to the amount of earnings taken into account in determining entitlement to those tax credits in order to

calculate or estimate the amount of earnings to be taken into account for the purposes of calculating net earnings, notwithstanding the fact that entitlement to those tax credits may have been determined by reference to earnings attributable to a period other than that specified in sub-paragraph (1).

(3) Where a person's earnings during the period of 52 weeks ending with the relevant week include a bonus or commission made in anticipation of the calculation of profits which is paid separately from, or in relation to a longer period than, the other earnings with which it is paid, the amount of that bonus or commission shall be determined for the purposes of the calculation of earnings by aggregating any such payments received in that period and dividing by 52.

(4) Where a calculation would, but for this sub-paragraph, produce an amount which, in the opinion of the Secretary of State, does not accurately reflect the normal amount of the earnings of the person in question, such earnings, or any part of them, shall be calculated by reference to such other period as may, in the particular case, enable the normal weekly earnings of that person to be determined more accurately, and for this purpose the Secretary of State shall have regard to –

   (a) the earnings received, or due to be received from any employment in which the person in question is engaged, has been engaged or is due to be engaged; and
   (b) the duration and pattern, or the expected duration and pattern, of any employment of that person.

PART III

SELF-EMPLOYED EARNER

7   Figures submitted to the Inland Revenue

(1) Subject to sub-paragraph (6) the net weekly income of the non-resident parent as a self-employed earner shall be his gross earnings calculated by reference to one of the following, as the Secretary of State may decide, less the deductions to which sub-paragraph (3) applies –

   (a) the total taxable profits from self-employment of that earner as submitted to the Inland Revenue in accordance with their requirements by or on behalf of that earner; or
   (b) the income from self-employment as a self-employed earner as set out on the tax calculation notice or, as the case may be, the revised notice.

(2) Where the information referred to in head (a) or (b) of sub-paragraph (1) is made available to the Secretary of State he may nevertheless require the information referred to in the other head from the non-resident parent and where the Secretary of State becomes aware that a revised notice has been issued he may require and use this in preference to the other information referred to in sub-paragraph (1)(a) and (b).

(3) This paragraph applies to the following deductions –

   (a) any income tax relating to the gross earnings from the self-employment determined in accordance with sub-paragraph (4);
   (b) any National Insurance contributions relating to the gross earnings from the self-employment determined in accordance with sub-paragraph (5); and
   (c) any premiums paid by the non-resident parent in respect of a retirement annuity contract or a personal pension scheme or, where that scheme is intended partly to provide a capital sum to discharge a mortgage or a charge secured upon the parent's home, 75 per centum of the contributions payable.

(4) For the purpose of sub-paragraph (3)(a), the income tax to be deducted from the gross earnings shall be determined in accordance with the following provisions –

  (a) subject to head (d), an amount of gross earnings equivalent to any personal allowance applicable to the earner by virtue of the provisions of Chapter I of Part VII of the Income and Corporation Taxes Act 1988 (personal relief) shall be disregarded;

  (b) subject to head (c), an amount equivalent to income tax shall be calculated in relation to the gross earnings remaining following the application of head (a) (the 'remaining earnings');

  (c) the tax rate applicable at the effective date shall be applied to all the remaining earnings, where necessary increasing or reducing the amount payable to take account of the fact that the earnings related to a period greater or less than one year; and

  (d) the amount to be disregarded by virtue of head (a) shall be calculated by reference to the yearly rate applicable at the effective date, that amount being reduced or increased in the same proportion to that which the period represented by the gross earnings bears to the period of one year.

(5) For the purposes of sub-paragraph (3)(b), the amount to be deducted in respect of National Insurance contributions shall be the total of –

  (a) the amount of Class 2 contributions (if any) payable under section 11(1) or, as the case may be, (3) of the Contributions and Benefits Act or under section 11(1) or (3) of the Contributions and Benefits (Northern Ireland) Act; and

  (b) the amount of Class 4 contributions (if any) payable under section 15(2) of that Act, or under section 15(2) of the Contributions and Benefits (Northern Ireland) Act,

at the rates applicable at the effective date.

(6) The net weekly income of a self-employed earner may only be determined in accordance with this paragraph where the earnings concerned relate to a period which terminated not more than 24 months prior to the relevant week.

(7) In this paragraph –

  'tax calculation notice' means a document issued by the Inland Revenue containing information as to the income of the self-employed earner; and

  'revised notice' means a notice issued by the Inland Revenue where there has been a tax calculation notice and there is a revision of the figures relating to the income of a self-employed earner following an enquiry under section 9A of the Taxes Management Act 1970 or otherwise by the Inland Revenue.

(8) Any request by the Secretary of State in accordance with sub-paragraph (2) for the provision of information shall set out the possible consequences of failure to provide such information, including details of the offences provided for in section 14A of the Act for failing to provide, or providing false, information.

8 Figures calculated using gross receipts less deductions

(1) Where –

  (a) the conditions of paragraph 7(6) are not satisfied; or

  (b) the Secretary of State accepts that it is not reasonably practicable for the self-employed earner to provide information relating to his gross earnings from self-employment in the forms submitted to, or as issued or revised by, the Inland Revenue; or

(c) in the opinion of the Secretary of State, information as to the gross earnings of the self-employed earner which has satisfied the criteria set out in paragraph 7 does not accurately reflect the normal weekly earnings of the self-employed earner,

net income means in the case of employment as a self-employed earner his earnings calculated by reference to the gross receipts of the employment less the deductions provided for in sub-paragraph (2).

(2) The deductions to be taken from the gross receipts to calculate net earnings for the purposes of this paragraph are –

(a) any expenses which are reasonably incurred and are wholly and exclusively defrayed for the purposes of the earner's business in the period by reference to which his earnings are determined under paragraph 9(2) or (3);

(b) any value added tax paid in the period by reference to which his earnings are determined in excess of value added tax received in that period;

(c) any amount in respect of income tax determined in accordance with sub-paragraph (4);

(d) any amount of National Insurance contributions determined in accordance with sub-paragraph (4); and

(e) any premium paid by the non-resident parent in respect of a retirement annuity contract or a personal pension scheme or, where that scheme is intended partly to provide a capital sum to discharge a mortgage or a charge secured upon the parent's home, 75 per centum of contributions payable.

(3) For the purposes of sub-paragraph (2)(a) –

(a) such expenses include –
   (i)   repayment of capital on any loan used for the replacement, in the course of business, of equipment or machinery, or the repair of an existing business asset except to the extent that any sum is payable under an insurance policy for its repair;
   (ii) any income expended in the repair of an existing business asset except to the extent that any sum is payable under an insurance policy for its repair; and
   (iii) any payment of interest on a loan taken out for the purposes of the business;
(b) such expenses do not include –
   (i)   repayment of capital on any other loan taken out for the purposes of the business;
   (ii) any capital expenditure;
   (iii) the depreciation of any capital assets;
   (iv) any sum employed, or intended to be employed, in the setting up or expansion of the business;
   (v)   any loss incurred before the beginning of the period by reference to which earnings are determined;
   (vi) any expenses incurred in providing business entertainment; or
   (vii) any loss incurred in any other employment in which he is engaged as a self-employed earner.

(4) For the purposes of sub-paragraph (2)(c) and (d), the amounts in respect of income tax and National Insurance contributions to be deducted from the gross receipts shall be determined in accordance with paragraph 7(4) and (5) of this Schedule as if in paragraph 7(4) references to gross earnings were references to taxable earnings and in this sub-paragraph 'taxable earnings' means the gross receipts of the earner less the deductions mentioned in sub-paragraph (2)(a) and (b).

9   Rules for calculation under paragraph 8

(1) This paragraph applies only where the net income of a self-employed earner is calculated or estimated under paragraph 8 of this Schedule.

(2) Where –

   (a) a non-resident parent has been a self-employed earner for 52 weeks or more, including the relevant week, the amount of his net weekly income shall be determined by reference to the average of the earnings which he has received in the 52 weeks ending with the relevant week; or
   (b) a non-resident parent has been a self-employed earner for a period of less than 52 weeks including the relevant week, the amount of his net weekly income shall be determined by reference to the average of the earnings which he has received during that period.

(3) Where a calculation would, but for this sub-paragraph, produce an amount which, in the opinion of the Secretary of State, does not accurately reflect the normal weekly income of the non-resident parent in question, such earnings, or any part of them, shall be calculated by reference to such other period as may, in the particular case, enable the normal weekly earnings of the non-resident parent to be determined more accurately and for this purpose the Secretary of State shall have regard to –

   (a) the earnings from self-employment received, or due to be received, by him; and
   (b) the duration and pattern, or the expected duration and pattern, of any self-employment of that non-resident parent.

(4) Where a person has claimed, or has been paid, working families' tax credit or disabled person's tax credit on any day during the period beginning not earlier than 8 weeks before the relevant week and ending not later than the date on which the calculation is made, the Secretary of State may have regard to the amount of earnings taken into account in determining entitlement to those tax credits in order to calculate or estimate the amount of earnings to be taken into account for the purposes of calculating net income, notwithstanding the fact that entitlement to those tax credits may have been determined by reference to earnings attributable to a period other than that specified in sub-paragraph (2).

10   Income from board or lodging

In a case where a non-resident parent is a self-employed earner who provides board and lodging, his earnings shall include payments received for that provision where those payments are the only or main source of income of that earner.

PART IV

TAX CREDITS

11   Working families' tax credit

(1) Subject to sub-paragraphs (2) and (3), payments by way of working families' tax credit under section 128 of the Contributions and Benefits Act, shall be treated as the income of the non-resident parent where he has qualified for them by his engagement in, and normal engagement in, remunerative work, at the rate payable at the effective date.

(2) Where working families' tax credit is payable and the amount which is payable has been calculated by reference to the weekly earnings of the non-resident parent and another person –

(a) where during the period which is used by the Inland Revenue to calculate his income the normal weekly earnings (as determined in accordance with Chapter II of Part IV of the Family Credit (General) Regulations 1987) of that parent exceed those of the other person, the amount payable by way of working families' tax credit shall be treated as the income of that parent;

(b) where during that period the normal weekly earnings of that parent equal those of the other person, half of the amount payable by way of working families' tax credit shall be treated as the income of that parent; and

(c) where during that period the normal weekly earnings of that parent are less than those of that other person, the amount payable by way of working families' tax credit shall not be treated as the income of that parent.

(3) Where –

(a) working families' tax credit is in payment; and

(b) not later than the effective date the person, or, if more than one, each of the persons by reference to whose engagement, and normal engagement, in remunerative work that payment has been calculated is no longer the partner of the person to whom that payment is made,

the payment in question shall only be treated as the income of the non-resident parent in question where he is in receipt of it.

12 Employment credits

Payments made by way of employment credits under section 2(1) of the Employment and Training Act 1973 to a non-resident parent who is participating in a scheme arranged under section 2(2) of the Employment and Training Act 1973 and known as the New Deal 50 plus shall be treated as the income of the non-resident parent, at the rate payable at the effective date.

13 Disabled person's tax credits

Payments made by way of disabled person's tax credit under section 129 of the Contributions and Benefits Act to a non-resident parent shall be treated as the income of the non-resident parent at the rate payable at the effective date.

PART V

OTHER INCOME

14 Amount

The amount of other income to be taken into account in calculating or estimating net weekly income shall be the aggregate of the payments to which paragraph 15 applies, net of any income tax deducted and otherwise determined in accordance with this Part.

15 Types

This paragraph applies to any periodic payment of pension or other benefit under an occupational or personal pension scheme or a retirement annuity contract or other such scheme for the provision of income in retirement whether or not approved by the Inland Revenue.

16 Calculation or estimate and period

(1) The amount of any income to which this Part applies shall be calculated or estimated –

   (a) where it has been received in respect of the whole of the period of 26 weeks which ends at the end of the relevant week, by dividing such income received in that period by 26;

   (b) where it has been received in respect of part of the period of 26 weeks which ends at the end of the relevant week, by dividing such income received in that period by the number of complete weeks in respect of which such income is received and for this purpose income shall be treated as received in respect of a week if it is received in respect of any day in the week in question.

(2) Where a calculation or estimate to which this Part applies would, but for this sub-paragraph, produce an amount which, in the opinion of the Secretary of State, does not accurately reflect the normal amount of the other income of the non-resident parent in question, such income, or any part of it, shall be calculated by reference to such other period as may, in the particular case, enable the other income of that parent to be determined more accurately and for this purpose the Secretary of State shall have regard to the nature and pattern of receipt of such income.

Child Support (Variations) Regulations 2000

SI 2001/156

PART I

GENERAL

1 Citation, commencement and interpretation

(1) These Regulations may be cited as the Child Support (Variations) Regulations 2000 and shall come into force in relation to a particular case on the day on which section 5 of the Child Support, Pensions and Social Security Act 2000 which substitutes or amends sections 28A to 28F of the Act is commenced in relation to that type of case.

(2) In these Regulations, unless the context otherwise requires –

'the Act' means the Child Support Act 1991;

'capped amount' means the amount of income for the purposes of paragraph 10(3) of Schedule 1 to the Act;

'Contributions and Benefits Act' means the Social Security Contributions and Benefits Act 1992;

'couple' has the same meaning as in paragraph 10C(5) of Schedule 1 to the Act;

'date of notification' means the date upon which notification is given in person or communicated by telephone to the recipient or, where this is not possible, the date of posting;

'date of receipt' means the day on which the information or document is actually received;

'home' has the meaning given in regulation 1(2) of the Maintenance Calculations and Special Cases Regulations;

'Maintenance Calculation Procedure Regulations' means the Child Support (Maintenance Calculation Procedure) Regulations 2000;

'Maintenance Calculations and Special Cases Regulations' means the Child Support (Maintenance Calculations and Special Cases) Regulations 2000;

'qualifying child' means the child with respect to whom the maintenance calculation falls to be made;

'relevant person' means –

    (a) a non-resident parent, or a person treated as a non-resident parent under regulation 8 of the Maintenance Calculations and Special Cases Regulations, whose liability to pay child support maintenance may be affected by any variation agreed;

    (b) a person with care, or a child to whom section 7 of the Act applies, where the amount of child support maintenance payable by virtue of a calculation relevant to that person with care or in respect of that child may be affected by any variation agreed; and

'Transitional Regulations' means the Child Support (Transitional Provisions) Regulations 2000.

(3) In these Regulations, unless the context otherwise requires, a reference –

    (a) to a numbered Part, is to the Part of these Regulations bearing that number;

    (b) to the Schedule, is to the Schedule to these Regulations;

    (c) to a numbered regulation, is to the regulation in these Regulations bearing that number;

(d) in a regulation, or the Schedule, to a numbered paragraph, is to the paragraph in that regulation or the Schedule bearing that number; and

(e) in a paragraph to a lettered or numbered sub-paragraph, is to the sub-paragraph in that paragraph bearing that letter or number.

2 Documents

Except where otherwise stated, where –

(a) any document is given or sent to the Secretary of State, that document shall be treated as having been so given or sent on the date of receipt by the Secretary of State; and

(b) any document is given or sent to any other person, that document shall, if sent by post to that person's last known or notified address, be treated as having been given or sent on the date that it is posted.

3 Determination of amounts

(1) Where any amount is required to be determined for the purposes of these Regulations, it shall be determined as a weekly amount and, except where the context otherwise requires, any reference to such an amount shall be construed accordingly.

(2) Where any calculation made under these Regulations results in a fraction of a penny, that fraction shall be treated as a penny if it is either one half or exceeds one half and shall be otherwise disregarded.

PART II

APPLICATION AND DETERMINATION PROCEDURE

4 Application for a variation

(1) Where an application for a variation is made other than in writing and the Secretary of State directs that the application be made in writing, the application shall be made either on an application form provided by the Secretary of State and completed in accordance with the Secretary of State's instructions or in such other written form as the Secretary of State may accept as sufficient in the circumstances of any particular case.

(2) An application for a variation which is made other than in writing shall be treated as made on the date of notification from the applicant to the Secretary of State that he wishes to make such an application.

(3) Where an application for a variation is made in writing other than in the circumstances to which paragraph (1) applies, the application shall be treated as made on the date of receipt by the Secretary of State.

(4) Where paragraph (1) applies and the Secretary of State receives the application within 14 days of the date of the direction, or at a later date but in circumstances where the Secretary of State is satisfied that the delay was unavoidable, the application shall be treated as made on the date of notification from the applicant to the Secretary of State that he wishes to make an application for a variation.

(5) Where paragraph (1) applies and the Secretary of State receives the application more than 14 days from the date of the direction and in circumstances where he is not satisfied that the delay was unavoidable, the application shall be treated as made on the date of receipt.

(6) An application for a variation is duly made when it has been made in accordance with this regulation and section 28A(4) of the Act.

5 Amendment or withdrawal of application

(1) A person who has made an application for a variation may amend or withdraw his application at any time before a decision under section 11, 16 or 17 of the Act, or a decision not to revise or supersede under section 16 or 17 of the Act, is made in response to the variation application and such amendment or withdrawal need not be in writing unless, in any particular case, the Secretary of State requires it to be.

(2) No amendment under paragraph (1) shall relate to any change of circumstances arising after what would be the effective date of a decision in response to the variation application.

6 Rejection of an application following preliminary consideration

(1) The Secretary of State may, on completing the preliminary consideration, reject an application for a variation (and proceed to make his decision on the application for a maintenance calculation, or to revise or supersede a decision under section 16 or 17 of the Act, without the variation, or not to revise or supersede a decision under section 16 or 17 of the Act, as the case may be) if one of the circumstances in paragraph (2) applies.

(2) The circumstances are –

    (a) the application has been made in one of the circumstances to which regulation 7 applies;

    (b) the application is made –

        (i) on a ground in paragraph 2 of Schedule 4B to the Act (special expenses) and the amount of the special expenses, or the aggregate amount of those expenses, as the case may be, does not exceed the relevant threshold provided for in regulation 15;

        (ii) on a ground in paragraph 3 of that Schedule (property or capital transfers) and the value of the property or capital transferred does not exceed the minimum value in regulation 16(4); or

        (iii) on a ground referred to in regulation 18 (assets) and the value of the assets does not exceed the figure in regulation 18(3)(a), or on a ground in regulation 19(1) (income not taken into account) and the amount of the income does not exceed the figure in regulation 19(2);

    (c) a request under regulation 8 has not been complied with by the applicant and the Secretary of State is not able to determine the application without the information requested; or

    (d) the Secretary of State is satisfied, on the information or evidence available to him, that the application would not be agreed to, including where, although a ground is stated, the facts alleged in the application would not bring the case within the prescription of the relevant ground in these Regulations.

7 Prescribed circumstances

(1) This regulation applies where an application for a variation is made under section 28G of the Act and –

    (a) the application is made by a relevant person and a circumstance set out in paragraph (2) applies at the relevant date;

    (b) the application is made by a non-resident parent and a circumstance set out in paragraph (3) or (4) applies at the relevant date;

    (c) the application is made by a person with care, or a child to whom section 7 of the Act applies, on a ground in paragraph 4 of Schedule 4B to the Act (additional cases) and a circumstance set out in paragraph (5) applies at the relevant date; or

(d) the application is made by a non-resident parent on a ground in paragraph 2 of Schedule 4B to the Act (special expenses) and a circumstance set out in paragraph (6) applies at the relevant date.

(2) The circumstances for the purposes of this paragraph are that –

(a) a default maintenance decision is in force with respect to the non-resident parent;

(b) the non-resident parent is liable to pay the flat rate of child support maintenance owing to the application of paragraph 4(1)(c) of Schedule 1 to the Act, or would be so liable but is liable to pay less than that amount, or nil, owing to the application of paragraph 8 of Schedule 1 to the Act, or the Transitional Regulations; or

(c) the non-resident parent is liable to pay child support maintenance at a flat rate of a prescribed amount owing to the application of paragraph 4(2) of Schedule 1 to the Act, or would be so liable but is liable to pay less than that amount, or nil, owing to the application of paragraph 8 of Schedule 1 to the Act, or the Transitional Regulations.

(3) The circumstances for the purposes of this paragraph are that the non-resident parent is liable to pay child support maintenance –

(a) at the nil rate owing to the application of paragraph 5 of Schedule 1 to the Act;

(b) at a flat rate owing to the application of paragraph 4(1)(a) of Schedule 1 to the Act, including where the net weekly income of the non-resident parent which is taken into account for the purposes of a maintenance calculation in force in respect of him is £100 per week or less owing to a variation being taken into account or to the application of regulation 18, 19 or 21 of the Transitional Regulations (reduction for relevant departure direction or relevant property transfer); or

(c) at a flat rate owing to the application of paragraph 4(1)(b) of Schedule 1 to the Act, or would be so liable but is liable to pay less than that amount, or nil, owing to the application of paragraph 8 of Schedule 1 to the Act, or the Transitional Regulations.

(4) The circumstances for the purposes of this paragraph are that the non-resident parent is liable to pay an amount of child support maintenance at a rate –

(a) of £5 per week or such other amount as may be prescribed owing to the application of paragraph 7(7) of Schedule 1 to the Act (shared care); or

(b) equivalent to the flat rate provided for in, or prescribed for the purposes of, paragraph 4(1)(b) of Part 1 of Schedule 1 to the Act owing to the application of –
(i) regulation 27(5);
(ii) regulation 9 of the Maintenance Calculations and Special Cases Regulations (care provided in part by a local authority); or
(iii) regulation 23(5) of the Transitional Regulations.

(5) The circumstances for the purposes of this paragraph are that –

(a) the amount of the net weekly income of the non-resident parent to which the Secretary of State had regard when making the maintenance calculation was the capped amount; or

(b) the non-resident parent or a partner of his is in receipt of working families' tax credit (as defined in section 128 of the Contributions and Benefits Act) or disabled person's tax credit (as defined in section 129 of that Act) and for this purpose 'partner' has the same meaning as in paragraph 10C(4) of Schedule 1 to the Act.

(6) The circumstances for the purposes of this paragraph are that the amount of the net weekly income of the non-resident parent to which the Secretary of State would have regard after deducting the amount of the special expenses would exceed the capped amount.

(7) For the purposes of paragraph (1), the 'relevant date' means the date from which, if the variation were agreed, the decision under section 16 or 17 of the Act, as the case may be, would take effect.

8 Provision of information

(1) Where an application has been duly made, the Secretary of State may request further information or evidence from the applicant to enable that application to be determined and any such information or evidence requested shall be provided within one month of the date of notification of the request or such longer period as the Secretary of State is satisfied is reasonable in the circumstances of the case.

(2) Where any information or evidence requested in accordance with paragraph (1) is not provided in accordance with the time limit specified in that paragraph, the Secretary of State may, where he is able to do so, proceed to determine the application in the absence of the requested information or evidence.

9 Procedure in relation to the determination of an application

(1) Subject to paragraph (3), where the Secretary of State has given the preliminary consideration to an application and not rejected it he –

(a) shall give notice of the application to the relevant persons other than the applicant, informing them of the grounds on which the application has been made and any relevant information or evidence the applicant has given, except information or evidence falling within paragraph (2);

(b) may invite representations, which need not be in writing but shall be in writing if in any case he so directs, from the relevant persons other than the applicant on any matter relating to that application, to be submitted to the Secretary of State within 14 days of the date of notification or such longer period as the Secretary of State is satisfied is reasonable in the circumstances of the case; and

(c) shall set out the provisions of paragraphs (2)(b) and (c), (4) and (5) in relation to such representations.

(2) The information or evidence referred to in paragraphs (1)(a), (4)(a) and (7), are –

(a) details of the nature of the long-term illness or disability of the relevant other child which forms the basis of a variation application on the ground in regulation 11 where the applicant requests they should not be disclosed and the Secretary of State is satisfied that disclosure is not necessary in order to be able to determine the application;

(b) medical evidence or medical advice which has not been disclosed to the applicant or a relevant person and which the Secretary of State considers would be harmful to the health of the applicant or that relevant person if disclosed to him; or

(c) the address of a relevant person or qualifying child, or any other information which could reasonably be expected to lead to that person or child being located, where the Secretary of State considers that there would be a risk of harm or undue distress to that person or that child or any other children living with that person if the address or information were disclosed.

(3) The Secretary of State need not act in accordance with paragraph (1) –

   (a) where regulation 29 applies (variation may be taken into account notwithstanding that no application has been made);

   (b) where the variation agreed is one falling within paragraph 3 of Schedule 4B to the Act (property or capital transfer), the Secretary of State ceases to have jurisdiction to make a maintenance calculation and subsequently acquires jurisdiction in respect of the same non-resident parent, person with care and any child in respect of whom the earlier calculation was made;

   (c) if he is satisfied on the information or evidence available to him that the application would not be agreed to, but if, on further consideration of the application, he is minded to agree to the variation he shall, before doing so, comply with the provisions of this regulation; or

   (d) where –

      (i)   a variation has been agreed in relation to a maintenance calculation;

      (ii) the decision as to the maintenance calculation is replaced with a default maintenance decision under section 12(1)(b) of the Act;

      (iii) the default maintenance decision is revised in accordance with section 16(1B) of the Act,

and the Secretary of State is satisfied, on the information or evidence available to him, that there has been no material change of circumstances relating to the variation since the date from which the maintenance calculation referred to in head (i) ceased to have effect.

(4) Where the Secretary of State receives representations from the relevant persons –

   (a) he may, if he considers it reasonable to do so, send a copy of the representations concerned (excluding material falling within paragraph (2)) to the applicant and invite any comments he may have within 14 days or such longer period as the Secretary of State is satisfied is reasonable in the circumstances of the case; and

   (b) where the Secretary of State acts under sub-paragraph (a) he shall not proceed to determine the application until he has received such comments or the period referred to in that sub-paragraph has expired.

(5) Where the Secretary of State has not received representations from the relevant persons notified in accordance with paragraph (1) within the time limit specified in sub-paragraph (b) of that paragraph, he may proceed to agree or not (as the case may be) to a variation in their absence.

(6) In considering an application for a variation, the Secretary of State shall take into account any representations received at the date upon which he agrees or not (as the case may be) to the variation from the relevant persons, including any representation received in accordance with paragraphs (1)(b), 4(a) and (7).

(7) Where any information or evidence requested by the Secretary of State under regulation 8 is received after notification has been given under paragraph (1), the Secretary of State may, if he considers it reasonable to do so, and except where such information or evidence falls within paragraph (2), send a copy of such information or evidence to the relevant persons and may invite them to submit representations, which need not be in writing unless the Secretary of State so directs in any particular case, on that information or evidence.

(8) The Secretary of State may, if he considers it appropriate, treat an application for a variation made on one ground as if it were an application made on a different ground, and, if he does intend to do so, he shall include this information in the notice and invitation to make representations referred to in paragraphs (1), (4) and (7).

(9) Two or more applications for a variation with respect to the same maintenance calculation or application for a maintenance calculation, made or treated as made, may be considered together.

PART III

SPECIAL EXPENSES

10 Special expenses – contact costs

(1) Subject to the following paragraphs of this regulation, and to regulation 15, the following costs incurred or reasonably expected to be incurred by the non-resident parent, whether in respect of himself or the qualifying child or both, for the purpose of maintaining contact with that child, shall constitute expenses for the purposes of paragraph 2(2) of Schedule 4B to the Act –

   (a) the cost of purchasing a ticket for travel;

   (b) the cost of purchasing fuel where travel is by a vehicle which is not carrying fare-paying passengers;

   (c) the taxi fare for a journey or part of a journey where the Secretary of State is satisfied that the disability or long-term illness of the non-resident parent or the qualifying child makes it impracticable for any other form of transport to be used for that journey or part of that journey;

   (d) the cost of car hire where the cost of the journey would be less in total than it would be if public transport or taxis or a combination of both were used;

   (e) where the Secretary of State considers a return journey on the same day is impracticable, or the established or intended pattern of contact with the child includes contact over two or more consecutive days, the cost of the non-resident parent's, or, as the case may be, the child's, accommodation for the number of nights the Secretary of State considers appropriate in the circumstances of the case; and

   (f) any minor incidental costs such as tolls or fees payable for the use of a particular road or bridge incurred in connection with such travel, including breakfast where it is included as part of the accommodation cost referred to in sub-paragraph (e).

(2) The costs to which paragraph (1) applies include the cost of a person to travel with the non-resident parent or the qualifying child, if the Secretary of State is satisfied that the presence of another person on the journey, or part of the journey, is necessary including, but not limited to, where it is necessary because of the young age of the qualifying child or the disability or long-term illness of the non-resident parent or that child.

(3) The costs referred to in paragraphs (1) and (2) –

   (a) shall be expenses for the purposes of paragraph 2(2) of Schedule 4B to the Act only to the extent that they are –

      (i) incurred in accordance with a set pattern as to frequency of contact between the non-resident parent and the qualifying child which has been established at or, where at the time of the variation application it has ceased, which had been established before, the time that the variation application is made; or

      (ii) based on an intended set pattern for such contact which the Secretary of State is satisfied has been agreed between the non-resident parent and the person with care of the qualifying child; and

   (b) shall be –

      (i) where head (i) of sub-paragraph (a) applies and such contact is continuing, calculated as an average weekly amount based on the expenses actually incurred over the period of 12 months, or such lesser period as the Secretary of State may consider appropriate in the circumstances of the case, ending immediately before the first day of the maintenance period from which a variation agreed on this ground would take effect;

(ii) where head (i) of sub-paragraph (a) applies and such contact has ceased, calculated as an average weekly amount based on the expenses actually incurred during the period from the first day of the maintenance period from which a variation agreed on this ground would take effect to the last day of the maintenance period in relation to which the variation would take effect; or

(iii) where head (ii) of sub-paragraph (a) applies, calculated as an average weekly amount based on anticipated costs during such period as the Secretary of State considers appropriate.

(4) For the purposes of this regulation, costs of contact shall not include costs which relate to periods where the non-resident parent has care of a qualifying child overnight as part of a shared care arrangement for which provision is made under paragraphs 7 and 8 of Schedule 1 to the Act and regulation 7 of the Maintenance Calculations and Special Cases Regulations.

(5) Where the non-resident parent has at the date he makes the variation application received, or at that date is in receipt of, or where he will receive, any financial assistance, other than a loan, from any source to meet, wholly or in part, the costs of maintaining contact with a child as referred to in paragraph (1), only the amount of the costs referred to in that paragraph, after the deduction of the financial assistance, shall constitute special expenses for the purposes of paragraph 2(2) of Schedule 4B to the Act.

11   Special expenses – illness or disability of relevant other child

(1) Subject to the following paragraphs of this regulation, expenses necessarily incurred by the non-resident parent in respect of the items listed in sub-paragraphs (a) to (m) due to the long-term illness or disability of a relevant other child shall constitute special expenses for the purposes of paragraph 2(2) of Schedule 4B to the Act –

    (a)   personal care and attendance;
    (b)   personal communication needs;
    (c)   mobility;
    (d)   domestic help;
    (e)   medical aids where these cannot be provided under the health service;
    (f)   heating;
    (g)   clothing;
    (h)   laundry requirements;
    (i)   payments for food essential to comply with a diet recommended by a medical practitioner;
    (j)   adaptations required to the non-resident parent's home;
    (k)   day care;
    (l)   rehabilitation; or
    (m)   respite care.

(2) For the purposes of this regulation and regulation 10 –

    (a) a person is 'disabled' for a period in respect of which –
        (i)   either an attendance allowance, disability living allowance or a mobility supplement is paid to or in respect of him;
        (ii)   he would receive an attendance allowance or disability living allowance if it were not for the fact that he is a patient, though remaining part of the applicant's family; or

(iii) he is registered blind or treated as blind within the meaning of paragraph 12(1)(a)(iii) and (2) of Schedule 2 to the Income Support (General) Regulations 1987;

and for this purpose –

(i) 'attendance allowance' means an allowance payable under section 64 of the Contributions and Benefits Act or an increase of disablement pension under section 104 of that Act, or an award under article 14 of the Naval, Military and Air Forces Etc., (Disablement and Death) Service Pensions Order 1983 or any analogous allowance payable in conjunction with any other war disablement pension within the meaning of section 150(2) of the Contributions and Benefits Act;

(ii) 'disability living allowance' means an allowance payable under section 72 of the Contributions and Benefits Act;

(iii) 'mobility supplement' means an award under article 26A of the Naval, Military and Air Forces Etc., (Disablement and Death) Service Pensions Order 1983 or any analogous allowance payable in conjunction with any other war disablement pension within the meaning of section 150(2) of the Contributions and Benefits Act; and

(iv) 'patient' means a person (other than a person who is serving a sentence of imprisonment or detention in a young offenders institution within the meaning of the Criminal Justice Act 1982) who is regarded as receiving free in-patient treatment within the meaning of the Social Security (Hospital In-Patients) Regulations 1975;

(b) 'the health service' has the same meaning as in section 128 of the National Health Service Act 1977 or in section 108(1) of the National Health Service (Scotland) Act 1978;

(c) 'long-term illness' means an illness from which the non-resident parent or child is suffering at the date of the application or the date from which the variation, if agreed, would take effect and which is likely to last for at least 52 weeks from that date, or, if likely to be shorter than 52 weeks, for the remainder of the life of that person; and

(d) 'relevant other child' has the meaning given in paragraph 10C(2) of Schedule 1 to the Act and Regulations made under that paragraph.

(3) Where the non-resident parent has, at the date he makes the variation application, received, or at that date is in receipt of, or where he will receive any financial assistance from any source in respect of the long-term illness or disability of the relevant other child or a disability living allowance is received by the non-resident parent on behalf of the relevant other child, only the net amount of the costs incurred in respect of the items listed in paragraph (1), after the deduction of the financial assistance or the amount of the allowance, shall constitute special expenses for the purposes of paragraph 2(2) of Schedule 4B to the Act.

12 Special expenses – prior debts

(1) Subject to the following paragraphs of this regulation and regulation 15, the repayment of debts to which paragraph (2) applies shall constitute expenses for the purposes of paragraph 2(2) of Schedule 4B to the Act where those debts were incurred –

(a) before the non-resident parent became a non-resident parent in relation to the qualifying child; and

(b) at the time when the non-resident parent and the person with care in relation to the child referred to in sub-paragraph (a) were a couple.

(2) This paragraph applies to debts incurred –

(a) for the joint benefit of the non-resident parent and the person with care;

(b) for the benefit of the person with care where the non-resident parent remains legally liable to repay the whole or part of the debt;

(c) for the benefit of any person who is not a child but who at the time the debt was incurred –

    (i)   was a child;

    (ii) lived with the non-resident parent and the person with care; and

    (iii) of whom the non-resident parent or the person with care is the parent, or both are the parents;

(d) for the benefit of the qualifying child referred to in paragraph (1); or

(e) for the benefit of any child, other than the qualifying child referred to in paragraph (1), who, at the time the debt was incurred –

    (i)   lived with the non-resident parent and the person with care; and

    (ii) of whom the person with care is the parent.

(3) Paragraph (1) shall not apply to repayment of –

  (a)   a debt which would otherwise fall within paragraph (1) where the non-resident parent has retained for his own use and benefit the asset in connection with the purchase of which he incurred the debt;

  (b)   a debt incurred for the purposes of any trade or business;

  (c)   a gambling debt;

  (d)   a fine imposed on the non-resident parent;

  (e)   unpaid legal costs in respect of separation or divorce from the person with care;

  (f)   amounts due after use of a credit card;

  (g)   a debt incurred by the non-resident parent to pay any of the items listed in sub-paragraphs (c) to (f) and (j);

  (h)   amounts payable by the non-resident parent under a mortgage or loan taken out on the security of any property except where that mortgage or loan was taken out to facilitate the purchase of, or to pay for repairs or improvements to, any property which is the home of the person with care and any qualifying child;

  (i)   amounts payable by the non-resident parent in respect of a policy of insurance except where that policy of insurance was obtained or retained to discharge a mortgage or charge taken out to facilitate the purchase of, or to pay for repairs or improvements to, any property which is the home of the person with care and the qualifying child;

  (j)   a bank overdraft except where the overdraft was at the time it was taken out agreed to be for a specified amount repayable over a specified period;

  (k)   a loan obtained by the non-resident parent other than a loan obtained from a qualifying lender or the non-resident parent's current or former employer;

  (l)   a debt in respect of which a variation has previously been agreed and which has not been repaid during the period for which the maintenance calculation which took account of the variation was in force; or

  (m) any other debt which the Secretary of State is satisfied it is reasonable to exclude.

(4) Except where the repayment is of an amount which is payable under a mortgage or loan or in respect of a policy of insurance which falls within the exception set out in sub-paragraph (h) or (i) of paragraph (3), repayment of a debt shall not constitute expenses for the purposes of paragraph (1) where the Secretary of State is satisfied that the non-resident parent has taken responsibility for repayment of that debt as, or as part of, a financial settlement with the person with care or by virtue of a court order.

(5) Where an applicant has incurred a debt partly to repay a debt repayment of which would have fallen within paragraph (1), the repayment of that part of the debt incurred

which is referable to the debt repayment of which would have fallen within that paragraph shall constitute expenses for the purposes of paragraph 2(2) of Schedule 4B to the Act.

(6) For the purposes of this regulation and regulation 14 –

    (a) 'qualifying lender' has the meaning given to it in section 376(4) of the Income and Corporation Taxes Act 1988; and

    (b) 'repairs or improvements' means major repairs necessary to maintain the fabric of the home and any of the following measures –

        (i) installation of a fixed bath, shower, wash basin or lavatory, and necessary associated plumbing;

        (ii) damp-proofing measures;

        (iii) provision or improvement of ventilation and natural light;

        (iv) provision of electric lighting and sockets;

        (v) provision or improvement of drainage facilities;

        (vi) improvement of the structural condition of the home;

        (vii) improvements to the facilities for the storing, preparation and cooking of food;

        (viii) provision of heating, including central heating;

        (ix) provision of storage facilities for fuel and refuse;

        (x) improvements to the insulation of the home; or

        (xi) other improvements which the Secretary of State considers reasonable in the circumstances.

13 Special expenses – boarding school fees

(1) Subject to the following paragraphs of this regulation and regulation 15, the maintenance element of the costs, incurred or reasonably expected to be incurred, by the non-resident parent for the purpose of the attendance at a boarding school of the qualifying child shall constitute expenses for the purposes of paragraph 2(2) of Schedule 4B to the Act.

(2) Where the Secretary of State considers that the costs referred to in paragraph (1) cannot be distinguished with reasonable certainty from other costs incurred in connection with the attendance at boarding school by the qualifying child, he may instead determine the amount of those costs and any such determination shall not exceed 35% of the total costs.

(3) Where –

    (a) the non-resident parent has at the date the variation application is made, received, or at that date is in receipt of, financial assistance from any source in respect of the boarding school fees; or

    (b) the boarding school fees are being paid in part by the non-resident parent and in part by another person,

a portion of the costs incurred by the non-resident parent in respect of the boarding school fees shall constitute special expenses for the purposes of paragraph 2(2) of Schedule 4B to the Act being the same proportion as the maintenance element of the costs bears to the total amount of the costs.

(4) No variation on this ground shall reduce by more than 50% the income to which the Secretary of State would otherwise have had regard in the calculation of maintenance liability.

(5) For the purposes of this regulation, 'boarding school fees' means the fees payable in respect of attendance at a recognised educational establishment providing full-time education which is not advanced education for children under the age of 19 and where some or all of the pupils, including the qualifying child, are resident during term time.

14 Special expenses – payments in respect of certain mortgages, loans or insurance policies

(1) Subject to regulation 15, the payments to which paragraph (2) applies shall constitute expenses for the purposes of paragraph 2(2) of Schedule 4B to the Act.

(2) This paragraph applies to payments, whether made to the mortgagee, lender, insurer or the person with care –

   (a) in respect of a mortgage or loan where –
      (i) the mortgage or loan was taken out to facilitate the purchase of, or repairs or improvements to, a property ('the property') by a person other than the non-resident parent;
      (ii) the payments are not made under a debt incurred by the non-resident parent or do not arise out of any other legal liability of his for the period in respect of which the variation is applied for;
      (iii) the property was the home of the applicant and the person with care when they were a couple and remains the home of the person with care and the qualifying child; and
      (iv) the non-resident parent has no legal or equitable interest in and no charge or right to have a charge over the property; or
   (b) of amounts payable in respect of a policy of insurance taken out for the discharge of a mortgage or loan referred to in sub-paragraph (a), including an endowment policy, except where the non-resident parent is entitled to any part of the proceeds on the maturity of that policy.

15 Thresholds for and reduction of amount of special expenses

(1) Subject to paragraphs (2) to (4), the costs or repayments referred to in regulations 10 and 12 to 14 shall be special expenses for the purposes of paragraph 2(2) of Schedule 4B to the Act where and to the extent that they exceed the threshold amount, which is –

   (a) £15 per week where the expenses fall within only one description of expenses and, where the expenses fall within more than one description of expenses, £15 per week in respect of the aggregate of those expenses, where the relevant net weekly income of the non-resident parent is £200 or more; or
   (b) £10 per week where the expenses fall within only one description of expenses, and, where the expenses fall within more than one description of expenses, £10 per week in respect of the aggregate of those expenses, where the relevant net weekly income is below £200.

(2) Subject to paragraph (3), where the Secretary of State considers any expenses referred to in regulations 10 to 14 to be unreasonably high or to have been unreasonably incurred he may substitute such lower amount as he considers reasonable, including an amount which is below the threshold amount or a nil amount.

(3) Any lower amount substituted by the Secretary of State under paragraph (2) in relation to contact costs under regulation 10 shall not be so low as to make it impossible, in the Secretary of State's opinion, for contact between the non-resident parent and the qualifying child to be maintained at the frequency specified in any court order made in respect of the non-resident parent and that child where the non-resident parent is maintaining contact at that frequency.

(4) For the purposes of this regulation, 'relevant net weekly income' means the net weekly income taken into account for the purposes of the maintenance calculation before taking account of any variation on the grounds of special expenses.

PART IV

PROPERTY OR CAPITAL TRANSFERS

16 Prescription of terms

(1) For the purposes of paragraphs 3(1)(a) and (b) of Schedule 4B to the Act –

    (a) a court order means an order made –
        (i) under one or more of the enactments listed in or prescribed under section 8(11) of the Act; and
        (ii) in connection with the transfer of property of a kind defined in paragraph (2); and
    (b) an agreement means a written agreement made in connection with the transfer of property of a kind defined in paragraph (2).

(2) Subject to paragraphs (3) and (4), for the purposes of paragraph 3(2) of Schedule 4B to the Act, a transfer of property is a transfer by the non-resident parent of his beneficial interest in any asset to the person with care, to the qualifying child, or to trustees where the object or one of the objects of the trust is the provision of maintenance.

(3) Where a transfer of property would not have fallen within paragraph (2) when made but the Secretary of State is satisfied that some or all of the amount of that property was subsequently transferred to the person currently with care of the qualifying child, the transfer of that property to the person currently with care shall constitute a transfer of property for the purposes of paragraph 3 of Schedule 4B to the Act.

(4) The minimum value for the purposes of paragraph 3(2) of Schedule 4B to the Act is the threshold amount which is £5000.

17 Value of a transfer of property – equivalent weekly value

(1) Where the conditions specified in paragraph 3 of Schedule 4B to the Act are satisfied, the value of a transfer of property for the purposes of that paragraph shall be that part of the transfer made by the non-resident parent (making allowances for any transfer by the person with care to the non-resident parent) which the Secretary of State is satisfied is in lieu of periodical payments of maintenance.

(2) The Secretary of State shall, in determining the value of a transfer of property in accordance with paragraph (1), assume that, unless evidence to the contrary is provided to him –

    (a) the person with care and the non-resident parent had equal beneficial interests in the asset in relation to which the court order or agreement was made;
    (b) where the person with care was married to the non-resident parent, one half of the value of the transfer was a transfer for the benefit of the person with care; and
    (c) where the person with care has never been married to the non-resident parent, none of the value of the transfer was for the benefit of the person with care.

(3) The equivalent weekly value of a transfer of property shall be determined in accordance with the provisions of the Schedule.

(4) For the purposes of regulation 16 and this regulation, the term 'maintenance' means the normal day-to-day living expenses of the qualifying child.

(5) A variation falling within paragraph (1) shall cease to have effect at the end of the number of years of liability, as defined in paragraph 1 of the Schedule, for the case in question.

PART V

ADDITIONAL CASES

18 Assets

(1) Subject to paragraphs (2) and (3), a case shall constitute a case for the purposes of paragraph 4(1) of Schedule 4B to the Act where the Secretary of State is satisfied there is an asset –

(a) in which the non-resident parent has the beneficial interest, or which the non-resident parent has the ability to control;

(b) which has been transferred by the non-resident parent to trustees, and the non-resident parent is a beneficiary of the trust so created, in circumstances where the Secretary of State is satisfied the non-resident parent has made the transfer to reduce the amount of assets which would otherwise be taken into account for the purposes of a variation under paragraph 4(1) of Schedule 4B to the Act; or

(c) which has become subject to a trust created by legal implication of which the non-resident parent is a beneficiary.

(2) For the purposes of this regulation 'asset' means –

(a) money, whether in cash or on deposit, including any which, in Scotland, is monies due or an obligation owed, whether immediately payable or otherwise and whether the payment or obligation is secured or not and the Secretary of State is satisfied that requiring payment of the monies or implementation of the obligation would be reasonable;

(b) a legal estate or beneficial interest in land and rights in or over land;

(c) shares as defined in section 744 of the Companies Act 1985, stock and unit trusts as defined in section 6 of the Charging Orders Act 1979, gilt-edged securities as defined in Part 1 of Schedule 9 to the Taxation of Chargeable Gains Act 1992, and other similar financial instruments; or

(d) a chose in action which has not been enforced when the Secretary of State is satisfied that such enforcement would be reasonable,

and includes any such asset located outside Great Britain.

(3) Paragraph (2) shall not apply –

(a) where the total value of the assets referred to in that paragraph does not exceed £65,000 after deduction of the amount owing under any mortgage or charge on those assets;

(b) in relation to any asset which the Secretary of State is satisfied is being retained by the non-resident parent to be used for a purpose which the Secretary of State considers reasonable in all the circumstances of the case;

(c) to any asset received by the non-resident parent as compensation for personal injury suffered by him;

(d) to any asset used in the course of a trade or business; or

(e) to property which is the home of the non-resident parent or any child of his.

(4) For the purposes of this regulation, where any asset is held in the joint names of the non-resident parent and another person the Secretary of State shall assume, unless evidence to the contrary is provided to him, that the asset is held by them in equal shares.

(5) Where a variation is agreed on the ground that the non-resident parent has assets for which provision is made in this regulation, the Secretary of State shall calculate the weekly value of the assets by applying the statutory rate of interest to the value of the assets and dividing by 52, and the resulting figure, aggregated with any benefit, pension or allowance which the non-resident parent receives, other than any benefits referred to in regulation 26(3), shall be taken into account as additional income under regulation 25.

(6) For the purposes of this regulation, the 'statutory rate of interest' means interest at the statutory rate prescribed for a judgment debt or, in Scotland, the statutory rate in respect of interest included in or payable under a decree in the Court of Session, which in either case applies on the date from which the maintenance calculation which takes account of the variation takes effect.

19 Income not taken into account and diversion of income

(1) Subject to paragraph (2), a case shall constitute a case for the purposes of paragraph 4(1) of Schedule 4B to the Act where –

    (a) the non-resident parent's liability to pay child support maintenance under the maintenance calculation which is in force or has been applied for or treated as applied for, is, or would be, as the case may be –

        (i) the nil rate owing to the application of paragraph 5(a) of Schedule 1 to the Act; or

        (ii) a flat rate, owing to the application of paragraph 4(1)(b) of Schedule 1 to the Act, or would be a flat rate but is less than that amount, or nil, owing to the application of paragraph 8 of Schedule 1 to the Act; and

    (b) the Secretary of State is satisfied that the non-resident parent is in receipt of income which would fall to be taken into account under the Maintenance Calculations and Special Cases Regulations but for the application to the non-resident parent of paragraph 4(1)(b) or 5(a) of Schedule 1 to the Act.

(2) Paragraph (1) shall apply where the income referred to in sub-paragraph (b) of that paragraph is a net weekly income of over £100.

(3) Net weekly income for the purposes of paragraph (2), in relation to earned income of a non-resident parent who is a student, shall be calculated by aggregating the income for the year ending with the relevant week (which for this purpose shall have the meaning given in the Maintenance Calculations and Special Cases Regulations) and dividing by 52, or, where the Secretary of State does not consider the result to be representative of the student's earned income, over such other period as he shall consider representative and dividing by the number of weeks in that period.

(4) A case shall constitute a case for the purposes of paragraph 4(1) of Schedule 4B to the Act where –

    (a) the non-resident parent has the ability to control the amount of income he receives, including earnings from employment or self-employment, whether or not the whole of that income is derived from the company or business from which his earnings are derived, and

    (b) the Secretary of State is satisfied that the non-resident parent has unreasonably reduced the amount of his income which would otherwise fall to be taken into account under the Maintenance Calculations and Special Cases Regulations by diverting it to other persons or for purposes other than the provision of such income for himself in order to reduce his liability to pay child support maintenance.

(5) Where a variation on this ground is agreed to –

(a) in a case to which paragraph (1) applies, the additional income taken into account under regulation 25 shall be the whole of the income referred to in paragraph (1)(b), aggregated with any benefit, pension or allowance which the non-resident parent receives other than any benefits referred to in regulation 26(3); and

(b) in a case to which paragraph (4) applies, the additional income taken into account under regulation 25 shall be the whole of the amount by which the Secretary of State is satisfied the non-resident parent has unreasonably reduced his income.

20 Life-style inconsistent with declared income

(1) Subject to paragraph (3), a case shall constitute a case for the purposes of paragraph 4(1) of Schedule 4B to the Act where –

(a) the non-resident parent's liability to pay child support maintenance under the maintenance calculation which is in force, or which has been applied for or treated as applied for, is, or would be, as the case may be –
  (i) the basic rate,
  (ii) the reduced rate,
  (iii) a flat rate owing to the application of paragraph 4(1)(a) of Schedule 1 to the Act, including where the net weekly income of the non-resident parent taken into account for the purposes of the maintenance calculation is, or would be, £100 per week or less owing to a variation being taken into account, or to the application of regulation 18, 19 or 21 of the Transitional Regulations (deduction for relevant departure direction or relevant property transfer);
  (iv) £5 per week or such other amount as may be prescribed owing to the application of paragraph 7(7) of Schedule 1 to the Act (shared care);
  (v) equivalent to the flat rate provided for in, or prescribed for the purposes of, paragraph 4(1)(b) of Schedule 1 to the Act owing to the application of –
    (aa) regulation 27(5);
    (bb) regulation 9 of the Maintenance Calculations and Special Cases Regulations (care provided in part by a local authority); or
    (cc) regulation 23(5) of the Transitional Regulations; or
  (vi) the nil rate owing to the application of paragraph 5(b) of Schedule 1 to the Act; and

(b) the Secretary of State is satisfied that the income which has been, or would be, taken into account for the purposes of the maintenance calculation is substantially lower than the level of income required to support the overall life-style of the non-resident parent.

(2) Subject to paragraph (4), a case shall constitute a case for the purposes of paragraph 4(1) of Schedule 4B to the Act where the non-resident parent's liability to pay child support maintenance under the maintenance calculation which is in force, or which has been applied for or treated as applied for, is, or would be, as the case may be –

(a) a flat rate owing to the application of paragraph 4(1)(b) of Schedule 1 to the Act, or would be a flat rate but is less than that amount, or nil, owing to the application of paragraph 8 of Schedule 1 to the Act; or

(b) the nil rate owing to the application of paragraph 5(a) of Schedule 1 to the Act,

and the Secretary of State is satisfied that the income which would otherwise be taken into account for the purposes of the maintenance calculation is substantially lower than the level of income required to support the overall life-style of the non-resident parent.

(3) Paragraph (1) shall not apply where the Secretary of State is satisfied that the life-style of the non-resident parent is paid for from –

(a) income which is or would be disregarded for the purposes of a maintenance calculation under the Maintenance Calculations and Special Cases Regulations;

(b) income which falls to be considered under regulation 19(4) (diversion of income);

(c) assets as defined for the purposes of regulation 18, or income derived from those assets;

(d) the income of any partner of the non-resident parent, except where the non-resident parent is able to influence or control the amount of income received by that partner; or

(e) assets as defined for the purposes of regulation 18 of any partner of the non-resident parent, or any income derived from such assets, except where the non-resident parent is able to influence or control the assets, their use, or income derived from them.

(4) Paragraph (2) shall not apply where the Secretary of State is satisfied that the life-style of the non-resident parent is paid for –

(a) from a source referred to in paragraph (3);

(b) from net weekly income of £100 or less; or

(c) from income which falls to be considered under regulation 19(1).

(5) Where a variation on this ground is agreed to, the additional income taken into account under regulation 25 shall be the difference between the income which the Secretary of State is satisfied the non-resident parent requires to support his overall life-style and the income which has been or, but for the application of paragraph 4(1)(b) or 5(a) of Schedule 1 to the Act, would be taken into account for the purposes of the maintenance calculation, aggregated with any benefit, pension or allowance which the non-resident parent receives other than any benefits referred to in regulation 26(3).

PART VI

FACTORS TO BE TAKEN INTO ACCOUNT FOR THE PURPOSES OF SECTION 28F OF THE ACT

21 Factors to be taken into account and not to be taken into account

(1) The factors to be taken into account in determining whether it would be just and equitable to agree to a variation in any case shall include –

(a) where the application is made on any ground –
   (i) whether, in the opinion of the Secretary of State, agreeing to a variation would be likely to result in a relevant person ceasing paid employment;
   (ii) if the applicant is the non-resident parent, the extent, if any, of his liability to pay child maintenance under a court order or agreement in the period prior to the effective date of the maintenance calculation; and

(b) where an application is made on the ground that the case falls within regulations 10 to 14 (special expenses), whether, in the opinion of the Secretary of State –
   (i) the financial arrangements made by the non-resident parent could have been such as to enable the expenses to be paid without a variation being agreed; or
   (ii) the non-resident parent has at his disposal financial resources which are currently utilised for the payment of expenses other than those arising from essential everyday requirements and which could be used to pay the expenses.

(2) The following factors are not to be taken into account in determining whether it would be just and equitable to agree to a variation in any case –

(a) the fact that the conception of the qualifying child was not planned by one or both of the parents;

(b) whether the non-resident parent or the person with care of the qualifying child was responsible for the breakdown of the relationship between them;

(c) the fact that the non-resident parent or the person with care of the qualifying child has formed a new relationship with a person who is not a parent of that child;

(d) the existence of particular arrangements for contact with the qualifying child, including whether any arrangements made are being adhered to;

(e) the income or assets of any person other than the non-resident parent, other than the income or assets of a partner of the non-resident parent taken into account under regulation 20(3);

(f) the failure by a non-resident parent to make payments of child support maintenance, or to make payments under a maintenance order or a written maintenance agreement; or

(g) representations made by persons other than the relevant persons.

PART VII

EFFECT OF A VARIATION ON THE MAINTENANCE CALCULATION AND EFFECTIVE DATES

22 Effective dates

(1) Subject to paragraph (2), where the application for a variation is made in the circumstances referred to in section 28A(3) of the Act (before the Secretary of State has reached a decision under section 11 or 12(1) of the Act) and the application is agreed to, the effective date of the maintenance calculation which takes account of the variation shall be –

(a) where the ground giving rise to the variation existed from the effective date of the maintenance calculation as provided for in the Maintenance Calculation Procedure Regulations, that date; or

(b) where the ground giving rise to the variation arose after the effective date referred to in sub-paragraph (a), the first day of the maintenance period in which the ground arose.

(2) Where the ground for the variation applied for under section 28A(3) of the Act is a ground in regulation 12 (prior debts) or 14 (special expenses – payments in respect of certain mortgages, loans or insurance policies) and payments falling within regulation 12 or 14 which have been made by the non-resident parent constitute voluntary payments for the purposes of section 28J of the Act and Regulations made under that section, the date from which the maintenance calculation shall take account of the variation on this ground shall be the date on which the maintenance period begins which immediately follows the date on which the non-resident parent is notified under the Maintenance Calculation Procedure Regulations of the amount of his liability to pay child support maintenance.

(3) Where the ground for the variation applied for under section 28A(3) of the Act has ceased to exist by the date the maintenance calculation is made, that calculation shall take account of the variation for the period ending on the last day of the maintenance period in which the ground existed.

23 Effect on maintenance calculation – special expenses

(1) Subject to paragraph (2) and regulations 26 and 27, where the variation agreed to is one falling within regulation 10 to 14 (special expenses) effect shall be given to the variation in the maintenance calculation by deducting from the net weekly income of the non-resident parent the weekly amount of those expenses.

(2) Where the income which is taken into account in the maintenance calculation is the capped amount and the variation agreed to is one falling within regulation 10 to 14 then –

  (a) the weekly amount of the expenses shall first be deducted from the actual net weekly income of the non-resident parent;
  (b) the amount by the which the capped amount exceeds the figure calculated under sub-paragraph (a) shall be calculated; and
  (c) effect shall be given to the variation in the maintenance calculation by deducting from the capped amount the amount calculated under sub-paragraph (b).

24 Effect on maintenance calculation – property or capital transfer

Subject to regulation 27, where the variation agreed to is one falling within regulation 16 (property or capital transfers) –

  (a) the maintenance calculation shall be carried out in accordance with Part 1 of Schedule 1 to the Act and Regulations made under that Part; and
  (b) the equivalent weekly value of the transfer calculated as provided in regulation 17 shall be deducted from the amount of child support maintenance which he would otherwise be liable to pay to the person with care with respect to whom the transfer was made.

25 Effect on maintenance calculation – additional cases

Subject to regulations 26 and 27, where the variation agreed to is one falling within regulations 18 to 20 (additional cases), effect shall be given to the variation in the maintenance calculation by increasing the net weekly income of the non-resident parent which would otherwise be taken into account by the weekly amount of the additional income except that, where the amount of net weekly income calculated in this way would exceed the capped amount, the amount of net weekly income taken into account shall be the capped amount.

26 Effect on maintenance calculation – maximum amount payable where the variation is on additional cases ground

(1) Subject to regulation 27, where this regulation applies the amount of child support maintenance which the non-resident parent shall be liable to pay shall be whichever is the lesser of –

  (a) a weekly amount calculated by aggregating an amount equivalent to the flat rate stated in or prescribed for the purposes of paragraph 4(1)(b) of Schedule 1 to the Act with the amount calculated by applying that Schedule to the Act to the additional income arising under the variation, other than the weekly amount of any benefit, pension or allowance the non-resident parent receives which is prescribed for the purposes of that paragraph; or
  (b) a weekly amount calculated by applying Part 1 of Schedule 1 to the Act to the additional income arising under the variation.

(2) This regulation applies where the variation agreed to is one to which regulation 25 applies and the non-resident parent's liability calculated as provided in Part 1 of Schedule 1 to the Act and Regulations made under that Schedule would, but for the variation, be –

(a) a flat rate under paragraph 4(1)(b) of that Schedule;

(b) a flat rate but is less than that amount or nil, owing to the application of paragraph 8 of that Schedule; or

(c) a flat rate under paragraph 4(1)(b) of that Schedule but for the application of paragraph 5(a) of that Schedule.

(3) For the purposes of paragraph (1) –

(a) any benefit, pension or allowance taken into account in the additional income referred to in sub-paragraph (b) shall not include –

(i) in the case of industrial injuries benefit under section 94 of the Contributions and Benefits Act, any increase in that benefit under section 104 (constant attendance) or 105 (exceptionally severe disablement) of that Act;

(ii) in the case of a war disablement pension within the meaning in section 150(2) of the Contributions and Benefits Act, any award under the following articles of the Naval, Military and Air Forces Etc., (Disablement and Death) Service Pensions Order 1983 ('the Service Pensions Order'): article 14 (constant attendance allowance), 15 (exceptionally severe disablement allowance), 16 (severe disablement occupational allowance) or 26A (mobility supplement) or any analogous allowances payable in conjunction with any other war disablement pension; and

(iii) any award under article 18 of the Service Pensions Order (unemployability allowances) which is an additional allowance in respect of a child of the non-resident parent where that child is not living with the non-resident parent;

(b) 'additional income' for the purposes of sub-paragraphs (a) and (b) means such income after the application of a variation falling within regulations 10 to 14 (special expenses); and

(c) 'weekly amount' for the purposes of sub-paragraphs (a) and (b) means the aggregate of the amounts referred to in the relevant sub-paragraph –

(i) adjusted as provided in regulation 27(3) as if the reference in that regulation to child support maintenance were to the weekly amount; and

(ii) after any deduction provided for in regulation 27(4) as if the reference in that regulation to child support maintenance were to the weekly amount.

## 27	Effect on maintenance calculation – general

(1) Subject to paragraphs (4) and (5), where more than one variation is agreed to in respect of the same period regulations 23 to 26 shall apply and the results shall be aggregated as appropriate.

(2) Paragraph 7(2) to (7) of Schedule 1 to the Act (shared care) shall apply where the rate of child support maintenance is affected by a variation which is agreed to and paragraph 7(2) shall be read as if after the words 'as calculated in accordance with the preceding paragraphs of this Part of this Schedule' there were inserted the words ', Schedule 4B and Regulations made under that Schedule'.

(3) Subject to paragraphs (4) and (5), where the non-resident parent shares the care of a qualifying child within the meaning in Part 1 of Schedule 1 to the Act, or where the care of such a child is shared in part by a local authority, the amount of child support maintenance the non-resident parent is liable to pay the person with care, calculated to take account of any variation, shall be reduced in accordance with the provisions of paragraph 7 of that Part or regulation 9 of the Maintenance Calculations and Special Cases Regulations, as the case may be.

(4) Subject to paragraph (5), where the variation agreed to is one falling within regulation 16 (property or capital transfers) the equivalent weekly value of the transfer calculated as provided in regulation 17 shall be deducted from the amount of child support maintenance the non-resident parent would otherwise be liable to pay the person with care in respect of whom the transfer was made after aggregation of the effects of any other variations as provided in paragraph (1) or deduction for shared care as provided in paragraph (3).

(5) If the application of regulation 24, or paragraph (3) or (4), would decrease the weekly amount of child support maintenance (or the aggregate of all such amounts) payable by the non-resident parent to the person with care (or all of them) to less than a figure equivalent to the flat rate of child support maintenance payable under paragraph 4(1)(b) of Schedule 1 to the Act, he shall instead be liable to pay child support maintenance at a rate equivalent to that rate apportioned (if appropriate) as provided in paragraph 6 of Schedule 1 to the Act.

(6) The effect of a variation shall not be applied for any period during which a circumstance referred to in regulation 7 applies.

(7) For the purposes of regulations 23 and 25 'net weekly income' means as calculated or estimated under the Maintenance Calculations and Special Cases Regulations.

28 Transitional provisions – conversion decisions

Where the variation is being applied for in connection with a subsequent decision within the meaning given in the Transitional Regulations, and the decision to be revised or superseded under section 16 or 17 of the Act, as the case may be, takes into account a relevant property transfer as defined and provided for in those Regulations –

(a) for the purposes of regulations 23 and 25 'capped amount' shall mean the income for the purposes of paragraph 10(3) of Schedule 1 to the Act less any deduction in respect of the relevant property transfer;

(b) for the purposes of regulation 26(3)(b) the additional income for the purposes of paragraph (1) of that regulation shall be after deduction in respect of the relevant property transfer;

(c) regulation 27(4) shall be read as if the aggregation referred to included any deduction in respect of the relevant property transfer; and

(d) regulation 27(5) shall be read as if after the reference to paragraph (3) or (4) there were a reference to any deduction in respect of the relevant property transfer.

29 Situations in which a variation previously agreed to may be taken into account in calculating maintenance liability

(1) This regulation applies where a variation has been agreed to in relation to a maintenance calculation.

(2) In the circumstances set out in paragraph (3), the Secretary of State may take account of the effect of such a variation upon the rate of liability for child support maintenance notwithstanding the fact that an application has not been made.

(3) The circumstances are –

(a) that the decision as to the maintenance calculation is superseded under section 17 of the Act on a change of circumstances so that the non-resident parent becomes liable to pay child support maintenance at the nil rate, or another rate which means that the variation cannot be taken into account; and

(b) that the superseding decision referred to in sub-paragraph (a) is itself superseded under section 17 of the Act on a change of circumstances so that the non-resident parent becomes liable to pay a rate of child support maintenance which can be adjusted to take account of the variation.

30 Circumstances for the purposes of section 28F(3) of the Act

The circumstances prescribed for the purposes of section 28F(3) of the Act (Secretary of State shall not agree to a variation) are –

(a) the prescribed circumstances in regulation 6(2) or 7; and
(b) where the Secretary of State considers it would not be just and equitable to agree to the variation having regard to any of the factors referred to in regulation 21.

PART VIII

MISCELLANEOUS

31 Regular payments condition

(1) For the purposes of section 28C(2)(b) of the Act (payments of child support maintenance less than those specified in the interim maintenance decision) the payments shall be those fixed by the interim maintenance decision or the maintenance calculation in force, as the case may be, adjusted to take account of the variation applied for by the non-resident parent as if that variation had been agreed.

(2) The Secretary of State may refuse to consider the application for a variation where a regular payments condition has been imposed and the non-resident parent has failed to comply with it in the circumstances to which paragraph (3) applies.

(3) This paragraph applies where the non-resident parent has failed to comply with the regular payments condition and fails to make such payments which are due and unpaid within one month of being required to do so by the Secretary of State or such other period as the Secretary of State may in the particular case decide.

32 Meaning of 'benefit' for the purposes of section 28E of the Act

For the purposes of section 28E of the Act, 'benefit' means income support, income-based jobseeker's allowance, housing benefit and council tax benefit.

PART IX

REVOCATION

33 Revocation and savings

(1) Subject to paragraph (2), the Child Support Departure Direction and Consequential Amendments Regulations 1996 shall be revoked with respect to a particular case with effect from the date that these Regulations come into force with respect to that type of case ('the commencement date').

(2) Where before the commencement date in respect of a particular case –

(a) an application was made and not determined for –
   (i) a maintenance assessment;
   (ii) a departure direction; or
   (iii) a revision or supersession of a decision;
(b) the Secretary of State had begun but not completed a revision or supersession of a decision on his own initiative;

(c) any time limit provided for in Regulations for making an application for a revision or a departure direction had not expired; or

(d) any appeal was made but not decided or any time limit for making an appeal had not expired,

the provisions of the Child Support Departure Direction and Consequential Amendments Regulations 1996 shall continue to apply for the purposes of –

(aa) the decision on the application referred to in sub-paragraph (a);

(bb) the revision or supersession referred to in sub-paragraph (b);

(cc) the ability to apply for the revision or the departure direction referred to in sub-paragraph (c) and the decision whether to revise or to give a departure direction following any such application;

(dd) any appeal outstanding or made during the time limit referred to in sub-paragraph (d); or

(ee) any revision, supersession or appeal or application for a departure direction in relation to a decision, ability to apply or appeal referred to in sub-paragraphs (aa) to (dd).

(3) Where, after the commencement date, a decision with respect to a departure direction is revised from a date which is prior to the commencement date, the provisions of the Child Support Departure Direction and Consequential Amendments Regulations 1996 shall continue to apply for the purposes of that revision.

(4) Where, under regulation 28(1) of the Transitional Regulations, an application for a maintenance calculation is treated as an application for a maintenance assessment, the provisions of the Child Support Departure Direction and Consequential Amendments Regulations 1996 shall continue to apply for the purposes of an application for a departure direction in relation to any such assessment made.

(5) For the purposes of this regulation –

(a) 'departure direction' and 'maintenance assessment' means as provided in section 54 of the Act before its amendment by the 2000 Act;

(b) 'revision or supersession' means a revision or supersession of a decision under section 16 or 17 of the Act before its amendment by the 2000 Act and 'any time limit for making an application for a revision' means any time limit provided for in Regulations made under section 16 of the Act; and

(c) '2000 Act' means the Child Support, Pensions and Social Security Act 2000.

SCHEDULE

Regulation 17(3)

EQUIVALENT WEEKLY VALUE OF A TRANSFER OF PROPERTY

1 (1) Subject to paragraph 3, the equivalent weekly value of a transfer of property shall be calculated by multiplying the value of a transfer of property determined in accordance with regulation 17 by the relevant factor specified in the Table set out in paragraph 2 ('the Table').

(2) For the purposes of sub-paragraph (1), the relevant factor is the number in the Table at the intersection of the column for the statutory rate and of the row for the number of years of liability.

(3) In sub-paragraph (2) –

Child Support – The New Law

(a) 'the statutory rate' means interest at the statutory rate prescribed for a judgment debt or, in Scotland, the statutory rate in respect of interest included in or payable under a decree in the Court of Session, which in either case applies at the date of the court order or written agreement relating to the transfer of the property;

(b) 'the number of years of liability' means the number of years, beginning on the date of the court order or written agreement relating to the transfer of property and ending on –

(i) the date specified in that order or agreement as the date on which maintenance for the youngest child in respect of whom that order or agreement was made shall cease; or

(ii) if no such date is specified, the date on which the youngest child specified in the order or agreement reaches the age of 18,

and where that period includes a fraction of a year, that fraction shall be treated as a full year if it is either one half or exceeds one half of a year, and shall otherwise be disregarded.

2   The Table referred to in paragraph 1(1) is set out below –

THE TABLE

Number of years of liability	Statutory Rate							
	7.0%	8.0%	10.0%	11.0%	12.0%	12.5%	14.0%	15.0%
1.	.02058	.02077	.02115	.02135	.02154	.02163	.02192	.02212
2.	.01064	.01078	.01108	.01123	.01138	.01145	.01168	.01183
3.	.00733	.00746	.00773	.00787	.00801	.00808	.00828	.00842
4.	.00568	.00581	.00607	.00620	.00633	.00640	.00660	.00674
5.	.00469	.00482	.00507	.00520	.00533	.00540	.00560	.00574
6.	.00403	.00416	.00442	.00455	.00468	.00474	.00495	.00508
7.	.00357	.00369	.00395	.00408	.00421	.00428	.00448	.00462
8.	.00322	.00335	.00360	.00374	.00387	.00394	.00415	.00429
9.	.00295	.00308	.00334	.00347	.00361	.00368	.00389	.00403
10.	.00274	.00287	.00313	.00327	.00340	.00347	.00369	.00383
11.	.00256	.00269	.00296	.00310	.00324	.00331	.00353	.00367
12.	.00242	.00255	.00282	.00296	.00310	.00318	.00340	.00355
13.	.00230	.00243	.00271	.00285	.00299	.00307	.00329	.00344
14.	.00220	.00233	.00261	.00275	.00290	.00298	.00320	.00336
15.	.00211	.00225	.00253	.00267	.00282	.00290	.00313	.00329
16.	.00204	.00217	.00246	.00261	.00276	.00283	.00307	.00323
17.	.00197	.00211	.00240	.00255	.00270	.00278	.00302	.00318
18.	.00191	.00205	.00234	.00250	.00265	.00273	.00297	.00314

3 The Secretary of State may determine a lower equivalent weekly value than that determined in accordance with paragraphs 1 and 2 where the amount of child support maintenance that would be payable in consequence of agreeing to a variation of that value is lower than the amount of the periodical payments of maintenance which were payable under the court order or written agreement referred to in regulation 16.

Social Security and Child Support (Decisions and Appeals) Regulations 1999, as amended

SI 1999/991

****

PART II

REVISIONS, SUPERSESSIONS AND OTHER MATTERS SOCIAL SECURITY AND CHILD SUPPORT

Chapter I – Revisions

****

3A Revision of child support decisions

(1) Subject to paragraph (2), any decision as defined in paragraph (3) may be revised under section 16 of the Child Support Act by the Secretary of State –

    (a) if he receives an application for the revision of a decision either –

        (i) under section 16; or

        (ii) by way of an application under section 28G,

    of the Child Support Act, within one month of the date of notification of the decision or within such longer time as may be allowed under regulation 4;

    (b) if –

        (i) he notifies the person who applied for a decision to be revised within the period specified in sub-paragraph (a), that the application is unsuccessful because the Secretary of State is not in possession of all of the information or evidence needed to make a decision; and

        (ii) that person reapplies for the decision to be revised within one month of the notification described in head (i) above, or such longer period as the Secretary of State is satisfied is reasonable in the circumstances of the case, and provides in that application sufficient information or evidence to enable a decision to be made;

    (c) if he is satisfied that the decision was erroneous due to a misrepresentation of, or failure to disclose, a material fact and that the decision was more advantageous to the person who misrepresented or failed to disclose that fact than it would have been but for that error;

    (d) if he commences action leading to the revision of the decision within one month of the date of notification of the decision; or

    (e) if the decision arose from an official error.

(2) Paragraph (1)(a) to (d) shall not apply in respect of a change of circumstances which –

    (a) occurred since the date on which the decision had effect; or

    (b) according to information or evidence which the Secretary of State has, is expected to occur.

(3) Subject to paragraph (7), in paragraphs (1) and (2) and in regulation 4(3) 'decision' means a decision of the Secretary of State under sections 11, 12 or 46 of the Child Support

Act, or a determination of an appeal tribunal on a referral under section 28D(1)(b) of that Act, or any supersession of a decision under section 17 of that Act.

(4) A decision made under section 12(2) of the Child Support Act may be revised at any time before it is replaced by a decision under section 11 of that Act.

(5) Where the Secretary of State revises a decision made under section 12(1) of the Child Support Act in accordance with section 16(1B) of that Act, that decision may be revised under section 16 of that Act at any time.

(6) Section 16 of the Child Support Act shall apply in relation to any decision of the Secretary of State –

(a) under section 41A or 47 of the Child Support Act; or
(b) that an adjustment shall cease or with respect to the adjustment of amounts payable under maintenance calculations for the purpose of taking account of overpayments of child support maintenance and voluntary payments,

as it applies in relation to any decision of the Secretary of State under sections 11, 12, 17 or 46 of that Act, or the determination of an appeal tribunal on a referral under section 28D(1)(b) of that Act.

(7) In paragraph (6)(b) and in regulations 6A(9), 6B(4)(d) and 30A 'voluntary payments' means the same as in the definition in section 28J of the Child Support Act and Regulations made under that section.

4 Late application for a revision

(1) The time limit for making an application for a revision specified in regulation 3(1) or (3) or 3A(1)(a) may be extended where the conditions specified in the following provisions of this regulation are satisfied.

(2) An application for an extension of time shall be made by the relevant person, the claimant or a person acting on his behalf.

(3) An application shall –

(a) contain particulars of the grounds on which the extension of time is sought and shall contain sufficient details of the decision which it is sought to have revised to enable that decision to be identified; and
(b) be made within 13 months of the date of notification of the decision which it is sought to have revised.

(4) An application for an extension of time shall not be granted unless the applicant satisfies the Secretary of State or the Board or an officer of the Board that –

(a) it is reasonable to grant the application;
(b) the application for revision has merit; and
(c) special circumstances are relevant to the application and as a result of those special circumstances it was not practicable for the application to be made within the time limit specified in regulation 3 or 3A.

(5) In determining whether it is reasonable to grant an application, the Secretary of State or the Board or an officer of the Board shall have regard to the principle that the greater the amount of time that has elapsed between the expiration of the time specified in regulation 3(1) and (3) and regulation 3A(1)(a) for applying for a revision and the making of the application for an extension of time, the more compelling should be the special circumstances on which the application is based.

(6) In determining whether it is reasonable to grant the application for an extension of time, no account shall be taken of the following –

    (a) that the applicant or any person acting for him was unaware of or misunderstood the law applicable to his case (including ignorance or misunderstanding of the time limits imposed by these Regulations); or

    (b) that a Commissioner, a Child Support Commisioner or a court has taken a different view of the law from that previously understood and applied.

(7) An application under this regulation for an extension of time which has been refused may not be renewed.

****

Chapter II – Supersessions

****

6A   Supersession of child support decisions

(1) Subject to paragraphs (7) and (8), the cases and circumstances in which a decision ('a superseding decision') may be made by the Secretary of State for the purposes of section 17 of the Child Support Act are set out in paragraphs (2) to (6).

(2) A decision may be superseded by a decision made by the Secretary of State acting on his own initiative where –

    (a) there has been a relevant change of circumstances since the decision had effect; or

    (b) the decision was made in ignorance of, or was based upon a mistake as to, some material fact.

(3) Subject to regulation 6B, a decision may be superseded by a decision made by the Secretary of State where –

    (a) an application is made on the basis that –

        (i) there has been a change of circumstances since the date from which the decision had effect; or

        (ii) it is expected that a change of circumstances will occur; and

    (b) the Secretary of State is satisfied that the change of circumstances is or would be relevant.

(4) A decision may be superseded by a decision made by the Secretary of State where –

    (a) an application is made on the basis that the decision was made in ignorance of, or was based upon a mistake as to, a fact; and

    (b) the Secretary of State is satisfied that the fact is or would be material.

(5) A decision, other than a decision made on appeal, may be superseded by a decision made by the Secretary of State –

    (a) acting on his own initiative, where he is satisfied that the decision was erroneous in point of law; or

    (b) where an application is made on the basis that the decision was erroneous in point of law.

(6) A decision may be superseded by a decision made by the Secretary of State where he receives an application for the supersession of a decision by way of an application made under section 28G of the Child Support Act.

(7) The cases and circumstances in which a decision may be superseded shall not include any case or circumstance in which a decision may be revised.

(8) Paragraphs (2) to (6) shall not apply in respect of a decision to refuse an application for a maintenance calculation.

(9) For the purposes of section 17 of the Child Support Act, paragraphs (2) to (6) shall apply in relation to any decision of the Secretary of State that an adjustment shall cease or with respect to the adjustment of amounts payable under a maintenance calculation for the purpose of taking account of overpayments of child support maintenance and voluntary payments, whether as originally made or as revised under section 16 of that Act.

6B Circumstances in which a child support decision may not be superseded

(1) Except as provided in paragraph (4), and subject to paragraph (3), a decision of the Secretary of State, appeal tribunal or Child Support Commissioner, on an application made under regulation 6A(3), shall not be superseded where the difference between –

(a) the non-resident parent's net income figure fixed for the purposes of the maintenance calculation in force in accordance with Part I of Schedule 1 to the Child Support Act; and

(b) the non-resident parent's net income figure which would be fixed in accordance with a superseding decision,

is less than 5% of the figure in sub-paragraph (a).

(2) In paragraph (1) 'superseding decision' means a decision which would supersede the decision subject to the application made under regulation 6A(3) but for the application of this regulation.

(3) Where the application for a supersession is made on more than one ground this regulation shall only apply to the ground relating to the net income of the non-resident parent.

(4) This regulation shall not apply to a decision under regulation 6A(3) where –

(a) the superseding decision is made in consequence of the determination of an application made under section 28G of the Child Support Act;

(b) the superseding decision affects a variation ground in a decision made under section 11 or 17 of the Child Support Act, whether as originally made or as revised under section 16 of that Act;

(c) the decision being superseded was made under section 12(2) of the Child Support Act, or was a decision under section 17 of that Act superseding an interim maintenance decision, whether as originally made or as revised under section 16 of that Act;

(d) the decision being superseded was a decision that an adjustment shall cease or with respect to the adjustment of amounts payable under maintenance calculations for the purpose of taking account of overpayments of child support maintenance and voluntary payments or was a decision under section 17 of the Child Support Act superseding that decision, whether as originally made or as revised under section 16 of that Act; or

(e) the superseding decision takes effect from the dates prescribed in regulation 7B(1) to (3), (19) or (20).

****

7B Date from which a decision superseded under section 17 of the Child Support Act takes effect

(1) Subject to paragraphs (17) to (22), where a decision is superseded by a decision made by the Secretary of State in a case to which regulation 6A(2)(a) applies on the basis of

information or evidence which was also the basis of a decision made under section 8, 9 or 10 of the Act, the decision under section 17 of the Child Support Act shall take effect from the first day of the maintenance period in which that information or evidence was first brought to the attention of an officer exercising the functions of the Secretary of State under the Child Support Act ('the officer').

(2) Where a decision is superseded by a decision made by the Secretary of State in a case to which regulation 6A(3)(a) applies and the relevant circumstance is that the non-resident parent or his partner has notified the officer that he or his partner had made a claim for a relevant benefit and, where the relevant benefit is payable, that the officer was notified within one month of notification of the award, the decision shall take effect from the first day of the maintenance period in which –

    (a) the non-resident parent or his partner notified the officer that he or his partner had made a claim for a relevant benefit, where entitlement to that benefit commences on or before the date of notification; or

    (b) entitlement to the relevant benefit commences, where that entitlement commenced after the date of notification.

(3) Where a decision is superseded by a decision made by the Secretary of State in a case to which regulation 6A(4) applies and the material fact is that the non-resident parent or his partner has notified the officer that he or his partner had made a claim for a relevant benefit before the Secretary of State notified him of an application for a maintenance calculation in accordance with regulation 5 of the Maintenance Calculation Procedure Regulations (notice of an application for a maintenance calculation) and, where the relevant benefit is payable, that the officer was notified within one month of notification of the award, the decision shall take effect from the first day of the maintenance period in which –

    (a) the non-resident parent or his partner notified the officer that he or his partner had made a claim for a relevant benefit, where entitlement to that benefit commences on or before the date of notification; or

    (b) entitlement to the relevant benefit commences, where that entitlement commenced after the date of notification.

(4) Subject to paragraphs (17) to (22), where the superseding decision is made in a case to which regulation 6A(3)(a)(i) applies and that decision supersedes one which has been made under section 12(2) of the Child Support Act, the decision shall take effect from the first day of the maintenance period in which the change of circumstances occurred.

(5) Where the superseding decision is made in a case to which regulation 6A(3)(a)(ii) applies, the decision shall take effect from the first day of the maintenance period in which the change of circumstances is expected to occur.

(6) Where the superseding decision is made in a case to which regulation 6A(6) applies and the relevant circumstance is that a ground for a variation is expected to occur, the decision shall take effect from the first day of the maintenance period in which the ground for the variation is expected to occur.

(7) Except in a case to which paragraph (1) applies, where the superseding decision is made in a case to which regulation 7C applies, that decision shall take effect from the first day of the maintenance period which includes the date which is 28 days after the date on which the Secretary of State gave notice to the relevant persons under that regulation.

(8) For the purposes of paragraph (7) –

    (a) where the relevant persons are notified on different dates, the period of 28 days shall be counted from the date of the latest notification;

(b) notification includes oral and written notification;

(c) where a person is notified in more than one way, the date on which he is notified is the date on which he was first given notification; and

(d) the date of written notification is the date on which it was given or sent to the person.

(9) Where –

(a) a decision made by an appeal tribunal or by a Child Support Commissioner is superseded on the ground that it was erroneous due to a misrepresentation of, or that there was a failure to disclose, a material fact; and

(b) the Secretary of State is satisfied that the decision was more advantageous to the person who misrepresented or failed to disclose that fact than it would otherwise have been but for that error,

the superseding decision shall take effect from the date on which the decision of the appeal tribunal or, as the case may be, the Child Support Commissioner took, or was to take, effect.

(10) Any decision made under section 17 of the Child Support Act in consequence of a determination which is a relevant determination for the purposes of section 28ZC of that Act shall take effect from the date of the relevant determination.

(11) Where a decision with respect to a reduced benefit decision is superseded because the decision ceases to be in force in accordance with regulation 16(a) of the Maintenance Calculation Procedure Regulations (termination of a reduced benefit decision), the superseding decision shall have effect –

(a) where the decision is in operation immediately before it ceases to be in force, from the last day of the benefit week during the course of which the parent concerned falls within the provisions of section 46(1) of the Child Support Act; or

(b) where the decision is suspended immediately before it ceases to be in force, from the date on which the parent concerned falls within the provisions of section 46(1) of that Act.

(12) Where a decision with respect to a reduced benefit decision is superseded because the decision ceases to be in force in accordance with regulation 16(b) of the Maintenance Calculation Procedure Regulations, the superseding decision shall have effect –

(a) where the decision is in operation immediately before it ceases to be in force, from the last day of the benefit week during the course of which the parent concerned complied with the obligations imposed by section 46(6)(b) of the Child Support Act; or

(b) where the decision is suspended immediately before it ceases to be in force, from the date on which the parent concerned complied with the obligations imposed by section 46(6)(b) of the Child Support Act.

(13) Where a decision with respect to a reduced benefit decision is superseded because the decision ceases to be in force in accordance with regulation 16(c) of the Maintenance Calculation Procedure Regulations, the superseding decision shall have effect from the last day of the benefit week in which entitlement to benefit ceased.

(14) Where a decision with respect to a reduced benefit decision is superseded because the decision ceases to be in force in accordance with regulation 16(d) of the Maintenance Calculation Procedure Regulations, the superseding decision shall have effect –

(a) where the decision is in operation immediately before it ceases to be in force, from the last day of the benefit week during the course of which the Secretary of State is supplied with information that enables him to make the calculation; or

(b) where the decision is suspended immediately before it ceases to be in force, from the date on which the Secretary of State is supplied with information that enables him to make the calculation.

(15) Where a decision with respect to a reduced benefit decision is superseded because the decision ceases to be in force in accordance with regulation 17(1) of the Maintenance Calculation Procedure Regulations (reduced benefit decisions where there is an additional qualifying child), the superseding decision shall have effect from –

(a) the last day of the benefit week preceding the benefit week which includes, in accordance with the provisions of regulation 11(3) of the Maintenance Calculation Procedure Regulations (amount of and period of reduction of relevant benefit under a reduced benefit decision), the first day on which the further decision comes into operation; or

(b) the first day on which the further decision would come into operation but for the provisions of regulation 14 of the Maintenance Calculation Procedure Regulations (suspension of a reduced benefit decision when a modified applicable amount is payable (income support)) or 15 (suspension of a reduced benefit decision when a modified applicable amount is payable (income-based jobseeker's allowance)) of those Regulations.

(16) Where a decision with respect to a reduced benefit decision is superseded because the decision ceases to be in force in accordance with regulation 18(2) of the Maintenance Calculation Procedure Regulations (suspension and termination of a reduced benefit decision where the sole qualifying child ceases to be a child or where the parent concerned ceases to be a person with care), the superseding decision shall have effect from the last day of the benefit week which includes the day on which the child ceases to be a child within the meaning of section 55 of the Child Support Act as supplemented by Schedule 1 to those Regulations, or the parent ceases to be the person with care.

(17) Where a superseding decision is made in a case to which regulation 6A(2)(a) or (3) applies and the relevant circumstance is the death of a qualifying child or a qualifying child ceasing to be a qualifying child, the decision shall take effect from the first day of the maintenance period in which the change occurred.

(18) Where a superseding decision is made in a case to which regulation 6A(2)(a) or (3) applies and the relevant circumstance is that the non-resident parent, person with care or the qualifying child has moved out of the jurisdiction, the decision shall take effect from the first day of the maintenance period in which the non-resident parent, person with care or qualifying child leaves the jurisdiction and jurisdiction is within the meaning of section 44 of the Child Support Act.

(19) Where a superseding decision is made in a case to which regulation 6A(2)(a) or (3) applies and the relevant circumstance is that the maintenance calculation has been made in response to an application which is treated as made under section 6 of the Child Support Act and –

(a) the person on whose application the calculation was made ('the applicant') asks the Secretary of State to cease acting; and

(b) the Secretary of State is satisfied that the applicant has ceased to fall within section 6(1) of that Act,

the decision shall take effect from the first day of the maintenance period after the applicant asks the Secretary of State to cease acting.

(20) Where a superseding decision is made in a case to which regulation 6A(2)(a) or (3) applies and the relevant circumstance is that both the non-resident parent and the person with care with respect to whom a maintenance calculation was made request the Secretary of State to decide that the maintenance calculation shall cease and he is satisfied that they are living together, the decision shall take effect from the first day of the maintenance period in which the later of the two requests was made.

(21) Where a superseding decision is made in a case to which regulation 6A(2)(a) or (3) applies and the relevant circumstance is that –

    (a) an application for a maintenance calculation is made under section 4 or 7 of the Child Support Act, or treated as made under section 6(3) of that Act, in respect of a non-resident parent; and

    (b) before the decision as to a maintenance calculation is made at least one other maintenance calculation is in force with respect to the same non-resident parent but to a different person with care and a different child,

the effective date of the maintenance calculation made in respect of the application shall be a date which is not later than 7 days after the date of notification to the non-resident parent and which is the day on which a maintenance period in respect of the maintenance calculation in force begins.

(22) Where a superseding decision is made in a case to which regulation 6A(3) applies and in relation to that decision a maintenance calculation is made to which paragraph 15 of Schedule 1 to the Child Support Act applies, the effective date of the calculation or calculations shall be the beginning of the maintenance period in which the change of circumstance to which the calculation or calculations relates occurred or is expected to occur and where that change occurred before the date of the application for the supersession and was notified after that date, the date of that application.

(23) In this regulation –

    'benefit week' in relation to income support has the same meaning as in regulation 2(1) of the Income Support Regulations, and in relation to jobseeker's allowance has the same meaning as in regulation 1(3) of the Jobseeker's Allowance Regulations;

    'partner' has the same meaning as in regulation 2 of the Income Support Regulations; and

    'relevant benefit' means a benefit which is prescribed in regulation 4 of the Maintenance Calculations and Special Cases Regulations for the purposes of paragraph 4(1)(b) of Part I of Schedule 1 to the Child Support Act, and child benefit as referred to in paragraph 10C(2)(a) of Part I of Schedule 1 to that Act.

7C Procedure where the Secretary of State proposes to supersede a decision under section 17 of the Child Support Act on his own initiative

Where the Secretary of State on his own initiative proposes to make a decision superseding a decision he shall notify the relevant persons who could be materially affected by the decision of that intention.

****

Chapter III – Other Matters

****

15B   Procedure in relation to an application made under section 16 or 17 of the Child Support Act in connection with a previously determined variation

(1) Subject to paragraph (3), where the Secretary of State has received an application under section 16 or 17 of the Child Support Act in connection with a previously determined variation which has effect on the maintenance calculation in force, he –

    (a) shall give notice of the application to the relevant persons, other than the applicant, informing them of the grounds on which the application has been made and any relevant information or evidence the applicant has given, except information or evidence falling within paragraph (2);

    (b) may invite representations, which need not be in writing but shall be in writing if in any case he so directs, from the relevant persons other than the applicant on any matter relating to that application, to be submitted to the Secretary of State within 14 days of notification or such longer period as the Secretary of State is satisfied is reasonable in the circumstances of the case; and

    (c) shall set out the provisions of paragraphs (2)(b) and (c), (4) and (5) in relation to such representations.

(2) The information or evidence referred to in paragraphs (1)(a), (4)(a) and (7), is –

    (a) details of the nature of the long-term illness or disability of the relevant other child which forms the basis of a variation application on the ground in regulation 11of the Variations Regulations (special expenses – illness or disability of relevant other child) where the applicant requests they should not be disclosed and the Secretary of State is satisfied that disclosure is not necessary in order to be able to determine the application;

    (b) medical evidence or medical advice which has not been disclosed to the applicant or a relevant person and which the Secretary of State considers would be harmful to the health of the applicant or that relevant person if disclosed to him;

    (c) the address of a relevant person or qualifying child, or any other information which could reasonably be expected to lead to that person or child being located, where the Secretary of State considers that there would be a risk of harm or undue distress to that person or that child or any other children living with that person if the address or information were disclosed.

(3) The Secretary of State need not act in accordance with paragraph (1) if –

    (a) he is satisfied on the information or evidence available to him, that he will not agree to a variation of the maintenance calculation in force, but if, on further consideration he is minded to do so he shall, before doing so, comply with the provisions of this regulation; and

    (b) were the application to succeed, the decision as revised or superseded would be less advantageous to the applicant than the decision before it was so revised or superseded.

(4) Where the Secretary of State receives representations from the relevant persons he –

    (a) may, if he considers it reasonable to do so, send a copy of the representations concerned (excluding material falling within paragraph (2) above) to the applicant and invite any comments he may have within 14 days or such longer period as the Secretary of State is satisfied is reasonable in the circumstances of the case; and

(b) where the Secretary of State acts under sub-paragraph (a), shall not proceed to make a decision in response to the application until he has received such comments or the period referred to in sub-paragraph (a) has expired.

(5) Where the Secretary of State has not received representations from the relevant persons notified in accordance with paragraph (1) within the time limit specified in sub-paragraph (b) of that paragraph, he may proceed to make a decision under section 16 or 17 of the Child Support Act in response to the application, in their absence.

(6) In considering an application for a revision or supersession the Secretary of State shall take into account any representations received at the date upon which he makes a decision under section 16 or 17 of the Child Support Act, from the relevant persons including any representations received in connection with the application in accordance with paragraphs (1)(b), (4)(a) and (7).

(7) Where any information or evidence requested by the Secretary of State under regulation 15A is received after notification has been given under paragraph (1), he may, if he considers it reasonable to do so and except where such information or evidence falls within paragraph (2), send a copy of such information or evidence to the relevant persons and may invite them to submit representations, which need not be in writing unless the Secretary of State so directs in any particular case, on that information or evidence.

(8) Where the Secretary of State is considering making a decision under section 16 or 17 of the Child Support Act in accordance with this regulation, he shall apply the factors to be taken into account for the purposes of section 28F of the Child Support Act set out in regulation 21 of the Variations Regulations (factors to be taken into account and not to be taken into account) as factors to be taken into account and not to be taken into account when considering making a decision under this regulation.

(9) In this regulation 'relevant person' means –

(a) a non-resident parent, or a person treated as a non-resident parent under regulation 8 of the Maintenance Calculations and Special Cases Regulations (persons treated as non-resident parents), whose liability to pay child support maintenance may be affected by any variation agreed;

(b) a person with care, or a child to whom section 7 of the Child Support Act applies, where the amount of child support maintenance payable by virtue of a calculation relevant to that person with care or in respect of that child may be affected by any variation agreed.

15C Notification of a decision made under section 16 or 17 of the Child Support Act

(1) Subject to paragraphs (2) and (5) to (11), a notification of a decision made following the revision or supersession of a decision made under section 11, 12 or 17 of the Child Support Act, whether as originally made or as revised under section 16 of that Act, shall set out, in relation to the decision in question –

(a) the effective date of the maintenance calculation;
(b) where relevant, the non-resident parent's net weekly income;
(c) the number of qualifying children;
(d) the number of relevant other children;
(e) the weekly rate;
(f) the amounts calculated in accordance with Part I of Schedule 1 to the Child Support Act and, where there has been agreement to a variation or a variation has otherwise been taken into account, the Variations Regulations;

(g) where the weekly rate is adjusted by apportionment or shared care or both, the amount calculated in accordance with paragraph 6, 7 or 8, as the case may be, of Part I of Schedule 1 to the Child Support Act; and

(h) where the amount of child support maintenance which the non-resident parent is liable to pay is decreased in accordance with regulation 9 of the Maintenance Calculations and Special Cases Regulations (care provided in part by local authority) or 11 (non-resident parent liable to pay maintenance under a maintenance order) of those Regulations, the adjustment calculated in accordance with that regulation.

(2) A notification of a revision or supersession of a maintenance calculation made under section 12(1) of the Child Support Act shall set out the effective date of the maintenance calculation, the default rate, the number of qualifying children on which the rate is based and whether any apportionment has been applied under regulation 7 of the Maintenance Calculation Procedure Regulations (default rate) and shall state the nature of the information required to enable a decision under section 11 of that Act to be made by way of section 16 of that Act.

(3) Except where a person gives written permission to the Secretary of State that the information in relation to him, mentioned in sub-paragraphs (a) and (b), may be conveyed to other persons, any document given or sent under the provisions of paragraph (1) or (2) shall not contain –

(a) the address of any person other than the recipient of the document in question (other than the address of the office of the officer concerned who is exercising functions of the Secretary of State under the Child Support Act) or any other information the use of which could reasonably be expected to lead to any such person being located;

(b) any other information the use of which could reasonably be expected to lead to any person, other than a qualifying child or a relevant person, being identified.

(4) Where a decision as to the revision or supersession of a decision made under section 11, 12 or 17 of the Child Support Act, whether as originally made or as revised under section 16 of that Act, is made under section 16 or 17 of that Act, a notification under paragraph (1) or (2) shall include information as to the provisions of sections 16, 17 and 20 of that Act.

(5) Where the Secretary of State makes a decision that a maintenance calculation shall cease to have effect –

(a) he shall immediately notify the non-resident parent and person with care, so far as that is reasonably practicable;

(b) where a decision has been superseded in a case where a child under section 7 of the Child Support Act ceases to be a child for the purposes of that Act, he shall immediately notify the persons in sub-paragraph (a) and the other qualifying children within the meaning of section 7 of that Act; and

(c) any notice under sub-paragraphs (a) and (b) shall specify the date with effect from which that decision took effect.

(6) Where the Secretary of State, under the provisions of section 16 or 17 of the Child Support Act, has made a decision that an adjustment shall cease, or adjusted the amount payable under a maintenance calculation, he shall immediately notify the relevant persons, so far as that is reasonably practicable, that the adjustment has ceased or of the amount and period of the adjustment, and the amount payable during the period of the adjustment.

(7) Where the Secretary of State has made a decision under section 16 of the Child Support Act, revising a decision under section 41A or 47 of that Act, he shall immediately notify the relevant persons so far as that is reasonably practicable, of the amount of child support maintenance payable, the amount of arrears, the amount of the penalty payment or fees to be paid, as the case may be, the method of payment and the day by which payment is to be made.

(8) Where the non-resident parent appeals against a decision made by the Secretary of State under section 41A or 47 of the Child Support Act and the Secretary of State makes a decision under section 16 of that Act, before the appeal is decided he shall notify the relevant persons, so far as that is reasonably practicable of either the new amount of the penalty payment or the fee to be paid or that the amount is no longer payable, the method of payment and the day by which payment is to be made.

(9) Paragraphs (1) to (3) shall not apply where the Secretary of State has decided not to supersede a decision under section 17 of the Child Support Act, and he shall, so far as that is reasonably practicable, notify the relevant persons of that decision.

(10) A notification under paragraphs (6) to (9) shall include information as to the provisions of sections 16, 17 and 20 of the Child Support Act.

(11) Where paragraph (9) applies, and the Secretary of State decides not to supersede under regulation 6B, he shall notify the relevant person, in relation to the decision in question of –

    (a) the fact that regulation 6B applies to the decision;
    (b) the non-resident parent's net income figure fixed for the purposes of the maintenance calculation in force in accordance with Part I of Schedule 1 to the Child Support Act;
    (c) the non-resident parent's net income figure provided by that parent to the Secretary of State with the application for supersession under regulation 6A(3);
    (d) the decision of the Secretary of State not to supersede; and
    (e) the right to appeal against the decision under section 20 of the Child Support Act.

(12) Where an appeal lapses in accordance with section 16(6) or 28F(5) of the Child Support Act, the Secretary of State shall, so far as that is reasonably practicable, notify the relevant persons that the appeal has lapsed.

****

PART IV

RIGHTS OF APPEAL AND PROCEDURE FOR BRINGING APPEALS

****

General Appeals Matters Including Child Support Appeals

30 Appeal against a decision which has been replaced or revised

(1) An appeal against a decision of the Secretary of State or the Board or an officer of the Board shall not lapse where the decision is treated as replaced by a decision under section 11 of the Child Support Act by section 28F(5) of that Act, or is revised under section 16 of that Act or section 9 before the appeal is determined and the decision as replaced or revised is not more advantageous to the appellant than the decision before it was replaced or revised.

(2) Decisions which are more advantageous for the purposes of this regulation include decisions where –

(a) any relevant benefit paid to the appellant is greater or is awarded for a longer period in consequence of the decision made under section 9;

(b) it would have resulted in the amount of relevant benefit in payment being greater but for the operation of any provision of the Administration Act or the Contributions and Benefits Act restricting or suspending the payment of, or disqualifying a claimant from receiving, some or all of the benefit;

(c) as a result of the decision, a denial or disqualification for the receiving of any relevant benefit, is lifted, wholly or in part;

(d) it reverses a decision to pay benefit to a third party;

(e) in consequence of the revised decision, benefit paid is not recoverable under section 71, 71A or 74 of the Administration Act or regulations made under any of those sections, or the amount so recoverable is reduced; or

(f) a financial gain accrued or will accrue to the appellant in consequence of the decision.

(3) Where a decision as replaced under section 28F(5) of the Child Support Act or revised under section 16 of that Act or under section 9 is not more advantageous to the appellant than the decision before it was replaced or revised, the appeal shall be treated as though it had been brought against the decision as replaced or revised.

(4) The appellant shall have a period of one month from the date of notification of the decision as replaced or revised to make further representations as to the appeal.

(5) After the expiration of the period specified in paragraph (4), or within that period if the appellant consents in writing, the appeal to the appeal tribunal shall proceed except where, in the light of the further representations from the appellant, the Secretary of State or the Board or an officer of the Board further revises his, or revise their, decision and that decision is more advantageous to the appellant than the decision before it was replaced or revised.

30A   Appeals to appeal tribunals in child support cases

Section 20 of the Child Support Act shall apply to any decision of the Secretary of State that an adjustment shall cease or with respect to the adjustment of amounts payable under a maintenance calculation for the purpose of taking account of overpayments of child support maintenance and voluntary payments, or a decision under section 17 of that Act, whether as originally made or as revised under section 16 of that Act.

31   Time within which an appeal is to be brought

(1) Where an appeal lies from a decision of the Secretary of State or the Board or an officer of the Board to an appeal tribunal, except in the case of a decision of the Secretary of State under section 3 or 3A of the Vaccine Damage Payments Act, the time within which that appeal must be brought is, subject to the following provisions of this Part –

(a) within one month of the date of notification of the decision against which the appeal is brought; or

(b) where a written statement of reasons for that decision is requested, within 14 days of the expiry of the period specified in sub-paragraph (a).

(2) Where the Secretary of State or the Board or an officer of the Board –

(a) revises, or following an application for a revision under regulation 3(1) or (3) does not revise, a decision under section 16 of the Child Support Act or under section 9, or

(b) supersedes a decision under section 17 of the Child Support Act or under section 10, the period of one month specified in paragraph (1) shall begin to run from the date of notification of the revision or supersession of the decision, or following an application for a revision under regulation 3(1) or (3), the date the Secretary of State or the Board or an officer of the Board issues a notice that he is or they are not revising the decision.

(3) An appeal against a certificate of recoverable benefits must be brought –

    (a) not later than one month after the date a person making a compensation payment discharges his liability under section 6 of the 1997 Act;

    (b) where the certificate is reviewed by the Secretary of State or the Board or an officer of the Board in accordance with regulations made under section 11(5)(c) of the 1997 Act, not later than one month after the date the certificate is confirmed, or, as the case may be, a fresh certificate is issued; or

    (c) where an agreement is made under which an earlier compensation payment is treated as having been made in final discharge of a claim made by or in respect of an injured person and arising out of the accident, injury or disease, not later than one month after the date of that agreement.

(4) Where a dispute arises as to whether an appeal was brought within the time limit specified in this regulation, the dispute shall be referred to, and be determined by, a legally qualified panel member.

(5) The time limit specified in this regulation for bringing an appeal may be extended in accordance with regulation 32.

32 Late appeals

(1) The time within which an appeal must be brought may be extended where the conditions specified in paragraphs (2) to (8) are satisfied, but no appeal shall in any event be brought more than one year after the expiration of the last day for appealing under regulation 31.

(2) An application for an extension of time under this regulation shall be made in accordance with regulation 33 and shall be determined by a legally qualified panel member.

(3) An application under this regulation shall contain particulars of the grounds on which the extension of time is sought, including details of any relevant special circumstances for the purposes of paragraph (4).

(4) An application for an extension of time shall not be granted unless the panel member is satisfied that –

    (a) if the application is granted there are reasonable prospects that the appeal will be successful;

    (b) it is in the interests of justice for the application to be granted.

(5) For the purposes of paragraph (4) it is not in the interests of justice to grant an application unless the panel member is satisfied that –

    (a) the special circumstances specified in paragraph (6) are relevant to the application; or

    (b) some other special circumstances exist which are wholly exceptional and relevant to the application,

and as a result of those special circumstances, it was not practicable for the application to be made within the time limit specified in regulation 31.

(6) For the purposes of paragraph (5)(a), the special circumstances are that –

    (a) the applicant or a spouse or dependant of the applicant has died or suffered serious illness;

    (b) the applicant is not resident in the United Kingdom; or

    (c) normal postal services were disrupted.

(7) In determining whether it is in the interests of justice to grant the application, the panel member shall have regard to the principle that the greater the amount of time that has elapsed between the expiration of the time within which the appeal is to be brought under regulation 31 and the making of the application for an extension of time, the more compelling should be the special circumstances on which the application is based.

(8) In determining whether it is in the interests of justice to grant an application, no account shall be taken of the following –

    (a) that the applicant or any person acting for him was unaware of or misunderstood the law applicable to his case (including ignorance or misunderstanding of the time limits imposed by these Regulations); or

    (b) that a Commissioner or a court has taken a different view of the law from that previously understood and applied.

(9) An application under this regulation for an extension of time which has been refused may not be renewed.

(10) The panel member who determines an application under this regulation shall record a summary of his decision in such written form as has been approved by the President.

(11) As soon as practicable after the decision is made a copy of the decision shall be sent or given to every party to the proceedings.

33 Making of appeals and applications

(1) An appeal, or an application for an extension of time for making an appeal to an appeal tribunal shall be in writing either on a form approved for the purpose by the Secretary of State or the Board or in such other format as the Secretary of State accepts or the Board accept as sufficient for the purpose and shall –

    (a) be signed by –

        (i) the person who, under section 4(1) of the Vaccine Damage Payments Act, section 20 of the Child Support Act, section 11(2) of the 1997 Act or section 12(2), has a right of appeal; or

        (ii) where the person in head (i) has provided written authority to a representative to act on his behalf, by that representative;

    (b) be sent or delivered to an appropriate office;

    (c) contain particulars of the grounds on which it is made; and

    (d) contain sufficient particulars of the decision, the certificate of recoverable benefits or the subject of the application, as the case may be, to enable that decision, certificate or subject of the application to be identified.

(2) In this regulation, 'an appropriate office' means –

    (a) in the case of an appeal under the 1997 Act against a certificate of recoverable benefits, the Compensation Recovery Unit of the Department of Social Security at Reyrolle Building, Hebburn, Tyne and Wear, NE31 1XB;

    (b) in the case of an appeal against a decision relating to a jobseeker's allowance, an office of the Department of Social Security or of the Department for Education and Employment;

(c) in the case of a contributions decision which falls within Part II of Schedule 3 to the Act, any National Insurance Contributions office of the Board, or any office of the Department of Social Security;

(cc) in the case of a decision made under the Pension Schemes Act 1993 by virtue of section 170(2) of that Act, any National Insurance Contributions office of the Board;

(d) in the case of an appeal under section 20 of the Child Support Act, an office of the Child Support Agency;

(dd) in the case of an appeal against a decision relating to working families' tax credit or disabled person's tax credit, a Tax Credits Office of the Board, and.

(ddd) in a case where the decision appealed against was a decision arising from a claim to a designated office, an office of a designated authority;

(e) in any other case, an office of the Department of Social Security.

(3) A form which is not completed in accordance with the instructions on the form –

(a) except where paragraph (4) applies, does not satisfy the requirements of paragraph (1), and

(b) may be returned by the Secretary of State or the Board to the sender for completion in accordance with those instructions.

(4) Where the Secretary of State is satisfied or the Board are satisfied that the form, although not completed in accordance with the instructions on it, includes sufficient information to enable the appeal or application to proceed, he or they may treat the form as satisfying the requirements of paragraph (1).

(5) Where an appeal or application is made in writing otherwise than on the approved form ('the letter'), and the letter includes sufficient information to enable the appeal or application to proceed, the Secretary of State or the Board may treat the letter as satisfying the requirements of paragraph (1).

(6) Where the letter does not include sufficient information to enable the appeal or application to proceed, the Secretary of State or the Board may request further information in writing ('further particulars') from the person who wrote the letter.

(7) Where a person to whom a form is returned or from whom further particulars are requested duly completes and returns the form or sends the further particulars and the form or particulars (as the case may be) are received by the Secretary of State or the Board within –

(a) 14 days of the date on which the form was returned to him by the Secretary of State or the Board,

(b) 14 days of the date on which the Secretary of State's or the Board's request was made ('the date of request'), or

(c) such longer period as the Secretary of State or the Board may direct,

the time for making the appeal shall be extended by 14 days from the date the form was returned, the date of request or the date of the Secretary of State's or the Board's direction, as the case may be.

(8) Where a person to whom a form is returned or from whom further particulars are requested does not complete and return the form or send further particulars within the period of time specified in paragraph (7) –

(a) the Secretary of State or the Board shall forward a copy of the form, or as the case may be, the letter, together with any other relevant documents or evidence to a legally qualified panel member, and

(b) the panel member shall determine whether the form or the letter satisfies the requirement of paragraph (1), and shall inform the appellant or applicant and the Secretary of State or the Board of his determination.

(9) Where –

(a) a form is duly completed and returned or further particulars are sent after the expiry of the period of time allowed in accordance with paragraph (7), and

(b) no decision has been made under paragraph (8) at the time the form or the further particulars are received by the Secretary of State or the Board,

that form or further particulars shall also be forwarded to the legally qualified panel member who shall take into account any further information or evidence set out in the form or further particulars.

(10) The Secretary of State may discontinue action on an appeal where the appeal has not been forwarded to the clerk to an appeal tribunal or to a legally qualified panel member and the appellant has given written notice that he does not wish the appeal to continue.

34 Death of a party to an appeal

(1) In any proceedings, on the death of a party to those proceedings (other than the Secretary of State or the Board), the Secretary of State or the Board may appoint such person as he thinks or they think fit to proceed with the appeal in the place of such deceased party.

(2) A grant of probate, confirmation or letters of administration to the estate of the deceased party, whenever taken out, shall have no effect on an appointment made under paragraph (1).

(3) Where a person appointed under paragraph (1) has, prior to the date of such appointment, taken any action in relation to the appeal on behalf of the deceased party, the effective date of appointment by the Secretary of State or the Board shall be the day immediately prior to the first day on which such action was taken.

PART V

APPEAL TRIBUNALS FOR SOCIAL SECURITY CONTRACTING OUT OF PENSIONS VACCINE DAMAGE AND CHILD SUPPORT

Chapter I – The Panel and Appeal Tribunals

35 Persons appointed to the panel

For the purposes of section 6(3), the panel shall include persons with the qualifications specified in Schedule 3.

36 Composition of appeal tribunals

(1) Subject to the following provisions of this regulation, an appeal tribunal shall consist of a legally qualified panel member.

(2) Subject to paragraphs (3) to (5), (8) and (9) an appeal tribunal shall consist of a legally qualified panel member and –

(a) a medically qualified panel member where –

      (i)   the issue, or one of the issues, raised on the appeal is whether the personal capability assessment is satisfied; or

      (ii) the appeal is made under section 11(1)(b) of the 1997 Act; or

  (b) one medically qualified panel member or two such members or one medically qualified panel member and an additional member drawn from the panel for the purposes described in paragraph (5) below where –

      (i)   the issue, or one of the issues, raised on the appeal (not being an appeal where the only issue is whether there should be a declaration of an industrial accident under section 29(2)) relates to either industrial injuries benefit under Part V of the Contributions and Benefits Act or severe disablement allowance under section 68 of that Act; or

      (ii) the appeal is made under section 4 of the Vaccine Damage Payments Act.

(3) An appeal tribunal shall consist of a financially qualified panel member and a legally qualified panel member where –

  (a) the issue raised, or one of the issues raised on appeal or referral, relates to child support or a relevant benefit; and

  (b) the appeal or referral may require consideration by members of the appeal tribunal of issues which are, in the opinion of the President, difficult and which relate to –

      (i)   profit and loss accounts, revenue accounts or balance sheets relating to any enterprise;

      (ii) an income and expenditure account in the case of an enterprise not trading for profit; or

      (iii) the accounts of any trust fund.

(4) Where the composition of an appeal tribunal would fall to be prescribed under both paragraphs (2) and (3), it shall consist of a medically qualified panel member, a financially qualified panel member and a legally qualified panel member.

(5) Where the composition of an appeal tribunal is prescribed under paragraphs paragraph (1), (2)(a), (3) or (9), the President may determine that the appeal tribunal shall include such an additional member drawn from the panel constituted under section 6 as he considers appropriate for the purposes of providing further experience for that additional member or for assisting the President in the monitoring of standards of decision making by panel members.

(6) An appeal tribunal shall consist of a legally qualified panel member, a medically qualified panel member and a panel member with a disability qualification in any appeal which relates to an attendance allowance or a disability living allowance under Part III of the Contributions and Benefits Act or a disabled person's tax credit under section 129 of that Act.

(7) In paragraph (2)(a)(i) above, 'personal capability assessment' has the meaning it bears in regulation 2(1) of the Social Security (Incapacity for Work) (General) Regulations 1995.

(8) A person shall not act as a medically qualified panel member of an appeal tribunal in any appeal if he has at any time advised or prepared a report upon any person whose medical condition is relevant to the issue in the appeal, or has at any time regularly attended such a person.

(9) Subject to paragraph (5), an appeal tribunal determining a misconceived appeal as a preliminary issue in accordance with regulation 48 shall consist of a legally qualified panel member.

37   Assignment of clerks to appeal tribunals: function of clerks

The Secretary of State shall assign a clerk to service each appeal tribunal and the clerk so assigned shall be responsible for summoning members of the panel constituted under section 6 to serve on the tribunal.

Chapter II – Procedure in Connection with Determination of Appeals and Referrals

38   Consideration and determination of appeals and referrals

(1) The procedure in connection with the consideration and determination of an appeal or a referral shall, subject to the following provisions of these Regulations, be such as a legally qualified panel member shall determine.

(2) A legally qualified panel member may give directions requiring a party to the proceedings to comply with any provision of these Regulations and may at any stage of the proceedings, either of his own motion or on a written application made to the clerk to the appeal tribunal by any party to the proceedings, give such directions as he may consider necessary or desirable for the just, effective and efficient conduct of the proceedings and may direct any party to the proceedings to provide such particulars or to produce such documents as may be reasonably required.

(3) Where a clerk to the appeal tribunal is authorised to take steps in relation to the procedure of the tribunal he may give directions requiring any party to the proceedings to comply with any provision of these Regulations.

38A   Appeals raising issues for decision by officers of Inland Revenue

(1) Where, on consideration of any appeal, it appears to an appeal tribunal that an issue arises which, by virtue of section 8 of the Transfer Act, falls to be decided by an officer of the Board, that tribunal shall –

(a)   refer the appeal to the Secretary of State pending the decision of that issue by an officer of the Board; and

(b)   require the Secretary of State to refer that issue to the Board;

and the Secretary of State shall refer that issue accordingly.

(2) Pending the final decision of any issue which has been referred to the Board in accordance with paragraph (1) above, the Secretary of State may revise the decision under appeal, or make a further decision superseding that decision, in accordance with his determination of any issue other than one which has been so referred.

(3) On receipt by the Secretary of State of the final decision of an issue which has been referred in accordance with paragraph (1) above, he shall consider whether the decision under appeal ought to be revised under section 9 or superseded under section 10, and –

(a)   if so, revise it or, as the case may be, make a further decision which supersedes it; or

(b)   if not, forward the appeal to the appeal tribunal which shall determine the appeal in accordance with the final decision of the issue so referred.

(4) In paragraphs (2) and (3) above, 'final decision' has the same meaning as in regulation 11A(3) and (4).

39   Directions concerning oral hearings

(1) Where an appeal or a referral is made to an appeal tribunal, the clerk to the appeal tribunal shall direct the appellant and any other party to the proceedings to notify the clerk

to the appeal tribunal in writing whether he wishes to have an oral hearing of the appeal or whether he is content for the appeal or referral to proceed without an oral hearing.

(2) Except in the case of a referral, a direction under paragraph (1) shall include a statement informing the appellant that, if he does not respond in writing to the direction within the period specified in paragraph (3), the appeal may be struck out in accordance with regulation 46.

(3) A notification given in accordance with paragraph (1) must be received by the clerk to the appeal tribunal within 14 days of the date of issue of the direction of the clerk to the appeal tribunal under paragraph (1) or within such longer period as the clerk to the appeal tribunal may direct.

(4) Where a party to the proceedings notifies the clerk to the appeal tribunal in accordance with paragraph (3) that he wishes to have an oral hearing of the appeal or referral, the appeal tribunal shall hold an oral hearing.

(5) The chairman, or in the case of an appeal tribunal which has only one member, that member, may of his own motion direct that an oral hearing of the appeal or referral be held if he is satisfied that such a hearing is necessary to enable the appeal tribunal to reach a decision.

40   Withdrawal of appeal or referral

(1) An appeal may be withdrawn by the appellant or an authorised representative of the appellant and a referral may be withdrawn by the Secretary of State the Board or an officer of the Board, as the case may be, either –

    (a) at an oral hearing; or
    (b) at any other time before the appeal or referral is determined, by giving notice in writing of withdrawal to the clerk to the appeal tribunal.

(2) If an appeal or a referral is withdrawn (as the case may be) in accordance with paragraph (1)(a), the clerk to the appeal tribunal shall send a notice in writing to any party to the proceedings who is not present when the appeal or referral is withdrawn, informing him that the appeal or referral (as the case may be) has been withdrawn.

(3) If an appeal or a referral is withdrawn (as the case may be) in accordance with paragraph (1)(b), the clerk to the appeal tribunal shall send a notice in writing to every party to the proceedings informing them that the appeal or referral (as the case may be) has been withdrawn.

41   Medical examination required by appeal tribunal

For the purposes of section 20(2) (medical examination required by appeal tribunal) the prescribed condition which must be satisfied is that the issue, or one of the issues, raised on the appeal –

    (a)   is whether the claimant satisfies the conditions for entitlement to –
        (i)   the care component of a disability living allowance specified in section 72(1) and (2) of the Contributions and Benefits Act;
        (ii) the mobility component of a disability living allowance specified in section 73(1), (8) and (9) of that Act;
        (iii) an attendance allowance specified in section 64 and 65(1) of that Act;
        (iv) a disability working allowance specified in section 129(1)(b) of that Act;
        . . .
        (vi) severe disablement allowance under section 68 of that Act;
    (b)   relates to the period throughout which the claimant is likely to satisfy the conditions for entitlement to an attendance allowance or a disability living allowance;

(c)   is the rate at which an attendance allowance is payable;

(d)   is the rate at which the care component or the mobility component of a disability living allowance is payable;

(dd)   is whether a person is incapable of work for the purposes of the Contributions and Benefits Act;

(f)   relates to the extent of a person's disablement and its assessment in accordance with Schedule 6 to the Contributions and Benefits Act;

(g)   is whether the claimant suffers a loss of physical or mental faculty as a result of the relevant accident for the purposes of section 103 of the Contributions and Benefits Act;

(h)   relates to any disease or injury prescribed for the purposes of section 108 of the Contributions and Benefits Act; or

(i)   relates to any payment arising under, or by virtue of a scheme having effect under, section 111 of, and Schedule 8 to, the Contributions and Benefits Act (workmen's compensation).

42 Non-disclosure of medical advice or evidence

(1) Where, in connection with an appeal or referral there is medical advice or medical evidence relating to a person which has not been disclosed to him and in the opinion of a legally qualified panel member the disclosure to that person of that advice or evidence would be harmful to his health, such advice or evidence shall not be required to be disclosed to that person.

(2) Advice or evidence such as is mentioned in paragraph (1) shall not be disclosed to any person acting for or representing the person to whom it relates or, in a case where a claim for benefit is made by reference to the disability of a person other than the claimant and the advice or evidence relates to that other person, shall not be disclosed to the claimant or any person acting for or representing him, unless a legally qualified panel member is satisfied that it is in the interests of the person to whom the advice or evidence relates to do so.

(3) A tribunal shall not be precluded from taking into account for the purposes of the determination advice or evidence which has not been disclosed to a person under the provisions of paragraph (1) or (2).

43 Summoning of witnesses and administration of oaths

(1) A chairman, or in the case of an appeal tribunal which has only one member, that member, may by summons, or in Scotland, by citation, require any person in Great Britain to attend as a witness at a hearing of an appeal, application or referral at such time and place as shall be specified in the summons or citation and, subject to paragraph (2), at the hearing to answer any question or produce any documents in his custody or under his control which relate to any matter in question in the appeal, application or referral but –

(a)   no person shall be required to attend in obedience to such summons or citation unless he has been given at least 14 days' notice of the hearing or, if less than 14 days' notice is given, he has informed the tribunal that the notice given is sufficient; and

(b)   no person shall be required to attend and give evidence or to produce any document in obedience to such summons or citation unless the necessary expenses of attendance are paid or tendered to him.

(2) No person shall be compelled to give any evidence or produce any document or other material that he could not be compelled to give or produce on a trial of an action in a court of law in that part of Great Britain where the hearing takes place.

(3) In exercising the powers conferred by this regulation, the chairman, or in the case of an appeal tribunal which has only one member, that member, shall take into account the need to protect any matter that relates to intimate personal or financial circumstances, is commercially sensitive, consists of information communicated or obtained in confidence or concerns national security.

(4) Every summons or citation issued under this regulation shall contain a statement to the effect that the person in question may apply in writing to a chairman to vary or set aside the summons or citation.

(5) A chairman, or in the case of an appeal tribunal which has only one member, that member, may require any witness, including a witness summoned under the powers conferred by this regulation, to give evidence on oath or affirmation and for that purpose there may be administered an oath or affirmation in due form.

44 Confidentiality in child support appeals or referrals

(1) In the circumstances specified in paragraph (2), for the purposes of paragraph 7 of Schedule 1 to the Act (President to secure confidentiality), in a child support appeal or referral, the prescribed material is –

(a) the address of the non-resident parent; the parent with care; the child; a parent of the child or any other person with care of the child; or

(b) any information the use of which could reasonably be expected to lead to the location of any person specified in paragraph (a).

(2) Except where the appeal is brought against a reduced benefit decision within the meaning of section 46(10)(b) of the Child Support Act, paragraph (1) applies where in response to an enquiry from the Secretary of State, the non-resident parent or, as the case may be, the parent with care, has within 14 days of issue of that enquiry notified the Secretary of State that he would like the information specified in paragraph (1) which relates to him to remain confidential.

(3) In this regulation, the expressions 'non-resident parent' and 'parent with care' have the meanings those expressions bear in section 54 of the Child Support Act.

45 Procedure following a referral under section 28D(1)(b) of the Child Support Act

(1) On a referral under section 28D(1)(b) of the Child Support Act an appeal tribunal may –

(a) consider two or more applications for a variation with respect to the same application for a maintenance calculation together; or

(b) consider two or more applications for a variation with respect to the same maintenance calculation together.

(2) In this regulation 'maintenance calculation' means a decision under section 11 or 17 of the Child Support Act, as calculated in accordance with Part I of Schedule 1 to that Act, whether as originally made or as revised under section 16 of that Act.

Chapter III – Striking Out Appeals

46 Appeals which may be struck out

(1) Subject to paragraphs (2) and (3), an appeal may be struck out by the clerk to the appeal tribunal –

(a) where it is an out of jurisdiction appeal and the appellant has been notified by the Secretary of State that an appeal brought against such a decision may be struck out;

(b) for want of prosecution including an appeal not made within the time specified in these Regulations; or

(c) subject to regulation 39(4), for failure of the appellant to comply with a direction given under these Regulations where the appellant has been notified that failure to comply with the direction could result in the appeal being struck out.

(2) Where the clerk to the appeal tribunal determines to strike out the appeal, he shall notify the appellant that his appeal has been struck out and of the procedure for reinstatement of the appeal as specified in regulation 47.

(3) The clerk to the appeal tribunal may refer any matter for determination under this regulation to a legally qualified panel member for decision by the panel member rather than the clerk to the appeal tribunal.

(4) Subject to regulation 48, a misconceived appeal may be struck out by a legally qualified panel member but such an appeal shall not be struck out unless the appellant has been given notice of –

(a) the intention to strike out the appeal,

(b) the ground on which the intention to strike out is based, and

(c) the requirement to notify the clerk to the appeal tribunal in writing of the matters specified in regulation 48(1)(a) or (b) and that failure to comply with this requirement may result in the appeal being struck out.

47 Reinstatement of struck out appeals

A legally qualified panel member may reinstate an appeal which has been struck out in accordance with regulation 46 or regulation 48 where –

(a) the appellant has made representations, or as the case may be, further representations in support of his appeal with reasons why he considers that his appeal should not have been struck out, to the clerk to the appeal tribunal, in writing within one month of the order to strike out the appeal being issued, and the panel member is satisfied in the light of those representations that there are reasonable grounds for reinstating the appeal;

(b) the panel member is satisfied that the appellant did not receive the notification required under regulation 46(4);

(c) the panel member is satisfied that the appeal is not an appeal which may be struck out under regulation 46; or

(d) the panel member is satisfied that notwithstanding that the appeal is one which may be struck out under regulation 46, it is not in the interests of justice for the appeal to be struck out.

48 Misconceived appeals

(1) Where the appellant has been given notice under regulation 46(4) of intention to strike out an appeal on the ground that it is a misconceived appeal that person must within 14 days of the issue of such notice notify the clerk to the appeal tribunal in writing that –

(a) he wishes the question of whether his appeal is misconceived to be determined by an appeal tribunal as a preliminary issue at an oral hearing, or

(b) he is content for an appeal tribunal to consider the question of whether his appeal is misconceived as a preliminary issue without an oral hearing and make representations in writing to the clerk to the appeal tribunal as to why he considers that the appeal is not misconceived.

(2) Where the appellant fails to notify or to make representations to the clerk to the appeal tribunal in writing as required in paragraph (1) within the period specified in that paragraph, a legally qualified panel member may strike out the appeal.

(3) Where the appellant notifies the clerk to the appeal tribunal under paragraph (1) within the period specified in that paragraph that he wishes an appeal tribunal to determine the question of whether his appeal is misconceived as a preliminary issue at an oral hearing, the appeal tribunal shall hold an oral hearing for that preliminary issue.

(4) Where the appeal tribunal determine as a preliminary issue that the appeal is a misconceived appeal, the appeal shall be struck out and the clerk to the appeal tribunal shall notify the appellant that the appeal is struck out.

(5) Where the appeal tribunal determine as a preliminary issue that the appeal is not a misconceived appeal –

- (a) the appeal tribunal shall refer the appeal and all the supporting documentation to the Secretary of State together with a statement of the reasons why the appeal tribunal considers that the appeal is not misconceived;
- (b) the clerk to the appeal tribunal shall notify the appellant of the referral of the appeal to the Secretary of State and send the appellant a copy of the reasons why the appeal tribunal considers that the appeal is not misconceived;
- (c) the Secretary of State may revise or supersede the decision against which the appeal is brought; and
- (d) if the Secretary of State does not revise or supersede the decision against the appeal is brought in the appellant's favour, the Secretary of State shall refer the appeal for determination by an appeal tribunal.

(6) Chapter IV of this Part shall apply to an oral hearing held under this regulation.

Chapter IV – Oral Hearings

49 Procedure at oral hearings

(1) Subject to the following provisions of this Part, the procedure for an oral hearing shall be such as the chairman, or in the case of an appeal tribunal which has only one member, such as that member, shall determine.

(2) Except where paragraph (3) applies, not less than 14 days notice (beginning with the day on which the notice is given and ending on the day before the hearing of the appeal is to take place) of the time and place of any oral hearing of an appeal shall be given to every party to the proceedings, and if such notice has not been given to a person to whom it should have been given under the provisions of this paragraph the hearing may proceed only with the consent of that person.

(3) Any party to the proceedings may waive his right to receive not less than 14 days notice of the time and place of any oral hearing by giving notice to the clerk to the appeal tribunal.

(4) If a party to the proceedings to whom notice has been given under paragraph (2) fails to appear at the hearing the chairman, or in the case of an appeal tribunal which has only one member, that member, may, having regard to all the circumstances including any explanation offered for the absence, proceed with the hearing notwithstanding his absence, or give such directions with a view to the determination of the appeal as he may think proper.

(5) If a party to the proceedings has waived his right to be given notice under paragraph (2) the chairman, or in the case of an appeal tribunal which has only one member, that member, may proceed with the hearing notwithstanding his absence.

(6) Any oral hearing shall be in public except –

(a) where the appellant requests a private hearing, or
(b) where the chairman, or in the case of an appeal tribunal which has only one member, that member, is satisfied that intimate personal or financial circumstances may have to be disclosed or that considerations of national security are involved, in which case the hearing shall be in private.

(7) Any party to the proceedings shall be entitled to be present and be heard at an oral hearing.

(8) A person who has the right to be heard at a hearing may be accompanied and may be represented by another person whether having professional qualifications or not and, for the purposes of the proceedings at the hearing, any such representative shall have all the rights and powers to which the person whom he represents is entitled.

(9) The following persons shall also be entitled to be present at an oral hearing (whether or not it is otherwise in private) but shall take no part in the proceedings –

(a) the President;
(b) any person undergoing training as a chairman or panel member of an appeal tribunal or as a clerk to an appeal tribunal;
(c) any person acting on behalf of the President in the training or supervision of panel members or in the monitoring of standards of decision-making by panel members;
(d) with the leave of the chairman, or in the case of an appeal tribunal which has only one member, with the leave of that member, and the consent of every party to the proceedings actually present, any other person; and
(e) a member of the Council on Tribunals or of the Scottish Committee of the Council on Tribunals.

(10) Nothing in paragraph (9) affects the rights of any person mentioned in sub-paragraphs (a) and (b) of that paragraph at any oral hearing where he is sitting as a member of the tribunal or acting as its clerk, and nothing in this regulation prevents the presence at an oral hearing of any witness or of any person whom the chairman, or in the case of an appeal tribunal which has only one member, that member, permits to be present in order to assist the clerk.

(11) Any person entitled to be heard at an oral hearing may address the tribunal, may give evidence, may call witnesses and may put questions directly to any other person called as a witness.

(12) For the purpose of arriving at its decision an appeal tribunal shall, and for the purpose of discussing any question of procedure may, notwithstanding anything contained in these Regulations, order all persons not being members of the tribunal, other than the person acting as clerk to the appeal tribunal, to withdraw from the hearing except that –

(a) a member of the Council on Tribunals or of the Scottish Committee of the Council on Tribunals, the President or any person mentioned in paragraph (9)(c); and
(b) with the leave of the chairman, or in the case of an appeal tribunal which has only one member, with the leave of that member, any person mentioned in paragraph (9)(b) or (d),

may remain present at any such sitting.

50   Manner of providing expert assistance

(1) Where an appeal tribunal require one or more experts to provide assistance to it in dealing with a question of fact of special difficulty under section 7(4), such an expert shall, if the chairman, or in the case of a tribunal with only one member, that member, so requests, attend at the hearing and give evidence and if the chairman or member sitting alone considers it appropriate, the expert shall enquire into and provide a written report on the question.

(2) A copy of any written report received from an expert in accordance with paragraph (1) shall be supplied to every party to the proceedings.

51   Postponement and adjournment

(1) Where a person to whom notice of an oral hearing is given wishes to request a postponement of that hearing he shall do so in writing to the clerk to the appeal tribunal stating his reasons for the request, and the clerk to the appeal tribunal may grant or refuse the request as he thinks fit or may pass the request to a legally qualified panel member who may grant or refuse the request as he thinks fit.

(2) Where the clerk to the appeal tribunal or the panel member, as the case may be, refuses a request to postpone the hearing he shall –

   (a) notify in writing the person making the request of the refusal; and
   (b) place before the appeal tribunal at the hearing both the request for the postponement and notification of its refusal.

(3) A panel member or the clerk to the appeal tribunal may of his own motion at any time before the beginning of the hearing postpone the hearing.

(4) An oral hearing may be adjourned by the appeal tribunal at any time on the application of any party to the proceedings or of its own motion.

(5) Where a hearing has been adjourned and it is not practicable, or would cause undue delay, for it to be resumed before a tribunal consisting of the same member or members, the appeal or referral shall be heard by a differently constituted tribunal and the proceedings shall be by way of a complete rehearing.

52   Physical examinations at oral hearings

For the purposes of section 20(3) an appeal tribunal may not carry out a physical examination except in a case which relates to –

   (a) the extent of a person's disablement and its assessment in accordance with section 68(6) of, and Schedule 6 to, the Contributions and Benefits Act;
   (b) the extent of a person's disablement and its assessment in accordance with section 103 of that Act;
   (c) diseases or injuries prescribed for the purposes of section 108 of that Act.

Chapter V – Decisions of Appeal Tribunals and Related Matters
Appeal Tribunal Decisions

53   Decisions of appeal tribunals

(1) Every decision of an appeal tribunal shall be recorded in summary by the chairman, or in the case of an appeal tribunal which has only one member, by that member.

(2) The decision notice specified in paragraph (1) shall be in such written form as shall have been approved by the President and shall be signed by the chairman, or in the case of an appeal tribunal which has only one member, by that member.

(3) As soon as may be practicable after an appeal or referral has been decided by an appeal tribunal, a copy of the decision notice prepared in accordance with paragraph (1) and (2) shall be sent or given to every party to the proceedings who shall also be informed of –

(a) his right under paragraph (4); and
(b) except in the case of an appeal under the Vaccine Damage Payments Act, the conditions governing appeals to a Commissioner.

(4) A party to the proceedings may apply in writing to the chairman, or in the case of a tribunal with only one member, to that member, for a statement of the reasons for the tribunal's decision within one month of the sending or giving of the decision notice to every party to the proceedings or within such longer period as may be allowed in accordance with regulation 54 and following that application the chairman or, as the case may be, that member shall record a statement of the reasons and a copy of that statement shall be sent or given to every party to the proceedings as soon as may be practicable.

(5) If the decision is not unanimous, the decision notice specified in paragraph (1) shall record that one of the members dissented and the statement of reasons referred to in paragraph (4) shall include the reasons given by the dissenting member for dissenting.

54   Late applications for a statement of reasons of tribunal decision

(1) The time for making an application for the statement of the reasons for a tribunal's decision may be extended where the conditions specified in paragraphs (2) to (8) are satisfied, but, subject to paragraph (13), no application shall in any event be brought more than three months after the date of the sending or giving of the notice of the decision of the appeal tribunal.

(2) An application for an extension of time under this regulation shall be made in writing and shall be determined by a legally qualified panel member.

(3) An application under this regulation shall contain particulars of the grounds on which the extension of time is sought, including details of any relevant special circumstances for the purposes of paragraph (4).

(4) The application for an extension of time shall not be granted unless the panel member is satisfied that it is in the interests of justice for the application to be granted.

(5) For the purposes of paragraph (4) it is not in the interests of justice to grant the application unless the panel member is satisfied that –

(a) the special circumstances specified in paragraph (6) are relevant to the application; or
(b) some other special circumstances are relevant to the application,

and as a result of those special circumstances it was not practicable for the application to be made within the time limit specified in regulation 53(4).

(6) For the purposes of paragraph (5)(a), the special circumstances are that –

(a) the applicant or a spouse or dependant of the applicant has died or suffered serious illness;
(b) the applicant is not resident in the United Kingdom; or
(c) normal postal services were adversely disrupted.

(7) In determining whether it is in the interests of justice to grant the application, the panel member shall have regard to the principle that the greater the amount of time that has elapsed between the expiration of the time within which the application for a copy of the statement of reasons for a tribunal's decision is to be made and the making of the

application for an extension of time, the more compelling should be the special circumstances on which the application is based.

(8) In determining whether it is in the interests of justice to grant the application, no account shall be taken of the following –

- (a) that the person making the application or any person acting for him was unaware of, or misunderstood, the law applicable to his case (including ignorance or misunderstanding of the time limits imposed by these Regulations); or
- (b) that a Commissioner or a court has taken a different view of the law from that previously understood and applied.

(9) An application under this regulation for an extension of time which has been refused may not be renewed.

(10) The panel member who determines the application shall record a summary of his decision in such written form as has been approved by the President.

(11) As soon as practicable after the decision is made a copy of the decision shall be sent or given to every party to the proceedings.

(12) Any person who under paragraph (11) receives a copy of the decision may, within one month of the decision being sent to him, apply in writing for a copy of the reasons for that decision and a copy shall be supplied to him.

(13) In calculating the time specified for applying in writing for a statement of the reasons for the tribunal's decision there shall be disregarded any day which falls before the day on which notice was given of –

- (a) a correction of a decision or the record thereof pursuant to regulation 56; or
- (b) a determination that a decision shall not be set aside following an application made under regulation 57.

55 Record of tribunal proceedings

(1) A record of the proceedings at an oral hearing, which is sufficient to indicate the evidence taken, shall be made by the chairman, or in the case of an appeal tribunal which has only one member, by that member, in such medium as he may direct.

(2) Such record shall be preserved by the clerk to the appeal tribunal for six months from the date of the decision made by the appeal tribunal to which the record relates and any party to the proceedings may within that period apply in writing for a copy of that record and a copy shall be supplied to him.

56 Correction of accidental errors

(1) The clerk to the appeal tribunal or a legally qualified panel member may at any time correct accidental errors in any decision, or the record of any such decision, of an appeal tribunal made under a relevant enactment, the Child Support Act or the Vaccine Damage Payments Act.

(2) A correction made to, or to the record of, a decision shall be deemed to be part of the decision or record of that decision and written notice of it shall be given as soon as practicable to every party to the proceedings.

(3) In this regulation and regulation 57, 'relevant enactment' has the same meaning as in section 28(3).

57   Setting aside decisions on certain grounds

(1) On an application made by a party to the proceedings, a decision of an appeal tribunal made under a relevant enactment, the Child Support Act or the Vaccine Damage Payments Act, may be set aside by a legally qualified panel member in a case where it appears just to set the decision aside on the ground that –

(a) a document relating to the proceedings in which the decision was made was not sent to, or was not received at an appropriate time by, a party to the proceedings or the party's representative or was not received at an appropriate time by the person who made the decision;

(b) a party to the proceedings in which the decision was made or the party's representative was not present at a hearing relating to the proceedings.

(2) In determining whether it is just to set aside a decision on the ground set out in paragraph (1)(b), the panel member shall determine whether the party making the application gave notice that he wished to have an oral hearing, and if that party did not give such notice the decision shall not be set aside unless the chairman, or in the case of an appeal tribunal which has only one member, unless that member is satisfied that the interests of justice manifestly so require.

(3) An application under this regulation shall –

(a) be made within one month of the date on which –
  (i) a copy of the decision notice is sent or given to the parties to the proceedings in accordance with regulation 53(3); or
  (ii) the statement of the reasons for the decision is given or sent in accordance with regulation 53(4),
  whichever is the later;

(b) be in writing and signed by a party to the proceedings or, where the party has provided written authority to a representative to act on his behalf, that representative;

(c) contain particulars of the grounds on which it is made; and

(d) be sent to the clerk to the appeal tribunal.

(4) Where an application to set aside a decision is entertained under paragraph (1), every party to the proceedings shall be sent a copy of the application and shall be afforded a reasonable opportunity of making representations on it before the application is determined.

(5) Notice in writing of a determination on an application to set aside a decision shall be sent or given to every party to the proceedings as soon as may be practicable and the notice shall contain a statement giving the reasons for the determination.

(6) The time within which an application under this regulation must be made may be extended by a period not exceeding one year where the conditions specified in paragraphs (7) to (11) are satisfied.

(7) An application for an extension of time shall be made in accordance with paragraph (3)(b) to (d), shall include details of any relevant special circumstances for the purposes of paragraph (9) and shall be determined by a legally qualified panel member.

(8) An application for an extension of time shall not be granted unless the panel member is satisfied that –

(a) if the application is granted there are reasonable prospects that the application to set aside will be successful; and

(b) it is in the interests of justice for the application for an extension of time to be granted.

(9) For the purposes of paragraph (8) it is not in the interests of justice to grant an application for an extension of time unless the panel member is satisfied that –

  (a) the special circumstances specified in paragraph (10) are relevant to that application; or
  (b) some other special circumstances exist which are wholly exceptional and relevant to that application,

and as a result of those special circumstances, it was not practicable for the application to set aside to be made within the time limit specified in paragraph (3)(a).

(10) For the purposes of paragraph (9)(a) the special circumstances are that –

  (a) the applicant or a spouse or dependant of the applicant has died or suffered serious illness;
  (b) the applicant is not resident in the United Kingdom; or
  (c) normal postal services were disrupted.

(11) In determining whether it is in the interests of justice to grant an application for an extension of time, the panel member shall have regard to the principle that the greater the amount of time that has elapsed between the expiry of the time within which the application to set aside is to be made and the making of the application for an extension of time, the more compelling should be the special circumstances on which the application for an extension is based.

(12) An application under this regulation for an extension of time which has been refused may not be renewed.

57A Provisions common to regulations 56 and 57

(1) In calculating any time specified for appealing to a Commissioner from a decision of an appeal tribunal there shall be disregarded any day falling before the day on which notice was given of a correction of a decision or the record thereof pursuant to regulation 56 or on which notice is given of a determination that a decision shall not be set aside following an application made under regulation 57, as the case may be.

(2) There shall be no appeal against a correction made under regulation 56 or a refusal to make such a correction or against a determination given under regulation 57.

(3) Nothing in this Chapter shall be construed as derogating from any power to correct errors or set aside decisions which is exercisable apart from these Regulations.

57B Interpretation of Chapter V

In Chapter V, except in regulation 58, 'Commissioner' includes Child Support Commissioner.

Applications for Leave to Appeal to a Commissioner (Not Including Child Support)

58 Application for leave to appeal to a Commissioner from an appeal tribunal

(1) An application for leave to appeal to a Commissioner from a decision of an appeal tribunal under section 12 or 13 shall –

  (a) be made within the period of one month commencing on the date the applicant is sent a written statement of the reasons for the decision against which leave to appeal is sought; and

(b) have annexed to it a copy of that written statement of the reasons for the decision.

(2) Where an application for leave to appeal to a Commissioner is made by the Secretary of State or the Board, the clerk to an appeal tribunal shall, as soon as may be practicable, send a copy of the application to every other party to the proceedings.

(3) Any party to the proceedings who is sent a copy of an application for leave to appeal in accordance with paragraph (2) may make representations in writing within one month of the date the application is sent.

(4) A person determining an application for leave to appeal to a Commissioner, shall take into account any further representations received from the applicant before the determination is made, and shall record his decision in writing and send a copy to every party to the proceedings.

(5) Where there has been a failure to apply for leave to appeal within the period of time specified in paragraph (1)(a) but an application is made within one year of the last date for making an application within that period, a legally qualified panel member may, if for special reasons he thinks fit, accept and proceed to consider and determine the application.

(6) Where in any case it is impracticable, or it would be likely to cause undue delay for an application for leave to appeal against a decision of an appeal tribunal to be determined by the person who was the chairman, or in the case of an appeal tribunal which has only one member, the member, of that tribunal, the application shall be determined by a legally qualified panel member.

****

INDEX

References are to paragraph numbers.